Language as Evidence

Victoria Guillén-Nieto • Dieter Stein
Editors

Language as Evidence

Doing Forensic Linguistics

palgrave
macmillan

Editors
Victoria Guillén-Nieto
Departamento de Filología Inglesa
University of Alicante
Alicante, Spain

Dieter Stein
Anglistik III Englische Sprachwissenschaft
Heinrich Heine University Düsseldorf
Düsseldorf, Germany

ISBN 978-3-030-84329-8 ISBN 978-3-030-84330-4 (eBook)
https://doi.org/10.1007/978-3-030-84330-4

Cover illustration: Zoonar GmbH / Alamy Stock Photo

This Palgrave Macmillan imprint is published by the registered company Springer Nature Switzerland AG.
The registered company address is: Gewerbestrasse 11, 6330 Cham, Switzerland

Preface

This volume aims to respond to calls for a survey of modern approaches to forensic linguistics, narrowly construed here as using linguistic science in an applied field with an extraordinary number of different types of challenges. It also tries to position forensic linguistics as a subtype of and with the claim to theoretical status and a theory of its own as part of larger forensic science.

Just as other scientific fields of enquiry, forensic linguistics has internal discussions about subjects, approaches, theories, methodologies and ethics. Because of this wide ambit of issues and the limited scope of a manageable volume, a selection had to be made that hopefully represents not a monoculture but a representative variety of approaches. The fact that a subject is not represented does not mean that it is less significant in itself. It only means that the editors have, at this point, made a choice that was deemed necessary.

The volume would not have seen the light of the day had it not been for several peoples' idealistic and unremunerated efforts. We are deeply indebted to Ingo Plag, Andrew Hammel, Donato Mancini and Borja

Navarro, who read and commented in detail on chapters of this volume. We are very grateful to Julika Weber for her thorough copy editing work. Special thanks also go to Anna Stein and Rebeca Ferrero for their assistance in technical translation.

Alicante, Spain
Düsseldorf, Germany
June 2021

Victoria Guillén-Nieto
Dieter Stein

Contents

Notes on Contributors

Janet Ainsworth is Professor of Law at Seattle University in the USA. Her research interests lie at the intersection of law, language and culture. She is President of the International Association of Forensic Linguists.

Patrizia Anesa is a researcher in English Language and Linguistics at the University of Bergamo in Italy and a member of the Research Centre on Specialised Languages (CERLIS). Her research interests lie mostly in the area of specialised discourse, with special reference to legal language. She also cooperates with several international organisations as a consultant in discourse, conversation and frame analysis.

Gea de Jong-Lendle is Senior Scientist and Lecturer in the Phonetics Arbeitsgruppe at the Philipps-University of Marburg in Germany. She holds a PhD in Linguistics from the University of Florida and an M.Phil. in Computer Speech and Language Processing from the University of Cambridge. Her research interests focus on the area of forensic phonetics and perceptive phonetics. As the Director of Forensic Research Associates, she has undertaken forensic investigations since 1994 for both prosecution and defence.

Mercedes Fernández-López is Senior Lecturer at the Commercial and Procedural Law Department at the University of Alicante. Her main line of research is evidence law (in civil and criminal law), on which she has published two monographs and numerous articles. Since 2008, Fernández has been a reserve judge at the Provincial Court of Alicante. She directs the Master's Degree in Law at the same University and the School of Legal Practice of Alicante.

Eilika Fobbe is Senior Scientist in Forensic Linguistics at the Bundeskriminalamt in Germany. After studying Indo-European linguistics, German and Sanskrit philology at the University of Göttingen, she received her doctorate in linguistics and worked as a postdoctoral fellow in the universities of Göttingen and Greifswald. In 2012, she published an introductory book on forensic linguistics that has become an important reference in Germany. Fobbe has also worked as an expert linguist for law firms and courts of justice.

Victoria Guillén-Nieto is Senior Lecturer in Applied Linguistics at the University of Alicante in Spain. She has published articles on trademarks linguistics, plagiarism detection and language crimes such as defamation, harassment and hate speech. Since 2009, she has served as an expert linguist in Spain, Switzerland, Sweden and the USA. From September 2019 to September 2021, she was President of the International Language and Law Association (ILLA) for Linguistics.

Andrew Hammel is a lawyer, defence counsel, writer and translator living in Düsseldorf, Germany. From 2003 to 2016 he taught Anglo-American Common Law and Comparative Law at the Heinrich Heine University Düsseldorf.

Julien Longhi is a Full Professor of Linguistics at the CY Cergy Paris Université in Paris and a Junior Member at the Institut Universitaire de France (IUF). He has published books, articles and edited volumes in semantics, pragmatics, discourse analysis and corpus linguistics. Longhi is working on two major projects: one investigating ideology detection in Twitter and the other looking at risk and security discourses in collaboration with security forces in France.

Martina Nicklaus is Senior Lecturer in the Department of Romance Languages at the Heinrich Heine University Düsseldorf, where she also received her PhD in Linguistics (Romance Languages). Her research interests lie in veracity assessment.

Dieter Alfred Stein is Emeritus Chair of English Linguistics at Heinrich Heine University Düsseldorf. One main focus of his work is language development; others deal with pragmatics, open access publishing, the linguistics of the Internet, language in the legal domain and forensic linguistics. In addition to teaching at his home university, he has taught at several foreign universities, including China, UCLA Los Angeles law school and the linguistic institute of the Linguistic Society of America.

Magdalena Szczyrbak is Assistant Professor in the Institute of English Studies at Jagiellonian University in Krakow. Her research interests lie primarily in discourse analysis and corpus-assisted discourse study applied to legal discourse and, particularly, to the study of stance and evaluation. She is the current President of the International Language and Law Asociation (ILLA) for Linguistics.

Hans van Halteren is Assistant Professor at the Centre for Language Studies (CLS), Radboud University Nijmegen. His research interests lie in corpus linguistics, computational linguistics and machine learning. Two of his focus areas are language variation and forensic linguistics, which are two aspects of the same natural language processing task.

Monika Zaśko-Zielińska is Associate Professor in the Institute of Polish Philology at the University of Wroclaw Bio -Monika Zaśko-Zielińska received her PhD in genre studies and habilitation on forensic linguistics at the University of Wroclaw. She has contributed to Polish Emo WordNet.

List of Figures

List of Tables

1

Introduction: Theory and Practice in Forensic Linguistics

Victoria Guillén-Nieto and Dieter Stein

1 The Field of Forensic Linguistics

It is a truism that language and the law are intricately and intensively related in many ways. The law, although determined by underlying ethical and moral principles, exists through language, is formulated on language and is executed in language. There are crimes that are committed in language, and there are crimes that are resolved by analysing discourse and texts that were produced in committing crime. Furthermore, language and law have many traits in common: Both are systems of norms and share important traits of normative systems (Stein, 2021).

V. Guillén-Nieto (✉)
Departamento de Filología Inglesa, University of Alicante, Alicante, Spain
e-mail: victoria.guillen@ua.es

D. Stein
Anglistik III Englische Sprachwissenschaft, Heinrich Heine University Düsseldorf, Düsseldorf, Germany
e-mail: stein@hhu.de

V. Guillén-Nieto, D. Stein (eds.), *Language as Evidence*,
https://doi.org/10.1007/978-3-030-84330-4_1

It is therefore very tempting to lump together all pursuits relating law and language in one category, an approach that has traditionally been followed by a number of volumes that have variously been given titles such as *Forensic linguistics. An introduction to language in the justice system* (Gibbons, 2003); *Forensic science and law. Investigative applications in criminal, civil and family justice* (Wecht & Rago, 2006), *Dimensions of forensic linguistics* (Gibbons & Turell, 2008), *The Routledge handbook of forensic linguistics* (Coulthard & Johnson, 2010) and *The Oxford handbook of language and law* (Tiersma & Solan, 2012).

The involvement of language with the law has several roots and is very unevenly distributed over different cultures and has quite a history by now. There is now also a body of metareflection on its history and the suggestions for future development in Vogel (2019), which contains a number of chapters on the developments of legal linguistics in different countries. Furthermore, there is at present an organised body of references on the open platform SOULL (*Sources of Language and Law*). Finally, the whole breadth of the field is represented by the conferences and activities in international associations such as the *International Association of Forensic Linguistics* (IAFL) and the *International Language and Law Association* (ILLA), the *International Journal of Speech, Language, and the Law* and the *International Journal of Language & Law* (JLL).

2 Differentiation of Disciplines

As scientific fields of inquiry mature they are getting more and more established and differentiated in the academic arena. An applied science area like Forensic Linguistics nurses on the more theoretical pursuits in legal linguistics, and the latter in turn on innovative thinking in linguistic areas, such as more recently in theories of genre and corpora, of the broad fields of pragmatics, of discourse and conversational analysis, in phonetic and statistical computational analysis, to name but a few. All this technical linguistic knowledge will trickle down to the applied level in forensic analysis and is constantly transforming approaches in all aspects of legal linguistics and in Forensic Linguistics. While certainly pragmatics has had the most impact on conceptualisations and formulations of problems

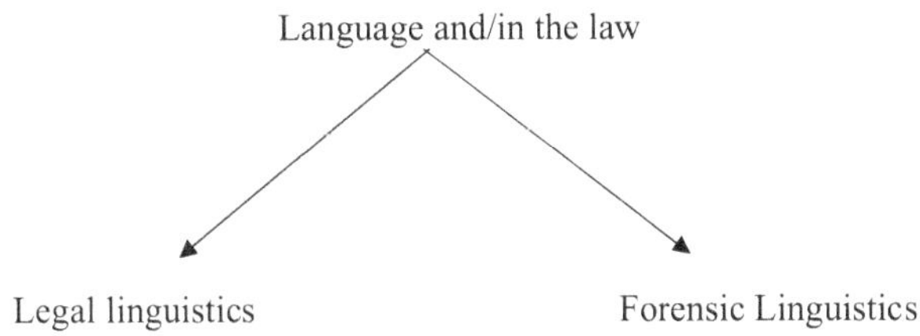

Fig. 1.1 Language and/in the law: disciplines

and issues in legal linguistics, such as in international law (Smolka & Pirker, 2016), it has also effected advances in Forensic Linguistics. The latter area is the one which is the focus of this volume. The formulation implies that it is a presupposition of this book, and its content, that, beyond the common ground and related origin as adumbrated above, it is now appropriate to speak of two separate subdisciplines of the area 'language and/in the law' and also consistently reflect this separation by a distinction in nomenclature.

In a way, the internal institutional and disciplinary distinctness depicted in Fig. 1.1 reflects what has happened in other sciences, including, for example, the so-called philologies: From a common historical take-off ground reflected in the term 'English' for university departments, it has become clear that the methodologies and epistemologies are too different and in need of disciplinary and organisational separation. This is reflected in the increasing association of the two sides with different neighbouring disciplines, with literature and cultural studies on the one side and more general linguistics on the other, while often retaining aspects of their common ground, but often with a problematic character of departmental cohabitation.

3 Forensic Linguistics: A Discipline of Its Own

Vogel (2019, p. 99) defines 'legal linguistics' as 'a branch of the discipline of language and legal science, with the linguistically-communicative 'constitution' of the societal institution of 'law'. The result of this pursuit is what Forensic Linguistics presupposes as a conceptual, institutional, organisational and processual structure for its tasks and activities. To that extent the link between the two branches of law and language is palpable. 'The law' in all of these facets defines the task for Forensic Linguistics, it defines actionability and what constitutes 'evidence' in the framework of activity types within the law.

Forensic Linguistics may have philosophical issues as an underpinning; it has no essential role in defining them. It presupposes them. This is the case in defining the setting for the practice of Forensic Linguistics. Different legal cultures define different roles for the forensic linguist, different privileges for calling in forensic experts and different processes of evaluation and discussions of forensic evidence in resolving concrete cases of real or purported crimes. This includes investigative activities by investigating agents.

Forensic Linguistics is basically 'action' and 'process' centred. It is involved in concrete decisions in real-time cases in the execution of the law. In practical cases a decision has to be made whether to bring a charge or, if the case is in court, a decision by the judge about guilty or not has to be made, with consequences for individual lives. Forensic Linguistics is intrinsically bound up, not with 'interpreting' the law—that is deciding which legal norm is applicable to the case once the judicial narrative has established the facts, but with establishing the facts on which a decision is to be based. Forensic Linguistics is placed prior to, and is a precondition for, interpretation—it is concerned with helping to establish the judicial narrative. It is in principle independent and a very different type of activity from legal interpretation and from legal and legal-theoretical considerations leading up to a decision. From this definition it is clear that different legal cultures with different internal structures of law will accord different tasks and different procedures to Forensic Linguistics so defined, as will be made clear in the contributions by Ainsworth (Chap. 2), Hammel (Chap. 3) and Fernández-López (Chap. 4) in this volume. So in dependence on the type of legal system, the temporally preceding, but logically posterior Forensic Linguistics will be partially different in methods, outlook, role and valuation at courts.

There is a fundamental difference in kind to the pursuit of timeless and abstract reflections about the doctrinal content of the law and its 'constitution' in the above citation by Vogel (2019, p. 99). Forensic Linguistics is the use of evidence from language use, based on records or 'texts', or 'traces'—not as the live substance, but as vestiges of the use of language, of communication or speech acts that took place in the past, however medially constituted, spoken, written, digital, in connection with the resolution of crime, and we suggest reserving the term 'Forensic Linguistics' for just that concrete task, as it is very distinct from all other activities and pursuits in the area of language and/in the law: in other words, 'a trace' of some sort that is suspected to be connected to a crime.

As a discipline, Forensic Linguistics has witnessed internal developments of different kinds, some of which will be discussed in separate places in the present introduction. The use of evidence from language used in connection with crimes on a major and systematic scale with an explicit scientific basis is, however, relatively recent, while other sciences have a longer history of being invoked to resolve crime, with arguably forensic medicine as the earliest case of a specific deployment of a science on a major systematic scale: 'Although most of what we now refer to as the forensic sciences did not begin to develop until the latter half of the 20th century, forensic medicine began to be recognised as a specialised branch of medicine, 'legal medicine' early in the 1800s.' (Lucas, 2014, p. 1805) A history of early applications of linguistic knowledge in the resolution of crime is given in Leonard et al. (2017). The first case of scientific application of modern technical linguistic knowledge is considered to be Svartvik (1968).[1]

It is instructive to compare the status of Forensic Linguistics, so defined and set off against legal linguistics, with the use of other sciences in forensics, some of them with a much longer standing in the forensic arena, such as medicine, psychology, entomology and artificial intelligence (Fadden & Disner, 2014). Forensic Linguistics, as part of the field of applied linguistics, stands in a paradigm with these sciences as they supply the technical knowledge of their fields that the application draws on. Forensic Linguistics belongs to the larger field of applied linguistics, fields of application of linguistic science that employ selected fields of scientific linguistic knowledge in applicational fields. An early discussion of status and peculiarities of Forensic Linguistics as an applied linguistic science is found in Kniffka (1990, p. IX) who claims that Forensic Linguistics is a subfield, to be established and consolidated, of applied linguistics.[2]

Scientific disciplines can to a large extent be characterised as questions that arise discipline-internally, whereas applied disciplines take knowledge from inside the canonised disciplines and try to answer questions that are posed in and from other areas. For instance, linguistics *is* not mathematics, but it applies tools from mathematics to explicitate properties of linguistic structures. Or forensic psychological veracity evaluation does not itself create new psychological concepts of analysis and description, but variously takes up such tools and applies them to an external domain of behaviour occurrence. Occasionally, these tools, as they originate from the home domain, do get modified in the process, as each empirical application of a tool or concept is a test for such tools or concepts.

But it will be clear that a forensic task context will always stand in a relationship of ad hoc application of knowledge from the canonical field, where these takings will be unconnected methodologically and epistemologically amongst each other: the results of a forensic medical evaluation is in principle completely unconnected from the application of linguistics to the same case. At best, they might point in the same direction. Sometimes they do not. And sometimes they may suggest calling in another discipline. And it is up to courts to achieve an evaluative comparison of the two. But an intrinsic scientific connexion between the two there is not, beyond some common ground in the rhetorical procedure of presenting evidence at court.

How completely different a forensic linguistic activity is from whatever pursuits are conducted under the rubric of legal linguistics becomes clear if we are aware of how much Forensic Linguistics is part of a paradigm of forensic uses of scientific knowledge. In principle, Forensic Linguistics, conducted in a professional way, is part of a forensic culture that defines a scientifically based application of scientific knowledge. The status and the distinguishing features of forensic activity—very different from anything else done in legal linguistics—apply to Forensic Linguistics in the same way as to other sciences, and the activities of Forensic Linguistics readily translate into the general framework of forensic science.

The development of a forensic science culture, such as called for by Mnookin et al. (2011) represents a watershed in a transition from an amateurish state of more or less dilettantist—in the positive sense of the historical 'dilettanti'—to a methodically reflected application of individual sciences to concrete cases. To what extent this highly transformative process has already taken place or is in the process of making is a matter of debate. Mnookin (2018) sees a glass at the same time half full and half empty. It is surely the case that this has progressed in different measure in different disciplines. The present volume is to be seen as an effort to contribute to further fill the glass and further entrench the disciplinary aims formulated in Kniffka (1990, pp. 1–55). The volume understands itself as further extending a developmental line of establishing the scientifically founded conception of a discipline of Forensic Linguistics in its own right opened up by Fobbe (2011), that is very separate from legal linguistics.

4 Forensic Linguistics as Part of Forensic Science Culture

Over the last two years there has been a more general discussion of the scientific nature and status of forensics, triggered by a perception that not all is well in this field. This perception has given rise to reports on the state of the art by top national research institutions. These reports in the US and GB and the ensuing discussions of the state of the art (and no longer a craft) are represented in Mnookin et al. (2011), Mnookin (2018), and Roux et al. (2015) who make an important conceptual distinction between different aspects of the wider forensic field:

> Forensics, the dominant model in the most developed countries, is defined as a series of enabling scientific disciplines that assist the criminal justice system as opposed to forensic science that is considered as a distinctive scientific discipline studying traces, the remnant of activity and/or presence, to address problems not only relevant to the court, but also to policing, intelligence and security, in general. In the forensics model, crime scene is considered as a separate police technical activity. (p. 7)

Therefore, part of the reorientation of the field is the widening of the perspective from local specialist to scientist with a much wider perspective. Forensic Linguistics is properly part of the larger field of forensic science and, therefore, has to take part in the discussions reflecting the state of the art of forensic science and suggestions for its elevation to a proper scientific discipline. Of the many reactions and suggestions generated in this discussion, the first and foremost one concerns an issue that goes to the very centre of the discipline as a scientific discipline. It is an open secret in the profession that Forensic Linguistics has on occasions suffered from presenting a less than favourable and convincing picture of itself to the legal world, and to judiciary, leading, in part, occasionally to evidence being disregarded. This does not refer to cases of conflicting evidence from different scholars, as it will always be the case that different types of 'traces' will be found, or 'traces' can be interpreted in different ways (cf. below), but to a type of case where there was a suggestion of lack of scientific technical knowledge. For instance, working in legal linguistics does not make you an expert in Forensic Linguistics, and working in traditional stylistics doesn't either. The essential step towards a Forensic Linguistics that it is part of a broader Forensic Science culture is the paramount requirement of first-rate academic training in their discipline. Mnookin et al. (2011, p. 100), tracing back the origin of forensics to the beginning of the last century, points out that 'Until recently, most forensic scientists had law enforcement backgrounds that typically did not include substantial formal training in science' and, even more worrying, 'even now, few forensic practitioners have Ph.D.-level training in science.' (Mnookin et al., 2011, p. 100) This situation, of course, with respect to a primary precondition for a scientific conduct of practice, was no basis for a scientific culture—'until recently', to wit.

5 Trace-Sign-Evidence

A task for further steps in the 'consolidation' of Forensic Linguistics is a conceptualisation of its activities in the more general framework of forensic science. It is common, in forensic science, to distinguish between a 'trace' and 'evidence', a distinction that is applicable in the same way in

Forensic Linguistics: The distinction is generally recognised in Forensic Science: 'Interestingly, the discovered physical trace is often called physical "evidence," whether at scene, laboratory, or court, although there is a huge difference in reality between these three settings.' (Hazard & Margot, 2014, p. 1790) The difference between the status of a 'trace' and 'evidence' is at least one step of interpretation:

> A trace exists in itself and does not have a meaning initially (although it can be measured), except that it is perceived as a support with an unexploited potential of information that might explain issues in the investigated cases. Once this potential is recognised, it is considered as a sign that potentially pertains to the class of *relevant traces*. (Hazard & Margot, 2014, p. 1790)

At the heart of it all is a suspicion that there might by a 'trace' that is connected to a crime:

> the trace as information whose origin was a material residue of the investigated event. More specifically, it is defined as a mark, a signal, or an object that is a visible sign (not always visible by naked eye) and a vestige indicating a former presence (source level information) and/or an action (activity level) of something where the latter happened. The physical trace is the common, elementary, and indispensable piece of the forensic puzzle. (Hazard & Margot, 2014, p. 1784)

> The first step is the *discovery*: this step corresponds to the intervention after the event when forensic science practitioners come into play. This implies successive reflections, decisions, and actions that will condition the latter stages of the forensic science process. The problem of finding, detecting, and recognizing relevant traces is not trivial; it requires a comprehensive study to understand the types and mechanisms of transfer. In any way, without the discovery of the trace (or a realisation of an abnormal absence), there is also no object of analysis or reasoning. The *meaning-making process*: the information carried by the trace may be a strong indicator of source and/or activity. According to variable utilitarian dimensions and basic logical steps (such as trace-to-source, source-to-trace, trace-to-trace relationships), forensic science practitioners evaluate the potential information content of the trace. (Delémont et al., 2014, p. 1784f)

Margot (2011) points to an issue that arises above all in adversarial systems when experts are hired by lawyers for the different sides: 'the illusion that scientists present evidence when they really provide an evaluative opinion/statement for the prosecution or for the defense as if they were party to the matter. In such situations, scientists take sides and become advocates' (p. 796). This issue arises as a problem exactly at the point when the evaluation or elevation of traces to the status of evidence has to be performed by the judge, with the tasks of assigning 'sign' status and establishing the historical facts on the one hand and the elevation to the status of evidence assigned to different actors in the court, depending on the legal system (cf. Chap. 3 in this volume). Both steps are essentially interpretive.

So it is really strictly speaking not possible for someone to have 'found evidence' for a crime or for innocence: one may have found a trace and this trace may be interpreted as a sign, but this is different, logically, technically and procedurally, from the interpreted status of 'evidence', that is presented and evaluated—in a very different linguistic genre of communication—in the court.

It is however, a fact, in practical forensic work that the finding from one field may turn up a trace that suggests looking at the crime facts from another angle. As a result, another scientific discipline may be called in to analyse the case from its perspective. To use an abstract case, a quality of a voice recording analysed forensically by a phonetician may suggest calling in a psychiatrist or medical scientist. There is, of course, the issue that under normal circumstances, in a Roman law situation, the court will strictly circumscribe the brief of a forensic linguist with a very precise task with very precise questions that really leave no room for comments or interpretations that would lead the forensic scientist farther afield and away from the discipline originally called in (cf. Chap. 4 in this volume).

While the logical steps of forensic inquiry as briefly outlined above, especially the distinction between the three steps involving the detection of traces, its 'meaning' assignment by interpreting it as a 'sign' of a potential criminal activity and the presentation to the court, easily translate into linguistic forensics, there are some interesting issues as to nature and reach of the linguistic 'trace'. In situations where discourse interpretation or conversational analysis is required, such as in the famous case of 'let him have it'—shoot him or hand over the gun to him—(cf. below) it would appear that all stages, from identifying the physical signal to the pragmatic interpretation of what type of proposition was 'meant', still work on establishing the trace. It is a peculiarity of language use that substantial interpretive, inductive and abductive processes are involved in even establishing the nature of the trace, and often enough methods from different perspectives have to be used, where such methods cannot claim to have exclusive rights as to the road to truth, but must be seen as complementary to each other in a situation of multiplicity of perspectives, as Ainsworth and Juola (2019) have pointed out in a recent survey of the state of the art that pretty much defines the current state developments of methodologies in the field.

Very often, in forensic issues, the trace involves some deviation from an expected value. The first initial input to the discovery of this type of trace is some very obvious, foregrounded or marked aspect of a segment of physically occurring language that registers with either the normal language user or the trained expert. Deviating always implies some baseline perception of normalcy, the departure from which registers with, or can be detected by, the informed specialist. This issue is treated in more detail in a type of case where the baseline is of paramount importance in the contribution by Nicklaus and Stein (this volume), with special emphasis on how circumscribed such a baseline must be, minimally in terms of idiolect and genre. There is the additional issue of perceived baseline and baseline deviation and its congruence or not with a factual baseline. The reader has at this point to be referred back to the citation above by Delémont et al. (2014, p. 1784f), who point to the complexities involved in establishing even the initial stages of discovery.

The problem is especially virulent in the case of statistical quantitative traces. What must be accorded the status of the trace is the result of statistical procedure after calculation of significance, not the individual occurrence of the form in question. Only if the statistical significance of the deviation from a baseline of expected occurrence is established can the next interpretive step, the 'semantic meaning-making process' be taken.

A statistical result, even if firmly established as a deviation relative to a valid baseline, is no evidence yet. It needs to be interpreted, in a next logical step, in order to become evidence, and, in yet another step, to be presented at court.

6 Forensic Linguistics as a Science

In the process of processing physical trace, linguistic disciplines like discourse analysis (Chaps. 5, 7, 11 and 12 in this volume) or translation (Chap. 10 in this volume) might have to be called in. This does not make them forensic disciplines in themselves, or justify classing translation, or even legal translation, as fields of Forensic Linguistics. Discourse analysis, guided by technical scientific knowledge from relevant fields like interpretive interactive cognitive pragmatics, is the requisite linguistic conceptual tool, and not in itself a 'homebase' forensic discipline. Between calls for 'the general forensic scientist' and the discipline specialist (the linguist as forensic), we would want to position ourselves more to the latter pole (without neglecting practice or training the former). It seems obvious that the idea of a scientist equally competent—in the sense advocated by Mnookin et al. (2011) and Mnookin (2018)—in linguistics and in the natural sciences is a non-starter. This would amount to a return to an amateurish level of mastery of all disciplines. There are a few salient cases of colleagues with the requisite competencies in linguistics and law—both disciplines are, after all, language-based, and there do exist conjoined university courses at degree level in both fields. These non-generalisable cases cannot detract from the fact that even internal subdisciplines of linguistics—for example phonetics and varieties linguistics are by now so specialised and so far from each other that even any call for a 'general' linguist to perform trace analysis must appear completely unrealistic—let alone a 'general scientist' who straddles natural science and linguistics.

The fact that traces and evidence from different fields may be interconnected and that the wider field of forensic activities has been put under scrutiny with respect to its standards has also given rise to an initiative to restructure the whole field: 'The dominant conception of forensic science as a patchwork of disciplines primarily assisting the criminal justice system—i.e. forensics—is in crisis or at least shows a series of anomalies and serious limitations.' (Roux et al., 2015, p. 1) Instead, the field should re-orient towards 'the study of its contribution along the whole chain of the judicial process, from the crime scene, to the presentation of forensic information in court'.

From this point of view, there can therefore not be a 'forensic science' as a stand-alone discipline, at least not as far as linguistics is concerned. There is essentially no such scientific discipline, or else it would be a something like a Bric-a-brac, postmodern science-bricolage that no one could take seriously. In addition, it would raise the serious issue of what slices of a science to include, given that every case is different and the knowledge required from each field would have to border on the infinite—a methodological issue that will surface in another guise below.

The issue can be exemplified by a look at two subdisciplines that are often cited in contexts of Forensic Linguistics. Forensic Linguistics is not the only discipline that is applied in character and is related to legal linguistics. Translation was actually the midwife of the contact between language and law in many countries and continues to be at the centre of intersecting interest between the two disciplines in francophone countries. Translation and interpretation are clearly applied disciplines with an important role to play in the world of law, but they are not involved in the resolution of crime and are not subject to further pragmatic constraints in their execution, and in consequence are not part of forensics. Language mediation services might be called for in some situations as ancillaries, but that does not make them an integral constitutive facet of Forensic Linguistics.

Discourse analysis is often invoked especially in oral genres in common law contexts where essential parts of the adjudication process takes place in court and in addition in connexion with police interviews. Again, the logical place of these activities is at the intersection of linguistic theory and its application on empirical data in a specific context of use—in this case in legal genres. But this does not make them forensic in the sense of being applied to the resolution of crime. They may be called in to help resolve a particular case. But this specific forensic use is not the standard use of discourse analysis in the world of law. It is mostly used to elucidate 'meaning making' (Foolen, 2019, p. 43; Wilson & Carston, 2019, p. 33) at court and in interaction with the police.

Mnookin et al. (2011) and Mnookin (2018) are representative for calls from the side of evidence scholarship for a reform of forensic science. Apart from the issue of relevant scientific training, she also mentions the professional use of statistics. This 'statistical turn' (Mnookin, 2018, p. 111) applies to two aspects: the replacement of 'reasonable degrees' of 'scientific certainty' (Mnookin, 2018, p. 113) by statistically calculated probabilities of chance occurrence as the basis for reliability judgements and the application of computational analyses of expectedness or deviations of distributions in constituting a trace. Analysis of language provides specific problems that are different in nature from assessing other physical data dealt with by natural sciences. The main issue here is that nearly each case needs to have an individual baseline of expectedness from which a significant deviation can be registered and which must be defined separately for this particular case: One cannot have a pre-constructed corpus as a baseline that is not circumscribed or specific enough. Something like 'written language' will not do. The issue is described in more detail in Chap. 6 in this volume. Such an adequately circumscribed baseline that needs to be combined with idiolectal aspects exists only in the very rarest of cases. This requirement, of course, has severely limiting consequences for the feasibility of automatic analyses, with all their undoubted methodological advantages like cutting out cognitive biases of all kinds. Faced with an imperative necessity to respond to the meta-scientific calls from the side of the 'statistical turn', linguistic forensics would be left with the uncomfortable option to deal only with cases that are amenable to such analysis or pass up on performing—a highly unrealistic scenario (Ainsworth and Juola, 2019) for theoretical, methodological and practical reasons.

The answer to this challenge can only be that 'scientific' is not identical to 'statistical' or 'computational', but the advantages of automatic analysis should be exploited where possible and where the data situation lends itself to a quantitative approach. But there are clear cases where both approaches can and, in fact, have to, be applied, such as in the case of language crimes from defamation to threats where interpretive (what speech act is 'I know where you live?') and quantitative and formal methods ('what is the typical syntactic shape of an insult?', based on a corpus of this type of crime) have to be applied, as paradigmatically implemented by Muschalik (2018) in a 'mixed method' approach. In terms of the conceptual forensic framework advocated here, there will be two different types of traces, the comparative conjunction of which will then have to be evaluated whether they singly or in a converging way (if so the case happens to be) are to be interpreted as evidence.

Linguistic forensics is also in a special position through the fact that the physical type of trace, the data input, is of vastly different types of data, such as represented in the present volume that call for vastly different types of technical scientific competencies. These types of data are amenable to computational analysis to very varying degrees. As, in addition, each case from a comparable field, say phonetic analysis, is different, there cannot be a blanket imperative to exclusively apply automatically accessible available data exclusively. As indicated above, this type of trace must be carefully evaluated with respect to the input parameters and output figures in order to be interpretable and transformable into evidence. In particular, statistical preferences cannot a priori be equated with causal connections, but need a further evaluational and integrational step of hermeneutic interpretation. In addition, input parameters will come from logically preceding hermeneutic and linguistic decisions—for example whether personal pronouns or 'negative emotions' are included in a measurement and counted must be based on a linguistic theory of the various very different types of functions of the same pronoun form and on a theory of what is an emotion and what types of emotions there are in which context and how they are linguistically realised. There is a massive amount of linguistics before even the first digit is counted, and what an expected distribution is and how any deviation can be evaluated in a Popperian fashion, is still a long way from trace to evidence.

7 The Pragmatics of Forensic Linguistics: Training Requirements

The claim to locate the forensic linguist in a comprehensive context of a forensic science in the sense advocated in the citation by Roux et al. (2015), suggesting training for a competence all the way from policing, trace analysis to presenting findings at court and suggesting their translation into evidence at court, defines competence and training requirements that go way beyond a scientific competence in a field of science—in this case linguistics—and, in addition, beyond anything the legal linguists would consider their briefs. This constitutes yet another main borderline within the area of language and law, in addition to the ones mentioned already. The legal linguist is a theoretician, but the forensic linguist has the practical task of having to act, to appear at court, know the rules of conducting and executing this part of the law, different in different legal cultures (cf. Chaps. 2, 3 and 4 in this volume) and also acquire a rhetoric for presenting evidence at court (cf. Chap. 5 in this volume). The rhetoric will have to be different and more persuasive in an agonistic system like the common law system than in most Roman law countries, where the forensic's contribution is more in the nature of an account, solicited by the judge, and not commissioned or even 'purchased' by counsel.

Apart from the challenge to 'translate' the results of trace analysis into a sign that may in turn be counted as 'evidence', the forensic linguist may be faced with a problem that is specific to the forensic linguist, and less to the forensic scientist from other fields. The legal profession is characterised by a specific ideology of language, which, to a large extent, as a professional requirement, is a reinforced version of the ideology of standardisation (Milroy & Milroy, 1999). These ideas tend to be very far from the potential of a technically up-to-date knowledge of the functioning of linguistic communication. Lawyers tend to think of language in terms of fixed chunks, correctly used, of form and function associations, in a fixed 'yes' or 'no', 'true' or 'not true', 'correct' or 'not correct' way, much in the nature of bricks, and tend not to be aware of the dynamic semiotisation processes as uncovered by a more modern pragmatic analysis of what goes on in discourse. In fact, much of the assumption of bi-uniqueness between form and function not only underlies ideas about amenabilities to formaliseability and quantitative procedures, but also underlies notions of literalness, which basically assumes a stable, direct and contextually undefiled association between form and meaning.

Lawyers and judges may be a priori mistrustful of linguistic expertise because of their own folklore and prescription-based view of what language is and how language analysis can or ought to be carried out. Above all, the judiciary is a profession with a very special relationship towards language. As pointed out at the beginning of this introductory chapter, the world of the law is tied up in an all-encompassing way with language, and everyone considers themselves an expert on language qua virtue of possessing, using and commenting on language, something that is not true for most natural sciences with a much clearer subject-object separation at least in their perception of the object. This puts the expert linguist in a very particular limelight and can define additional burdens in the forensic process, in addition to the ones imposed by the newly formulated requirements of rigorous scientific standards and training.

It is very often difficult to pinpoint exactly the birth of a new discipline, but as indicated above, an essential criterion for its canonisation as a scientific discipline (for being granted money, for establishing degree courses, giving doctorates and devoting chairs) is putting an end to a state of affairs characterised by Mnookin et al. (2011, p. 106): 'forensic practitioners even today typically lack doctoral-level science training. Judgment honed by experience is the primary coin of the realm, not formal empirical study or statistical modeling.'

It should at this point be highlighted that the first truly scientific application on a major scale with consequences for a court decision of modern linguistic science (Svartvik, 1968) was performed by an eminent professional linguist, who co-authored a standard and most widely used linguistic description of morphology and syntax of English (Quirk et al., 1972). Svartvik typifies a class of linguistic professionals who now play a major role in the analysis of language in the forensic context.

So the issue is not the birth of Forensic Linguistics, but rather a second coming of the discipline on new founding stones in several respects, such as early invoked by Kniffka (1990) and Chaski (2013). The predominance in the field of scientifically not well-trained 'practitioners' has of course meant that there is neither time nor incentive to publish: the lots of time it takes to work scientifically and to prepare peer-reviewed publication and spend days and money on copy-editing, has meant that there is not much motivation to publish and expose underlying theory and practice to open scientific discourse and criticism—a precondition for any discipline that is worth its money. There is, of course, another motivation for not publishing: to the extent proprietary methods are developed and money is charged for their application, making a professional secret public means loss of income—an important factor above all in systems where service providers are private companies, and not state agents. Money is the great crux of Forensic Linguistics. The more service providers are acting as businesses the greater the danger is that the 'hired gun' culture will be conducive to seek and produce features that can serve as 'evidence' in the direction of their funders—a situation that calls for an explicit code of professional ethics (cf. Chap. 1 in this volume).

The lack of published scientific work was explicitly noted in the Report by the 2009 National Academy of Science, as cited by Mnookin et al. (2011, p. 105):

> The simple reality is that the interpretation of forensic evidence is not always based on scientific studies to determine its validity. This is a serious problem. There is a notable dearth of peer-reviewed, published studies establishing the scientific bases and validity of many forensic methods.

The dearth of a body of published, peer-reviewed work means, in turn, that there is no basis on which new generations of forensic linguists can be trained. Another inhibiting factor relates to the very nature of practical forensic work: understandably enough, it is often ~~enough~~ immunised by non-disclosure agreements.

A substitute that at first sight seems an attractive prospect for use in research and training is the use of laboratory data. This seems to work for different fields of Forensic Linguistics in vastly varying degrees. There is no doubt that it will be a successful procedure in author identification. For this purpose, a programme can validly be tested in concrete, not crime-related, training cases. Training must include the necessary competence in handling computerised empirical data even in cases where the statistical methods are in the process of being developed (cf. Chap. 8 in this volume). In other cases, where verbal behaviour is directly analysed without the possibility of a formal measurement of identity or deviation, like in lie or deception detection, the use of laboratory data is dangerously misleading:

> While there is no question that the laboratory provides much greater control and precision than conducting research in real world contexts, it does so, I believe, at the expense of utility. That is, the context of the laboratory is so different from the contexts of many crimes, particularly violent crimes, that using the lab to study memory in the forensic context is pointless. The gain in control and precision is vacuous.[3] (Yuille, 2013, p. 9)

And later:

> The cure for methodolotry [sic] is that we have to abandon our faith in the laboratory/experimental method as the appropriate methodology for studying forensic questions. We have to stop forcing the questions to conform to the methodology and instead adapt the methodologies to the needs of the particular question.[4] (Yuille, 2013, p. 19)

These postulates are formulated for forensic activities in general. So they equally apply to linguistic forensic analysis which in many ways is faced with the same methodological issues as more narrowly forensic linguistic research. In fact, major psychological procedures in veracity evaluation include linguistic aspects (cf. Chap. 6 in this volume).[5] The reservations regarding experimental research apply with a vengeance to 'experimental' research on lying and deceit, where large body of research must face substantial criticism with respect to its methodological validity: 'Although there is a large literature on evaluating truthfulness, it is marred by several problems that impact its generalisability to real-world settings. A major problem with this body of research is that it has been conducted predominately in the controlled setting of the laboratory. It is argued that, by relying almost exclusively on the laboratory, researchers have committed the offence of methodolotry' (cf. Yuille, 2013). Researchers' strong belief in the utility of controlled research has led them to rely on laboratory analogues to study truthfulness and deceit. More weight has been placed on methodological concerns than on issues concerning generalisability and applicability. In the modal experiment on deception, undergraduate research participants tell the truth or lie about some activity or opinion. The motives to fool others are usually weak (e.g. a small monetary incentive or course credit) and the consequences of being caught in such low-stakes lies have no significant personal or social consequences. The end result is that more is known about how to trigger effects using laboratory designs in undergraduate students instructed to lie under low consequence paradigms than how real-world deception and its detection takes place.

Another methodological problem is the over-reliance on group designs. While group designs that compare truth tellers and liars meet stringent research requirements, the practice of evaluating truthfulness focuses on one individual, typically in the context of an interview, and therefore necessitates a single-subject design for analysis. (Cooper et al., 2013, 2014).

Apart from the difference between research context and real-life context that is targeted by Cooper et al. (2013, 2014), the complexities involved in going from the trace of a linguistic surface form back to the cognitive processes underlying them (the aim of veracity evaluation) currently seem insurmountable. The whole processes of choice and strategy involved in going from a communicative goal of an individual in a specific utterance situation to the selection of a form are simply not amenable to reductive process such as a controlled laboratory experiment would require—a lesson taught by modern interactive pragmatics. Going the other way round, analysing a linguistic form and trying to reconstruct backwards the cognitive state that led to the form is the bane of much forensic activity: 'Was the act intentional?' 'Is the function of the discourse to consciously mislead the partner?' 'Is the utterance meant to hurt and offend?' 'What in fact was the intended meaning of an utterance?' These issues may be relevant in everyday communication, but in a legal context they must be made explicit, as well as the type of reasoning behind both use and explicit analysis, as 'guilty' or 'not guilty' depend on it. It is a fact of language—and one of the central challenges for Forensic Linguistics—that there is no bi-uniqueness between function and form, and there is a multitude of knowledge and motivation types that intervenes between form and function. The interpretive reconstruction of these steps is a task of establishing the trace. This, then, the very nature of the tasks, is another characterising feature of Forensic Linguistics that defines training requirements.

So the call to include for the 'statistical turn' (Mnookin, 2018, p. 111) should be taken, at least as far as Forensic Linguistics is concerned, to imply the competence, the aptitude and the judicious inclusion of quantitative methods and laboratory data where this is appropriate, and not in a blanket and monolithic way (cf. Chap. 10 in this volume).

Therefore, the frequent non-availability of original cases in their life context and the impossibility of their laboratory emulation defines a very specific challenge for training, and consequently the quality of practical work, in the field. This, in turn, means that original data cannot be used for training purposes. Proper scientific training implies that cases be presented in teaching in their very full internal and external contexts: A disputed case of evidence in the context of perjury discussing—for example 'Did the defendant lie and commit perjury?'—needs to be subjected to a thorough analysis in terms of discourse-pragmatically analysed full contextual situation. Not only is there not full access to the trace—'text' (nothing short of a videotape will really do) of the communication that took place, but it is always extremely difficult to trace the full 'meaning-making' processes that went on mutually in the cognitions of the participants.

And this is, after all, what the judges need to ultimately have as a basis for 'evidence' status: 'Did she or he want to or incite to kill or not?' More precisely, 'did she or he intend to kill or to incite to kill or not?' There is, after all, a difference between a first- and second-degree murder charge. The full range of scientific knowledge especially in terms of modern scientific knowledge of pragmatics and discourse analysis required to analyse a criminal case lege artis is illustrated through the analysis of the famous 'Derek Bentley case', where the reconstruction of the meaning-making process hinges on the intention and understanding of 'Let him have it, Chris' and its full context, as well as the discourse conditions of the police-produced 'text' trace (Coulthard et al., 2017, pp. 163–171). The reconstruction of the communicational trace—the internal information-flow structure of the communication both in the actual origin and the processing in the police report—also highlights another communicational issue that constitutes yet another challenge for the competence of the forensic linguist in the latter end of her or his activity: how can the analytic reasoning be presented to the court and the judge in a way that is far from a folklore or stereotypical ideas about language on the side of the recipients in the court? This highlights another training requirement for the forensic linguist: how to 'sell' the analysis to the court.

Forensic Linguistics is not a classical scientific field with epistemological tenets and procedures in itself with a unified set, or schools of such sets, organised in theories, concepts and methods, but a field of application of such pre-existing knowledge sets and theories. This is true for most fields of applied linguistics. Language acquisition and language teaching are in the same situation: they take up pre-existing linguistic theories of what language is like and predict, on the basis of constraints derived from them, how the acquisition and the teaching of these properties will function: whether in formal or functional terms, or what versions of them, will give you different types of processes and theories of acquiring and teaching.

However, in language acquisition the 'applicational' field is much more homogeneous than in Forensic Linguistics, and therefore much more amenable to one coherent theory or at least type of theory. This is very different in Forensic Linguistics. The only typifying constraining parameter is 'language use in a context deemed potentially criminal' by agents of the legal system. This in itself is nowhere near constituting anything like a 'genre', which could then suggest a unified type of methodology, or something that could be taught as a unified subject. So, from the perspective of Forensic Linguistics, it does not make sense to establish a subject 'General Forensic Linguistics', or train a 'General Forensic Linguist', but as Chaski (2013) emphasises: 'Scientifically respectable and judicially acceptable methods for author identification should be: a. developed independent of any litigation; b. tested for accuracy outside of any litigation' (p. 334).

Each case for Forensic Linguistics in principle belongs to a different type of genre. There cannot be, from this point of view, the same type of unity of approach as in, for instance, the analysis of oral genres (like a cross-exam) at court in an adversarial system. This individuality of application cases and its recalcitrance to methodological unification makes Forensic Linguistics an applied linguistics species of a very special kind.

As a consequence, the lack of typefiability and the individuality of cases strongly constrains the type of applicable theoretical knowledge, and the type of linguistic approach. Few generalisations seem, therefore, applicable to which type of linguistic knowledge is applicable to solving a case from the linguistic point of view. It would appear that these are mostly not system-based or compositional approaches, but broadly speaking usage-based and functional approaches.

It is probably safe to say that a thorough technical knowledge not below a PhD-level training in more functional than formal linguistics is a minimum requirement. Other necessary areas of training for the forensic linguist are: (a) experimental design, (b) scientifically based methods and tools, (c) statistical analysis, (d) the rules of evidence, (e) scholarly and legal ethics, (f) writing the evaluative report, (g) giving expert opinion and (g) courtroom interaction.

8 This Volume

This volume purports to be part of the reaction to the calls for a renewal of Forensic Linguistics. This is where the present volume aims to make a contribution. As a scientific discipline, there is no pretence of finality or completeness, just a measure of broad consensus, at this point of writing, that what is presented here represents the present state of the art, represented by practitioners of the field, all of them with (at least) doctoral degrees.

Since the earlier textbooks of the field, linguistic research has advanced on many fronts so that the applicability to forensic issues and the sophistication of the methods of analysis have increased accordingly and warrant an update of substantial parts of the field. As two examples one can cite the use of computers, corpora and artificial intelligence and the changes in the perspectives of pragmatics, especially the turn towards interactive cognitive pragmatics. On the other hand, the new technical medial affordances have created new types of crimes.

As behoves a true scientific field, there is variation and controversy in approaches and ample internal discussion, some of which is focused in the discussions at ILLA Focus Conferences on Forensic Linguistics. While it is clear that the editors have personal preferences in their perspectives on the field, care has been taken to present, not a theoretical monoculture, but a glimpse on the broader spectrum with the claim of scientific foundation from outside the practice of forensic analysis itself, but with concrete analyses for exemplification to the extent possible given obvious, and obviously massive, data protection constraints.

This volume aims to provide a non-dogmatic introduction to the field of Forensic Linguistics and its areas of expertise. While the volume is scientifically based and draws on the most modern published work in the specialised areas represented, it does not purport to be a comprehensive survey of the most recent work in all fields because it would burst the quantitative boundaries of a volume as it is intended. The volume's intention is also didactic to the extent that it aims to introduce the range of methods in the field and what counts as scientific procedure. At the same time, it defines, in the process, the necessary breadth of knowledge required before forensic practice can be embarked upon professionally. This approach appears necessary as there is a growing number of courses of study that give the impression that there are not always enough standardised levels of science-based knowledge available, which may lay practitioners in the field open to the charge of dilettantism and thereby damage the field as a whole.

The book is divided into two different but at the same time closely related parts. Part I (Chaps. 2–5) focus on the role of the linguist as expert witness in common law and civil law jurisdictions. Part II (Chaps. 6–13) brings together some of the major areas of expertise of forensic linguistics and their investigative methodologies. Whereas some of them are well-established areas of expertise—that is authorship identification, speaker identification, plagiarism detection and the authenticity of suicide notes—others such as statement veracity assessment and cyberlanguage crimes such as online scams and terrorist threats are emerging and currently developing. For didactic purposes, the chapters in Part II share the same structure: (1) introductory definition of the area of inquiry, (2) the state of the art, theories and controversies in the area, (3) description and explanation of the most significant methodologies, (4) exemplary case study and (5) conclusions and suggestions for further research. In what follows we give an overview of the contents of the volume chapters.

In Chap. 2, 'Serving Science and Serving Justice: Ethical Issues Faced by Forensic Linguists in Their Role as Expert Witnesses', Janet Ainsworth introduces the figure of the expert witness emphasising their commitment to empirically based science and fair justice. Ainsworth foregrounds and discusses in detail seven aspects of the legal process that potentially raise ethical issues for expert witnesses: (1) the ethical issues involved in being retained by an attorney for a party, (2) the ethical issues involved in turning down participation in a case, (3) the ethical issues involved in expert witness compensation, (4) the ethical issues involved in analysing a case, including confirmation bias and motivation bias on the part of the expert, (5) the ethical issues involved in preparing to testify under oath, (6) the ethical issues involved in drafting expert reports and (7) the ethical issues involved in communications during the trial.

Chapters 3 and 4 discuss the legal doctrines ruling the use of expert witnesses in common law and civil law jurisdictions. Specifically, in Chap. 3, 'Linguistic Expert Evidence in the Common Law', Andrew Hammel traces the history of the expert witness in the common law from eighteenth century to the present time. The chapter further describes the change in court admissibility criteria in US legal decisions as a result of *Frye* and *Daubert* standards. Lastly, the chapter analyses the current relevant legal standards for qualification as an expert witness and expert opinion in the common law jurisdictions, with special emphasis on US law.

In Chap. 4, 'Expert Evidence in Civil Legal Systems', Mercedes Fernández-López foregrounds the fact that, contrary to common law jurisdictions, expert witnesses are not regulated in detail and not even expressly provided for in all civil law jurisdictions. The chapter describes the main regulatory differences governing expert evidence in civil legal systems—that is who has the initiative to propose the expert evidence (the court and/or the parties), how the experts are selected and how the evidence is practised. The chapter further discusses the probative value of expert opinion and its influence on the court decision.

In Chap. 5, 'Interacting with the Expert Witness: Courtroom Epistemics Under a Discourse Analyst's Lens', Magdalena Szczyrbak's primary concern is to explain, from a discourse analysis perspective, how, in a court trial, expert witnesses interact with the counsel while negotiating the status and validity of their expert knowledge. Specifically, using data from a US murder trial, the chapter analyses the discursive mechanisms involved in the presentation of expert knowledge in an institutional setting marked by power and epistemic asymmetries. Furthermore, the chapter demonstrates the usefulness of corpus-assisted discourse studies for identifying some of the linguistic choices expert witnesses make affecting the weight and credibility attributed to their testimony.

In Chap. 6, 'A Lie or Not a Lie, That Is the Question. Trying to Take Arms Against a Sea of Conceptual Troubles: Methodological and Theoretical Issues in Linguistic Approaches to Lie Detection', Martina Nicklaus and Dieter Stein provide a survey of key theoretical and methodological issues in statement veracity assessment—an area traditionally dominated by forensic psychologists—from a linguistic perspective. The chapter first examines the controversial notion of *truth*. It then gives an overview of psychological and other approaches verifying the truthfulness or untruthfulness of verbal reports. At the heart of the chapter is the discussion of the methodological burdens the expert linguist must deal with when assessing statement veracity. Among the most outstanding ones is the scarcity of 'ground truth' data *external* to the assessment against which the result of linguistic analysis can be checked. The authors argue that an additional methodological burden is related to the *internal* assessment—that is a linguistic form may have different discourse-related functions depending on the speech event and communication genre. Furthermore, the same form may even have different argumentative values in different individuals. The chapter illustrates the identification and analysis of linguistic indicators in statement veracity assessment through a selected sample of true and untrue statements of minors claiming sexual abuse. The chapter ends claiming the inclusion of linguistic cues in statement veracity assessment tests on a systematic and technical linguistic basis, as well as the need for further refinement in the definition and application of linguistic categories in psychological tools of analysis.

Chapter 7, 'Authorship Identification', by Eilika Fobbe focuses on authorship identification from a qualitative linguistic perspective. The chapter begins with the definitions of basic terms such as 'text', 'author' and 'authorship', and explains the differences between the types of subtasks the expert linguist may have to deal with under the general task of authorship identification—that is 'attribution', 'verification', 'profiling', 'imitation' and 'obfuscation'. Subsequently, the chapter outlines the state of the art in the expert area of authorship identification pointing out the controversies in the area. At the core of the discussion are the differences between qualitative linguistic approaches and quantitative automatic approaches to authorship identification. After defining some relevant theoretical concepts—that is 'idiolect', 'style' 'genre', 'text type', 'inter-author variation' and 'intra-author variation'—the chapter explains qualitative linguistic methodologies such as error analysis and style analysis. The theoretical discussion is illustrated through the analysis of a live case of severe arson in a city in the south-west of Germany where an anonymous offender had set several shops on fire. The police wanted to know from the BKA forensic linguist whether the author of the anonymous emails to the State police threatening to continue the arson in the case was the same as the one who had written the extorsion letter found at the crime scene in an earlier case.

The area of automatic authorship identification has experimented considerable advance over the last few years, with the development of promising scientific research into information retrieval and deep learning—a subfield of machine learning concerned with the design of algorithms inspired by the structure and function of the brain called artificial neural networks. Deep learning can assist the forensic linguist in automatically deciding the features and patterns that best characterise an author's idiolect, classify texts depending on the set features and patterns, and allot texts to their corresponding authors effectively (cf. Chaps. 8 and 13). In Chap. 8, 'Automatic Authorship Investigation', Hans van Halteren investigates deep-learning-based-authorship identification. The author organises the discussion around several key questions such as: 'How much undisputed and disputed text is necessary for a reliable judgement?' 'How many features and which features are needed?' 'Which statistical or machine learning method should be used in comparing the various authors' feature measurements?' And 'to which degree are the frequencies also influenced by the communicative situation and by the text topic?' van Halteren conducts an experiment on automatic authorship verification based on romance fiction books—published by the British publisher Mills and Boon in the 1990s—included in the *British National Corpus*. The experiment aims at comparing the efficiency of a deep-learning-based authorship identification approach to the traditional automatic authorship identification method. The chapter concludes by delineating further lines of research regarding the deep learning approach, which may bring some radical changes in automatic authorship investigation over the next years.

In Chap. 9, 'Speaker Identification', Gea de Jong-Lendle analyses how voice analysis can assist in solving a crime. Forensic phonetics is the sub-area of phonetics that deals with the analysis of voice—and speech—for the purpose of criminal investigations. The chapter first gives an overview of the different types of tasks that forensic phoneticians carry out when investigating a case, and then describes and demonstrates methodological strategies using materials from live cases.

In Chap. 10, 'Plagiarism Detection: Methodological Approaches', Victoria Guillén-Nieto deals with the expert area of plagiarism detection. The chapter examines the problems challenging the expert linguist's work, laying emphasis on the evaluation of text similarity. Subsequently, the chapter discusses the main plagiarism frameworks, and addresses the latest research in computer-based plagiarism detection methods and their implementation in automated plagiarism detection systems. Furthermore, the chapter points to the essential complementary role that qualitative linguistic analysis plays in plagiarism detection and foregrounds the relevance of context in understanding and interpreting the data appropriately. Lastly, the author provides the reader with a step-by-step guide to the elaboration of the expert opinion at the same time she analyses a live case of plagiarism between Spanish translators of Oscar Wilde's *The nightingale and the rose* (1888). The author employs an integrative method combining a computer-based approach using *CopyCatch Gold* v2 (Woolls, 2002) and a qualitative linguistic approach. Finally, for the elaboration of the evaluative report conclusions, the author uses an inductive probability scale.

In Chap. 11, 'The Linguistic Analysis of Suicide Notes', Monika Zaśko-Zielińska deals with the authenticity of suicide notes. The chapter first defines the suicide note as a communication genre, describes its generic features and points to the difficulties involved in the linguistic analysis of such texts, especially their short length, their mixed features of written and spoken register, and their emotional basis, among others. The chapter discusses the current state of the art of suicide notes analysis. Furthermore, it explains in detail the linguistic methodologies employed in the analysis of suicide notes, foregrounding the assistance of corpus linguistics and genre theory in delineating a safe 'baseline' against which suspicious suicide notes can be compared and contrasted. The chapter subsequently analyses in detail an exemplary case study involving the authenticity of a questioned suicide note. The method the author employs is empirically based and results from the qualitative and quantitative analyses of a collection of 614 authentic suicide notes from the *Polish Corpus of Suicide Notes* (PCSN) and compiled as part of the experimental *Corpus of Forged Suicide Notes*.

The last two chapters of the volume are devoted to language cybercrimes. With the advent of internet, old crimes have reinvented themselves and other crimes have emerged. Because cybercrime is mostly transnational, legal and investigative procedures are seriously challenged and thereby need incessant updating to deal with the continually evolving phenomenon of cybercrime. Similarly, electronic criminal genres have made linguists abandon the traditional idea of a genre as encapsulated in a fixed template and thus adopt more dynamic views allowing research into the spatial and temporal discontinuity of the integrative units of online genres and multiple authorship. Furthermore, the analysis of language cybercrimes often involves the analysis and processing of large population data that is only plausible with the assistance of artificial intelligence. The analysis of language cybercrime has also prompted the development of scientific research in information retrieval and deep learning.

In Chap. 12, 'Fighting Cybercrime Through Linguistic Analysis: The case of online romance scams', Patrizia Anesa analyses the criminal genre of online romantic scams. The chapter shows the narrative structure and lexical choices the scammer uses to gain the victim's trust and ultimately defraud them. The chapter illustrates the linguistic analysis of online romantic scams through a corpus of authentic romance scams. The author uses a computer-based approach to scams analysis based on word frequencies and keyness analysis. The author claims that this method is specifically designed for early detection and prevention measures against scammers.

In Chap. 13, 'Linguistic Approaches to the Analysis of Online Terrorist Threats', Julien Longhi investigates online terrorist threats. The chapter shows the application of a combined approach integrating semantic analysis, textometry and deep learning, to a case of online terrorist threat taken from the author's collaboration with the French Gendarmerie. As in the case of Chap. 12, the type of analysis employed by the author is designed for early detection and prevention measures of online terrorist threats.

As shown above, the volume contents are wide-ranging regarding the areas of expertise, and it also integrates the best of both worlds: qualitative linguistic-based approaches with quantitative computer-based approaches. The purpose of each chapter in Part II is to 'teach' the reader, either student or practitioner, either academic or professional, good research practices through a detailed analysis of an exemplary case study. The novice reader in Forensic Linguistics may be disappointed to know that there is no single valid method or recipee to analyse a forensic text. In each case, the forensic linguist must carefully define the speech events, study the data, make general observations, formulate null and alternative hypotheses, choose the most convenient linguistic and non-linguistic tools to find the trace that every forensic text leaves, analyse the data objectively, systematically, and accurately, and reach conclusions grounded in the findings obtained. The method employed must be scientifically based, capable of being repeated by the same forensic linguist, and replicable by other forensic linguists to meet general court admissibility criteria (Ainsworth & Juola, 2019). Apart from a sound technical linguistic—and non-linguistic—knowledge, forensic linguistic analysis demands observation skills and scientific creativity—the ability to form mental images and visualise and/or to think in terms of various possibilities—to identify a trace, transform it into language facts that, once validated by the judge or jury as evidence, may assist the court to deliver a fair decision.

Notes

1. A much earlier case of an application of professional linguistic knowledge to the resolution of a crime of falsification with major political consequences for the political power of the Pope in the middle age was brought to our attention by Emma Stein: the 'Donation of Constantine' was shown by Lorenzo Valla—priest and early linguist—to be a falsification (Harari, 2017, p. 263f).

2. "Der vorliegende Band müßte eigentlich "Texte zu Praxis und Theorie.." heißen; diese Formel gibt es im Deutschen aber wie den Ausdruck "Stand der Praxis" nicht. …Der Band möchte nämlich,…zur Konsolidierung "forensischer Linguistik", eines konstituierenden Teilfachs der Angewandten Linguistik, beitragen." (Kniffka, 1990, p. IX).
3. As a concrete example for the discrepancy between different types of witnesses and laboratory experiments in the case of veracity evaluation of with respect to lying 'clues' see Hettler (2012, p. 144).
4. That this is seen as a general issue in psychology—and linguistics is to be included here—is formulated as follows: 'the reliance on laboratory research has had a profound negative effect on the discipline, retarding our understanding of many psychological phenomena in the forensic field. In the title to this chapter I used the term "methodolotry". I use the term to characterize the reliance among psychologists on the use of standard experimental design in laboratory-based research (…) This method—conducting research in a relatively sterile context and manipulating some factors while other factors are controlled—is the dominant method of conducting psychological research.' (Yuille, 2013, p. 3)
5. Cf Hettler (2012) for a discussion of theoretical and methodological issues in procedures used in psychological veracity evaluation.

References

Ainsworth, J., & Juola, P. (2019). Who wrote this?: Modern forensic authorship analysis as a model for valid forensic science. *Washington University Law Review, 96*(5), 1161–1189.

Chaski, C. (2013). Best practices and admissibility of forensic author identification. *Journal of Law & Policy, 21*(2), 333–376.

Cooper, B., Griesel, D., & Ternes, M. (Eds.). (2013). *Applied issues in investigative interviewing, eyewitness memory, and credibility assessment.* Springer.

Cooper, B., Hugues, F., Herve, F., & Yuille, J. (2014). Evaluating truthfulness: Interviewing and credibility assessment. In G. Bruinsma & D. Weisburd (Eds.), *Encyclopedia of criminology and criminal justice* (pp. 1413–1426). Springer. https://doi.org/10.1007/978-1-4614-5690-2_534

Coulthard, M., & Johnson, A. (Eds.). (2010). *The Routledge handbook of forensic linguistics.* Taylor & Francis.

Coulthard, M., Johnson, A., & Wright, D. (Eds.). (2017). *An introduction to forensic linguistics: Language in evidence* (2nd ed.). Routledge.

Delémont, O., Lock, E., & Ribaux, O. (2014). Forensic science and criminal investigation. In G. Bruinsma & D. Weisburd (Eds.), *Encyclopedia of criminology and criminal justice* (pp. 1754–1763). Springer. https://doi.org/10.1007/978-1-4614-5690-2_145

Fadden, L., & Disner, S. F. (2014). *Forensic linguistics*. In G. Bruinsma & D. Weisburd (Eds.), *Encyclopedia of criminology and criminal justice* (pp. 1547–1555). Springer. https://doi.org/10.1007/978-1-4614-5690-2_534

Fobbe, E. (2011). *Forensische Linguistik. Eine Einführung*. Gunter Narr.

Foolen, A. (2019). Quo vadis Pragmatics? From adaptation to participatory sense-making. *Journal of Pragmatics, 145*, 29–46.

Gibbons, J. (2003). *Forensic linguistics. An introduction to language in the justice system*. Blackwell.

Gibbons, J., & Turell, M. T. (Eds.). (2008). *Dimensions of forensic linguistics* (AILA Applied Linguistics Series, 5). John Benjamins Publishing Company.

Harari, Y. N. (2017). *Homo Deus. Eine Geschichte von Morgen*. Beck.

Hazard, D., & Margot, P. (2014). Forensic science culture. In G. Bruinsma & D. Weisburd (Eds.), *Encyclopedia of criminology and criminal justice* (pp. 1782–1795). Springer.

Hettler, S. (2012). *Wahre und falsche Zeugenaussagen. Evaluation von Zeugenaussagen mit unterschiedlichem Wahrheitsgehalt mittels erweitertem Kanon inhaltlicher Kennzeichen*. AV Akedemiker Verlag.

Kniffka, H. (Ed.). (1990). *Texte zu Theorie und Praxis forensischer Linguistik*. Niemeyer.

Leonard, R., Ford, J., & Christensen, T. (2017). Forensic linguistics: Applying the science of linguistics to issues of the law. *Hofstra Law Review, 45*, 881–897.

Lucas, D. (2014). Forensic science in the nineteenth and twentieth centuries. In G. Bruinsma & D. Weisburd (Eds.), *Encyclopedia of criminology and criminal justice* (pp. 1805–1819). Springer. https://doi.org/10.1007/978-1-4614-5690-2

Margot, P. (2011). Commentary on the need for a research culture in the forensic sciences. *UCLA Law Review, 58*, 725–779.

Milroy, J., & Milroy, L. (1999). *Authority in language. Investigating standard English* (3rd ed.). Routledge.

Mnookin, J. (2018). The uncertain future of forensic science. *DAEDALUS, 147*, 99–118.

Mnookin, J., et al. (2011). The need for a research culture in the forensic sciences. *UCLA Law Review, 58*, 725. https://www.uclalawreview.org/the-need-for-a-research-culture-in-the-forensic-sciences-2/

Muschalik, J. (2018). *Threatening in English. A mixed method approach*. Benjamins. e-Book ISBN: 9789027264633. https://doi.org/10.1075/pbns.284

Quirk, R., Greenbaum, S., Leech, G., & Svartvik, J. (1972). *A grammar of contemporary English*. Longman.

Roux, C., Talbot-Wright, B., Robertson, J., Crispino, F., & Ribeaux, O. (2015). The end of the (forensic science) world as we know it? The example of trace evidence. *Philosophical Transactions of the Royal Society B, 370*, 20140260. https://doi.org/10.1098/rstb.2014.0260

Smolka, J., & Pirker, B. (2016). International law and pragmatics—An account of interpretation in international law. *International Journal of Language and Law, 5*, 1–40.

Sources of Language and Law. https://legal-linguistics.net/

Stein, D. (2021). Sprache und Recht: das Recht als Forschungsobjekt der Sprachwissenschaft. In E. Vogenauer (Ed.), *Schiedsgerichtsbarkeit und Rechtssprache Festschrift für Volker Triebel*. Beck.

Svartvik, J. (1968). *The Evans statements: A case for forensic linguistics*. University of Göteborg.

Tiersma, P., & Solan, L. (Eds.). (2012). *The Oxford handbook of language and law*. Oxford University Press.

Vogel, F. (ed.) 2019. Legal linguistics beyond borders: Language and law in a world of media, globalisation and social conflicts. In Berlin, Duncker, & Humblot (Eds.), *Relaunching the international language and law association (ILLA)*. ISBN978-3-428-85423-3.

Wecht, C., & Rago, J. T. (2006). *Forensic science and law. Investigative applications in criminal, civil and family justice*. CRC and Taylor & Francis.

Wilson, D., & Carston, R. (2019). Pragmatics and the challenge of 'non-propositional' effects. *Journal of Pragmatics, 145*, 31–38.

Woolls, D. (2002). *CopyCatch Gold v2*. CL Software. UK.

Yuille, J. (2013). The challenge for forensic memory research: Methodolotry. In B. Cooper, D. Griesel, & M. Ternes (Eds.), *Applied issues in investigative interviewing, eyewitness memory, and credibility assessment* (pp. 3–19). Springer.

2

Serving Science and Serving Justice: Ethical Issues Faced by Forensic Linguists in Their Role as Expert Witnesses

Janet Ainsworth

1 Introduction

Linguists who research issues at the intersection of language and the law sometimes find themselves being consulted for their expertise to assist in legal cases. The typical practice in civil law countries is for judges to appoint experts to provide pertinent science-based evidence on behalf of the court, whereas in common law countries, the usual way in which expert evidence is brought to bear in legal cases is through an expert being retained to testify by the legal counsel of one of the parties. Despite this major difference in the civil law and common law systems' procurement of expert witness evidence, many of the ethical issues presented to the expert witness are similar regardless of legal system, and in some cases, turn out to be identical. This chapter is written from the perspective of an

J. Ainsworth (✉)
Seattle University, Seattle, WA, USA
e-mail: jan@seattleu.edu

V. Guillén-Nieto, D. Stein (eds.), *Language as Evidence*,
https://doi.org/10.1007/978-3-030-84330-4_2

author who spent several years litigating cases in the United States, but given the convergence in the use of expert evidence in civil law litigation and arbitration, it is expected the ethical and practical problems faced by expert witnesses in common law cases will be increasingly shared in civil law systems as well.

Lawyers have their own set of ethical issues and norms in practice, governed in the United States by the Rules of Professional Responsibility. Those rules are enforced by state bar associations; lawyers who break ethical rules can be disciplined, even ultimately disbarred for life. However, scientific experts such as linguists do not have the benefit of written, enforceable codes of ethics within their own discipline, although linguist Gail Stygall (2009) has suggested that such a code of ethics for forensic linguistics might be a valuable project to implement. Nor can linguists who serve as expert witnesses rely on the ethical regulations pertaining to lawyers, since the ethical rules defining improper conduct for lawyers differ substantially from the appropriate ethical constraints on experts offering their expertise to assist in court. With this in mind, this chapter will outline some of the main ethical concerns that linguists need to be aware of if they are approached to assist in a legal case.

2 The Ethics of Agreeing to Serve as an Expert in a Case

When attorneys are about to take on a new case, they must first determine whether they have a conflict of interest with regard to the potential new client. Lawyers cannot undertake to represent a client whose interests may adversely impact the interests of the lawyer's pre-existing clients—and this is true even if the earlier client's case is long since finished and the case file closed. Linguists, however, do not have this constraint. Linguists are free to testify on behalf of a party in one case, and against that same party in another case. Unlike the lawyer—who has a continuing duty of loyalty to all of their clients—the linguist's only duty of loyalty is to the science of linguistics.

The linguist's ethical considerations in agreeing to assist in a case come out of that loyalty to the science of linguistics. Linguistics is a field with many, many specialised sub-fields. No linguist could ever aspire to having equal expertise in all of the many branches of linguistics. The question that the linguist must first address before agreeing to serve as an expert is whether they have the necessary expertise to provide useful information to the fact-finding process in the appropriate resolution of this particular case. It is not invariably necessary that an expert witness have conducted research or have written peer-reviewed scholarship in the specific area of linguistics at issue in the case—although the ideal expert witness will have done so. This is a situation in which the perfect is the enemy of the good—as long as the linguist is fully conversant and up-to-date with the pertinent literature in the area in question, that linguistic expert can ethically agree to participate in the case.

This preliminary question—do you have enough expertise in the branch of linguistics pertaining to the matter at issue?—is one that the potential expert witness has an ethical duty to consider carefully before agreeing to participate in the case. Just because the would-be retaining attorney thinks a linguist is the right expert for the case does not relieve that linguist from making that judgement independently. Lawyers, after all, generally have no understanding of linguistics at all, and may be unaware that a dialectologist is probably not the right expert for a case turning on syntactic analysis of a statute, for example. Nor can the linguist rely on a determination of the judge qualifying them as an expert in the case. Judges do have the 'gatekeeping' obligation to make a legal ruling on whether a proffered witness is qualified to give expert evidence in a case (see *Daubert v. Merrill-Dow Pharmaceuticals*, 1993), but judicial lack of scientific background in the expert's field means that a judge may often be willing to qualify someone as an expert witness despite the proffered expert's actual lack of expertise in the area at issue in the case. Neither a lawyer's willingness to retain a linguist as an expert nor a judge's ruling that the linguist will be permitted to testify as an expert should relieve that linguist of the ethical obligation to turn down an appointment as an expert if it is beyond the scope of expertise possessed. The sole loyalty of the linguist in court is to the science of linguistics; providing evidence in areas in which the linguist lacks full expertise is to betray that loyalty.

3 Can the Expert Ethically Switch Sides if their Examination of the Facts Warrants Testifying for Opposing Counsel instead?

Consider the relatively common situation in which a linguist is contacted by a lawyer interested in retaining them as an expert witness, but the linguist, upon examining the factual record in the case, concludes that they cannot be helpful to the lawyer's case—in fact, their evidence, if admitted, would directly harm that lawyer's case. Clearly, the lawyer will not be calling this linguist to the witness stand in their case, after the potential expert witness has informed the lawyer that their testimony would not be helpful. May the linguist then offer their services to the other side of the case? Or, even assuming that the linguist does not volunteer to do so, if the other side offers to retain that linguist as an expert, is it ethical to agree? Again, legal ethics in a parallel situation are not a helpful guide to the linguist here. A lawyer who was fired by a client could not subsequently agree to work for the opposing side of the case because of the continuing duty of loyalty that lawyers owe to their clients, even their former clients. In contrast, expert witnesses have no duty to promote the interests of the clients of former or would-be retaining lawyers. So, at least in theory, an expert could work for the other side of a case from the side which originally contacted the expert hoping to retain them for their expert evidence. In practice, however, it is very often the case that, by the time that the expert makes the determination that they cannot be helpful to the attorney who originally sought to retain them, that expert is already privy to confidential information—client confidences and secrets and the developing trial strategy of the lawyer. If that is the case, as it usually is, then it is not permissible to defect to the other side—the expert will have to decline testifying in this case for either side.

4 What Are the Ethical Issues of Being Financially Compensated for Your Participation in the Case?

Being paid for your time and expertise is not inherently unethical, of course. The judge and the attorneys in the case are being paid for their time and professional expertise in court, and the expert likewise has professional expertise that warrants being compensated for their time and effort in serving as an expert witness. As noted above, if at some point in the preparation of the case, the expert realises that they cannot be helpful to the side that has retained them, that expert by that time will have already spent considerable effort on the case. It is ethical and entirely reasonable for the expert to demand to be compensated for the time spent determining whether they have the appropriate expertise and whether their expert analysis would likely be helpful to the retaining lawyer.

In fact, it is a wise practice for any expert who is being retained to require an upfront consulting fee from the lawyer to compensate for the work done analysing whether the expert can provide useful evidence in the case. That payment, however, is much less than the expert would have ultimately received if they had proceeded to later stages of participation in the case, including drafting an expert report and testifying as to their expert opinions. If the reason that the expert witness is turning down further participation in the case is that the expert's analysis turns out to favour the other side of the case, the expert has by then likely lost the chance to offer their services to the opposing side. To compensate the expert for the lost opportunity to participate in the case further, the initial consulting fee can ethically include not just compensation for the work of the initial case assessment but also the cost of the potential lost opportunity of testifying on the other side. This potential 'lost opportunity' cost must be discounted to take into account the fact that the future lost work was not actually performed, but it is ethical and reasonable for the upfront consulting fee to include a nominal amount to represent that potential 'lost opportunity' to work on behalf of opposing counsel.

Note that lawyers, at least in most legal fields, may ethically represent a client on a contingency basis—that is, the compensation of the lawyer will depend on whether the client wins the case. This is justified by the fundamental ethical norm of lawyering—that the duty of the lawyer is to unswervingly act in the client's interests. Since the client is nearly always interested in winning the case, having the lawyer's compensation turn on winning the client's case puts them both squarely on the same side. For expert witnesses, however, the ethical obligation of the expert is not to the case or to the client in the case, but to the science. If the compensation for the expert witness turned on the success of the case for the side for which the expert testified, the expert's financial stake in the case could cause the expert to be tempted to shade their testimony in a way that was to their personal financial benefit. For that reason, contingency fee compensation for expert witnesses is unethical and should not be allowed (Parker, 1991).

One controversial practice in recent American litigation practice is the upfront payment of experts by retaining attorneys not to appear for current or potential opposing counsel in future cases. These so-called lock-up fees are supposedly designed to compensate the expert for the loss of opportunities to represent opposing counsel in future cases, but in reality, they often are intended to deprive opposing counsel of valuable potential expertise. This practice raises serious access to justice concerns when used to deprive litigants in future cases of expert testimony. After all, linguists with sufficient qualifications to be expert witnesses may be few and far between in a particular geographic area. Paying the only available linguistics expert a 'lock-up' fee could, as a practical matter, prevent litigants from having any meaningful ability to appropriately raise language questions in their cases. Although it is ethical to take some nominal fee to compensate an expert for work they must forego for opposing counsel in a case due to the opinion the expert has in that case, it is ethically questionable to take payment from a lawyer conditioned on not testifying in cases other than the present case. To do so is to collaborate in denying access to justice for litigants in the future.

One final ethical consideration, which has significant ramifications for access to justice, is whether expert witnesses should have the ethical mandate to appear as witnesses for litigants who lack the financial resources to compensate the expert for their work—that is, to supply their analysis and testimony *pro bono*. The American Bar Association does not require that attorneys perform *pro bono* services as a condition of licensure, but there is a strong professional norm supporting the obligation to provide free or discounted legal services to promote access to justice (Sandefur, 2007). Especially for experts who provide expert witness services regularly, a precatory obligation to do so on occasion on a *pro bono* basis as an ethical imperative would be consistent with an understanding that a legal system open to all is a public good worth supporting.

5 What Are the Ethical Issues Involved in Preparing a Science-Based Analysis in a Case?

Once a linguist has agreed to be retained as an expert by an attorney, the linguist's overriding commitment is to the integrity of the science of linguistics. That unswerving commitment to science is the source of the unique role of expert witnesses in the law. Because experts have specialised knowledge, they can assist judges and juries in better understanding the issues and evidence in the case and in making better decisions. Expert witnesses are allowed to do things in their testimony that ordinary 'fact' witnesses cannot—they are permitted to give opinions about the interpretation to be given to evidence, they can testify about facts outside their own personal observation, and they can even take into account information in forming their expert opinions that would not otherwise be admissible in court. With these special privileges as witnesses come special responsibilities—the expert witness has an obligation to the justice system to be objective in analysis and to 'tell it like it is', rather than how the lawyer who retains the witness would like it to be.

This is a hard truth for the lawyers who retain expert witnesses to fully accommodate, because lawyers hire expert witnesses for one reason and one reason only—to win the case. This is consistent with the lawyer's paramount ethical commitment—to loyally serve the interests of their client. When a lawyer retains an expert witness, it is because the lawyer hopes that the expert will provide helpful information for the client's cause. If the expert cannot do so, the lawyer has no obligation to provide expertise to the court that hurts their case—in fact, in such a case, the lawyer would have an ethical duty to resist the admission of that expert information into evidence. It is the single-mindedness of this role of the lawyer that provides some of the tension in the relationship between the expert witness and the retaining lawyer. As an expert witness, an expert must work in close cooperation with the lawyer who retains them, because the expert's science-based analysis may open up new areas of argument for the lawyer, or may foreclose strategies that the lawyer had originally considered using. A lawyer's narrative theory of the case is a dynamic one, unfolding and changing as case preparation continues, and the science-based expertise provided by the expert witness is one of the key ingredients for that case preparation. Naturally, the retaining lawyer is hopeful that the expert will turn out to be helpful to the client's case, which means the lawyer will therefore work diligently with that expert to see whether their analysis of the evidence can further bolster that case.

In working with a linguist in preparation for trial, the lawyer will likely ask them many questions about the theoretical linguistic underpinnings of their expert analysis. Assuming that the linguist is qualified by the judge to permit them to testify in court, the lawyer needs to understand enough about the pertinent areas of the linguistic science in order to make that expert testimony clear and comprehensible to the jury. The retaining lawyer also needs to be prepared to rebut misleading cross-examination strategies used by opposing counsel. In addition, the lawyer will want to be sure that no stone has been left unturned in utilising the professional expertise of the linguist. The expert is likely to be pressed by the retaining lawyer: 'Are there additional things you could testify to that would be helpful to the client?' 'Could you frame your conclusions in stronger, or less limited, ways?' 'Have you considered all the possible ways in which your conclusion could be impeached by opposing counsel or by an expert witness on the other side?' All of these questions are completely ethical on the part of the lawyer, given their prime ethical requirement to represent the client's interests with the utmost attention and diligence. But questions like these can present ethical temptations for the expert witness.

Because the retaining lawyer must work so closely with the expert witness in the course of trial preparation, it is only natural that the expert comes to feel part of the retaining lawyer's team of attorneys, paralegals and investigators putting together the case. There is a natural tendency of any witness to identify with the side that has called them in the case, and this tendency is enhanced by the close working relationship needed to develop the testimony of the expert witness so that it can best assist the jury in deciding the case. One request that lawyers often make of their retained experts is to review the expert report of the opposing party's expert witness and assist the retaining lawyer in developing a good cross-examination strategy to undermine that expert's credibility. Helping the retaining lawyer to show that the other side's expert should not be relied upon further cements the expert witness's self-identification with the retaining lawyer's side of the case (Meier, 1986, p. 274). The further along in the case an expert gets, the greater the sense the expert develops that they are on the 'right' side of the case, which therefore justly should prevail (Nunberg, 2009, p. 231). That psychodynamic makes it perilously easy for the expert to cross the line and become the 'hired gun' willing to provide whatever testimony would be most helpful to the retaining lawyer. Lawyers have a professional obligation to their clients and would not be serving their ethical obligations if they did not vigorously press experts for the most favourable testimony possible. Expert witnesses, it must be remembered, instead owe their professional allegiance to science, not to the lawyer and client in any particular case.

6 What Ethical Issues Exist in the Preparation of an Expert's Report and their Testimony at Trial?: Biasing Information from the Attorney

The process of working with the attorney to develop expert opinions pertinent to a case raises a number of ethical and practical problems for the expert witness. For example, the retaining lawyer will supply the expert with what the lawyer considers the relevant facts of the case, and the expert will be asked to provide an expert opinion about the meaning of those facts in their analysis. In presenting the facts to the expert, the lawyer may ask the expert to ignore certain facts—facts that the expert, however, may believe could be relevant in providing a scientifically valid expert analysis. This means that the expert is frequently put in the uncomfortable position of having to educate the retaining lawyer about why factual omissions or unsupported factual assumptions might make their analysis incomplete or even completely invalid.

There has been increasing attention paid to the problem of confirmation bias when expert witnesses have been exposed to evidence in the case beyond that needed for their analysis. Exposure to facts that are extraneous to the facts needed for the expert's analysis can cause the expert to draw conclusions about the overall strength of the case. That understanding, in turn, can undermine the expert's objectivity in the necessary scientific analysis. Once the expert has concluded that the client-litigant ought to win the case, they will come to see the facts in the case needed for their analysis through the lens of that belief that justice prevailing and the client winning are identical. Worse yet, the expert whose analysis has been distorted in this way seldom is aware that this has happened. There is a growing body of empirical evidence that strongly shows confirmation bias on the part of experts who have been exposed to unnecessary but nevertheless biasing information in the case.

Here is one example of that research into confirmation bias on the part of expert witnesses. Itiel Dror and his colleagues were interested in the degree to which experienced FBI fingerprint analysts were affected in their fingerprint analyses by unrelated information they had about the case in question. The FBI's fingerprint analysts had been severely embarrassed by a case in which they matched the latent prints left in a terrorist train bombing in Spain with reference prints of an Oregon attorney named Brandon Mayfield. The FBI went public with their 'solution' to the case, only to have Spanish authorities reject their findings in favour of a suspect who better matched the latent prints, who was resident in Spain at the time of the bombing, and who had a history of association with radical terrorism. Obviously, the individual identified by the Spanish authorities was a more plausible suspect in the case than the Oregon attorney Brandon Mayfield, who the FBI conceded at that point was not involved in the bombing. The episode, however, raised the unsettling question: How could the best-trained fingerprint analysts in the world have made such a mistake?

To attempt to find an answer to that troubling question, Dror arranged for five highly experienced FBI fingerprint analysts to make their own examination of the Mayfield prints to see if they would have found them a non-match if they had conducted the FBI analysis in that case (Dror et al., 2006). However, the fingerprints that each analyst were actually given were not the Mayfield prints at all; instead, each was given latent and reference prints that in an earlier case they had classified as being 'clear matches'. Yet, when told the prints they were examining were the 'Mayfield' prints, three of the five said they would have called them 'clear non-matches', one said that he could not decide either way, and only one said, consistent with his original analysis, that in his opinion the prints were a match. In other words, when told that the fingerprints in question were the now-known-to-be-non-matching Mayfield prints, four of the five analysts changed their minds about fingerprints that they had earlier called definite matches.

After the results of this experiment came out, some objected that the extraneous 'information'—that these were the infamous Mayfield prints—was too strong a biasing fact, and did not warrant a conclusion that this kind of confirmation bias would occur under more ordinary circumstances. So, Dror and his co-researchers (Dror & Charlton, 2006) conducted a parallel test; again, using experienced FBI fingerprint analysts, who, as in the Mayfield experiment, were given fingerprints that they had earlier either called 'clear matches' or 'clear non-matches'. This time, the analysts were giving biasing information more typical of the kind of routine biasing information given to experts in the process of developing their testimony. In this experiment, analysts who had earlier called the prints 'clear matches' were given information that the comparison prints were from someone apparently in jail when the crime occurred, but in case that alibi information turned out to be incorrect, the analyst was needed to examine the fingerprints in question. Analysts who had earlier called the prints 'clear non-matches' were given the biasing information that the suspect in the case had confessed and already agreed to plead guilty, but in case the suspect changed his mind about the guilty plea, the analyst was needed to examine the fingerprints. Again, just as in the Mayfield experiment, most of the analysts given extraneous information that the suspect was either very likely guilty or very likely not guilty, reversed their earlier analysis of the prints and tendered conclusions in line with the extraneous information rather than their earlier fingerprint analysis. Dror and his colleagues (Dror & Hampikian, 2011) have gone on to replicate this kind of experiment in DNA analysis—probably the gold standard in expert scientific evidence—with the same results: biasing information can impact the conclusions that expert witnesses draw doing what they believe are objective evaluations without them being aware of having been biased.

As we now are becoming aware, biasing information—even information which is not intended to be biasing—is incredibly powerful in affecting our perceptions and in the conclusions that we draw from those perceptions. Yet, surveys of experts reveal that most experts underappreciate the powerful impact of confirmation bias in general, and few of them believe that they, personally, would be affected in their professional science-based decision-making (Kukucka et al., 2017). The best way to avoid falling into the cognitive bias trap is for experts to avoid obtaining any information about the case except the specific data and information that the expert requires for their analysis. Many scientific experts are now aware of confirmation bias in scientific analysis, but most of them believe they personally are immune. By limiting the information received from the retaining lawyer to only that necessary for their expert witness report, the possibilities for bias to creep into the expert's analysis are reduced considerably.

7 What Are the Ethical Considerations in Preparing Expert Reports?: The Changing Face of Pre-trial Discovery

After a lawsuit has been filed, both sides to the lawsuit have continuing obligations to provide opposing counsel with information about the testimony that they expect to present at trial. The days of 'trial by ambush' are over. The process of mutual exchange of anticipated evidence is called the discovery phase of the trial, and it is governed by legal rules that include sanctions on attorneys who fail to turn over required discoverable evidence (Federal Rules of Evidence 615, 1975). In recent years, the discovery rules have placed new obligations on expert witnesses with respect to the process through which they develop their expert opinions in a case. Specific legal rules require expert witnesses to prepare written reports summarising their evidence, which the retaining lawyers are obligated to turn over to opposing counsel before trial.

One critical ethical concern that these discovery obligations pose for expert witnesses is the growing trend of courts to require expert witnesses to turn over notes and preliminary drafts of their final filed expert report. While traditionally those notes and drafts were not discoverable by opposing counsel, today courts are much more likely to find that opposing counsel is entitled to those documents as well as to the final expert report (Easton & Romines, 2003). Some expert witnesses have concluded that, if their notes and drafts are indeed discoverable by the other side, then the best practice is to destroy such materials to avoid them falling into the hands of opposing counsel. This strategy is both unethical and unwise. A trial judge could bar an expert's testimony entirely on the grounds that the destruction of drafts interfered with opposing counsel's potential cross-examination of the expert. Even if the trial judge permitted the expert to testify despite the destruction of notes or drafts, that expert could be subjected to a withering cross-examination insinuating that the notes and drafts had been destroyed in order to attempt to hide unfavourable information. Worse yet, opposing counsel may be entitled to have the jury specifically instructed that the jury is allowed to assume that the destroyed material would have been unfavourable to the party offering the witness (Huang & Muriel, 1998). An attorney, faced with the possibility of having the jury instructed that they may conclude that the reason the expert's notes were destroyed is because they would have harmed their side of the case, might well decide not to put the expert on the stand at all. Best ethical practices with respect to notes and drafts of final expert reports is for the expert to retain them and pass them on to the retaining lawyer. It is that lawyer's responsibility to turn them over to opposing counsel in discovery if the lawyer believes that is required; the expert witness has discharged their ethical duties once the notes and drafts are in the possession of the retaining lawyer.

Retaining those notes and drafts of expert reports is especially crucial whenever the retaining attorney has seen a draft report before the ultimately filed expert report is finalised. There are good reasons for the retaining attorney to request to see a preliminary version of the expert report—it can assist the lawyer in honing their theory of the case, in preparing for the direct examination of the expert witness, and in anticipating potential cross-examination questioning of the expert. The retaining lawyer may have questions and suggestions concerning the substance of the draft report. It should be emphasised that there is nothing ethically improper about this. The lawyer putting an expert on the stand must ethically seek to have that testimony framed in the light most favourable to the client, as long as that testimony is not factually compromised. Having said that, however, opposing counsel in cross-examination may well argue to the jury that an earlier version of the expert's report used language that was less favourable to the client than was contained in the ultimate report. This line of cross-examination is particularly potent if those changes to the final report occurred after a draft was seen by the retaining lawyer. These issues suggest that experts be judicious and careful in their notes and drafts to present their analysis in ways that are as true as possible to the science underlying their analysis. Correction in the final filed expert report of misstatements or unwarranted conclusions in early drafts is always possible, of course. However, by opening the door to cross-examination of the final draft as being unreliable due to later corrections to the draft, the expert may unwittingly undermine the credibility of the science behind the report. Careless drafting that could be misleading about the scientific principles and their application in the case could betray the expert witness's prime ethical obligation—to the integrity of the science that they are presenting to the court.

In a related discovery issue, opposing counsel will have the right to access any reports the expert may have prepared in other cases involving similar issues to the one at trial. Any apparent inconsistencies or discrepancies can be the basis of cross-examination, so it is important that expert reports be written to be as consistent as possible with the expert's reports in earlier cases. Of course, the retaining lawyer can try to clear up what superficially look like inconsistencies or contradictions between the expert's report in this case with what the expert wrote in earlier expert reports, but this problem is better to avoid in the first place by careful drafting in light of what the expert has written in earlier reports.

The same problem can occur when an expert's report appears to contradict things that the expert has written in their published scholarly writing. The expert should review their publications pertinent to the issue in the case and should make counsel aware of potential areas of cross-examination based on apparent inconsistencies or contradictions. Sometimes, inconsistencies arise because of advances in the field since the time of the earlier publication. Highlighting them in the final expert report can avoid the misleading implication that the expert report should be considered unreliable because of its inconsistency with an earlier position or approach. Linguistics, like all sciences, progresses over time, and that march of progress can result in new methods that supersede older ones. A good expert report can make this point salient for the court. Sometimes, what superficially appear to be contradictions between the expert report and earlier scholarly work are in fact not contradictions at all. Terminology can change over time. Facts that differ can justify differing conclusions in one analysis from the conclusions of another. Because the prime ethical obligation that the linguist expert witness has is to the linguistic science involved, the expert should be vigilant to avoid inadvertently discrediting the science of linguistics in the expert report or in their testimony.

8 What Are the Ethical Considerations in Testifying at Depositions?

In American civil litigation, the first time an expert witness is likely to have face-to-face contact with opposing counsel is during the deposition process, which occurs before trial during the pre-trial preparation phase of litigation. In a deposition, a witness is questioned by opposing counsel under oath. The retaining counsel who will be calling the expert witness at trial will be present at the deposition, which will be recorded to provide a record of the testimony, but no judge is present to resolve disputes.

The absence of a judge as a referee in depositions can result in some awkward situations for the expert witness. For example, the retaining lawyer may object to a question put to the expert witness, arguing that the question will reveal inadmissible information. Opposing counsel may respond by insisting that the witness answer the question, and that any evidentiary objections be dealt with later at trial. Another problem can occur if the retaining lawyer interrupts a question by opposing counsel and seeks to consult with the expert privately before the expert answers the question. If that happens, opposing counsel may well object, insisting that the deposition questioning continue without a break for consultation with the retaining attorney. Opposing counsel might even threaten the expert with being held in contempt for refusing to answer the questions. At this point, the expert is caught in the middle of a dispute between the lawyers, with no judge to rule on who is right and who is not.

Naturally, the expert witness in a situation like this is often unsure of what to do. The first consideration is this: the retaining lawyer represents only the interests of the client, and not the expert witness. Because the retaining lawyer is not representing the interests of the expert witness, that lawyer cannot give the witness legal advice about what to do. Nor do they have the right to tell the expert what to do in this situation—the expert witness is not a member of the trial team to be given marching orders by the lawyer in charge of the case. The most prudent course when there is a conflict between the lawyers at a deposition is for the expert witness to decline to answer the questions at issue at that time. Not answering preserves the status quo until a judge can later rule on the objection, since once an answer is given, the cat is irretrievably out of the bag. Once there is a judicial order to answer, however, the expert should comply with it, even if the retaining lawyer believes the judge has made a mistake in issuing the order. If the lawyer feels that the judge has made an error in issuing the order to answer, the retaining lawyer can pursue a stay of the order pending appeal, which is likely to be granted if the basis for the retaining lawyer's objection is that the expert witness is being asked to reveal legally privileged information. In the final analysis, the expert witness cannot and should not take sides in a fight between the lawyers, and can and must obey an order by the judge to answer or not to answer.

9 What Are the Ethical Considerations of Communications that Occur During Trial?

While a trial is underway, there are ethical constraints on witnesses and other participants in the trial regarding communication with other people that might have a role in the case. A hard and fast position banning any communication, even innocent pleasantries, between trial participants is intended to preserve the appearance of fairness in the justice system. For that reason, speaking outside of the courtroom with judges, jurors or even other witnesses in the case is improper—regardless of the topic of the conversation. Amazingly, judges have been known to try to have private conversations with expert witnesses while a case was in progress—sometimes because they realise that the witness has expertise that could have application in another case before them, sometimes because they have questions about the case at hand that were not addressed by the lawyers, and sometimes just because they are intellectually curious. Regardless of the judge's motivation, though, the expert should be aware that this kind of out-of-court communication could result in a mistrial for the case being tried. If an expert witness is approached by the judge outside of being on the witness stand, the expert should politely decline the invitation to conversation and report the situation to retaining counsel.

It is very common for expert witnesses to run into jurors in the courthouse or elsewhere. A friendly smile is unproblematic, but even an innocent conversation about matters completely outside the case could be misconstrued if seen and reported by someone. Obviously, any attempt by a juror to discuss the case must be firmly refused and reported to retaining counsel.

A judge may impose limits regarding contact between an expert witness and other witnesses during the trial. Witnesses are routinely excluded from the courtroom while other witnesses in the case are testifying to avoid the testimony of one affecting the other (Federal Rules of Evidence 615). Often the judge will specifically order that witnesses not speak to other potential witnesses until both have already testified. An expert witness should always check with the retaining lawyer about whether the judge in the case has imposed any such limitations, and, if so, should be careful to abide by them. It is easy to inadvertently violate this kind of order. Suppose a linguist is sitting on a bench in the hallway of the courthouse waiting to testify as an expert witness when along comes the linguist who is waiting to testify for the other side in the case. It can be awfully tempting to chat, especially if the expert on the other side is someone you know well—which is often the case in a field like linguistics. If there has been an order barring communication with other witnesses, however, this innocent chat could result in a mistrial and possibly sanctions by the judge (State v. Sherman, 1995).

10 Conclusion: The Importance of Linguists in Accurate and Just Dispute Resolution

Witnesses with special scientific knowledge are an indispensable resource to the justice system. From the point of view of the expert witness, however, participation in litigation may well expose a tension between the apparent role demands of being a participant on one side of a contested dispute and the over-arching obligations that the expert has to the integrity of their scientific field. It is only experts who understand how subtle those issues can be that can proof themselves against these professional pitfalls and perils. An appreciation of the fundamental differences between the ethical demands placed on lawyers and the ethical demands inherent in being an expert witness can make the linguist called to be an expert witness both a more effective participant in the justice system and a more responsible member of the linguistics community by upholding its standards of science-based knowledge.

References

Daubert v. Merrill Dow Pharmaceuticals, 509 U.S. 579 (1993).

Dror, I. E., Charlton, D., & Péron, A. E. (2006). Contextual information renders experts vulnerable to making erroneous identifications. *Forensic Science International, 156*(1), 74–78.

Dror, I. E., & Charlton, D. (2006). Why experts make errors. *Journal of Forensic Identification, 56*(4), 600–616.

Dror, I. E., & Hampikian, G. (2011). Subjectivity and bias in forensic DNA mixture interpretation. *Science and Justice, 51*(4), 204–208.

Easton, S. D., & Romines, F. D. (2003). Dealing with draft dodgers: Automatic production of drafts of expert witness reports. *Review of Litigation, 22*, 355–384.

Federal Rules of Evidence 615 (1975).

Huang, S. W., & Muriel, R. H. (1998). Spoliation of evidence: Defining the ethical boundaries of destroying evidence. *American Journal of Trial Advocacy, 22*, 191–214.

Kukucka, J., Kassin, S. M., Zapf, P. A., & Dror, I. E. (2017). Cognitive bias and blindness: A global survey of forensic science examiners. *Journal of Applied Research in Memory and Cognition, 6*(4), 452–459.

Meier, P. (1986). Damned liars and expert witnesses. *Journal of the American Statistical Association, 81*, 269–276.

Nunberg, G. (2009). Is it ever okay not to disclose work for hire? *International Journal of Speech, Language, and the Law, 16*(2), 227–235.

Parker, J. L. (1991). Contingent expert witness fees: Access and legitimacy. *Southern California Law Review, 64*, 1363–1391.

Sandefur, R. L. (2007). Lawyers' pro bono service and American-style civil legal assistance. *Law & Society Review, 41*(1), 79–112.

State v. Sherman, 662 A. 2d 767 (Conn. App. 1995).

Stygall, G. (2009). Guiding principles: Forensic linguistics and codes of ethics in other fields and professions. *International Journal of Speech, Language and the Law, 16*(2), 253–266.

3

Linguistic Expert Evidence in the Common Law

Andrew Hammel

1 Introduction

This chapter will trace the origins of expert testimony in common-law courtrooms, and its relevance to the admissibility and use of linguistic expert evidence. The article will begin with a brief discussion of the common law and a review of the main differences between common and civil-law systems. In Section 2, I will trace the origins of the adversarial model of trial procedure, which took modern form in England in the seventeenth and eighteenth centuries. In Section 3, I will turn to the origins of expert witness testimony, which are intricately bound up with developments in the adversarial trial and in the role of the jury. In Section 4, I will describe the advent of expert witnesses within the common-law system. In Section 5, I will lay out the modern approach to expert evidence in the common law, which requires judges to evaluate the suitability of experts' qualifications and the reliability of their proposed

A. Hammel (✉)
Düsseldorf, Germany
e-mail: Andrew.Hammel@uni-duesseldorf.de

V. Guillén-Nieto, D. Stein (eds.), *Language as Evidence*,
https://doi.org/10.1007/978-3-030-84330-4_3

conclusions. Finally, in Section 6, I will address the special topic of linguistic expert evidence, which is routinely accepted in common-law courts to help judges and juries understand a broad variety of questions.

2 What Is the Common Law?

The 'common law' (often referred to by comparative-law specialists as 'English-origin legal systems') is customarily defined as the group of legal systems based on English law as it developed in the late medieval and early modern period. The common-law legal family currently includes England and Wales, the United States, Australia, Canada, New Zealand and India. There are also hybrid systems which incorporate certain common-law elements, but which combine them with ideas drawn from other legal inheritances. These include Scotland, which mixes common law with Roman law, South Africa, which incorporates elements of indigenous African law and Dutch law, and Louisiana, which, uniquely among American states, combines common-law elements with those drawn from the French, or more specifically Napoleonic, legal tradition.

The common-law legal tradition is usually described by distinguishing it from the civil law, the other great tradition of modern legal orders. Civil law—'European legal origin systems'—still governs most of continental Europe, Latin America and many other nations. The distinctions between the common law and other traditions have been defined, debated and disputed for centuries, but a brief and necessarily simplified sketch will help define the contours of the following discussion. Civil-law jurisdictions draw on the great codification systems and principles of Roman law, which left its legacy throughout the Roman empire. Modern civil-law legal systems stress rationality, predictability and uniformity in legal decision-making. To achieve this, civil-law jurisdictions enact expansive uniform national codes for most core legal areas and establish politically insulated civil-service systems for the judiciary. Judges typically begin their careers straight out of university in civil-law jurisdictions. In civilian trials the judge, thoroughly trained and conscious of the mandate of objectivity, leads, shapes and directs the process of fact-gathering. Judges are expected to hew closely to the statutes governing a particular case, downplaying their own profiles and personalities in the service of 'legal certainty'—the requirement of stability and predictability in the law. Lawyers play an important but ultimately subservient role: They must accept the facts established by the judge, but can stress those aspects of the record favourable to their clients, and petition the judge to summon helpful witnesses. The underlying model of the civil law posits that all parties will work *more or less* cooperatively to uncover as much information about the issues as possible.

The common law first took shape in the late medieval era in England. Common-law court proceedings, including trials, first took recognisable modern form in the seventeenth and eighteenth centuries in Great Britain. Like Roman law, common law was also spread far and wide by empire. Until the twentieth century, the main source of law in common-law jurisdictions was court decisions, which were recorded, redacted and published in the form of 'reporters'. As the number of reported decisions—and commentaries on them—accumulated, a deep and broad tradition emerged which furnished workable rules for most ordinary legal disputes. This meant, in turn, that Parliament was not obliged to pass the kinds of ambitious synoptic codes favoured in civil-law countries. As long as Parliament found *existing* rules already established by judges to be appropriate, it was not obliged to act. Parliament could thus turn its attention to specialised or emerging areas of law which had yet to become the focus of judicial attention.

In common-law trials the judge acts as a 'referee', not an active participant. Lawyers drive the development of the trial: they gather the evidence, summon and question witnesses, and deliver arguments to a jury of laypersons. The common-law judge's role is not to guide the proceedings, but merely to regulate them. He or she may intervene to enforce the rules, and must decide disputes which arise among the lawyers, but does not actively try to influence the focus of the evidence. Yet the comparatively passive role of common-law judges during trials contrasts with their crucial role in law formation. It is universally accepted that although common-law judges are obliged to apply the provisions of the law and constitution, they enjoy considerable freedom to interpret the laws to adapt to changing circumstances, and—when faced with novel questions in need of prompt solutions—to 'legislate from the bench'. Civil law judges enjoy much less freedom. They are expected to hew extremely closely to the relevant statute, and to apply it to the facts without distortion or filters. They are also not obliged to consult previous decisions by other courts—even higher courts within their own chain of command—although they often do so in practice, to avoid successful appeals. The assumption behind this rule is that a well-crafted statute will generate the right outcomes when straightforwardly applied by *any* conscientious judge—therefore a strict hierarchy is unnecessary. In common-law systems, by contrast, courts are bound to obey rulings handed down by higher courts in comparable cases. This rule, called 'stare decisis', ensures consistency in the law's development which the civil law achieves by grand codifications.

Of course, this discussion is necessarily brief and superficial, and ignores many contrary trends, such as the increasing tendency towards codification within common-law systems, and the fact that there are many legal areas in the civil-law world which evince considerable influence from common-law ideas and practices—especially adversarial lawyering. Many scholars even speak of a convergence of the two major legal families. However, the subject of this chapter—expert testimony—is one in which the common law and civil law continue to follow significantly different paths.

3 The Emergence of the Trial Jury and its Influence on the Common Law

The English common-law criminal trial began taking its modern form in the middle of the eighteenth century (Langbein, 2005). Until that time, trials had largely been informal affairs in which a judge questioned a few witnesses and then issued a ruling, often merely by giving a short speech analysing the evidence and deciding the case. Before the eighteenth century, the institution of the jury, although firmly established for many kinds of cases, was still regulated largely by local custom or tradition. Although Magna Carta had guaranteed 'free men' the right to a trial by 'the lawful judgment of [their] peers' in 1215, this right was drastically limited in scope and effect. Nevertheless, it formally enshrined the idea of trial by jury in English law for the first time. The institution gained in popularity, although rules governing the selection and powers of juries varied widely and were sometimes dictated by local custom. In many cases, the roles of witness and juror overlapped; a judge might summon a few local men of good reputation to help him understand the case. As one commentator notes:

> As soon as they were chosen, they were expected to make their own inquiries, in effect gathering the evidence against the suspect, and have been described as 'neither exactly accusers, nor exactly witnesses; they are to give voice to common repute'. (Ryan, 2014, pp. 89-90, citing Pollock & Maitland, 1895, p. 642)

Some judges, faced with specialised issues of animal husbandry or commercial practice, chose jurors from among these trades, effectively choosing a jury of experts. Rules governing jury selection and the jury's authority and mission gradually became more detailed and consistent. The major impetus for the formalisation of nationwide rules governing courtroom procedure and trial by jury was the Bill of Rights of 1689, which explicitly mentioned jury trials.

Throughout the eighteenth century, general rules of trial procedure were established, often by case law. These rulings permitted the accused to be represented by counsel—something which was formerly forbidden—regulated the composition and competencies of juries in criminal cases, and established rules of admissibility to ensure juries would be presented only with relevant and reliable evidence. These developments culminated in the Juries Act 1825, the first piece of legislation to establish comprehensive uniform national rules governing English juries. Now almost totally superseded, the Act specified that juries could be composed only of males between the ages of 21 and 60 who owned property above a certain value. Women were not permitted to serve on juries until 1919 (Choo & Hunter, 2018, p. 194).

With the increasing reliance on juries came a concept which would play a critical role in the debate over expert testimony: the 'province of the jury'. Now that judges and juries shared the responsibility of deciding cases, which issues should be reserved for decision by the experienced judge, and which could be safely committed to the discretion and understanding of respectable citizens? Eventually, a broad consensus was established: It was the role of the judge to decide which law applied to the case and to decide purely or mainly legal questions, while the jury decided questions of fact and judged the credibility of witnesses.

Developments in civil—or private-law—cases followed a somewhat different trajectory. Private-law procedure in England was shaped by the system of *writs*: complex, technical templates for legal actions. These writs, which often bore obscure Latin names, had to be carefully prepared and authorised; the smallest error could lead to a dismissal of an otherwise-compelling case. Nevertheless, when a writ was successfully pleaded and the preliminaries had been accomplished, a trial, often by jury, would be held. The rules governing civil trials differed from those governing criminal trials, but with regard to expert witnesses, the similarities are so numerous that there is little reason to distinguish between criminal and civil proceedings. Modern juries have far fewer prerogatives than their historical counterparts: Jurors are ordered not to perform any independent investigation of the case, and to limit their consideration solely to the facts presented at trial, setting aside their own experience or expertise. Nevertheless, juries still exercise decisive influence on common-law procedure. The possibility that an assortment of laypeople may end up answering important legal questions informs almost every aspect of common-law trial procedure, even in cases where no jury serves.

One of the many structural issues jury participation raises is: Who decides which kinds of questions at trial, the jury or the judge? An example may clarify the matter. Jenkins sells a mare to Craven for €200. Craven asks whether the mare is fertile; Jenkins assures him that she is. Jenkins does not tell Craven that the mare has been inseminated once but did not become pregnant. Jenkins believes that the mere fact that the mare failed to become pregnant once does not mean she is barren. Craven, for his part, assumed that there were no indications the mare might be infertile. If he had known there were, he would have paid only €50 for her. After trying to impregnate the mare, again without success, Craven sues for damages.

Under the division of responsibilities created by the common law, the judge first decides whether the allegations in Craven's writ, if proven, would satisfy an existing definition of a recognised legal wrong—in this case, likely some form of fraud. The judges rule that Craven's story, if proven true, would satisfy the definition of fraud. The lawsuit can proceed. The judge now empanels a jury, which, under the judge's guidance, takes over the task of hearing the evidence, resolving factual disputes, and ultimately resolving the case. They hear evidence from Craven, Jenkins and other witnesses surrounding the circumstances of the sale. The judge performs a gatekeeping function here: He decides whether witnesses have *personal* knowledge relevant to the case, and will decide which questions from counsel are relevant and appropriate, and which are irrelevant or potentially misleading. For instance, the judge may learn from Bartleby, a fellow horse-dealer, that Jenkins was accused of concealing a horse's medical problems in another case. However, this was a mere rumour, and no charges or claims were ever brought. The judge rules that Bartleby may not say anything about this rumour *before the jury*, since this could unfairly prejudice them against Jenkins.

After these preliminary rulings, the witnesses testify before the jury. The jury decides, based on their personal examination of the testifying witnesses, who is telling the truth, and who is exaggerating or lying. The jury then decides whether the definition of fraud has been met, under the careful supervision of the judge, who explains the law to them. To help structure their deliberations, juries are usually instructed to answer simple 'yes' or 'no' questions: Did Jenkins have a duty to inform Craven that attempts to inseminate the mare had previously failed? If you find he did, did Jenkins' failure to fulfil that duty cause Craven to buy the horse? After deciding these questions, the jury hands back its *verdict* form. The judge examines the answers, judging whether the jury has properly fulfilled its task, and whether elements of a cause of action for fraud have been fulfilled. If they have, the judge enters a 'judgement' finding Jenkins liable for fraud.

The task of deciding basic questions of fact and law is known in the common law as the *province of the jury*. The example above shows the traditional division of labour: the judge handles the law, whether it is the legal theory governing the case or the laws of evidence determining what witnesses may and may not say. This is the *province of the judge*. The jury then makes any credibility evaluations, if necessary, and determines the 'historical facts' of the case: Did Jenkins tell Craven about the previous failed insemination? If not, did he have a duty to do so? Did Jenkins' assurances cause Craven to buy the horse, or would Craven have bought it anyway, for instance because he simply liked the breed? After determining these facts, the jury applies the law to them by answering the questions put forward in the charge. The existence of the jury requires a fundamentally different approach from civil law systems (cf. Chap. 4), in which judges control the entire process of determining the law and applying it to the facts.

At this point—where the law is applied to the facts—the American and British approaches differ somewhat. British judges are expected to issue a *summing up* before the jury begin deliberations. In the summing up, the judge verbally instructs the jurors on the applicable law, then gives the jury a brief précis of and commentary on the evidence, trying to stay as neutral as possible, but also warning jurors against common errors of logic or legal misconceptions (Madge, 2006, p. 817). In the United States, the judge is strictly forbidden from commenting on the evidence. He or she issues the jury a written 'charge' which the jury can take with them into the deliberation room. American judges are also forbidden to comment on the evidence presented to the jury, on the grounds that the judge could, whether consciously or not, exert undue influence on the jury's decision-making. This concern to preserve the province of the jury is also recognised in English law. Even though the judge is entitled to comment on the evidence—a privilege intended in part to prevent the jury from being overmastered by advocates' rhetoric—the jury always has the last call, as shown by a model summing-up phrase suggested for use in English and Welsh courts:

> [if], when I review the evidence, I do not mention something please do not think you should ignore it. And if I do mention something please do not think it must be an important point. Also, if you think that I am expressing any view about any piece of evidence, or about the case, you are free to agree or to disagree because it is your view, and yours alone, which counts. (Judicial College, 2020, pp. 4-3)

Even while instructing and guiding the jury, thus, judges must still respect its autonomy. Another method of protecting juror autonomy is the hypothetical question. Instead of asking whether (for instance) the level of alcohol in the *defendant's blood* interfered with *his* ability to drive, the expert is asked whether the alcohol level detected in the defendant's blood would likely interfere with a person's ability to drive, given that the person shared the defendant's general characteristics. The distinctions may seem trivial, but it is considered necessary to leave to the jury the ultimate decision of whether something an expert said was likely (or certain) to happen in a similar case in fact *did* happen in the case before them.

The transition to a jury of one's peers, rather than a specially summoned panel of experts, marked a change in how judges decided cases involving complex technical issues such as animal husbandry, mining, agriculture or commercial practices. Formerly, the custom had been to empanel jurors who *themselves* had expertise in these areas and who swore an oath to analyse the evidence impartially. With the trend towards 'lay' juries, as they came to be known, the emphasis changed. The judge expected to let the jurors make their own decisions. Further, jurors, who now had no special expertise in the technical issues driving the lawsuit, were ordered to decide based solely on the evidence presented in the courtroom, without regard to their own specialised experience or expertise. They were permitted to use general common sense and everyday experience, but not their own training or education in (for instance) hydrodynamics, auto repair or the treatment of personality disorders. This new requirement of impartial juries was arguably a step forward in excluding bias and arbitrariness from the courtroom, but it raised an urgent new question: How could courts, or juries of ordinary citizens, reach reliable decisions concerning technical issues they may be unfamiliar with?

4 The Arrival of Experts in the Adversarial System

The advent of the partisan expert witness accompanied the emergence of the adversarial trial in English courts in the eighteenth century. Before 1700, as legal historian John Langbein notes, a criminal trial 'was expected to transpire as a lawyer-free contest of amateurs' (Langbein, 1999, p. 314). However, the unreliability of such trials, coupled with the notoriously harsh English 'bloody code' which imposed the death penalty for numerous offences, soon gave rise to scandal. Professional informants known as *thief-takers* teamed up with unscrupulous lawyers to manufacture evidence against innocent defendants, all with the aim of obtaining cash rewards for convictions. To respond to calls for reform, the Crown created professional prosecution agencies which enforced higher ethical standards. The increasingly professional nature of prosecution resulted in a corresponding need for a professional defence—at least for defendants able to pay the fees. The previous rule forbidding lawyers from representing defendants in court was abolished, and legal assistance became commonplace for those who could afford it.

During the eighteenth century, English law gradually refined the model of the 'adversarial' courtroom trial which persists to this day. Under this model, each party to a case is represented by their own legal advocates. In civil—that is, private-law cases—these advocates are private lawyers hired by each of the two parties to represent that party's interests. In criminal cases, the Crown—the sovereign whose laws were being enforced, and who was represented by the word 'Rex' or 'Regina'—was usually represented by a private lawyer, although this role could sometimes be performed by government officials. The defendant in a criminal case was now entitled to hire a private lawyer for his or her defence. Crucially, these private lawyers were the main actors in developing evidence for their respective sides. Lawyers for each side of the case were responsible for gathering and presenting evidence, documents, and witness testimony favourable to its side of the dispute. Langbein (2005) ably describes the shift of power from judges to lawyers and juries:

> By the later eighteenth century, when the rise of adversary criminal justice had caused the judges to yield increasing control over the conduct of criminal trials to the lawyers, the judges' authority over the formulation of jury verdicts was weakening. The judges kept their command over the pardon power, but they surrendered the power to fine disobedient juries; they moderated their use of the power to comment upon the evidence; [and] the power to reject verdicts became contentious… (p. 350).

As we will see, this gradual shift helped cement the most controversial aspects of the adversarial system, since it raised the prospect that trials might be won and lost based in part, or in whole, on the ability of narrowly partisan lawyers to convince laypeople.

The epistemological model of the adversarial system is combat, the 'crucible of meaningful adversarial testing', as one US Supreme Court case has described it (*Cronic v. United States*, p. 656). Each side introduces evidence and arguments beneficial to its own case, and directly attacks and undermines the other side's presentation. Critical scrutiny and cross-examination, like a sculptor's tools, prune away the weakest arguments and evidence, and the finished image—the closest approximation to the truth—gradually emerges. The adversarial system had its critics from the start. First, they complained, this approach turned the search for the truth into a kind of undignified, quasi-gladiatorial spectacle. To gain advantage before the jury, lawyers might try to ambush witnesses with unexpected or inappropriate questions, probe their personal lives for unflattering information, or provoke them into an angry outburst—even when these tactics contributed nothing to the search for truth. Another closely related argument is that the adversarial approach makes the skill of the lawyers crucial to the outcome of a case: The side with the cleverest or most aggressive lawyer might prevail regardless of the evidence. Comparative scholar John Langbein, who has studied European and English-origin legal systems extensively, has cast doubt on the value of cross-examination. Citing famed evidence scholar John Henry Wigmore, Langbein observes:

> Wigmore's celebrated panegyric—that cross-examination is 'the greatest legal engine ever invented for the discovery of truth'—is nothing more

> than an article of faith...Judge Frankel explains why: 'The litigator's devices, let us be clear, have utility in testing dishonest witnesses, ferreting out falsehoods, and thus exposing the truth. But to a considerable degree these devices are like other potent weapons, equally lethal for heroes and villains.'...In the hands of many of its practitioners, cross-examination is not only frequently truth-defeating or ineffectual, it is also tedious, repetitive, time-wasting, and insulting. (Langbein, 1985, p. 833 n. 41, citations omitted)

The fact that expert witnesses emerged at the time the adversarial system was taking shape meant that they—like other witnesses—became entangled in the adversarial structure of court proceedings. Expert witnesses represented a new institution in English law which combined elements of the role of both witness and juror. As early as 1670, English courts described the contrasting roles of the jury and the witness:

> A witness swears to what he has seen and heard … to what hath fallen under his senses. But a juryman swears to what he can infer and conclude from the testimony by the act and force of the understanding. (Bushell's Case, 1670)

This division of epistemological labour forbids lay witnesses from stating their opinions. Yet this rule would effectively prevent any expert input: Since juries were no longer selected for their expertise, and witnesses were permitted to convey only facts, not opinions, there was no way for expert witness' conclusions to be formally integrated into the trial process—although of course judges and litigants used work-arounds to overcome this obstacle. A little over a century later, a landmark case resolved the situation by explicitly permitting expert testimony based solely on the expert's own knowledge. In *Folkes v. Chadd* (1782), Lord Mansfield held that there was no bar to experts testifying about their opinions, even if they had no personal experience of the subject matter of the trial. Even though the expert in *Folkes* had never visited the artificial embankment which was allegedly ruining a local harbour—the focus of the lawsuit, and thus had no first-hand personal knowledge to relate—he could apply his specialised mathematical understanding to facts established by *other people*, thus generating an opinion which could help the court resolve the case. As legal scholar Tal Golan noted, the expert in the case, Smeaton, had in fact visited the embankment, but Mansfield was not aware of this. More importantly, Mansfield 'did not find it important to refer to the crucial fact that Smeaton's courtroom appearance in the Wells Harbor case was different—Smeaton had not served as a court-nominated consultant or arbitrator, but had appeared as a partisan witness selected and paid for by one of the parties to represent its case before the jury' (Golan, 1999, p. 13).

Folkes and its successors thus opened the way forward for partisan expert testimony not based on personal experience, paving the way for the full integration of expert testimony into the modern adversarial trial. Advocates soon found that expert testimony, backed as it was by the expert's experience and qualifications, could be quite influential. Thus, if one side of a lawsuit hired an expert witness, the other side had no choice but to hire one of its own or risk a decisive tactical disadvantage. The result was often less than edifying: One renowned expert might conduct a series of experiments decisively proving a certain result, and another, equally prominent expert would then perform his own experiments and reach the opposite result. Courts and commentators often deplored the spectacle. Lord Chief Justice Dallas, summing up evidence at an 1821 trial involving just such a contradiction, observed that:

> these two days...are not days of triumph, but days of humiliation for science; for when I find that their science ends in this degree of uncertainty and doubt, and when I observe that [the expert witnesses] are drawn up in such martial and hostile array against each other, how is it possible for me to form, at a moment, an opinion on such contradictory evidence? (Parkes, 1820, p. 317)

The debate about expert witnesses in English courts raged for most of the nineteenth century. Opponents decried the damage done by 'battles of the experts' to the legitimacy and reputation of science. These battles were also problematic from a structural perspective. Many social forces, including the industrial revolution, had begun a transformation of science from a gentlemanly leisure pursuit into a full-time, regimented career within institutions such as universities and companies. Commentators regarded the spectacle of men of science attacking each other's methods and even character in high-profile trials as a danger to the burgeoning field of professional, institutionalised scientific research. Yet, in adversarial trials, such direct frontal attacks, and searing cross-examinations, were critical to the search for the truth. The genteel decorum of academic debate found itself in grating conflict with the free-for-all of the common-law courtroom—a conflict which survives to this day. The proposed solution is almost as old as the controversy:

> [T]hroughout the second half of the nineteenth century, men of science repeatedly demanded that the English legal system reform its procedures of expert testimony and employ the scientific expert independent of the parties either as part of a special tribunal or as an advisor to the court. However, even those in the legal profession who empathised with the frustrated scientific community were well aware that the operation of fundamental principles of the adversarial system rendered the reforms proposed by the scientific community unworkable. (Golan, 1999, pp. 22-23)

This argument persists to the present day. In an influential 1998 article, American legal scholar Scott Brewer called for American judges to make more extensive use of their power to appoint neutral experts (which is permitted by Rule 706 of the Federal Rules of Evidence, discussed below), but regarded this as only a stopgap reform. What is truly needed, Brewer argues, is a 'two-hat' system in which the decision-maker in a case (hat 1) involving scientific evidence is himself or herself an expert in the field (hat 2):

> [Potential models] include turning over many decisions currently made by private litigation to public administrative agencies staffed with trained scientists, relying on blue ribbon scientifically trained juries, scientific expert magistrate judges, or even special science courts staffed by scientifically trained judges. (Brewer, 1998, p.1677)

Defenders of the adversarial approach, however, see expert witnesses as bringing an extra measure of reliability and probity to court proceedings. Cross-examination and contrary arguments can be unpleasant, but experts should hardly expect their testimony to be accepted without debate, and most are protected from any real harm to their reputations by their independence, status and—not infrequently—private wealth. The witnesses themselves also appreciated the substantial sums such testimony could command, since official salaries were often meagre.

Yet the integration of scientific expert testimony into court proceedings raised a host of difficult legal and epistemological issues. What level of expertise and/or qualification could entitle someone to testify as an expert witness? Should expert witnesses be bound by the same rules which applied to everyone else in common-law trials? What areas of inquiry qualified as truly 'scientific'? When two expert witnesses reached diametrically opposed conclusions, how should judges or juries resolve the dispute? These questions continue to shape the debate over expert scientific witnesses to this day. They also raise a host of ethical issues concerning how to reconcile partisan testimony within a lawyer-driven adversarial system with the need to preserve the image and substance of scientific rectitude and objectivity (cf. Chap. 2 of this volume).

5 The Modern Gatekeeping Framework for Expert Testimony in the United States and England

The first and most important difference between expert and lay witnesses is that experts, as we have seen, may state their opinions. After laying out their procedure and methodology and describing the results of any experiments they may have concluded, experts may state their opinion on critical issues: Did the bullet come from the defendant's gun? Was the type of rubber used in the defendant company's tyres prone to failure in cold temperature? Did the defendant pharmaceutical company's medication cause the plaintiff's birth defects? By the twentieth century, scientific expert testimony had become an ingrained feature of both criminal and civil trials in the common-law world. Expert testimony was especially frequent in criminal trials, since many modern forms of proof, such as fingerprint comparison, blood typing and ballistics comparisons, could scarcely be offered without expert support. Defences based on an offender's disturbed mental state were also heavily dependent on expert testimony, and prosecutors found themselves obliged to present their own expert testimony to combat these defences.

The increasing importance of *scientific* expert testimony raised thorny issues concerning qualifications and the nature of science. The first order of business was to define the term 'expert'. Traditionally, the definition has been quite broad: An American treatise from 1883 defined an expert as 'one who is skilled in any particular art, trade, or profession, being possessed of peculiar knowledge concerning the same' (Rogers, 1891, p. 2). Thus, anyone who had special knowledge going beyond that of the average juror could qualify. But when experts testified about abstruse scientific subjects, how were courts to tell whether the witness' conclusions were based on sound methods?

The rule which dominated in American courts for most of the twentieth century originated, oddly enough, in a brief opinion by a lower federal court, the Court of Appeals for the District of Columbia (*Frye v. United States*, 1923). A defendant on trial for murder had attempted to introduce the results of an early form of lie detector test called the 'systolic pressure' test. The test purportedly showed his protestations of innocence to be truthful. The court first noted the general rule that expert testimony may be introduced to assist the jury in assessing a topic which 'does not lie within the range of common experience or common knowledge, but requires special experience or special knowledge'. The court then proceeded directly to another point: When is the science undergirding an expert opinion sufficiently established to be admissible in court? The court reasoned:

> Just when a scientific principle or discovery crosses the line between the experimental and demonstrable stages is difficult to define. Somewhere in this twilight zone the evidential force of the principle must be recognised, and while courts will go a long way in admitting expert testimony deduced from a well-recognised scientific principle or discovery, the thing from

> which the deduction is made must be sufficiently established to have gained general acceptance in the particular field in which it belongs. (ibid., p. 1014)

The court held, without further explanation, that the systolic blood pressure test did not meet this standard.

Since the question in *Frye* was one of evidence and not of constitutional law, the court's ruling had no binding effect on any American state court, to say nothing of courts in other common-law countries. Yet the judges in *Frye* had been lucky: They confronted an issue which had not been squarely addressed before by any prominent court. Their ruling struck a chord with its simplicity and ease of application, for it became enormously influential. Throughout the United States and parts of the common-law legal world, *Frye* gave rise to what became known as the 'general acceptance' test: Expert scientific testimony will be deemed admissible only if it is based on a scientific theory or process which has gained 'general acceptance' in the scientific community. This standard continues in force in many American states.

The next major development in the United States was the adoption of the Federal Rules of Evidence (or FRE) in 1975. The FRE were an ambitious crystallisation and codification of hundreds of years of common-law court rulings on questions of evidence and admissibility. Rule 702 of the FRE, which governs admissibility of expert testimony, originally read as follows:

> If scientific, technical, or other specified knowledge will assist a trier of fact to understand the evidence or to determine a fact in issue, a witness qualified as an expert by knowledge, skill, experience, training, or education, may testify thereto in the form of an opinion or otherwise if…the testimony is the product of reliable principles and methods.

The FRE benefited from a quirk of American legal federalism. American states are each individual sovereign entities, and they can and do enact fully independent legal codes governing everything from divorce law to corporate law. However, some federal legislation—which is technically binding only on US federal courts—has proven highly influential, for several reasons. The first is prestige: A code of legislation developed by a respected 'blue-ribbon' panel of experts from across the nation cannot help but be influential. The second is a desire to avoid reinventing the wheel. If the federal court system adopts a set of rules which appear to work well in practice, a state which has yet to pass its own laws in this area can simply copy the federal solution with a few adjustments to fit local circumstances.

Thus, when the US Supreme Court hands down a decision interpreting the Federal Rules of Evidence, the consequences may be felt nationwide. That is precisely what happened in *Daubert v. Merrell Dow Pharmaceuticals*. The plaintiffs in a massive class-action suit alleged that the drug Bendectin had caused birth defects, and sued its maker, Merell Dow. Yet the evidence was anything but cut-and-dried. Bendectin did not cause birth defects in all women who took it, or even a majority. The rates of birth defects among women who took it were only slightly higher than in those who had not, and many other factors could have played a role. To prove their case, therefore, the plaintiff's lawyers relied on complex statistical inferences and a 're-analysis' of previous studies. The defendant, Merrell Dow Pharmaceuticals, filed a motion to exclude the plaintiffs' expert opinion on the basis that the statistical techniques used in the re-analysis failed to satisfy the *Frye* test of general acceptance.

The Supreme Court accepted the case to decide on the current status of the *Frye* test. Had the 1923 decision in *Frye* been abrogated—that is replaced—by the 1975 adoption of the FRE? The Supreme Court held that it had. Rule 702, as we have seen, required expert testimony to be 'the product of reliable principles and methods'. The Court fleshed out this bare-bones definition with a series of 'considerations' lower courts could take into account when deciding whether to permit expert scientific evidence:

(1) whether the theory or technique in question can be and has been tested;
(2) whether it has been subjected to peer review and publication;
(3) its known or potential error rate;
(4) the existence and maintenance of standards controlling its operation; and

(5) whether it has attracted widespread acceptance within a relevant scientific community. (*Daubert v. Merrell Dow Pharmaceuticals*, 1993, pp. 12–15).

Several years later, the Court was called on to answer a related question. We recall that an expert does not have to be a scientist, but rather can be anyone with specialised knowledge of aid to the jury. In *Kumho Tires v. Carmichael*, the plaintiff argued that a tyre blowout had been caused by a manufacturing defect, not by general wear or underinflation. The plaintiff proffered the testimony of an engineer who stated that in his expert opinion, it was impossible for an automobile tyre to fail in a certain way unless it had a manufacturing defect. The Court was required to determine whether the *Daubert* criteria, developed in the context of scientific expert testimony, apply to the testimony of a non-scientist expert based merely on his experience? The Court ruled that it did. Although some of the *Daubert* criteria had no relevance to this form of testimony, the Court stressed *Daubert* was not a straitjacket; it merely proposed 'considerations' which lower courts could apply depending on the context, keeping in mind the ultimate goal of ensuring reliable expert testimony.

Daubert and *Kumho* established the modern law of expert witness evidence in the USA. The decisions have been received largely positively by courts and practitioners and have not led to significant confusion in practice. However, they have also been criticised by American legal scholars, which is normal in the robust culture of American legal academic debate. This would hardly be the first time that decisions which generated workable rules were nevertheless critiqued by law professors and interdisciplinary experts, and it will surely not be the last. *Daubert* has also been somewhat influential in the common-law legal family. No prior high Court had given such sustained consideration to the question of the reliability of expert testimony, and the Court's approach struck many observers as relatively straightforward and sensible. *Daubert* has, therefore, been cited and discussed throughout the common-law world. UK law has, as we have seen, traditionally shared with the United States a flexible definition of an 'expert'. The leading modern case, *R. v Turner*, states simply that expert evidence is admissible:

> to furnish the court with…information which is likely to be outside the experience and knowledge of a judge or jury. If on the proven facts a judge or jury can form their own conclusions without help, then the opinion of an expert is unnecessary. (R v Turner, 1975, QB 834, p. 841)

However, no English court has yet succinctly articulated a standard comparable to *Daubert* for defining what exactly constitutes expertise reliable enough to be invoked in court. One reason the issue is less pressing is that juries are used less frequently in English courtrooms, since they rarely decide private-law cases:

> The courts of England and Wales, Scotland and Northern Ireland have not developed standards for the admissibility of expert evidence comparable to those set out in *Daubert*. American judges have taken on a 'gatekeeping' role, largely in response to concern about the perceived gullibility of civil juries. British juries, by contrast, play little part in civil proceedings, and in those types of civil action where jury trial is still possible—notably libel—cases involving complex scientific evidence are tried by a judge alone. A more pressing concern for British judges has been to reduce the length and cost of civil litigation, and we shall see that this has led to some major reforms in the use of experts. (Ward, 2004, p. 41)

In the UK, thus, it has been the area of criminal law—where jury trials have been more common—which has been the focus of most reform efforts. One such effort was undertaken by the Law Commission, Britain's semi-private legal consultancy thinktank. The House of Commons' Science and Technology Committee had found that expert evidence was being allowed in criminal cases 'too readily, with insufficient scrutiny', sometimes leading to wrongful convictions (Law Commission, 2011, p. 1), and requested the Law Commission study the issue.

The result of the consultation was a substantial report by the Law Commission entitled 'Expert Evidence in Criminal Proceedings in England and Wales' (Law Commission, 2011). The impulse for reform, the Commission noted, came from numerous recent cases in which questionable expert testimony had led to unsafe convictions. One defendant had been convicted in part on comparison of an 'earprint', and others had been convicted of injuring or killing children based on discredited theories (ibid., pp. 1-3). The Commission outlined the reasons expert evidence is subject to special rules. First and foremost, 'Expert witnesses stand in the very privileged position of being able to provide the jury with opinion evidence on matters within their area of expertise and outside most jurors' knowledge and experience' (ibid., p. 3). There is also the danger that the jury 'may simply defer' to the expert (ibid., p. 4). This is dangerous because judges tend to have a very 'laissez-faire' attitude towards allowing expert testimony despite the fact that, quoting an Associate Professor William O'Brian of the University of Warwick, 'virtually all of the areas of "forensic science", with the exception of DNA evidence, have quite dubious scientific pedigrees' (ibid., p. 5).

The Law Commission discussed the *Daubert* standard extensively. While crediting the United States Supreme Court for addressing the issue head-on, the Commission noted that Daubert has been subjected to extensive criticism:

> We note that the equivalent reliability test in the United States…has been criticised as insufficiently effective for criminal proceedings because, amongst other things, it provides the trial judge with a wide discretion in the determination of evidentiary reliability and that appeals in relation to the application of this test are judged against a very narrow "abuse of discretion" standard of review. We believe that the assessment of evidentiary reliability in respect of matters which are not case-specific, principally questions of underlying scientific methodology, should be addressed anew in the Court of Appeal…not according to whether the trial judge acted within the parameters of a wide discretion. (ibid., p. 83)

Unlike their colleagues in civil-law systems, judges in first-instance trial courts in common-law legal systems enjoy a great deal of leeway to conduct cases as they see fit. This is based on the common-sense notion that trial judges have direct daily contact with the litigants and issues in their cases, and therefore have a sounder basis for making decisions than appeals courts. When it comes to ordinary questions of whether evidence should be admissible, a trial judge's decision will not be overturned unless it constitutes an 'abuse of discretion'—an extremely forgiving standard which means most challenges will fail. The Law Commission did not question the overall validity of this standard but argued that it is inappropriate for the general issue of whether an expert's testimony is sufficiently scientifically reliable. Unlike decisions about the credibility of witnesses or the effect of a certain piece of evidence on the jury in a specific case, the soundness of a particular scientific claim is an abstract question which any informed commentator can answer.

The Law Commission's proposals were intended to address this, and other, supposed deficiencies in the system. It is interesting to note that, like American commentators, the Law Commission felt a strong temptation to order judges to appoint 'neutral' experts to avoid unseemly 'battles of the experts'. However, its Report notes:

> on account of the adversarial nature of criminal proceedings in England and Wales, it is reasonable to assume that many trial judges may be reluctant to enter the arena [of appointing experts] in the absence of an explicit authority permitting this. (ibid., p. 91)

The Report, therefore, suggested introducing such an explicit statutory authorisation for the first time, while simultaneously noting that it should only be used in exceptional cases, to avoid delaying proceedings.

In any event, Parliament chose not to introduce new legislation. Instead, in 2014, the Ministry of Justice extensively re-organised and amended the Criminal Rules of Evidence (CRE) used in British courts in 2014. The rule changes granted judges the power to appoint neutral experts in Rule 19 of the CRE. The Criminal Practice Directions for Rule 19 governing expert evidence recommend that courts evaluate 'the extent and quality of the data' used by the expert, the reliability of any inferences made, the accuracy of 'any method' used by expert, the extent to which written material used by the expert has been 'reviewed' by third parties, whether the opinion relies on material outside the expert's specialty, the completeness of the information the expert relied on, whether the expert's opinion lies within the mainstream of the field, and whether the expert's methods rely on 'established practice' in the field (UK Ministry of Justice, Criminal Procedure Rules and Practice Directions, 2020, p. 33).

The discussion so far has revolved principally around criminal cases. It is an interesting question whether standards should differ depending on whether a case is criminal or civil (private) in nature. Given that a defendant's very freedom is at stake in criminal trials—and that they are more likely to involve a jury—one could argue the standards should be higher when the state is prosecuting a person accused of crime. Yet if the principle at stake is merely to ensure that the decision-maker receives the most reliable evidence possible, the nature of the case is secondary. In any event, the UK Supreme Court, in a recent case originating from Scotland, recently surveyed cases from several common-law jurisdictions and held that the admissibility of 'skilled' witness evidence (as it is known in Scottish law) should be determined by four factors: (1) whether the proposed evidence will assist the court in reaching a decision, (2) whether the witness has the required knowledge and experience, (3) whether the witness will be impartial in his or her presentation and assessment of the evidence and (4) whether there is a reliable body of knowledge or experience to underpin the expert's evidence (Kennedy v Cordia Services LLP 2016, paras. 38-61).

As we have seen, the admissibility of expert witness testimony is handled quite similarly across the common-law world. In both the US and the UK, courts have the authority to summon neutral expert witnesses on their own, but generally leave this task to the parties, especially in jury trials. Expert testimony is liberally allowed based on a broad initial definition, but courts have articulated a loose catalogue of considerations which courts can use to ensure that testimony is reliable, backed by adequate research or experience, and within the expert's specialty. Courts are generally receptive to expert testimony in the belief that any shortcomings in one expert's approach will be highlighted by the competing expert, as provided for by the common law. Expert evidence will, however, be excluded if it lies well outside the mainstream, uses novel techniques or theories, or generates inconsistent results.

6 Forensic Linguistics: Language as Evidence, Linguists as Experts

The term 'forensic linguistics' was first used by Swedish professor Jan Svartvik in 1968. (Ariani et al., 2014, p. 223). Svartvik (1968) analysed the case of Timothy Evans, a Welsh miner with intellectual disabilities who had been convicted, sentenced to death and executed (in 1950) on the basis of statements he had given to police confessing to the murder of his wife and daughter. His guilt was called into question shortly thereafter, when the bones of many additional murder victims who could not have been killed by Evans were discovered in the house in which Evans had lived. They had been killed by John Christie—a serial killer who, by sheer coincidence, had lived in the same building as Evans. Evans was eventually pardoned posthumously in 1966. Controversy raged around the issue of whether Evans' confessions were accurate. Svartvik subjected them to a thorough analysis, finding ultimately that although there were many suspicious discrepancies between the statements, there was too little evidence to permit a conclusive judgment on the accuracy of Evans' confessions.

Although Svartvik seems to have coined the term 'forensic linguistics', linguists had been giving expert testimony for quite some time and continue to do so. Given the relatively liberal common-law standards for admitting expert testimony, it should come as no surprise that linguists and language professionals have been introduced to address a broad array of subjects in common-law courtrooms. They do not, however, always testify as classically 'scientific' expert witnesses. Linguistics, as a branch of the humanities, rarely generates 'falsifiable' hypotheses which can be tested empirically—although such hypotheses, and experiments, of course exist within linguistics. More often, however, linguists testify based on their experience and understanding, in a context well-defined by Judge Learned Hand, who spoke of 'general truths derived from … specialised experience' (Hand, 1901, p. 54). There has been little controversy specifically about the role of *linguistic* expert testimony; controversies which arise are generally similar to ones which may crop up in any case involving expert evidence.

The most common controversy in the context of linguistic expert evidence revolves around two issues. First, since every juror uses language, the linguist expert must bring a sufficient level of specialised expertise to distinguish him or her from the jurors themselves. Most jurors, for example, can identify the accent of a native Spanish speaker speaking English, and would not need a linguist to help answer the question at this level of generality—that is, with no need to identify an unusual dialect. This question is the sort of question which jurors are expected to answer based on their general understanding and experience. A second question is how much influence the linguist expert's conclusions may have. As legal scholar and linguist Larry Solan writes, linguistic experts rarely provide the decisive evidence in a case; often, they end up being more of a 'semantic tour guide'—providing the decider of fact with background information helping it make more reliable judgments (Solan, 1998).

A 1994 survey of linguistic evidence in North American courtrooms identified dozens of specific applications in legal cases (Levi, 1994). These included localising the accents of persons who placed anonymous threat calls, distinguishing between closely related trademarked words or prefixes (phonetics and morphology), gauging the readability of official bureaucratic notifications to people with limited education (syntax), judging whether jury instructions in a capital murder case were unambiguous (semantics), and assessing whether a working-class plaintiff's answers to complex legal questions in a deposition were honest (pragmatics). The author also notes that expert testimony from linguists often blurs the boundaries between classifications which appear distinct within the academic specialty of linguistics. This is a common phenomenon in the courtroom, where the distinct boundaries between academic subfields dissolve under the insistent pressure to produce useful evidence in specific cases.

Linguistic expert testimony has been well-received in American courts and courts in other common-law jurisdictions. Tiersma and Solan (2002) explained why:

> At least in theory, linguistic evidence should fare quite well regardless of the evidentiary standard that is applied. Linguistics is a robust field that relies heavily on peer-reviewed journals for dissemination of new work.

> Furthermore, much of the expert testimony offered is in keeping with very basic literature in the field. For example, when a linguist is asked to testify about a criminal defendant's proficiency in English, the expert has available a number of well-accepted instruments and a great deal of learning on which to base an analysis. (p. 225)

Further, as noted above, linguists often act more as 'tour guides' than as aggressive partisan experts opining on issues which will determine the outcome of a case. Thus, the risk that they will 'usurp the province of the jury' is usually seen as negligible. Nevertheless, Solan and Tiersma note that courts have been reluctant to permit expert testimony to identify speakers or authors, testimony relying on discourse analysis, and linguistic evidence concerning interpretation of contracts and jury instructions. In each case, courts held that these matters were either for the jury to decide or could be resolved by standard tools of legal analysis.

Another reason linguistic expert evidence is rarely the focus of intense controversy during court proceedings has to do with that perennial topic of contention between experts and lawyers: How much certainty is the expert willing to testify to? Another contributor to this volume (see Chap. 7) has helpfully described the scale of probabilities customarily used by linguists to describe how confident they are that a certain author created a certain text. The highest level of certainty is 'exceedingly high probability'. Lawyers will see an analogy to DNA testing: A DNA analysis can only show the likelihood that another human being, chosen at random, contributed the DNA found at the crime scene. This probability may be 1 in 10 billion—that is the denominator may be larger than the entire population of humans—but still, technically, this does not constitute absolute *positive* proof that the suspect left the DNA. Even the most skilled linguist using the most advanced algorithms will rarely be able to state a definitive conclusion, which is why 'absolute certainty' is not listed as a potential expert judgment. This remaining uncertainty means that linguistic evidence will almost never be the *sole* issue in any case. This is especially true of criminal cases, in which the typical standard of proof the prosecution must meet is proof beyond a reasonable doubt. Prosecutors may use linguistic evidence as a key piece of a mosaic pointing to the defendant's guilt, but they will still have to gather the other pieces of the mosaic. They may have to satisfy themselves with a mere statement from the linguist that the defendant 'cannot be excluded' as the author of the text. The defence, for its part, will highlight for the jury or judge all of the factors—from methodological disputes to small corpora to mere random chance—which caused the linguist to frame his or her conclusions cautiously. This incommensurability between legal and scientific epistemology crops up constantly and often causes significant tactical problems for lawyers. Nevertheless, there is no way around it: Science is a process of continuous questioning and refinement ideally driven by ideals of honest and careful inquiry. The legal system, by contrast, must come to final, binary yes-or-no conclusions even in the presence of considerable doubt and uncertainty.

7 Conclusion

Courts and legislatures in virtually all Western legal systems, and many others besides, permit expert witnesses to give evidence to help decision-makers understand complex issues and reach accurate verdicts. The standards for defining an 'expert' are generally quite broad, and differ little even across the common civil law divide, as shown by Chap. 4 in this volume: Essentially, an expert is anyone who has specialised experience and understanding going beyond what an average juror or judge could be reasonably expected to possess. Beyond this core of agreement, however, legal systems differ, sometimes dramatically, in how they handle expert evidence. In the early modern era, the common law took a distinctive path which marks its handling of these issues to this day: it integrated expert witnesses into the emerging adversarial system. This helped entrench lawyers' control over the trial: Not only did they determine which witnesses would be heard, they also determined which expert judgments would be heard by the jury. From the very beginning, critics deplored the phenomenon of 'duelling experts' as a discredit to both science and law. Yet the adversarial instinct has, so far, prevented widespread acceptance of court-appointed 'neutral' experts in the civil-law mould, even though many common-law jurisdictions (including the USA and UK) explicitly grant judges this choice.

Linguists have generally had little difficulty being qualified as experts under the tests applicable in most common-law countries. The only questions emerge in two main areas. First, courts may exclude linguistic testimony because it invades the province of the jury: that is the linguist proposes to testify on an issue which an ordinary juror could be expected to form a reliable opinion based on their own life experience and common sense, without the need for expert guidance. Second, linguistic testimony has been excluded or limited based on questions of reliability, falsifiability and general acceptance when it involves novel techniques or comparisons which have not been subjected to robust testing and review. Yet these are unusual cases: Linguists generally face little difficulty being qualified as experts and have been used by parties to shed light on a vast array of issues, from the historical understanding of legal terms to the likelihood that a welfare recipient will be able to comprehend welfare-agency notices. Perhaps one reason for their widespread acceptance is that linguistic expert witnesses are often not called to testify concerning the ultimate issue at trial, but rather to provide background knowledge, helping the decision-maker (whether judge or jury) understand how the study of language can help them reach a just and reliable resolution to a legal dispute.

References

Ariani, M. G., Sajedi, F., & Sajedi, M. (2014). Forensic linguistics: A brief overview of the key elements. *Procedia - Social and Behavioral Sciences, 158*, 222–225.

Brewer, S. (1998). Scientific expert testimony and intellectual due process. *Yale Law Journal, Yale Law Journal, 107*, 1535–1681.

Bushell's Case, 124 Eng. Rep. 1006 (C.P. 1670).

Choo, A. L. T., & Hunter, J. (2018). Gender discrimination and juries in the 20th century: Judging women judging men. *International Journal of Evidence and Proof, 22*(3), 192–217.

Daubert v. Merrell Dow Pharmaceuticals 509 U.S. 579 (1993).

Frye v. United States, 293 F. 1013 (D.C. Cir. 1923).

Golan, T. (1999). The history of scientific expert testimony in the English courtroom. *Science in Context, 12*, 7–32.
Hand, L. (1901). Historical and practical considerations regarding expert testimony. *Harvard Law Review, 15*, 40.
Judicial College, *The crown court compendium, part I: Jury and trial management and summing up*. December 2020 (Retrieved from: https://www.judiciary.uk/publications/crown-court-compendium-published/)
Kennedy v Cordia (Services) LLP, [2016] UKSC 6.
Langbein, J. H. (1985). The German advantage in civil procedure. *University of Chicago Law Review, 52*(4), 823.
Langbein, J. H. (1999). The prosecutorial origins of defence counsel in the eighteenth century: The appearance of solicitors. *The Cambridge Law Journal, 58*(2), 314–365.
Law Commission (2011). Expert evidence in criminal proceedings in England and Wales. Retrieved on February 15th, 2021, from https://assets.publishing.service.gov.uk/government/uploads/system/uploads/attachment_data/file/229043/0829.pdf
Madge, N. (2006). Summing up—A judges' perspective. *Criminal Law Review, September 2006*, 817-827.
Ministry of Justice of the United Kingdom, Criminal Procedure Rules and Practice Directions (2020). Retrieved on March 23rd, 2021, from https://assets.publishing.service.gov.uk/government/uploads/system/uploads/attachment_data/file/938591/crim-practice-directions-V-evidence-2015.pdf
Ministry of Justice of the United Kingdom, A Guide to the Criminal Procedure Rules 2014 (S.I. 2014/1610) Retrieved on March 23rd, 2021, from https://www.justice.gov.uk/courts/procedure-rules/criminal/docs/2014/criminal-procedure-rules-2014.pdf
Parkes, S. (1820). Observations on the chemical part of the evidence given on a late trial. *The Journal of Science and the Arts, 10*(XI), 316–354.
Pollock, F., & Maitland, F. (1895). *The history of English law before the time of Edward I* (Vol. 2). Cambridge University Press.
Rogers, H.W. (1891). The law of expert testimony. *Central Law Journal Co.*, St. Louis, Mo. (2d ed.).
R v Turner, [1975] QB 834.
Solan, L. R. (1998). Linguistic experts as semantic tour guides. *Forensic Linguistics, 5*(2), 87–106.
Svartvik, J. (1968). The Evans statements: A case for forensic linguistics. Part I. *Acta Universitatis Gothoburgensis, 20*, 7–44.

Tiersma, P., & Solan, L. R. (2002). The linguist on the witness stand: Forensic linguistics in American courts. *Language, 78*, 221–239.

Ward, T. (2004). Expert testimony issues in the UK. *Security Journal, 17*(3), 41–49.

4

Expert Evidence in Civil Law Systems

Mercedes Fernández-López

1 Introduction

It is not easy to identify common general principles that describe the expert witness's regulation and function in continental procedures. These principles, in a sense, are not entirely clear, and are sometimes far from what might be expected. While it is true that there are some differences regarding the role of the expert in common law and civil law systems, there is no doubt that expert testimony within the legal procedure raises common problems. The different legal cultures that inspire continental and common law procedural systems condition, to a great extent, how expert evidence is approached, but we must not forget that the phenomenon of globalisation is also present in the legal field, minimising the

This piece of research shows part of the results of the research project DER2017-87516-P (funded by the Spanish Ministry of Economy, Industry and Competitiveness).

M. Fernández-López (✉)
University of Alicante, Alicante, Spain
e-mail: mercedes.fernandez@ua.es

V. Guillén-Nieto, D. Stein (eds.), *Language as Evidence*,
https://doi.org/10.1007/978-3-030-84330-4_4

differences between the legal systems. The same globalising phenomenon also drives significant attempts made by the European institutions to harmonise substantive and procedural rules in cross-border litigation, which has grown exponentially and has become a major issue in both the public and private legal sectors. In this context, it is useful and relevant to identify the areas in which European countries offer different answers to the same legal problem, as in the case of expert evidence. Hence, from the perspective of European continental or civil law, this chapter aims to discuss the different ways in which a selected sample of civil law jurisdictions—that is Spain, France, Germany, Austria, Italy and Poland—regulate the judicial intervention of experts concerning three main aspects: (a) the legal status of the expert and how their independence is guaranteed, (b) the procedure for procuring expert evidence and the influence of the judge and the parties in practice (from the appointment of the expert to the ratification of his or her report in the court trial) and (c) the court's evaluation of the expert evidence when assembling the body of evidence on which the legal decision is based. However, firstly, it is necessary to clarify what an expert is and what consideration is given to his or her intervention in civil court proceedings.

2 The Expert Is Not a Witness

The first fundamental characteristic needed to understand this type of evidence correctly is this: the expert is not a witness. The Anglo-Saxon term *expert witness* can be misleading because, in continental legal systems, there are substantial differences between those who testify as witnesses and those who do so based on their specialised knowledge. Although both types of testimonies—witness and expert witness—make up the so-called personal evidence—this is what Anglo-Saxon countries emphasise by considering the expert witness a qualified type of witness due to his or her knowledge, the truth is that they have few points of connection. The essential difference between the witness and the expert lies in the content of their contribution to the proceedings. The witness offers personal information regarding the subject matter of the case; their knowledge is specific and exclusive to the facts of the case, either because they have witnessed the facts directly or because they have been told about the facts by the person who witnessed them. By contrast, the expert offers the judge general and abstract technical, scientific or artistic knowledge necessary to assess the facts and reach a conclusion about them. In sum, the witness provides information of an exclusively personal nature, while the information that the expert offers to the court is of a technical nature (Cortés Domínguez & Moreno Catena, 2017; Taruffo, 2008). The expert is appointed because the facts to be examined require some expert assessment that the judge cannot perform due to the lack of expert knowledge and required qualifications to do so. For example a lay witness can provide valuable information, known personally or through third parties, about how the defendant intentionally damaged the victim's vehicle with a golf club; the witness knows how many times the car was struck, the specific location of the dents and/or the situation before and after the incident. The witness may thus corroborate the prosecution's version, implicating the defendant as the perpetrator of the crime. However, lay testimony is not always sufficient; sometimes, there are no identified lay witnesses who can help to clarify the facts. It is in such a case that the expert witness' contribution becomes an essential means of proof of how the events may have occurred—for example which instrument might have been used to cause the damage, how much damage was done (to determine the seriousness of the crime) and, if applicable, the extent of the monetary compensation to the victim. Only if the eyewitness is, by chance, an expert in the assessment of material damages, could he or she provide, in addition to information on how the events occurred, a useful damage estimate. However, in such a case the witness would not be an expert witness in the strict sense—that is a third party called upon to assess events which have already occurred, because the witness' statement will not be accompanied by any technical report.

In Spanish civil law, expert witnesses are regulated in Article 370.4 of the Spanish Civil Procedure Law (hereinafter 'LEC'):

> Where the witness has scientific, technical, artistic or practical knowledge of the subject matter to which the facts of the examination relate, the court shall admit statements which by such knowledge the witness adds to his or her answers on the facts.[1]

From the quote above, it is clear that the law grants the expert the principal attribute of witness. The expert must act in conformity with this status, although he or she must also agree to warn the court about any possible loss of impartiality as described by Art. 343 LEC. This way, the Spanish legislator limits the technical scope of eyewitness testimony to the assessments they can make at the court trial. Consequently, the eyewitness will be admitted as a witness to the facts and not because of the expert knowledge they can provide; the eyewitness statement will deal with the facts that they know based on knowledge gained outside the courtroom. When the eyewitness has expert knowledge, they can also give their opinion on the facts about which they testify. This fact has special repercussions in the field of healthcare liability for facts attributed to one or several members of a medical or multidisciplinary team when the other members of the team are aware of such facts, who will be called as witnesses. The information the expert witness can provide the court of justice with is particularly valuable to complement the evidence given by the eyewitness. Apart from the category of eyewitness and expert witness, the expert is called upon to assist the court in assessing the facts or to help the court to acquire certainty about the facts (Art. 355.1 LEC).

Therefore, the information the expert provides to the court of justice can serve two purposes. On the one hand, such information can offer a technical interpretation of facts introduced through other means of evidence. In the golf-club example, this could include assessment of the damages caused, the possible existence of a causal relationship between the injuries presented by the victim and the legal wrong they claim to have suffered, or a technical assessment of the credibility of the victim's statement. On the other hand, the expert may provide relevant facts to when specific knowledge and skills are required. For example by judging the authenticity of an artwork in a fraud offence, or affirming the statistical probability that a certain person wrote a handwritten note found at a crime scene. It is not easy to draw the line between these two purposes, since the expert's interpretation of the facts often involves introducing new relevant facts—for example when coroner concludes that death was caused by asphyxiation and excludes poisoning. Therefore, what is important is that the expert provides information—either *ex novo* or known, but interpreted in the light of their knowledge in a way which serves to clarify the facts (Murray & Stürner, 2004).

3 The Expert Must Be Independent

One of the goals of legal proceedings is the discovery of the truth, since this is a necessary presupposition to legitimise the final judicial resolution of a case. A trial resulting in a decision obviously untethered to reality would carry no weight and enjoy no public acceptance. For this reason, mechanisms and remedies have been established to overturn judicial decisions that do not conform to the facts—for example appeals and the review of judgments which, despite having become final and therefore irrevocable, have nevertheless been revealed to be manifestly unjust. Furthermore, procedural systems are openly committed to this end by regulating evidentiary systems which seek a fair balance between the admission of all relevant means of evidence and the guarantee that the evidence that is produced will provide reliable information. Therefore, a common feature to all civil legal systems analysed in this chapter is the effort to preserve the impartiality of the expert in order to reduce, as far as possible, any suspicion of lack of neutrality. Experts are also given a special status because they are considered assistants to the judge. This fact explains why special precautions have to be taken to preserve their independence. A consequence of the independence requirement is the provision of mechanisms to monitor possible causes of loss of impartiality which may affect the quality and neutrality of the expert report.

The German Code of Civil Procedure (hereinafter known by its German acronym ZPO) provides that experts can be challenged on the same grounds as judges, as set out in Arts. 42–45 ZPO. In Austria, when an expert's independence is in question, the Federal court decides whether the expert can issue a report in the criminal case to which they were appointed (Popa & Necula, 2013). In Poland, an expert may be challenged if there are circumstances that might compromise their impartiality (Art. 196 §2 y §3 Criminal Procedure Code [CPC]). In Spain, an expert may be proposed by any of the parties or by the court in both civil and criminal cases. A dual system of control over the expert's impartiality is established according to how they are appointed. While the experts proposed by the parties are subject to the 'objection' system (Arts. 124.2 and 343 LEC), a judicially appointed expert—always at the request of the parties in the civil sphere, but also *ex officio* in the criminal sphere—is subject to the 'challenge' system (Arts. 124.1 LEC and 468 of the Spanish Criminal Procedure Act [from now on LECrim]) and, subsidiarily (only in the civil sphere) to the 'objection' system, to determine the concurrence of an objective cause of possible loss of impartiality. Cortés Domínguez and Moreno Catena (2017) explains the rationale for this dual system of control over the expert's impartiality based on the different conception of the expert as an assistant to the judge (when appointed by the court) and as an assistant to the parties (when appointed by a party). This distinction appears unsustainable for various reasons. Firstly, because the expert is called upon to perform the same function and their impartiality must be preserved in any case. Secondly, because in criminal proceedings both forms of appointment coexist and no system is established to question the impartiality of the experts appointed by the parties.

The concurrence of one of the grounds for objection provided for in Art. 343.1 LEC, which are based on the existence of a personal relationship with the parties, their advocates or representatives,[2] or of a direct or indirect interest in the lawsuit, does not exclude the intervention of the expert, who may issue their report and ratify it in the trial; it is exclusively a warning or reprobation that the opposing party addresses the court—not binding in any way—to question the reliability of the report based on the occurrence of an objective cause of lack of impartiality of the expert. Such reprobation will be considered by the judge when passing judgement and may result in the report being deprived of evidentiary weight. On the other hand, the challenge of an expert—a figure that has its origin in preserving the independence of judicial personnel and which extends to the judicially appointed expert—entails, if it is upheld, the replacement of the challenged expert by another, also judicially appointed. The grounds on which an expert may be removed through a challenge, which in part coincide with those for objection, also include the grounds for the challenge of judges and magistrates (Art. 219 of the Spanish Judiciary Law [from now on LOPJ]), as well as the existence of prior professional relationships with the litigant who is opposed to the one who is challenged and the preparation of a prior report against the challenger in the same or a different case (Art. 124.3.1ª LEC).

4 The Submission of Expert Evidence and the Appointment of the Expert

An essential difference between expert evidence in common law and civil law jurisdictions concerns the proposal of expert evidence and who is to appoint the expert. In countries within the common law system, it is the parties who propose the experts who will intervene in the legal proceedings in support of the parties' position at trial, and the court only appoints them in exceptional circumstances (a possibility provided for in Rule 706 of the *Federal Rules of Evidence* but hardly implemented in practice). However, in civil law systems, it is usual for the court to nominate the expert, which indicates that the figure of the expert is considered an assistant to the court for interpreting data and evaluating evidence. The European Court of Human Rights (ECHR) has held that the system of judicial appointment, which is common to practically all continental European systems, allows for the presumption of the expert's impartiality. The expert therefore acts as assistant to the court of justice in matters that require specific knowledge and skilled expertise (Judgement of the ECHR of April 4, 2013 [C.B. v. Austria]). However, as mentioned, this system coexists in some countries (such as Spain) with the appointment of experts by the parties in support of their respective theses (Popa & Necula, 2013).

In Germany, the appointment of experts (*Sachverständige*) is, as a general rule, the judicial body's task, which can do so either *ex officio* or at the parties' request (Ansanelli, 2019, p. 1260). The expert will only be appointed by the parties once they have agreed on who will issue the report. According to Art. 404 ZPO, the judge may limit the number of experts involved to a single expert. The experts may be chosen either from among those who have passed a selection process (screening procedures for publicly appointed and sworn experts) or from among those already recognised by the state. This is common practice in specialised areas managed by the respective professional associations that also establish selection procedures), or from among the experts who have the approval of certifying bodies, because they meet the quality standards of ISO 9001 (Lösing, 2020). In both civil law and criminal law proceedings, the court in charge of the prosecution and the public prosecutor who conducts the investigation have broad powers to appoint the expert, who may not necessarily be included in the official lists of accredited experts at the state level.

Similarly, the civil court in France is responsible for appointing the expert from those included in the lists of experts of *Le Conseil national des compagnies d'experts de justice*. The expert's inclusion in such lists is valid for five years. After this period, the expert's inclusion can be renewed, provided that the expert successfully completes specific training courses in the relevant fields. In criminal law, an expert who is not on such official lists may report on a case at the request of an investigating judge only exceptionally (Arts.157 and 159 *Code de procédure pénale* [from now on CPP]).

In Italy, the court also manages the expert's appointment. Whereas Italian civil proceedings (Arts. 61 and 191 to 193 of the *Codice di procedura civile* [from now on CPC] refer to the figure of *the consulente tecnico d'ufficio*, criminal proceedings refer to the figure of the expert. Both figures are considered assistants to the judge in Italy. In the Italian procedure, the *ex officio* appointment coexists with the possibility of the parties appointing an expert. In this case, the expert is referred to as a *consulente Tecnico de parte*; it is their job to rebut the methods employed and the conclusions reached by the expert the judge has appointed (Art. 201 CPC).

In turn, the Polish Code of Civil Procedure (from now on CCP) provides for the appointment of experts by the court itself, *ex officio* or at the request of a party, when the subject matter of the case requires (Art. 278 §1 CCP), and such experts must be appointed from the lists of professionals available to the district courts. In criminal proceedings, all experts in a given field, not only those on official lists, are obliged to provide their services as experts if required to do so (Art. 195 Polish Criminal Procedure Code [from now on CPC]).

The Spanish system for appointing an expert is somewhat different because, as mentioned, there are two coexisting forms of designation: either judicial or by the parties. Neither of these forms of designation has prominence over the other. In civil law, the initiative to propose expert evidence always lies with the parties, because the proceeding revolves around the facts and the evidence they provide to the court, these being matters of private law. Nevertheless, the appointment of the expert can be made freely by the parties or can be made by the court at the request of one or both of the parties, by mutual agreement. In the latter case, the expert is proposed from among those available on the official lists of experts established by the professional associations. Only in the area of non-dispositive civil proceedings, characterised by the presence of public interest (e.g. family proceedings or proceedings relating to the civil status of individuals), judges may take the initiative to agree on the practice of the means of evidence they deem necessary and, among them, the appointment of experts (Art. 752.1 LEC). In criminal proceedings, the LECrim contains very little expert evidence regulation, which the LEC regulation must complement. Unlike in civil proceedings, the judge in charge of the criminal investigation has the power to order all means of evidence that may be relevant to the clarification of the facts (Art. 456 LECrim) (as is the case of the French legal system (Solaro & Jean, 1987, p. 33) and the Belgian legal system (Art. 61 quinquies Code d'instruction criminelle [from now on CIC])), without prejudice to the fact that the parties may appoint experts at their own expense (Art. 471 LECrim). In Spain, the *ex officio* expert opinions on criminal matters are usually entrusted to the State Security Forces and Corps and the Legal Medicine and Toxicology services. At the same time, parties are free to use the professionals they deem appropriate.

5 The Intervention of the Judge and the Parties in the Practice of Expert Evidence

Another issue that must be addressed is how expert evidence is conducted and the intervention of the judge and the parties in such practice.

In German law, not all experts are obliged to issue a report, only those who are required to do so by the court. In that case, the written report (according to § 411a ZPO) can be used in different proceedings concerning the same facts but between different people. This would be the case, for example, in mass tort proceedings, if the report made in the context of one of the proceedings provides relevant information for the resolution of the other. Therefore, unless the court expressly requests or authorises the expert to issue a written report, the expert's intervention will be limited to being questioned by the judge and by the attorneys for the parties. However, given his or her status as a court-appointed expert, cross-examination is usually less exhaustive than that of a party-appointed expert (Timmerbeil, 2003). This difference lies in the fact that the party-appointed expert is considered a witness and thereby, the rules regarding witness statements govern their procedural intervention (Taruffo, 2008). The party-appointed experts express their opinion in writing but are not questioned at a court trial. This fact is undoubtedly related to the low value that judges give to the expert opinion in Germany (Timmerbeil, 2003). This view is shared in Polish courts of justice, where the opinion of experts appointed by the parties is presupposed to support their thesis. Besides, in Poland, it is the civil judicial body that decides whether the expert gives a written report or only gives an oral report (Art. 278 §3 CPC and Art. 200 CPC), as well as whether it is necessary to ask the expert to clarify, orally or in writing, certain points of their report to ensure that the parties can ask any questions they deem necessary. The judge may appoint a second expert when they deem that another opinion is necessary (Art. 286 CPC and Art. 201 CPC), while in criminal law the court may decide that several experts should issue reports, either separately or jointly (Art. 193 §3 CPC).

By contrast, in other European countries expert evidence has absolute autonomy concerning testimonial evidence and is regulated greatly. For instance, in French criminal proceedings, the investigating judge appoints the expert, determines the subject matter of the expert report and receives the results. However, the parties and their attorneys may challenge those results by questioning the expert (Art. 165 CPP), even if they have themselves appointed an expert to examine the judicially appointed expert's actions during the investigation phase preceding the trial.

Apart from the expert's role in assisting the court in evaluating the evidence and/or interpreting the facts at trial, it is essential that the expert can be questioned by both the court and the parties. The so-called principle of contradiction must be the basis for considering all the evidence. In particular, the principle of contradiction must be applied to evidence of a personal nature (witnesses and experts). This principle implies that the parties should have the opportunity to question the expert on the subject matter of his or her report (oral or written). In this regard, and although respect for the principle of contradiction makes it possible to assess compliance with the requirements derived from due process, the ECHR has endorsed that the possibility of submitting the expert report to contradiction does not necessarily occur in the act of trial. To the ECHR, it is also acceptable that in some systems such cross-examination takes place in the early stages of the process, just as it happens in countries where this examination takes place in the investigative stage (Bujosa Vadell, 2017, p. 62) prior to trial.

Finally, it is important to note that, as a general rule, the expert examination of evidence is carried out autonomously. However, the Spanish LEC allows the judge to agree—*ex officio* or at the request of the parties—to hold the expert examination jointly with the judicial examination, so that the expert can make observations during the judge's examination (Arts. 356 and 358 LEC). German civil procedure also allows the judge to agree *ex officio* on the participation of an expert in the on-site examination (§144 I (1) ZPO).

6 The Evaluation of Expert Evidence

As opposed to the common law system, where special controls are imposed on the quality of expert evidence at the time of its procedural admission, in civil law countries such controls occur at the time of its evaluation. However, the admission of expert evidence is carried out under the classic and general criteria of relevance and usefulness for the discovery of the truth. It is noteworthy that there is only a brief mention regarding the scientific criteria that the evidence must meet to support the expert opinion (Champod & Vuille, 2011). Indeed, the principle of a free appraisal of expert evidence governs in all the procedural systems analysed in this chapter. However, that freedom must be exercised reasonably for purposes of assessing the reliability of the expert opinion and the evidential weight that it should be given. There are no formal rules governing how the judge values the expert evidence, because the judge retains exclusive competence to evaluate such evidence. However, the judge must always do so under the principle of 'good reasoning' (*sana crítica*); the judge must explain in their legal decision the reasons for acceptance or rejection of the expert's conclusions (Timmerbeil, 2003). Indeed, the expert opinion is one of the evidentiary elements—in some cases, qualified, or, to a certain extent, privileged, due to the expert's specialised knowledge—based on which the judicial decision will be made. Therefore, the result of the joint evaluation of the evidence may be contrary to what the expert has stated in his or her report, because it will not necessarily prevail over the rest of the evidence, if the other evidence leads to a different and better-founded decision. Expert opinion does not always offer a solution for solving the case. In other words, sometimes the expert opinion refers only to a tangential aspect of the facts. For example the assessment of damages or the authorship of a message. Sometimes the expert opinion cannot individually explain the facts, but is compatible with different versions of them, such as when a DNA report reveals that the defendant had sexual relations with the plaintiff but cannot conclude whether or not they were consensual, or when the expert opinion can identify the geographical origin of a particular speaker but cannot guarantee his or her specific identity.

In the above-mentioned examples, the rest of the evidence will make it possible to lean on the judicial decision in a direction that will not necessarily align with the expert's opinion, or which may even be contrary to that opinion. Furthermore, in legal systems such as Spain, the experts appointed by the parties and the judge may hold different and even contradictory opinions. In this case, the judge must make a reasonable decision about the expert opinions that will be relevant and useful for making their legal decision.

One of the main problems with expert evidence in civil law systems is the judges' tendency to give inordinate weight to the expert's opinion literally, especially when that expert has been judicially appointed. This has been called 'epistemic deference' and finds its *raison d'être* in the inadequate knowledge of the judicial body to assess the reliability of the expert report or of the expert who subscribes it (Champod & Vuille, 2011; Timmerbeil, 2003; Vázquez Rojas, 2014). Although this problem is found whenever expert evidence is introduced, it is especially conspicuous in the case of scientific evidence (Gascón Abellán, 2016). Scientific evidence poses two types of problems. First, although the expert's opinion is not legally binding, judges hardly question it (Yein Ng, 2014), except when contradictory expert opinions are presented. Therefore, the judge does not have the competence to do an effective critical analysis of the expert's information, which, *de facto*, takes the place of the judge as a decision-maker (Champod & Vuille, 2011; Timmerbeil, 2003, p. 180).

The second, related problem is the serious risk incurred by the absence of control over the content of expert opinions. Without such control, purportedly expert information, which in fact has no valid scientific basis, can be introduced into judicial procedure, and can mislead the judge into making serious errors (Gascón Abellán, 2016, p. 350).

When judges have several reports at their disposal, they may sometimes decide to give greater value to some reports over others, without being able to reasonably justify their decisions. This issue is particularly problematic if one takes into account that, in civil law systems, there is a judicial duty to provide reasons that must extend not only to the legal norms that are considered applicable, but also to the facts of the case and the evidence on which the decision is based. The requirement to state reasons is seen as one of the limits to the judge's over-reliance on the expert opinion, since the decision must state the judge's reasons for accepting the expert's conclusions (Yein Ng, 2014), but that limit may be inadequate to solve the problem.

One way of overcoming such problems would require the joint effort of judges and experts, especially in forensic identification sciences. For example the conclusions of a forensic report on authorship identification should be expressed in terms of statistical probability or plausibility that could help the judge to make the legal decision about the case (Gascón Abellán, 2016). In this regard, a particularly noteworthy initiative is that of ENFSI (*European Network of Forensic Science Institutes*), whose project is to write guides for the explication of the conclusions in the main types of forensic reports.[3] It is also important to note that judges should receive basic scientific training to understand and interpret the main types of reports appropriately:

> (…) education is necessary. Without it, there will always be a risk of accepting as solid knowledge that which has little basis or ends up making the evidence say what it does not and cannot say, and the fairness of the decision may be compromised. Without education, the cognitive basis of the legal decision is weakened, and the risk of error becomes stronger.[4] (Gascón Abellán, 2016, p. 365)

As Champod and Vuille (2011, p. 53) have pointed out, the proper understanding of scientific evidence depends on the judges' ability to evaluate such evidence critically. For this reason, it is essential not only that forensic reports are scientifically reliable, but also judges are well trained to assess such reports.

7 Conclusions

This chapter has analysed the differences and similarities of a selected sample of European civil law jurisdictions concerning expert evidence. In general, these differences are responsive to the roles and powers concerning expert evidence attributed to the parties and the judge in each legal system. Whereas in common law systems the proposition and practice of expert evidence rest, as a general rule, on the parties, in civil law systems the judge has greater control over the evidence, although the role of the parties is also fundamental. The parties assume the evidentiary strategy, both in civil and criminal proceedings. This is the case except during the criminal investigation phase; the countries that maintain the figure of the investigating judge recognise broad powers of the latter for the practice of investigative acts and means of evidence. The production of evidence by a party is a central procedural principle. This principle is consistent with the dispositive principle—around which civil proceedings are structured—and with the accusatory principle, which in criminal proceedings seeks to guarantee judicial impartiality by reserving the leading role in taking evidence to the parties. After all, the parties are the ones who are interested in proving the facts to which the evidence to be taken refers. At the same time, judges remain in a neutral position and limit themselves to evaluating the evidence available to pass a judgement. Hence, it is the parties who propose the means of evidence that they intend to use, reserving for the judge the decision on the admission of the proposed evidence—for example the admission of the statement of a witness or the inadmissibility of expert evidence unrelated to the litigation—and the direction of the evidentiary activity to be carried out in the court trial—for example the inadmissibility of questions to the witnesses that are reiterative or impertinent.

Moreover, within the framework of such powers, in all the legal systems analysed here judges retain the competence to appoint the experts who will intervene to report on the disputed facts. In criminal law, this is usually the case, since criminal courts generally turn to official bodies to obtain such opinions; in civil law, they usually turn to the experts—individuals and legal entities—who populate the official lists available to the Administration of Justice, which are managed by them in some cases and, in others, by professional associations. Nevertheless, these powers coexist in many cases, as we have seen, with the possibility—more or less extensive—of the parties themselves appointing private experts who hold a specialised opinion on the facts on which they base their procedural positions. Such experts, appointed by the parties, may or may not concur with experts appointed by the court. However, the evidentiary weight of the experts appointed by the parties tends to be lower, and in some cases, it is considered negligible. Of all the systems analysed here, the one with the most special characteristics is the Spanish system, which generally provides for the selection of experts by the parties. In the Spanish system, the experts selected by the parties are alternative to one and coexistent with their judicial appointment, at the request of a party or even *ex officio* by the court itself.

The growing tendency in civil law countries to cede control to the judge over expert evidence is a reflection of the change in the procedural paradigm in the area of evidentiary activity. There is a growing interest in the discovery of the truth as one of the main purposes of judicial process, beyond, no doubt, the particular interest that parties may have in the facts and the allegations they may offer to the court of justice. It is also an unambiguous recognition of the procedural relevance that expert evidence, especially scientific evidence, has acquired (Ansanelli, 2019). The appointment of the expert, the determination of the number of experts to be called upon to contribute, or the definition of the object of the expertise, are in the domain of judicial powers that do not necessarily affect the parties' powers of evidentiary initiative, but rather seek to exercise a certain control over the quality of information that may enter the process by means of such evidence.

This same purpose is also behind the various mechanisms that, as we have seen, are articulated in all the systems discussed here to guarantee the impartiality of the expert. It is possible to challenge judicially appointed experts and, consequently, to remove them from the proceedings and replace them with others. In the Spanish legal context, it is also possible to question the impartiality of the experts provided by the other party through the 'objection system.' Through this objection system, a warning regarding the impartiality of the expert is provided to the court, a warning which must be taken into account when assessing the forensic report along with the rest of the evidence.

While impartiality alone does not guarantee the accuracy of a forensic report, *ex ante* mechanisms seek to screen out information that could mislead the court because it comes from experts who lack due impartiality. Apart from the problem of the expert's impartiality, other more important problems need to be taken into consideration, such as disagreements between different experts or scientific weaknesses in their conclusions (Vázquez Rojas, 2014). Therefore, in all civil law systems, the judge has the power to question the expert on their reports and to request any clarifications deemed necessary. In the case of the French legal system, the expert can even be asked for clarifications during the process of drafting the report. Later, when the expert is called upon to intervene orally, the judge may question them or appoint another expert who can highlight the weaknesses of the methodology employed, or the expertly scrutinise conclusions reached in their forensic reports.

Another control mechanism *ex post* is also provided for in all civil law systems through the requirement that judicial decisions be justified with reasoning. The purpose of the reasoning requirement is to ensure that the expert's forensic report is reliable, relevant and consistent with the rest of the evidence that forms the basis of the judicial decision, while assuring that the judge has adequately understood the scientific bases for the report. Indeed, all the European civil law jurisdictions examined here, in which the principle of free evaluation of the evidence prevails, require judges to state the reasons for their evaluation, and require that the reasons for this assessment be expressed in the judgement. In the case of jury decisions, this requirement can be very difficult to comply with. The reasoned assessment of evidence is not only a means to guarantee the principle of publicity of judicial decisions, but it essentially guarantees parties the right to appeal erroneous decisions, ultimately, guarantees the right to due process.

Furthermore, the similarities between European procedural systems and their ways of regulating expert evidence are relative. Although some characteristic features bring such legal systems closer to each other and, at the same time, set them against the common law systems, there is no homogeneous set of procedural rules. On the contrary, the differences detected demonstrate the need to improve regulatory harmonisation, for two purposes. First, regulatory harmonisation would make it possible for experts to provide their professional services in different European countries. To this end, European registries of experts should be created (Champod & Vuille, 2011). Second, regulatory harmonisation would allow a forensic report produced in the context of one proceeding to have evidentiary value in other State proceedings, which would be particularly valuable in cross-border civil and criminal litigation. The more general need remains to harmonise the various mechanisms of judicial protection, to achieve genuine European integration. Gascón Inchausti (2017) identifies the two core matters around which there must be agreement regulatory harmonisation to be minimally realistic. The first concerns the power of parties to summon experts of their own choice, without the evidentiary value of their forensic report being nullified, or considered intrinsically lower than that of the forensic report made by the judicially appointed expert. The second concerns whether or not judges should be allowed to appoint experts *ex officio*, that is, without a prior request from any of the parties to the dispute. Once legal answers to both questions have been harmonised, it will be possible to address other technical issues, such as the experts' requirements, their duties, the manner of presentation of their results or the costs of the forensic report (Gascón Inchausti, 2017). Currently, however, these issues, on which there remain challenging differences between legal systems, make it difficult to make judicial use of cross-border expert evidence, since the rules internal to each system—regarding the status of the expert, or how they are appointed, and other matters—are unlikely to be complied with in the other systems, despite the existence of European legal rules aimed at facilitating the cross-border procuration of evidence (Peiteado Mariscal, 2017).

Notes

1. Original version: 'Cuando el testigo posea conocimientos científicos, técnicos, artísticos o prácticos sobre la materia a que se refieran los hechos del interrogatorio, el tribunal admitirá las manifestaciones que en virtud de dichos conocimientos agregue el testigo a sus respuestas sobre los hechos.'
2. The Spanish system of technical assistance is somewhat peculiar concerning that in other European countries that are analysed here since defence and procedural representation are split up and attributed to different subjects: the lawyer (defence) and the court attorney (representation).
3. The guidelines are available at: http://enfsi.eu/documents/forensic-guidelines/.
4. Original version: '(…) la educación resulta necesaria. Sin ella existirá siempre el riesgo de aceptar como conocimiento sólido lo que en rigor

tiene escaso fundamento, o de terminar haciéndoles decir a los datos arrojados por las pruebas lo que no dicen ni pueden decir, con lo que la justicia de la decisión puede quedar comprometida. Sin educación la base cognoscitiva de la decisión judicial se debilita y el riesgo de error se hace más fuerte.'

References

Ansanelli, V. (2019). L'utilizzazione della prova scientifica nel proceso civile. Cenni di Diritto comparato. *Rivista di Diritto Procesuale*, 4–5.

Bujosa Vadell, L. (2017). La prueba pericial en la jurisprudencia del Tribunal Europeo de Derechos Humanos. In J. Picó i Junoy (Ed.), *Peritaje y prueba pericial*. Bosch Editor.

Champod, C., & Vuille, J. (2011). Scientific evidence in Europe—Admissibility, evaluation and equality of arms. *International Commentary on Evidence, 9*(1), 1–68.

Cortés Domínguez, V., & Moreno Catena, V. (2017). *Derecho procesal civil. Parte general*. Tiran lo Blanch.

Gascón Abellán, M. (2016). Conocimientos expertos y deferencia del juez (apuntes para la superación de un problema). *Doxa. Cuadernos de Filosofía del Derecho, 39*.

Gascón Inchausti, F. (2017). ¿Hacia una armonización de la prueba pericial en Europa? In J. Picó i Junoy (Ed.), *Peritaje y prueba pericial*. Bosch Editor.

Lösing, N. (2020). La prueba pericial en el proceso civil alemán. In J. Picó i Junoy (Ed.), *La prueba pericial a examen. Propuestas de lege ferenda*. Bosch Editor.

Murray, P. L., & Stürner, R. (2004). *German civil justice*. Carolina Academic Press.

Peiteado Mariscal, P. (2017). Obtención de prueba pericial en la Unión Europea. In J. Picó i Junoy (Ed.), *Peritaje y prueba pericial*. Bosch Editor.

Popa, G., & Necula, I. (2013). Study on expert status in the European judicial system, AGORA. *International Journal of Juridical Sciences, 3*, 161–168.

Solaro, C., & Jean, J. P. (1987). El proceso penal en Francia. *Jueces para la Democracia, 2*.

Taruffo, M. (2008). *La prueba*. Marcial Pons.

Timmerbeil, S. (2003). The role of expert witnesses in German and U.S. civil litigation. *Annual Survey of International & Comparative Law, 9*(1), 163–187.

Vázquez Rojas, C. (2014). *La Prueba pericial. Entre la deferencia y la educación*. Girona: Universitat de Girona.

Yein Ng, G. (2014). Study on the role of experts in judicial systems of the Council of Europe Member States. *CEPEJ-GT-QUAL(2014)2Rev*, Strasbourg, September 1. https://static1.squarespace.com/static/534f89eee4b0aedbe40ae270/t/558a6d15e4b0dfba0a2afcc8/1435135253774/3rev_2014_CEPEJ-GT-QUAL_RoleExperts_en.pdf

5

Interacting with the Expert Witness: Courtroom Epistemics Under a Discourse Analyst's Lens

Magdalena Szczyrbak

1 Knowledge and Authority in the Courtroom

Displaying knowledge, or lack thereof, is a significant issue in the Anglo-American adversarial system, even more so in trials involving expert witnesses whose testimony is subject to strict rules of evidence. Expert witnesses' specialised knowledge, experience, skill and training help the trier of fact to draw conclusions about disputed actions or events and evaluate the evidence (cf. Hammel, this volume). Unlike ordinary (or percipient) witnesses, who may report what they have personally experienced or observed, expert witnesses offer their assessments based on sufficient facts or data and form opinions with a reasonable degree of scientific (or discipline) certainty. This difference translates into specific

M. Szczyrbak (✉)
Jagiellonian University, Kraków, Poland

University of Pardubice, Pardubice, Czech Republic
e-mail: magdalena.szczyrbak@uj.edu.pl

V. Guillén-Nieto, D. Stein (eds.), *Language as Evidence*,
https://doi.org/10.1007/978-3-030-84330-4_5

linguistic behaviour, with the expert witnesses trying to make their expertise look credible in the eyes of the jury and the counsel attempting to either validate the testimony or discredit its evidentiary validity.

That said, the search for *truth* is not the primary goal of the adversarial trial process, which prioritises argumentation, persuasion and verbal dexterity, with which the participants persuade the jury that their version of reality is more plausible than that constructed by their opponent (Cotterill, 2003, p. 9). To achieve their interactional goals, lawyers and witnesses 'incorporate several interpersonal, linguistic, and evidential strategies designed to persuade the fact-finder about the truthfulness of their claims', which is in stark contrast to 'the impersonal, objective, and empirical practices of sound scientific research in the quest for truth' (Matoesian, 1999, p. 492). As is clear, presentational style affects the reception of courtroom testimony and seemingly minor changes in the delivery of evidence 'produce major differences in the evaluation of testimony on such key factors as credibility, competence to testify, the intelligence of speaker, and the like' (O'Barr, 1982, p. xii). Put differently, if *form*, subsuming not only stylistic variation but also paralinguistic features and non-verbal cues, does not correspond to *content*, hearers may question the validity and sincerity of the message (O'Barr, 1982, p. 1).

Against this background, this chapter looks at expert witnesses' interactional behaviour in a jury trial from a discourse-analytic perspective. It demonstrates how expert witnesses—acting within the adversarial system's constraints—interact with counsel while negotiating the validity of their expertise and highlights several discursive strategies in counsel-expert witness talk. Using data from a criminal trial, the chapter shows the relevance of selected linguistic concepts such as *speaker commitment*, *epistemicity* and *evidentiality*. It also explains what stances the witnesses and the counsel adopt and the interactional resources they use to position themselves vis-à-vis their interactants and their knowledge claims.

2 Expert Testimony in Earlier Linguistic Research

Expert testimony has been thoroughly examined from legal, psychological and philosophical perspectives. Alongside this vast scholarship—addressing, among other issues, the relationship between epistemology and scientific evidence (see, e.g., Haack, 2014; Ward, 2017)—several linguistic and discourse-analytic studies look at the role of language and reveal discursive mechanisms in jury trials involving expert witnesses. Earlier research on courtroom discourse has been informed by various analytical models and theoretical paradigms, including Conversation Analysis, Interactional Sociolinguistics, Critical Discourse Analysis and Corpus-Assisted Discourse Studies, and it has covered four major areas: (a) interactional dynamics in the courtroom; (b) question-answer strategies in lawyer-witness talk; (c) testimony styles and their effect on juries and (d) power and ideology in courtroom talk (Cotterill, 2003, p. 3). Within these areas, the following aspects related to expert witnesses have been particularly prominent: expert identity construction, power and status asymmetries in lawyer-expert witness talk, the status of scientific evidence, and the (in)comprehensibility of expert testimony to juries. I discuss these issues below.

Expert witness identity has been examined, for example, by Matoesian (1999) who observes that it is constructed through linguistic and interactional processes—that is, by performing expert knowledge in real-time discursive interaction,[1] which determines the persuasive impact the testimony has on the jury. In a different study based on historical data, Chaemsaithong (2012), in turn, demonstrates how a medical expert builds his authority through discursive practices: establishing self through self-categorisation as an expert and negotiating his discursive rights and speaking roles by counteracting power asymmetries. As he concludes, expert identity is constructed both through work practice (onsite performance) and during court testimony (offsite performance) (Chaemsaithong, 2012, p. 482). In her oft-quoted book on the O.J. Simpson trial, Cotterill (2003, pp. 169–170), likewise, discusses the expert witness's performance of work practice in the courtroom, pointing to the essentially facilitative function of the expert witness, whose role consists chiefly in providing specialised knowledge to jurors, so that they can form independent opinions about the evidence (Cotterill, 2003, p. 169).[2] In addition to listing qualities of admissible expert evidence (cf. Hammel, this volume), Cotterill (2003, pp. 173–182) indicates ways in which the expert witness's *expertness* is demonstrated by lawyers who use the language of deference in references to the expert witness in opening argument and who legitimise the expert witness by drawing on their qualifications and professional affiliations in direct examination. The witnesses themselves validate their expert status by invoking specialised concepts and terminology, and recontextualising them for the lay jury's benefit. A more recent study by Clarke and Kredens (2018), on the other hand, explores ways in which one group of expert witnesses—that is, forensic linguists, conceptualise their professional identity outside of the workplace context. As the authors argue, forensic linguists construct their professional identities by drawing on such resources as customary practices and procedures, professional and social duty, and experts' knowledge and expertise, and they appreciate the social value of their expert witness work (Clarke & Kredens, 2018, p. 97).[3]

Related to professional identity are power and status asymmetries in courtroom interaction between legal professionals, who control the flow of information, and expert witnesses, who are drawn into what superficially represents dyadic talk, but what constitutes fundamentally unidirectional discourse (Eades, 2010, p. 57). It has been argued that although both lawyers and expert witnesses are experts in their respective fields and represent multiple layers of expertise or an inter-professional relationship (Cotterill, 2003, pp. 166–167),[4] once on the lawyer's territory, expert witnesses become subject to procedural frameworks and interactional mechanisms which significantly limit their opportunity to claim authority and demonstrate expertise (Renoe, 1996). At the same time, it has been suggested that power asymmetries are to some extent neutralised given that expert witnesses have more freedom in their responses than do lay witnesses, which results, for instance, in fewer lawyer-initiated interruptions, longer narrative spans and attempts at re-orienting talk through challenging lawyers on the content of their questions (Cotterill, 2003).

Previous research has also looked at the status of scientific evidence and the (in)comprehensibility of expert testimony to jurors (cf. Hammel, this volume). The very nature of the adversarial system—whose fact-finding principles are clearly at odds with those pursued in scientific inquiry aimed at discovering the truth—has been the subject of numerous studies (see, e.g., Haack, 2014; Ward, 2017). It has, for instance, been argued that 'the parallel discourse worlds of science and law' co-exist in court, but that it is the legal system that takes primacy in determining who is competent to present an authoritative version of the truth (Cotterill, 2003, pp. 170–171). From this perspective, the expert witness is not expected to impart objective scientific truths but rather to 'finesse reality through the use of language' (Matoesian, 1999, p. 492) and support the retaining counsel's narrative loyally. At the same time, it has been posited that to be properly understood, scientific concepts need to be communicated in plain language—which, as Storey-White (1997) suggests, means balancing between accessibility and scientific precision—and in conformity with the values and ethical beliefs of the lay audience (Anesa, 2011, p. 173).

As noted above, research on expert testimony addresses various discoursal phenomena and highlights the role of language in the mediation of expert knowledge and the negotiation of its status in conformity with the adversarial system's rules. With that in mind, in what follows, I turn my attention to related linguistic concepts—including speaker commitment, epistemicity and evidentiality—explaining their relevance to counsel-expert witness talk and demonstrating how they may be usefully applied to identify the interactional mechanisms which underpin the construction of legal truth and expert knowledge in jury trials.

3 Subjectivity, Speaker Commitment and Knowledge Claims in Interaction

3.1 Subjectivity and Speaker Commitment

Subjectivity and speaker commitment may be approached as cognitive and philosophical constructs or as interactional phenomena which underpin naturally occurring communication. Broadly defined, linguistic subjectivity is concerned with the manifestation of *subject* or *self* in 'the exercise of language' (Benveniste, 1971, p. 226) and, as a multidimensional phenomenon, it is realised on different levels of linguistic expression. Simply put, it is 'a speaker's imprint' or even 'an incarnation' of 'perceiving, feeling, *speaking subjects*' (Finegan, 1995, p. 2). The speaker's perspective, or point of view, determines the choice of linguistic resources to communicate his or her *stance*, that is, 'personal feelings, attitudes, value judgments, or assessments' (Biber et al., 1999, p. 972). This aspect applies as well to how speakers qualify the information—marking personal (subjectivity) or shared responsibility (intersubjectivity) for its validity—and how they assess the source of information, depending on how they want their utterance to be interpreted in the interaction (Mushin, 2001, p. 58).

Whereas studies on the linguistic marking of attitude reflect various scholarly interests and theoretical orientations (see, e.g., Englebretson, 2007; Hunston, 2000; Kärkkäinen, 2003; Ochs, 1996; Sidnell, 2014; White, 2003; Zuczkowski et al., 2017), they commonly draw on two notions—that is, *epistemicity* and *evidentiality*. Epistemicity, or epistemic stance, is understood as 'knowledge or belief vis-à-vis some focus of concern, including degrees of certainty of knowledge, degrees of commitment to the truth of propositions and sources of knowledge, among other epistemic qualities' (Ochs, 1996, p. 410). Descriptions of evidentiality, on the other hand, fall into two groups: those that equate evidentiality with a grammatical marking of information source (Aikhenvald & Dixon, 2014) and those that embrace grammatical, lexical and other means of marking information source which, in this view, may be indicative of the reliability of the information (Chafe, 1986).

While, admittedly, marking information source and its assessment are conceptually different (de Haan, 2005), they are sometimes difficult to separate in English, and there is no unanimity among scholars as to their mutual relation. Some suggest that the two intersect, while others see them as mutually inclusive or exclusive (cf. Dendale & Tasmowski, 2001, pp. 341–342). It has also been suggested that the expression of evidentiality and epistemicity is of a scalar nature (Fetzer, 2014, p. 337).

Irrespective of the ongoing debate on the boundary between epistemicity and evidentiality, the two may be seen as constitutive elements of *epistemological stance* (Mushin, 2001) or, phrased differently, *epistemological positioning* (Bednarek, 2006). Epistemological stance is defined as individuals' construal of information based on their assessment of the epistemological status of the information (Mushin, 2001, p. 58). The range of stances that speakers or writers may adopt depends on their 'assessment of how they acquired their information based on both cultural conventions and interactive goals' (Mushin, 2001, p. 59). Epistemological positioning, similarly, refers to 'the linguistic expression of assessments concerning knowledge', and it encompasses the basis of knowledge (evidentiality); the certainty of knowledge (epistemic modality); the (un)expectedness of knowledge (mirativity) and the extent (limitation) of knowledge (Bednarek, 2006, pp. 637–638). Both models can be useful in analysing linguistic representations of various states of affairs in diverse communicative contexts ranging from casual talk to institutional interaction.

3.2 Knowledge Claims in Interaction

Whether in everyday conversation or professional communication, the management of knowledge in dialogue has been the focus of numerous conversation-analytic studies (see, e.g., Heritage, 2012; Sidnell, 2014; Stivers et al., 2011), which argue that the communication of knowledge in interaction depends not only on the speaker's *epistemic stance*, which is 'encoded, moment by moment, in turns at talk', but also on their *epistemic status*, which is 'based upon the participants' evaluation of one another's epistemic access and rights to specific domains of knowledge and information' (Heritage, 2012, p. 7).[5] The two tend to be congruent[6] but it may also be the case that speakers try 'to appear more, or less, knowledgeable than they really are' (Heritage, 2012, p. 33) or that they 'exploit non-congruent actions in order to resist, subvert and renegotiate their epistemic status' (Mondada, 2013, p. 600). Thus, in handling their rights to talk about certain topics or domains of knowledge, they manage their *(epistemic) authority* (Heritage & Raymond, 2005).

Indices of epistemic stance—marking the interactional management of knowledge but not necessarily the speaker's actual mental state—include, among other markers, verbal and non-verbal expressions of knowing, thinking and believing, epistemic modals, adverbials of degrees of certainty, adverbials of commitment, adverbials of mitigation and unqualified equative expressions with copula *be* (Strauss & Feiz, 2014, p. 280). Importantly, since speaker commitment to the truth value of the proposition is generally taken for granted (Simon-Vandenbergen & Aijmer, 2007, p. 2), full commitment is often zero-marked, thus 'reflecting the workings of our cultural models regarding knowledge, whereby information is assumed to be true unless otherwise indicated' (Marín-Arrese, 2009, p. 259).

That is not to say that knowledge may not be explicitly marked. Among the explicit markers of one's belief or knowledge, through which 'the speaker voices personal views belonging to the realm of strictly individual experiences or attitudes' (Nuyts, 2001, p. 122) are the cognitive predicates *know*, *think* and *believe*. Although *I know* and *I don't know* mark knowledge or lack of knowledge, respectively, they may perform a range of other interactional functions which need to be considered in analyses of spoken data. To start with, *I know* is linked to contrasting actions: it may serve as a marker of solidarity and co-alignment or as a marker of challenge and dismissiveness, thus indexing the speaker's stance vis-à-vis an issue or event, or a set of beliefs (Strauss & Feiz, 2014, pp. 280–281). In a similar vein, *I don't know* signals insufficient knowledge. However, it may also fulfil other rhetorical goals, as shown in studies on everyday conversation and courtroom examinations (Beach & Metzger, 1997), medical interaction (Lindström & Karlsson, 2016) or political discourse (de Candia & Venuti, 2013). While standalone *I don't know*, with its literal meaning, operates as a disclaimer of knowledge, other interactional uses are linked to six functions: (1) avoiding assessment; (2) prefacing disagreement; (3) avoiding explicit disagreement; (4) avoiding explicit commitment; (5) minimising impolite beliefs and (6) indicating uncertainty (Tsui, 1991). As earlier work on adversarial interaction suggests, *I don't know* responses resist something about the question and the disclaiming of knowledge enables witnesses to avoid confirming and disconfirming information, and thus to construct neutral ground or a posture of innocence (Beach & Metzger, 1997).[7]

Along the same lines, negative assertions like *I don't know* or *I cannot remember* may be perceived as a reflection of *aphony* (Brandt, 2004, p. 7

as cited in Marín-Arrese, 2009, p. 238), detachment or non-commitment or as disclaimers of responsibility. As Marín-Arrese (2009, p. 246) puts it, negatively asserted information is 'flawed in evidentiary validity, since the speaker expressly refrains from assigning any validity to the information'. On the other hand, negative polarity statements with belief verbs—like *I don't think* or *I don't believe*—have been shown to perform distinctly (contrary) speech acts which differ from affirmative assertions in terms of the background presuppositions and the speaker's beliefs and communicative goals (Givón, 2018). In agreement with this, it has been posited that affirmative declaratives be explicated as 'speaker knows *p*, hearer does not know *p*', whereas negative declaratives as 'hearer wrongly believes in *p*, speaker knows better'. What follows from this is that negative declaratives indicate disagreements about facts and the negotiation of how reality is to be construed by the interactants.

The resources which speakers mobilise to make their stances known in discourse may be viewed along experiential, cognitive and communicative dimensions, which signal varying degrees of the explicitness/implicitness/opaqueness of the role of the speaker as well as index personal or shared responsibility for the information (Marín-Arrese, 2009, p. 238). Experiential (or evidential) stance (e.g. *I see, I heard*) concerns the perceptual aspect of how the information was acquired; cognitive (or epistemic) stance (e.g. *I know, I believe*) stresses the cognitive, or mental, frame of reference and communicative stance relies on the 'here-and-now speech acts' (Brandt, 2004, p. 7 as cited in Marín-Arrese, 2009, p. 250) and is communicated through the language of reporting and attribution (e.g. *as I'm saying, I would say*). Varying degrees of speaker commitment, in turn, are illustrated by the following examples: *I saw, I think, I have to say* (explicit personal responsibility), *as you can see, we all know, we can say* (explicit shared responsibility), *may, perhaps, it is possible* (implicit personal responsibility) and *it seems, that meant, it was noted* (opaque personal/shared responsibility) (Marín-Arrese, 2009, p. 262).

The three dimensions of stance, experiential, cognitive and communicative, will be exemplified in the analysis of counsel-expert witness talk in the case study reported below.

4 Negotiating Knowledge in Counsel-Expert Witness Talk: A Case Study

The study builds on the existing work on the complexities of counsel-witness-jury interaction (Heffer, 2005), and it examines selected strategies associated with the negotiation of knowledge and the construction of expertness in a criminal trial. It extends the focus of earlier research to include indicators of experiential, cognitive and communicative stance (Marín-Arrese, 2009). Intended as a corpus-assisted discourse study, it adopts a corpus-driven approach (Tognini-Bonelli, 2001) and uses personal pronouns as *access points* to identify these parts of the discourse, which may reveal the stance-related strategies of the interactants. This procedure, involving a close reading of the transcript data, helps to identify the interactional role of selected epistemic markers and enables a form-to-function mapping. What it does not account for, however, are the non-linguistic aspects of witness questioning subsuming 'such forms as gaze, gesture, facial expressions, prosodic features and other non-verbal vocalisations' (Heffer, 2005, p. 48). In other words, since written transcripts are a collection of physically observable surface forms rather than a record of the whole communicative event, they are an imperfect representation of spoken discourse. As such, they do not provide enough information on what non-linguistic elements caused the speakers' cognitive actions. This limitation notwithstanding, the findings presented here provide insight into the lexico-grammatical expression of attitude, and they can inspire related studies into the multimodal construction of expert witness stance, whether in adversarial or civil-law proceedings.

The transcripts used in the analysis come from the trial of David Westerfield, a self-employed engineer charged with abducting and murdering his neighbours' daughter, seven-year-old Danielle van Dam. The trial, which received extensive coverage in the US, took place in San Diego, California, between June and September 2002. The jury found the defendant guilty of first-degree murder, kidnapping and possession of child pornography, and the judge sentenced him to death. The trial's principal expert witnesses included forensic entomologists, anthropologists and computer specialists (for a discourse analysis of the Westerfield trial, see Anesa, 2011). The trial was deemed suitable for the analysis since it involved different types of expert witnesses, including forensic entomologists whose testimony was a major focus during the trial. The entomological evidence presented by the specialists called by the defence proved crucial for establishing the defendant's alibi. On the other hand, the top US forensic entomologist hired by the prosecutor produced inaccurate and confusing testimony as well as admitted to having made basic mathematical errors in his assessment of the insect activity on the victim's body. Irrespective of this, considering the entirety of the forensic evidence presented in court, the defendant was found guilty. To reveal how the expert witnesses in this trial expressed their stances, I have examined four days of testimony provided by three entomologists and one anthropologist called by the defence.[8] This sample was considered to be sufficient for the purpose of illustrating selected discursive strategies underpinning the negotiation of knowledge claims. Using this material, I show how expert knowledge is claimed, disclaimed, attributed and contested in counsel-expert witness interaction. It might also be added that although the data used in this study come from an adversarial trial, the same analytical approach could be applied in examinations of expert testimony delivered during trials in civil-law jurisdictions. To demonstrate how knowledge claims are negotiated in hostile, asymmetrical interaction, in what follows, I consider the interplay of pronouns (*I, you, we*),[9] markers of experiential stance (*look*), cognitive stance (*know, think, believe*) and communicative stance (*tell, talk, say*) as well as negation, all of which resurfaced most visibly in the cluster analysis of the corpus data carried out with the use of *WordSmith Tools* (2012). Although the study focuses on recurrent patterns which were found among the most common three-word clusters (i.e. strings of words that follow each other) with the pronouns *I*, *you* and *we* (Table 5.1), it is not intended as quantitative analysis, and it does not claim exhaustiveness.

I-clusters

Among the *I*-clusters linked to explicit personal responsibility, the negative assertions *I don't know*, *I don't recall*, *I don't think* and *I don't believe* (cognitive stance) proved most common, alongside *I'm not*-type

Table 5.1 The most common clusters with *I*, *you* and *we*

I	You	We
I don't	*you told us*	*we don't*
I'm sorry	*you have a*	*we have a*
I don't know	*didn't you*	*we look at*
I'm not	*do you have*	*we're talking*
I didn't	*do you recall*	*if we have*

utterances (marking cognitive or communicative stance). In this section, I illustrate ways in which the expert witnesses used negatively asserted information to disclaim knowledge or contest the claims put forward by the counsel. For space reasons, I have limited the discussion to selected examples that are reproduced with their interactional contexts.

In the data, the stance of non-commitment was shown chiefly through the deployment of *I don't know*, one of the cognitive predicates concerned with internal (or private) domains of reference to which the speaker has privileged access (Fetzer, 2014, p. 70). As shown in (1), standalone *I don't know* marks lack of knowledge. Such is also the case in (2), where the witness also provides a reason for not knowing. When found in other interactional configurations, however, *I don't know* conveyed other meanings. In (3), for instance, it signals lower certainty; in (4), it marks limited knowledge and in (5), it is a discourse marker which signals both word search and, at the same time, an attack on the witness's credibility.[10]

(1) standalone *I don't know*—lack of knowledge [W][11]

Q.: Do you have any idea what the weather conditions are in the imperial county desert region in February?
A.: I would guess dry.
Q.: I'm not talking about guess. Do you know?
A.: In my opinion, it would probably be dry.
Q.: Temperature range where?
A.: ***I don't know.***
Q.: What do you mean by dry?
A.: Lack of moisture is dry.
Q.: How dry?

*A.: **I don't know.***

(2) *I don't know*—lack of knowledge + reason for not knowing [W]

Q.: You give an x-ray of a suspected broken arm to four qualified medical doctors. Wouldn't you expect them all to be able to read it the same, reaching the same conclusion?

*A: **I don't know**. I'm not a radiologist.*

(3) *I don't know* + candidate answer—marking lower certainty [W]

Q.: How many hours have you put in on this case, sir?

*A.: **I don't know**. Quite a few now.*

Q.: I assume you're being paid.

A.: Yes, I am.

(4) *I don't know*—marking limited knowledge [W]

Q.: Would bleach on the body affect their reproductive cycle?

*A.: I don't think it would affect their reproductive cycle because the reproduction has already been done when they lay the eggs. And as far as the bleach affecting, **I don't know**.*

(5) Discourse marker use of *I don't know*—word search [W]

*Q: Sir, I would like to show you a document, just ask you whether or not this is, **I don't know**, your curriculum vitae, your resume.*

A.: Yes, sir. That's a copy of my resume.

Just like *I don't know*, the next two items—that is *I don't think* and *I don't believe*, focus on the speaker's mental operations, that is, they convey cognitive stance. However, while *I don't know* is linked to non-commitment and detachment, *I don't think/believe* marks the speaker's contrary opinion and denial of the prior speaker's presumed belief. As an illustration of this, consider (6) and (7), where the witnesses deny the counsel's attributions in a 'I-know-better-and-here-is-what-I-know' move introducing the interpretation with which they identify—and the knowledge claim to which they commit themselves—paraphrasable as 'I don't think/believe A is true, I aver B'.

(6) *I don't think*—resistance to knowledge attribution [W]

Q.: Did you look at that report?
A.: Yes, I did.
Q.: Did you agree or disagree with it in particular areas?
A.: I agree with it in general.
Q.: Did you have specific disagreements with it in particular, specific areas?
*A.: **I don't think** I would term it a specific disagreement.*
Q.: Okay.

(7) *I don't believe*—resistance to knowledge attribution [W]

Q.: Even if the body had been wrapped as Mr Dusek was talking to you about it, you just testified today I think it would delay your calculations or the onset of the ovipositioning for five days. Is that your testimony?
*A.: **I don't believe** I used five days.*
Q.: What did—
A.: I said several days.

Finally, in the data, *I'm not*-type utterances formed three patterns and the witnesses employed them either to signal non-commitment, that is to refrain from assigning any validity to the claims advanced in the prior turns or to contest the knowledge attributed to them. This is illustrated in (8), where the witness conveys lack of certainty, in (9), where he disclaims having expert knowledge in an area outside of his field and in (10), where he resists the knowledge claim attributed to him by the counsel and commits himself to a different claim.

(8) *I'm not (really/exactly/a hundred per cent) sure (whether)*—lack of certainty [W]

Q.: Which ways do the breezes customarily blow around here?
*A.: **Well, I'm not a hundred percent sure**.*
Mr. Feldman: Foundation.
The Court: Sustained.

(9) *I'm not a (botanist/radiologist/specialist in)*—disclaiming expert knowledge [W]

Q.: You also see where this child had been exposed to animal activity?
A.: That is part of the reports, yes.
Q.: Do you accept that, or do you reject that?
*A.: **I'm not a specialist in** animal damage.*
Q.: So, are you telling us then that you are accepting those findings by other people better qualified than you or your opinions here?
A.: As far as the testimony of those people who have examined animal damage on decedents, yes.

(10) *I'm not saying/telling you*[12]—resistance to knowledge attribution [W]
Q.: So you're telling us that the maggots would have eaten through the skin to create the maggot mass?
*A.: **No, I'm not telling you that**. I'm telling you they came in through the natural pelvic openings.*

The above excerpts, taken together, demonstrate the function of negation in the expert witness's turns: on the one hand, the prominence of non-commitment (*I don't know; I'm not sure*) and, on the other, of contestation (*I don't think; I don't believe; I'm not telling you*). All these utterances convey the witnesses' cognitive stances based on the knowledge to which they have privileged access. Given the role of expert witnesses in the trial and the fact that the testimony is provided under oath as well as the expectation that they make assessments based on sufficient facts or data and not on what they experienced or observed, visual perception markers (*I saw, I have seen*), when used by the expert witnesses, concerned their assessment of the evidence (as in Q: *The one maggot was in the head? A: That's all I saw.*). As might be expected, hearsay evidentials (*I heard, I have heard*) were not attested at all, which, too, results from the tight legal constraints allowing only certain types of hearsay.

you-clusters
Turning now to *you*-clusters, they were employed by the counsel in the examinations of expert witnesses but designed 'with the third-party juror addressee in mind' (Cotterill, 2003, p. 4).[13] Since such questioning does not seek to reveal the truth but rather aims at constructing a more

compelling narrative and convincing the jurors of the correctness of the preferred version of events, counsel rely on external (or public) domains of reference (Fetzer, 2014, p. 70) in their attempt to 'elicit all or part of the desired master story' (Gibbons, 2005, p. 158).

One of such tactics, marking communicative stance, is the *(I think) you told us (that)* schema exploited by the counsel to elicit the desired response by challenging the witness's earlier testimony and pressing for a particular version of events, as shown in (11). In the data, *you told us (that)* was followed by positive agreement questions, for example, *Is that right?* or *Is that a fair statement?*, which helped the counsel to establish the trajectory of the questioning before asking further questions aiming to elicit more elements of the desired master story—provided the opposing counsel did not object as in (11). In addition to this, by using 'us', the counsel acknowledged other recipients (judge and jurors) and could polarise the audience, trying to influence their perception of the expert witness.

(11) *you told us (that)* + confirmation-seeking question(s)—challenging the witness's testimony [C]

*Q.: There was a question concerning maggot mass. With regard to the maggot mass, Sir, that is—**I think you told us** that is a subject of professional disagreement within your scientific community, **is that right?***

A.: That's right.

Q.: Counsel asked you a question that implicated or inferred that there was something wrong with using maggot mass to factor in post-mortem estimates?

Mr Dusek: Objection, argumentative as phrased.

The Court: As phrased. Rephrase it, and I'll allow it, Mr Feldman.

Two types of question produced a similar effect: negative grammatical yes/no questions (e.g. *Didn't you (just) tell us/indicate/criticise/make statements…?*) and positive checking tag questions (e.g. *Well, you recalculated dr. Goff's numbers, didn't you?*) which were argumentative and which preceded other leading questions with checking tags[14] (e.g. *wouldn't it?; couldn't you?*), as in (12).[15] Here, the expert witness vs *us* divide is evident as well, and the counsel tries to foreground these elements of the testimony which tie in with his narrative.

(12) *didn't you*—challenging the witness's testimony [C]

Q.: ***Didn't you just tell us*** *that you took the high and low from Brown Field and did an average?*
A.: *I calculated the accumulated degree days based on the daily average.*
Q.: *But you had the hourly temperatures, so you could compute them every hour, couldn't you?*
A.: *You could do that if you chose.*
Q.: *And that would be the best method to give us the minimum P.M.I., wouldn't it?*
A.: *Not necessarily.*
Q.: *Don't you, as an entomologist, want the hourly temperatures?*

we-clusters

In the case of shared responsibility markers with the pronoun 'we', the referential domains of 'we' varied depending on where in the interaction and how the pronoun was used. *We don't*-type utterances were found among the most common *we*-clusters in the data, and, just like the affirmative *we have*, they exemplified demonstrative language used to create objects of joint attention and draw the hearers' attention to the presence or absence of relevant evidence, as demonstrated in (13). In such instances, 'we', inclusive of the courtroom audience, referred to the physically co-present participants and the here-and-now context of the interaction. In other cases, like in the phrase *we look* shown in (14), 'we', inclusive of the scientific community of expert witnesses but exclusive of the courtroom audience, was used to claim authority, to show common values with other forensic entomologists and to explain how 'things get done' in this community. Finally, in *we're talking*, exemplified in (15), 'we' referred, again, only to the physically co-present participants and the ongoing discourse.

(13) *we don't have*—displaying lack of evidence [C]

Q.: Okay. So basically, what you're telling us now is that where you went to, what you saw, is not the same as that which is depicted in 2-B because it's been changed. We know that. Is that a fair statement?
A.: The foliage has been cut down. It's still elevated above the roadside.
*Q.: **But we don't have** the foliage, **correct?***
A.: Not all of it.
*Q.: **We don't have** the area we can see in D because it's been cleared, **right?***
A.: It's been cleared out. I can't say, you know, to what extent.

(14) *we look*—displaying expert knowledge [W]
Q.: Does that tell us when the body arrived at the recovery site, Dehesa Road?
A.: No, it doesn't.
Q.: Why not?
A.: Because we're merely estimating a period of insect activity. There's nothing to indicate that body was there for—when it got there previously. We have no way of knowing from the entomological standpoint.
Q.: Is that because the entomologist can't say that or because you're not good enough to say that?
*A.: **We look** at insects. The entomology cannot say that. As **we look** at insects, **we look** at what insects have most probably done.*

(15) *we're talking*—displaying expert knowledge [W]
Q.: And when we use the post-mortem interval, what are you talking about as the beginning of that period?
*A.: When **we're talking** about the post-mortem interval, **we're talking** about when presumably of the time that an individual was deceased to the time they were recovered or discovered.*
Q.: From the time of death?
A.: That's correct.

5 Conclusions and Suggestions for Further Research

The chapter has described some of the discursive mechanisms that underlie the presentation and contestation of expert knowledge in a criminal trial, aiming to deepen understanding of the interactional patterns found in jury trials as well as processes of constructing evidence and legal truth. Specifically, the analysis has revealed some of the communicative instruments that expert witnesses and counsel employ to mark their experiential, cognitive and communicative stances and show the foundation of their knowledge claims within the adversarial system's constraints.

In the case study reported here, the most common *I*-clusters in the expert witnesses' turns relied on internal, that is private, frames of reference and signalled explicit responsibility for the information or its lack (*I don't know*, *I don't think*, *I don't believe*—cognitive stance), while *you*- and *we*-clusters relied on external, that is public, frames of reference accessible to all interactants (*you told us (that)*; *didn't you (just) tell us/indicate*; *we're talking*—communicative stance; *we have/we don't have*; *we look*—experiential stance). The latter betrayed the speaker's awareness of audience design (Bell, 1984, 2001) and were used to display knowledge and present the preferred narrative, or master story, to benefit other discourse participants. As became clear, there was a correlation between participant status and the type of stance adopted in the testimony (expert witness—cognitive and experiential stance; counsel—communicative and experiential stance). The analysis also revealed that taken-for-granted disclaimers of knowledge like *I don't know* need not communicate aphony (Brandt, 2004), but rather different states of knowledge, and so their meaning should each time be considered in their interactional context. Simultaneously, the study highlighted the role of negative polarity assessments that signalled either non-commitment or contrary opinions.

That said, it needs to be acknowledged that the corpus-assisted approach is not best suited to identifying averrals and knowledge claims which are zero-marked. Given its focus on the most frequent lexico-grammatical patterns, it fails to detect less common ways of communicating stances, which tend to be dispersed in discourse and inevitably ignores less tangible, context-sensitive carriers of subjectivity (Stein & Wright, 1995) as well as non-verbal aspects of epistemic assessments (Roseano et al., 2015) which are not amenable to automated analysis. However, despite its limitations, the corpus-assisted approach to written courtroom data—representing 'once-was-discourse' (Partington et al., 2013, p. 2)—helps to identify points of access to the testimony styles and types of stances which may then be subject to a more detailed qualitative analysis. The approach may be adopted in forensic linguistic research to elucidate the role of discourse-pragmatic strategies in establishing legal truth in courtroom proceedings, both in adversarial systems and civil-law jurisdictions. In particular, by comparing the presentational styles of expert witnesses, pseudo/quasi-expert witnesses such as law enforcement officers (Cotterill, 2003, p. 50) and ordinary witnesses, the analyst may provide more insights into the differences between the epistemological resources employed by respective participants and assess their possible effect on the perception of the witnesses' credibility. Such findings may be of value not only to forensic linguists or legal scholars but also expert witnesses themselves who may thus gain a better understanding of the discursive practices they engage in, and of the role their linguistic performance plays in the construction of plausibility and the delivery of expert evidence with 'a reasonable degree of scientific certainty'.

Notes

1. In recent scholarship, identity is no longer regarded as something that people are, but rather as something that they perform using language (Bucholtz & Hall, 2005). This issue applies to professional identity as well, which, on the one hand, concerns an individual's self-concept (it is cognitive) and, on the other, the profession's collective identity, which is co-constructed through a shared repertoire of resources including specific vocabulary and routines (it is social) (Clarke & Kredens, 2018, p. 82 drawing on Angouri & Marra, 2011 and Li & Ran, 2016).
2. From a legal perspective, an expert is someone who 'is recognised as having a special competence to draw inferences from evidence within a certain domain', and whose competence 'typically derives from access to a large body of evidence and from socialisation into specialised ways of

perceiving and reasoning about evidence of that kind' (Ward, 2017, p. 263).

3. Forensic linguists' reports of their own experience of providing expert evidence can be found, for example, in Shuy (1993, 2006) and Coulthard (2005, 2020).
4. For a discussion about the distribution of knowledge and expertise in institutional talk involving multiple professional voices, see Linell (1998).
5. However, the usefulness of this 'unwarranted theoretical construct' has been questioned by Lymer et al. (2017).
6. '(…) if we agree that you have greater authority and/or more rights than I do, then we have achieved epistemic primacy congruence (…). Conversely, if we disagree over who has greater authority and/or more rights, then we are in an epistemically incongruent situation' (Stivers et al., 2011, p. 16).
7. It has also been noted that the *I don't know* response, which can 'stand for a variety of states of knowledge', reduces the witness's credibility (Brennan, 1994, p. 207), especially in the cross-examination of children who are unaccustomed to the 'strange language' used in court.
8. The trial transcripts were downloaded from https://www.unposted.com (date of last access: 3 March 2020).
9. This excludes from the analysis implicit/opaque personal/shared responsibility markers (such as *perhaps, it seems, it was noted*) and limits its scope to explicit personal/shared markers.
10. To see the multifunctionality and meaning potentials of selected discourse markers (or pragmatic markers/particles), go to, for example, Aijmer (2013).
11. The letters W and C refer to the expert witness and the counsel, respectively.
12. For a discussion of the progressive of mental and communication verbs in courtroom talk, see Szczyrbak (2021).
13. For a discussion of the trial as a complex genre, see Heffer (2005) and, in particular, the description of participant roles in witness examination (Heffer, 2005, pp. 47–50).
14. Question tags have a built-in bias towards one answer, and they 'typically seek confirmation of the speaker's point of view' (Biber et al., 1999, p. 1113). In the words of Gibbons, they are 'strengthening devices' which place 'a degree of pressure for agreement upon the interlocutor' and which are more coercive than simple polar questions (2005, p. 101).

15. For the relation between question type and coerciveness, see Berk-Seligson (1999, p. 36).

References

Aijmer, K. (2013). *Understanding pragmatic markers. A variational pragmatic approach*. Edinburgh University Press.

Aikhenvald, A. Y., & Dixon, R. M. W. (2014). *The grammar of knowledge. A cross-linguistic typology*. Oxford University Press.

Anesa, P. (2011). *Courtroom discourses: An analysis of the Westerfield jury trial.* PhD dissertation, University of Verona.

Angouri, J., & Marra, M. (2011). 'OK one last thing for today then': Constructing identities in corporate meeting talk. In M. Marra & J. Angouri (Eds.), *Constructing identities at work* (pp. 85–100). Palgrave Macmillan.

Beach, W. A., & Metzger, T. R. (1997). Claiming insufficient knowledge. *Human Communication Research, 23*, 560–585.

Bednarek, M. (2006). Epistemological positioning and evidentiality in English news discourse—A text-driven approach. *Text & Talk, 26*(6), 635–660.

Bell, A. (1984). Language style as audience design. *Language in Society, 13*, 145–204.

Bell, A. (2001). Back in style: Reworking audience design. In P. Eckert & J. R. Rickford (Eds.), *Style and sociolinguistic variation* (pp. 139–169). Cambridge University Press.

Benveniste, E. (1971). Subjectivity in language. In M. E. Meek (Ed.), *Problems in general linguistics* (pp. 223–230). University of Miami Press.

Berk-Seligson, S. (1999). The impact of court interpreting on the coerciveness of leading questions. *Forensic Linguistics, 6*(1), 30–56.

Biber, D., Johansson, S., Leech, G., Conrad, S., & Finegan, E. (1999). *The Longman grammar of spoken and written English*. Longman.

Brandt, P. A. (2004). Evidentiality and enunciation. A cognitive and semiotic approach. In J. I. Marín-Arrese (Ed.), *Perspectives on evidentiality and modality* (pp. 3–10). Editorial Complutense.

Brennan, M. (1994). Cross-examining children in criminal courts: Child welfare under attack. In J. Gibbons (Ed.), *Language and the law* (pp. 199–216). Longman.

Bucholtz, M., & Hall, K. (2005). Identity and interaction: A sociocultural linguistic approach. *Discourse Studies, 7*(4–5), 585–614.

Chaemsaithong, K. (2012). Performing self on the witness stand: Stance and relational work in expert witness testimony. *Discourse and Society, 23*(5), 465–486.
Chafe, W. (1986). Evidentiality in English conversation and academic writing. In W. Chafe & J. Nichols (Eds.), *Evidentiality: The linguistic coding of epistemology* (pp. 261–272). Ablex.
Clarke, I., & Kredens, K. (2018). 'I consider myself to be a service provider': Discursive identity construction of the forensic linguistic expert. *The International Journal of Speech, Language and the Law, 25*(1), 79–107.
Cotterill, J. (2003). *Language and power in court. A linguistic analysis of the O. J. Simpson trial.* Palgrave Macmillan.
Coulthard, M. (2005). The linguist as expert witness. *Linguistics and the Human Sciences, 1*(1), 39–58.
Coulthard, M. (2020). Experts and opinions: In my opinion. In M. Coulthard, A. May, & R. Sousa-Silva (Eds.), *The Routledge handbook of forensic linguistics* (pp. 523–538). Routledge.
de Candia, S., & Venuti, M. (2013). 'I don't know the answer to that question': A corpus-assisted discourse analysis of White House press briefings. *Critical Approaches to Discourse Analysis across Disciplines, 7*(1), 66–81.
de Haan, F. (2005). Encoding speaker perspective: Evidentials. In Z. Frajzyngier, D. Rood, & A. Hodges (Eds.), *Linguistic variation and language theories*. John Benjamins.
Dendale, P., & Tasmowski, L. (2001). Introduction: Evidentiality and related notions. *Journal of Pragmatics, 33*, 339–348.
Eades, D. (2010). *Sociolinguistics and the legal process*. Multilingual Matters.
Englebretson, R. (Ed.). (2007). *Stancetaking in discourse: Subjectivity, evaluation, interaction* (Pragmatics & Beyond New Series, 164). John Benjamins.
Fetzer, A. (2014). Foregrounding evidentiality in (English) academic discourse: Patterned co-occurrences of the sensory perception verbs *seem* and *appear*. *Intercultural Pragmatics, 11*(3), 333–355.
Finegan, E. (1995). Subjectivity and subjectivisation: An introduction. In D. Stein & S. Wright (Eds.), *Subjectivity and subjectivisation* (pp. 1–15). Cambridge University Press.
Gibbons, J. (2005). *Forensic linguistics: An introduction to language in the justice system*. Blackwell.
Givón, T. (2018). *On understanding grammar* (Rev. ed.). John Benjamins.
Haack, S. (2014). *Evidence matters. Science, proof, and truth in the law*. Cambridge University Press.

Heffer, C. (2005). *The language of jury trial. A corpus-aided analysis of legal-lay discourse*. Palgrave Macmillan.

Heritage, J. (2012). Epistemics in action: Action formation and territories of knowledge. *Research on Language and Social Interaction, 45*(1), 1–29.

Heritage, J., & Raymond, G. (2005). The terms of agreement: Indexing epistemic authority and subordination in talk-in-interaction. *Social Psychology Quarterly, 68*(1), 15–38.

Hunston, S. (2000). Evaluation and the planes of discourse: Status and value in persuasive texts. In S. Hunston & G. Thompson (Eds.), *Evaluation in text: Authorial stance and the construction of discourse* (pp. 176–207). Oxford University Press.

Kärkkäinen, E. (2003). *Epistemic stance in English conversation: A description of its interactional functions, with a focus on 'I think'* (Pragmatics & Beyond New Series, 115). John Benjamins.

Li, C., & Ran, Y. (2016). Self-professional identity construction through other-identity deconstruction in Chinese televised debating discourse. *Journal of Pragmatics, 94*, 47–63.

Lindström, J., & Karlsson, S. (2016). Tensions in the epistemic domain and claims of no-knowledge: A study of Swedish medical interaction. *Journal of Pragmatics, 106*, 129–147.

Linell, P. (1998). Discourse across boundaries: On recontextualisation and the blending of voices in professional discourse. *TEXT, 18*(2), 143–157.

Lymer, G., Lindwall, O., & Ivarsson, J. (2017). Epistemic status, sequentiality, and ambiguity: Notes on Heritage's rebuttal. Unpublished manuscript. Uppsala University, Sweden.

Marín-Arrese, J. I. (2009). Commitment and subjectivity in the discourse of a judicial inquiry. In R. Salkie, P. Busuttil, & J. van der Auwera (Eds.), *Modality in English* (pp. 237–268). Mouton de Gruyter.

Matoesian, G. (1999). The grammaticalisation of participant roles in the constitution of expert identity. *Language in Society, 28*(4), 491–521.

Mondada, L. (2013). Displaying, contesting and negotiating epistemic authority in social interaction: Descriptions and questions in guided visits. *Discourse Studies, 15*(5), 597–626.

Mushin, I. (2001). *Evidentiality and epistemological stance. Narrative retelling*. John Benjamins.

Nuyts, J. (2001). *Epistemic modality, language and conceptualisation: A cognitive-pragmatic perspective*. John Benjamins.

O'Barr, W. (1982). *Linguistic evidence. Language, power, and strategy in the courtroom*. Academic.
Ochs, E. (1996). Linguistic resources for socialising humanity. In J. J. Gumperz & S. C. Levinson (Eds.), *Rethinking linguistic relativity* (pp. 407–437). Cambridge University Press.
Partington, A., Duguid, A., & Taylor, C. (2013). *Patterns and meanings in discourse. Theory and practice in corpus-assisted discourse studies (CADS)*. John Benjamins.
Renoe, C. E. (1996). Seeing is believing: Expert testimony and the construction of interpretative authority in an American trial. *International Journal for the Semiotics of Law, 9*, 115–137.
Roseano, P., González, M., Borràs-Comes, J., & Prieto, P. (2015). Communicating epistemic stance: How speech and gesture patterns reflect epistemicity and evidentiality. *Discourse Processes, 53*(3), 135–174.
Scott, M. (2012). *WordSmith Tools* (version 6). Stroud: Lexical Analysis Software.
Shuy, R. W. (1993). *Language crimes: The use and abuse of language evidence in the courtroom*. Blackwell.
Shuy, R. W. (2006). *Linguistics in the courtroom: A practical guide*. Oxford University Press.
Sidnell, J. (2014). The architecture of intersubjectivity revisited. In N. Enfield, P. Kockelman, & J. Sidnell (Eds.), *The Cambridge handbook of linguistic anthropology* (Cambridge Handbooks in Language and Linguistics) (pp. 364–399). Cambridge University Press.
Simon-Vandenbergen, A. M., & Aijmer, K. (2007). *The semantic field of modal certainty. A corpus-based study of English adverbs*. Mouton de Gruyter.
Stein, D., & Wright, S. (Eds.). (1995). *Subjectivity and subjectivisation*. Cambridge University Press.
Stivers, T., Mondada, L., & Steensig, J. (2011). *The morality of knowledge in conversation*. Cambridge University Press.
Storey-White, K. (1997). KISSing the Jury: The advantages and limitations of the 'keep it simple' principle in the presentation of expert evidence to courts and juries. *Forensic Linguistics, 4*(2), 280–287.
Strauss, S., & Feiz, P. (2014). *Discourse analysis. Putting our worlds into words*. Routledge.
Szczyrbak, M. (2021). 'I'm thinking' and 'you're saying': Speaker stance and the progressive of mental verbs in courtroom interaction. *Text & Talk, 41*(2), 239–260.
Tognini-Bonelli, E. (2001). *Corpus linguistics at work*. John Benjamins.

Tsui, A. B. M. (1991). The pragmatic functions of 'I don't know'. *TEXT, 11*(4), 607–622.

Ward, T. (2017). Expert testimony, law and epistemic authority. *Journal of Applied Philosophy, 34*(2), 263–277.

White, P. (2003). Beyond modality and hedging: A dialogic view of the language of intersubjective stance. *Text, 23*, 259–284.

Zuczkowski, A., Bongelli, R., & Riccioni, I. (2017). *Epistemic stance in dialogue. Knowing, unknowing, believing*. John Benjamins.

6

A Lie or Not a Lie, That Is the Question. Trying to Take Arms Against a Sea of Conceptual Troubles: Methodological and Theoretical Issues in Linguistic Approaches to Lie Detection

Martina Nicklaus and Dieter Stein

1 Relevance

The first part of the Shakespeare quotation, slightly adapted, defines the research question of this chapter, the second part defines the methodological focus. Lying and deceiving are relevant to the law in several respects. In a way, the law runs on statements and 'texts' that are presumed to be true. This is why veracity evaluation is of prime importance

M. Nicklaus (✉)
Department of Romance Languages, Heinrich Heine University Düsseldorf, Düsseldorf, Germany
e-mail: nicklaus@phil.hhu.de

D. Stein
Anglistik III Englische Sprachwissenschaft, Heinrich Heine University Düsseldorf, Düsseldorf, Germany
e-mail: stein@hhu.de

V. Guillén-Nieto, D. Stein (eds.), *Language as Evidence*,
https://doi.org/10.1007/978-3-030-84330-4_6

for the functioning of the law as a process. False statements in contracts may invalidate the contract or may entail punishment, or may even put yourself into peril in the case of a false confession, or others in the case of perjury. Lying and deceiving may be subject to punishment as perjury in certain—and certainly not all—genres in legal contexts. The main context where lying is forensically relevant in the resolution of crime are various contexts in the legal and judicial process: From false accusations via false testimony to perjury. A major role in processes involved in the resolution of crime, and in court proceedings in particular, in the establishment of what happened, is what the facts are and what the final judicial narrative will be on which the legal norm is based on evidence given in and through language.

The area treated in this chapter is arguably the one where the methodological difficulties for both research and practical analysis are most serious, and where nevertheless a great amount of experimentation and trial and error is taking place, because of the very attractiveness of the topic and the completely understandable and in itself reasonable ~~to~~ attempt to find 'objective' diagnostic criteria. Such an avenue would—equally naturally—be preferable for the legal world which of necessity needs to rely on 'hard' facts in establishing truth. Naturally, there is a tendency to stick to what is 'objectively observable', such as surface features in the physical text that can also be identified in an error-free way by a machine. It will, however, be argued here that this expectation can hardly be met on an appreciable scale at the present stage of research. In order to calibrate expectations in a reasonable way, in fact, the topic of this contribution might even better be 'how not to do', rather than 'how to do'.

This contribution will first (Sect. 2) try to define 'a lie', moving from a static idea of a lie as a kind of a truth value of a segment or a proposition in a text or utterance to a more dynamic notion of lying. Section 3 will summarise psychological approaches to the identification of lies, Sect. 4 will look at traditional linguistic diagnostic features that have variously been employed in attempts to identify linguistic markers of lies or lying. The chapter goes on to discuss some central theoretical concepts that constrain the usefulness of linguistic diagnostic markers of lying, focusing on the concept of the genre as, apart from idiolectal regularities, the other major baseline of analysis. Section 5 takes up recent orientations in pragmatics to re-focus the search for interpretable linguistic behaviour away from observed forms to their interpretation as manifestations of cognitive and interactive discourse processes involved in lying using a concrete example from investigated cases as exemplification.

A final remark is in order regarding the use of the terms 'marker', 'cue' and 'trace'. These terms refer, on the one hand, to the same initial, uninterpreted phenomenon. However, they are also part of different approaches: 'marker' is embedded in a more linguistic-surface approach, much like linguistic markers of varieties. The term 'cue' is current in psycholinguistic approaches, and the term 'trace' comes from the theory of criminal investigation.

2 What Is a Lie?

2.1 Initial Definitions

The issue of lying and deception has long been a major subject for research in both psychology and philosophy. The most comprehensive treatment in forensic context is Fobbe (2011, pp. 186–229). The present contribution has a much narrower focus. The main tenor of previous larger-scale empirical work on identifying lying and deception is summarised by Hauch et al. (2015) in a meta-study of computational studies of lie-detection cues: 'A potential reason why only small to medium effect sizes were found in general could be that most computer programs simply count single words without considering the semantic context' (p. 330).

This chapter will focus on the methodological side of what is meant by 'semantic context' in the citation. We will argue that the crucial dimension for enabling larger studies with data type and quality that might eventually be amenable to computational analysis is the genre. This focus is on methodological aspects in identifying properties of the linearised utterance or text that can be taken to be diagnostic for whatever defines a lie and it suggests to widen the scope of approach, as far as linguistics is concerned, to encompass pragmatics in general and a modern development in cognitive-interactive pragmatics in particular. The contribution goes beyond the discussion of methodological issues and tries to exemplify the application of a cognitive-pragmatic dimension of genre analysis on narratives embedded in interviews in the context of child abuse cases.

This chapter will deal with lies only, not with the much broader concept of deception. With respect to *deception* it is convenient to follow Vrij et al.'s (2011) definition of deception that includes a lie. In the present context, we deem Vrij's (2008, p. 15) definition of deception to be sufficient: 'a successful or unsuccessful attempt, without forewarning, to create in another a belief which the communicator considers to be untrue' (p. 15). In principle, this definition also includes animals as the subject and the object of deception—a very common phenomenon. This attempt may be verbal or non-verbal, or may include components of both. Lies may be considered a subclass of deception that, following Horn (2017), are illocutional in character, with deception a perlocutionary act, defined by its effect on the addressee. Although it is entirely possible to deceive without using language, lying is not possible without using language. It is the more intrinsically linguistic activity (Horn, 2017, p. 31), as also evidenced by a set of linguistic contrasts (Horn, 2017, p. 31).

2.2 Pragmatic Approaches

However, beyond this more narrow speech act theoretical view, we wish to enlarge our perspective towards a more cognitive-interactive view of what goes on in lying and that includes the effect on the hearer (it may also be in principle a reader, or several such persons). We will for simplicity's sake refer to the addressee of a lie as 'hearer', and to the producer of a lie as 'speaker'. We do not conceive of the producer of a lie as a lonely organism, but as one who does what the speaker is doing in order to manipulate his hearer. This perspective appears especially necessary if we extend the purview of our analysis from the utterance of sentences, or sentence-like utterances, to portions of a larger stretch of discourse such as are frequently solicited in the context of psychological witness evaluations.

For the purpose of this discussion, we will accept a more narrowly circumscribed view of lying here: linguistically realised intentional falsehood, with the intention of changing the other person's cognitive content such that it will contain assumptions that are not in agreement with the 'facts' that the speaker assumes are in the speaker's knowledge at the time of speaking. Heffer (2020, p. 55) makes an illuminating distinction (arguably legally relevant) between withholding, misleading and lying. For the purpose of the present discussion we will simply subsume the three categories under the term 'lying'. Heffer's definition essentially includes and presupposes an element of uttering a false proposition, but goes beyond a more surface-based definition in explicitly including the intention of the speaker. It appears uncontroversial to say that lying is a case of where we have to include an interactive discourse situation, with, in a judicial or legal context, an asymmetrical power situation and with non-identical intentions, putting very special constraints on any notion of intention, let alone shared intentions or utterance interpretation as an archaeology of mutually shared intentions.

In discussing the notion of 'a lie', we have to distinguish three levels:

1. Common and lay usage: what is the famous man in the street's idea of a lie, or when does she or he use the term 'lie' naively and unreflectedly?
2. The linguist's technical characterisation of No 1
3. What counts as a lie in a formal legal process?

No 1 notion of lie must be disregarded here. The scope of this chapter are methodological issues in identifying type 2 lies, which, in the course of certain genres in court proceedings such as testimony or cross-examination, can then be classed as perjury. Note that this fact alone, the dependency of the communicative status of a lie, already points to the indispensability of the notion of genre in establishing 'lie-hood'.

We will later argue that it is difficult to maintain any notion of a kind of 'degree zero' lie aloof from its communicative and interactive genre embedding (Georgakopoulou, 2020, p. 6). Obviously, No 2 concept and No 3 concepts are not the same. In the domain of law, a lie is not automatically perjury (Douglis, 2018) and not all cases of perjury would automatically classify as lies in different linguistic approaches at court. The different rulings in the famous Bronston case is a case in point (Horn, 2017, pp. 35–37). In addition, it is obviously the case that different legislatures elevated lies to the status of perjury in different ways and in different contexts.

What is important is the fact that the liar really engages in a twofold lie. Not only in trying to induce the hearer to introduce false 'contextual effects' (in terms of relevance theory) as permanent contents in the cognition and memory of the hearer, but the liar is also engaged in establishing or creating an impression of credibility with the communication partner, otherwise the lie would not work, and the intended contextual effect would not materialise. The liar also has to perform 'deception management' (Carter, 2014, p. 137) as an additional meta-activity. So there is really a double workload to perform by the liar. This is relevant for the interpretation of a technical lie in the speech act sense as a lie in the judicial genre-relevant sense: a lie will attain the status of an act of perjury only in a context of assurance or pretence of credibility. The legal gravity of a lie is enhanced if, in a court hearing, the questioning party had the opportunity of asking additional clarifying questions—an opportunity available, but not taken in the famous Bronston case (Douglis, 2018) and a condition not normally obtaining in a bread-and-butter lie in a normal conversation in everyday life.

Two more complications in the notion of a lie as intentionally providing false information must be mentioned. Obviously, you do not lie in cases of accidental truth. A major vitiating factor in veracity evaluations are spontaneous changes in memory and changes in memory induced through repeated retellings, especially in cases of traumatisations. Generally, the assumption of an objective truth, while indispensable for the judiciary, is problematic on several counts (Linde, 2015, p. 4f; Newman et al., 2014). Although the discussion of psychiatric factors in memory determination is beyond the scope of this paper, it should be pointed out that the case to be discussed in more detail in Sect. 5 belongs to a class of cases in which it is known that beyond the more general 'false memory syndrome' traumatisation in cases of child abuse can lead to additional uncertainties and memory loss over a period of time and also to a later recovery of memory. This type of factor must be taken into account in principle, maybe not in each and every case of analysis, when interpreting the validity of 'linguistic cues', to the extent they can at all be established on some level of generality.

Eades (2012) has explicitly discussed the problematic nature of the belief in stable degree zero propositional truth that is engraved in stone and that can be dug out unchanged repeatedly at any later occasion and which still is one of the main criteria for truth evaluations of testimony—a principle or an ideology (Eades, 2012) that must appear questionable in the light of much discourse-based research that stresses the co-creational character of discourse (Foolen, 2019, p. 43) on each new utterance occasion.

The most general, often popularly assumed, logical form of the use of linguistic forms of utterances in the identification of lies in a legal context is as follows: 'If linguistic form x occurs then lie, if form y then true'. This is often accompanied by expectations that there is something like a 'style' of lying, tied—as in the notion of 'text type'—to the occurrence of linguistic surface features like full noun versus pronoun or similar. These are simplistic expectations and must be discarded.

In the following we will turn to issues related to the definition of the 'X', the notion of the 'linguistic form' in a lie. Before doing so, it must be said that this discussion is necessarily restricted in its validity by its exclusion of all suprasegmental and paralinguistic information. Restricting the discussion to linearised surface morphemes, in other words to one aspect of the physical 'text' amounts to restricting it to the properties, although with the system-given meaning potentials of an epiphenomenon of a discourse that has taken place in the past. Such a restriction implies above all the non-availability of all other information that is available to the discourse participants in an online interaction. Above all, it tends to encourage a view of language that overlooks a perspective suggested by recent pragmatics of a discourse as an online process that involves 'a series of interactively made decisions' (Jaszczolt, 2019, p. 18).

3 Current Lie-Detection Approaches

The most widely used instruments in evaluating witnesses for veracity of their testimony in legal contexts are assessment techniques that include linguistic criteria. The most common of these techniques are *Statement Validity Assessment* (SVA) and *Scientific Content Analysis* (SCAN) (Vrij, 2008, p. 9, 2015b, p. 4); Vrij et al. (2021, s.p.) list further, less common techniques: *Assessment Criteria Indicative of Deception, Strategic Use of*

Evidence, and *Verifiability Approach*. A very specialised instrument geared to a very restricted context is *VeriPol*, created in Spain in 2018 by Quijano-Sánchez et al., designed to detect insurance fraud. Among researchers, on the other hand, the so-called *Reality Monitoring* technique (RM), designed in 1981 (Johnson & Raye, 1981), is very popular in the field of deception detection (Vrij, 2008, p. 9). None of these techniques is perfectly convincing, since to date 'current scientific knowledge cannot yet provide a comprehensive understanding of deceptive verbal behaviour' (Nahari et al., 2019, p. 3).

The above-mentioned techniques share three features. Firstly, they draw on the assumption that linguistic designs of true and false statements differ significantly, a hypothesis that has been put forward explicitly by the 'pioneer' of statement validity assessment in Germany, Udo Undeutsch (cf. Steller & Köhnken, 1989, p. 219; cf. Undeutsch, 1967, pp. 125–126). The so-called *Undeutsch-Hypothese* has been taken up or confirmed in various contexts. Newman et al. (2003), for example, the developers of the lexicometric software LIWC[1] that has been tested in various studies for lie detection (e.g. Almela et al., 2013) assume: 'Although liars have some control over the content of their stories, their underlying state of mind may "leak out" through the way that they tell them […]' (p. 665).

Secondly the above-mentioned techniques involve the application of cue lists, more precisely lists of linguistic markers that are assumed to identify true or fabricated statements respectively. Regardless of the overall quality of these techniques (cf. Sect. 3.4), the integration of such verbal cues in the assessment-procedure seems to be reasonable in any case, since 'findings about verbal cues are less variable and are more strongly related to deception' (Bogaard et al., 2016, p. 1).

Thirdly, in a more or less implicit manner all deception tests seem to aim at universally applicable procedures. Universal validity however might remain an illusion as Nahari's et al. example concerning the use of pronouns suggests (2019, pp. 17–18): 'The cue 'extensive use of first person pronouns' seems to be related to deception in North African British speakers and to truthtelling in white British speakers'.[2] Dead certain, general indicators for lies, like 'Pinocchio's nose' (Luke, 2019) probably do not exist, not even at a linguistic level, as supposed by Smith (2001,

p. 5) who wonders 'whether linguistic indicators apply uniformly to all people'. And more recently Sporer et al. (2021) relativising the results of some studies, warn: 'not all criteria may be equally valid for all types of populations' (p. 24; similar: Sporer, 2004, p. 78). The following sections are intended to describe how the best established (Bogaard et al., 2016, p. 2) deception detection techniques work, and provide some observations concerning the advantages and disadvantages of such techniques; Sect. 3.1 analyses SVA, Sect. 3.2, RM and Sect. 3.1., SCAN. Section 3.4 discusses some aspects of current research concerning the deception cues' validity.

What will not be considered here are some less serious approaches, based on physiological effects, uncovered without mercy as 'charlatanry' by Ericsson and Lacerda (2007, p. 169) or, more moderately, as 'problematic' by Vrij (2008, p. 342). Ericsson & Lacerda tested two commercially available lie-detection tools that claim to be based on scientific findings, for example in voice analysis. Both tools turned out not only to lack any scientific underpinning but also to be 'totally unreliable' (Ericsson & Lacerda, 2007, p. 191). Vrij (2008, p. 342) discusses the so-called *Comparison Question Test* that is supposed to elicit various bodily activities to be registered by polygraphs. The successful application of this test seems to depend largely 'on the skills of individual examiners' (Vrij, 2008, p. 342) which confirms the unreliability of physiological cues. Measuring brain activities, however, could be promising, according to Vrij (2008, p. 372).

Furthermore, we only focus on verbal lie-detection techniques (or on the verbal part of these techniques) and exclude all non-language based, nevertheless sometimes rather popular techniques such as *Behavioral Analysis Interview* frequently used in US police interviews (cf. Vrij et al., 2014, p. 133). Vrij's *Cognitive Lie Detection Approach* (Vrij et al., 2017), being a more promising strategy for police interviews, is excluded as well. This technique is not intended to help in the linguistic analysis but to puzzle liars to produce inconsistent statements. The—eventually false—statements obtained in this way are verified without any cue list or other linguistic instruments:

> The observers [in various studies, MN] were never coached about which cues to pay attention to. In other words, it appears that observers pick up these cues naturally, and a training programme about such cues does not seem to be necessary. (Vrij et al., 2017, p. 12)

3.1 *Statement Validity Assessment* (SVA)

SVA is the most common method to verify testimonies in forensic contexts in Germanophone countries. In Germany, SVA has even been authorised through a ruling of the German Supreme Court in 1999[3] as a technique to be used in experts' reports at court. This method, German: *Glaubwürdigkeitsbegutachtung*[4] is the central issue within *Aussagepsychologie* ('psychology of statement/testimony'), the oldest branch of forensic psychology (cf. Greuel, 2001, p. 6), that developed in Germany and Sweden at the beginning of the twentieth century (cf. Undeutsch, 1967, p. 29).

SVA is an integrated method that considers three aspects of the statement and its author: eye-witness ability ('Aussagetüchtigkeit'), quality of testimony ('Aussagequalität') and reliability of testimony ('Aussagezuverlässigkeit' cf. Greuel, 2001, pp. 16–40; Nicklaus & Stein, 2020). Linguistic expertise becomes relevant only when analysing the second aspect, the quality of the testimony—that is its content and structure.

When evaluating quality, the SVA specialists, mostly psychologists, apply the so-called criteria-based content analysis (CBCA) to the originally oral but recorded and thoroughly transcribed testimonies. CBCA is based on Undeutsch's *Realkennzeichen* ('reality criteria') established in 1967 (cf. Undeutsch, 1967, pp. 127–156). Steller and Köhnken (1989, p. 220) provide a revision of these criteria taking up the criticism put forward concerning Undeutsch's and some similar proposals (cf. Steller & Köhnken, 1989, pp. 221–222). It is this revised version of the reality criteria that is used in CBCA today. There is also one terminological innovation in Steller and Köhnken's proposal: it is no longer the witness' credibility that the psychological experts assess but the statements' degree of experience-relatedness (Steller & Köhnken, 1989, p. 218; Greuel, 2001, p. 42). In other words, the psychological experts have to locate the statement on a scale between 'self-experienced' and 'invented' (Sporer et al., 2021, p. 2). Arntzen, Volbert and Steller point out that quality could also be assessed concerning the intraindividual consistency of content in various statements regarding the same crime (Arntzen & Michaelis-Arntzen, 2011, pp. 52–53; Volbert & Steller, 2014, p. 396).

SVA with integrated linguistic quality analysis is supposed to be performed by psychological experts only, not by 'practitioners whose guidance comes from hands-on experience but with minimal formal training' (Vrij et al., 2014, p. 134). The individual interviews might last several hours, a fact that certainly contributes to 'rapport-building' as required in Nahari et al. (2019, p. 10) and Cooper et al. (2014, p. 1422) for successful forensic interviews.

The list of cues, the *Content Criteria*, is applied only to transcripts of 'considerable length' (Hauch et al., 2017, p. 820; Greuel, 2001, p. 213; Vrij, 2005, p. 15) and only within a complete SVA. Furthermore, the transcripts are written with extreme accuracy, reproducing errors and typically spoken language phenomena, like discourse particles or self-corrections. These conditions certainly increase the reliability of SVA, and in fact, SVA seems to be a quite successful method to detect linguistic deception in real cases, even though Hauch et al. (2017, p. 829) point out that there have been many cases where experts' interpretations diverged to some degree. Unfortunately, 'no reliable data regarding the accuracy of SVA assessments in real life cases are currently available' (Vrij, 2015b, p. 11), whereas data of laboratory studies do exist in abundance and show an accuracy rate of 70% (Vrij, 2008, p. 235[5], 2015b, p. 12). In a more recent study Vrij admits, referring to the unsatisfactory laboratory outcome for some lie-detection cues (Vrij et al., 2021, s.p.), that generally higher accuracy rates could be obtained in real life than in laboratory environments.

Another advantage of SVA, including CBCA, is the determination of an individual linguistic baseline (cf. Sect. 4) within every single interview by asking the interviewee to report a special—and verifiable—event in the past. The elicited narration meets, to a certain extent, the requirements for valid baselines in lie detection, as listed by Verigin et al. (2020, s.p.). The 'within-examinee comparisons', a desideratum put forward in

Nahari et al. (2019, p. 18; also in Hettler, 2012, p. 34 and p. 139; Greuel, 2001, p. 36) to verify deception tests, are thus established within SVA-interviews.

German SVA experts, whose reports are highly valued at court and often decide cases,[6] are extremely careful before presenting any assessment. The final evaluation confirms that the statement is experience-based only if all SVA components—that is ability, quality and reliability—provide solid proof. This might be a disadvantage when verbally less skilful but honest witnesses produce inconsistent, confusing accounts that might be misjudged as not presenting enough truth features at the 'quality'-level. Note that this technique is almost exclusively applied in sexual abuse cases in which the victim-witness' statement is crucial.

There remains dissatisfaction with the fact that Content Criteria are truth-criteria—and only truth-criteria. The occurrence of these criteria is supposed to constitute evidence that the reported facts are 'self-experienced' (Sporer et al., 2021, p. 2). However, the absence of these criteria does not indicate deception, a deficiency criticised in Nahari et al. (2019, p. 8). Moreover, the criteria themselves are still too vague and 'vary widely with respect to the precision with which they are operationalised' (Hauch et al., 2017, p. 820; following Sporer, 2004, p. 91). The criterion 'spontaneous corrections', defined by different authors as 'amendment', 'specification', 'correction' and even 'explanation', would need specification (for a deeper discussion cf. Nicklaus & Stein, 2020, pp. 42–43). More precise definitions would increase interrater reliability and simplify the assessing, making the evaluation more systematic and less time-consuming.

3.2 *Scientific Content Analysis* (SCAN)

Unlike SVA, SCAN is used to analyse originally written statements as part of police interviews worldwide (Vrij, 2008, p. 281; Bogaard et al., 2016, p. 2). Police officers assess these written statements with the help of a cue list that contains criteria such as 'placing of emotion within the statement' or 'spontaneous corrections' (Smith, 2001, pp. 11, 13; see also comments on criteria in Vrij, 2008, pp. 283–287). Some of the criteria are equivalent to CBCA-Criteria but are interpreted differently (Vrij,

2008, pp. 282–283). This discrepancy might be due to 'different predictions concerning liars' strategies' (Vrij, 2008, p. 283) and the different linguistic realisation of the verified data: the SCAN-data reflect written, CBCA-data spontaneous spoken language.

Smith (2001), in a rather comprehensive presentation and evaluation of SCAN, underlines that it is *not* supposed to provide immediate deception detection, but to identify hints: SCAN 'claims to be able to detect instances of potential deception' (Smith, 2001, p. 1). The critical segments identified then 'need to be examined in more depth' during the subsequent forensic procedures, as Smith adds later (2001, p. 9; see also Vrij, 2008, p. 291). Smith cites several individual examples where SCAN deception cues, like 'language change', did indeed turn up false statements. In one of the reported cases, the suspect used synonyms for nouns or varied the determiner in noun phrases to refer to the same offence-related fact: 'that vehicle', 'the car', 'the vehicle', 'the dark-coloured car' (Smith, 2001, p. 10). Variations of this type are interpreted as 'change in language' and, therefore, as indicators for lying. In this particular case, the suspect did indeed not tell the truth. This seemingly diffuse criterion proved to be quite reliable in Bogaard's verification of the SCAN method (Bogaard et al., 2016, p. 5), with otherwise rather disappointing results (in line with Vrij et al., 2014, p. 134).

As far as training is concerned, some of the SCAN-users did attend workshops (Smith, 2001, p. 1) but training seems not to be compulsory for police to date—and does not seem to significantly increase the accuracy of evaluations either, even if carried out by experienced police officers (Smith, 2001, pp. 23–24).

One obvious advantage of SCAN for police interviews seems to be its (apparently) easy application. This might be due to some immediately identifiable *formal* criteria, like 'improper use of pronouns', identified in Smith's study (2001, p. 30) as the most popular criterion the assessments were based on. Compared to the conventional written recording of statements, the authentic written data (Smith, 2001, p. 10) are preferable: there is no editing of the suspect's style, no ironing out of mistakes, self-corrections or discourse-related elements that often happen in police officers' transcriptions.

SCAN-criteria are intended for the analysis of written reports only. Though having the interviewees write their statement down need not be a disadvantage *per se*, this procedure makes sense for deception detection only if the written accounts are evaluated regarding the individual baseline, which is not established in SCAN. The individual's linguistic skills might be more different to written language than to speech—that is the individual written deceptive and non-deceptive styles differ significantly between individuals. The ability to vary lexical elements in written accounts using synonyms (feature: 'change of language') might well be the consequence of constant language training in certain communication-related professional backgrounds. Unfortunately, research regarding the validity of SCAN is 'scarce' (Bogaard et al., 2016, p. 2) and did not yield encouraging results (Vrij et al., 2014, p. 134; Bogaard et al., 2016, p. 2; Smith, 2001, p. 7)

3.3 *Reality Monitoring* (RM)

RM as a theoretical model was designed by the psychologists Marcia Johnson and Carol Raye in 1981 to understand how individuals distinguish 'the representations of externally and internally generated events' (Johnson & Raye, 1981, p. 79). The authors found evidence that individuals not only connect memories of external events 'with better spatial, temporal and sensory information' but that they also tacitly assume this to be so (Johnson & Raye, 1981, p. 82). The reality monitoring approach has stimulated research worldwide (cf. Vrij, 2008, p. 261), without being transformed to be used in practice, in any case. Reality monitoring has also been used in various studies concerning deception detection (Vrij, 2008, pp. 278–279). RM presupposes that memories of external events are the fundament of true statements and should therefore present, among others, the above-quoted features of memories, that is better spatial, temporal, sensory information related to external events (Sporer, 2004, p. 64).

According to Vrij (2008, p. 261), the reality monitoring approach is theoretically well-founded. Some of the RM features attributed to truth telling overlap with CBCA-Criteria, for example 'sensory information in true reports', which might be interpreted as a confirmation of these features. Vrij (2015b, p. 19) resumes an overall accuracy of 70% in the studies reported. Sporer et al. (2021) are still convinced that the RM approach and CBCA-criteria could be integrated into lie detection,[7] if methods to test their accuracy are refined and the cues standardised (Sporer et al., 2021, pp. 25–26; Sporer, 2004, p. 91).

The main disadvantage of RM—at least when it is considered a lie-detection technique—lies in the vague description of cues (Sporer, 2004, p. 66; Vrij, 2008),—but this seems to be a general shortcoming in relevant studies, as criticised by Luke (2019, p. 647): 'The paradigm in which deception-cue data are collected offer unusually high flexibility in coding and analysis'.

3.4 Testing the Detection Cues

Tests with simulated lying to verify cue validities are extremely popular and constitute a 'rapidly growing area of research' (Nahari et al., 2019, p. 2). However, already in 2001, Smith pointed out that laboratory studies 'do not reflect real life-settings' (Smith, 2001, p. 5; Cooper et al., 2014, p. 1414), the results, therefore, must be interpreted with some reservations. Simulated lying concerning the topic *of abuse*, the main application field for CBCA, is even impossible for research purposes due to ethical reasons (Steller, 1989, p. 145; Vrij, 2008, p. 220; Vrij et al., 2014, p. 133). In recent publications the benefit of studies based on simulated lying and applied statistical methods (Kleinberg et al., 2019; Luke, 2019; Sporer et al., 2021) is put under scrutiny. Sporer (in line with Kleinberg et al., 2019, p. 7), for example, criticises the omission of cross-validation in many studies. According to Sporer et al. (2021, p. 29), this methodological step should be included to verify the techniques' robustness and accuracy. Furthermore, Sporer provides evidence for 'dramatic decreases' (Sporer et al., 2021, p. 14) in the accuracy of most common deception cues when the data are cross-validated.

A further weakness of almost all laboratory tests is the discarding of situation-related aspects, the so-called ecological aspects, a desideratum put forward by Hardin (2019, p. 70), when she is calling for more 'empirical testing', but also by practitioners (Nahari et al., 2019, p. 16). First of all, the absence of a baseline as a comparative value (cf. Sect. 4) is a serious flaw. The inclusion of such an individual linguistic profile, 'the general verbal ability' or the 'self-presentational skills of communicators' (Sporer, 2004, p. 78), as a comparative figure has been recommended at least indirectly on various occasions—for example Greuel, 2001, p. 36; Smith, 2001, p. 6; Sporer, 2004, p. 78; Cooper et al., 2014, p. 1414; Nahari et al., 2019, p. 19; Sporer et al., 2021, p. 24). Nevertheless, even the compensation of the baseline deficit, as realised in the study of Verigin et al. (2020), does not seem to improve the accuracy of deception detection in simulated settings. Verigin et al. (2020) presented to their raters several transcribed, predominantly true statements that contained some crucial—true or false—segments. The raters were asked to identify the false segments correctly. Although some baseline was available in the surrounding text, the evaluations were disappointing and confirmed the doubts raised against fake liars' texts. As an alternative to laboratory research, Nahari et al. (2019) recommend using the 'untapped source of insight into real-world lying by debriefing experienced liars' (p. 11) to understand better how deception works.

Another 'ecological' factor with some impact on lying behaviour is the type of general communicative activity, the genre. Already in 2004, Sporer observes a 'need to place more emphasis on the nature of the communication situation' (p. 29). More recently, he suggests establishing a 'base rate of occurrence for specific types of events' for the supposed detection cues (Sporer et al., 2021, p. 27).

Strangely enough, while the methodological procedures in studies that are supposed to test the accuracy of detection tools are severely criticised (Luke, 2019; Sporer et al., 2021), identifying the data (the cues) only rarely or only indirectly is questioned. Vrij et al. (2021), in their critical article, provide only vague, even arbitrary, cue definitions for their tests. As far as the cue 'detail' is concerned, the authors provide an example, considered as one sentence,[8] and add the assumed number of 'details' (nine) without further explanation. Nevertheless, the interrater reliability between the two coders turns out to be 'excellent' (Vrij et al., 2021, s.p.). However, the expected difference in detail-reporting being truth-tellers to present more details could not be proven (Vrij et al., 2021, s.p.). Furthermore, the accuracy of the transcriptions, that are, after all, the basis of ratings and statistical analysis, is never questioned; the transcripts' good quality seems to be taken for granted (Sporer, 2004, p. 71; Verigin et al., 2020, s.p.).

However, 'standardising coding schemes', which means standardising and refining cue definitions, certainly *is* called for (e.g. Nahari et al., 2019, p. 19; Sporer, 2004, p. 91; regarding SCAN: Vrij, 2008, p. 290). Sporer et al. (2021, p. 25) can demonstrate the coders' considerably different interpretations of some deception criteria, such as 'sensory information'. Standardising coding, that is, standardising the identification of verbal features, might well be the field where research in lie detection could benefit most from linguists' expertise.

Taken together, the above represents a collection of features or criteria that have been empirically applied in standard procedures of evaluations of veracity. Hettler (2012) has pointed out that the basis for setting up the above-mentioned criteria in evaluation techniques of veracity has been an inductive, experience-based process in application, where success in correlating with ground truth factors has led to a further refinement of the criteria up to their present, widely used shape.

Nevertheless, as these findings stand, they often represent an unsatisfyingly simple correlation between frequency and cause: frequencies and causes need an intervening interpretive link of theory connection. Two elements of this procedure in widespread practice would appear to be missing. One is a theory or several theories that would explain what is going on in the minds or cognitions of speakers who produce lies. After all, lying is a complex cognitive operation, of which we assume that it leaves, amongst other traces, a verbal 'trace'. Based on such a model, the other element is an explanation of exactly why a particular correlation exists between a specific trace—cue or marker—and what is going on in the minds of speakers, which amounts to a functional-cognitive explanation of the trace.

The same applies to the obvious assumption that there should be an explanatory link to a neighbouring discipline like linguistics that studies the properties of the language produced, the productional sources of language use and the discourse-based function of individual expressions on several levels.

In the last section of this paper (Sect. 4), we will try to exemplify how such a link can be established based on a pragmatics-based view of discourse. So, there are four levels of analysis that are variously and selectively not coherently addressed in current practical and theoretical—to the extent they exist—approaches:

1. practical psychological approaches and psychological theories;
2. interactive, cognitive-based discourse models of language use, production and interpretation;
3. the observed linguistic productions as 'text' or as ongoing production of discourse, interpretive; and
4. formal statistical properties of the distribution of linguistic elements.

It would appear that Nos 1 and 2 are psychological and linguistic approaches, with two a model of internal processes involved in lying, whereas No 4 turns up formal data that would require interpretation in terms of either 1 and 2 or both 1 and 2.

4 The Problem of Individual Linguistic 'Deception Cues'

4.1 Types of Cues

So what does it mean to say a particular linguistic structure indicates or is diagnostic of a lie? The term 'lie' has to be reduced to a cognitive process of a specific type. These surface cues are thought to be correlative with or diagnostic of this special cognitive work or effort to cover up the divergence between the speaker's knowledge and the knowledge she wants to insert in the addressee's cognition. In most work on truth evaluation, the problematic assumption is that this will be the same in very different contexts, in stark contradiction to what we know about the co-creational processes involved and discussed above (Sect. 2), legal or non-legal.

To go back to the naive assumption referred to in Sect. 2 ('If form X occurs then lie, if form Y then true'), several surface structures have been discussed with varying degrees of statistical confidence as indicative of the speaker's intention to lie. The overwhelming impression in overlooking the literature on linguistic access to lies and deception is the great number of linguistic expressions that have been cited—or have been hypothesised, suspected or experimentally tested—as indicative of lying. We will take up as a selection of frequently mentioned forms the list of content features discussed in Adams and Jarvis (2006) as well as in Taylor et al. (2017) and in Fobbe (2011, pp. 210–227):

1. unique sensory detail (a marker of veracity);
2. emotion/positive affect (a marker of lying);
3. equivocation ('maybe', 'kind of' (more in lying));
4. quotation (a marker of veracity);
5. negation (less negation in lying than in truth telling);
6. decreased first-person usage, with an increase of third-person usage (a marker of lying); and
7. length of prologue

The exemplary markers enumerated here are of different kinds: some refer to grammatical forms, some to the expression of types of content, others to features of discourse elements of various extensions. For purposes of analysis, we will refer to the whole range as 'cues' or 'content' types. The great number of types of cues that are supposed to be indicative of lying makes it a priori clear that what is required is 'an underlying interactional explanation for the differences across the literature regarding the astounding variety in form, function and frequency of deception cues' (Carter, 2014, p. 137). Before suggesting an alternative approach that takes away the focus from considering each surface cue in itself and tries to identify its diagnostic value it must be pointed out that there is a wide range of occurrence domains for each of these cues. For instance, only some are eligible to occur in one genre, others in another. So, apart from very few cues, there is a low level of generality and a highly constrained applicability concerning usability contexts.

The overall impression of the applicability, apart from issues to be discussed below, is the one expressed by Vrij et al. (2011, p. 110f) and Hauch et al. (2015, p. 330) that there is little general validity of the cues that have been mentioned recently and that individual cues have to be much more strictly relativised in terms of context, which means in terms of genre and subgenres, and individual case types.

In particular, there is conflicting evidence for nearly all widely discussed cues such as first-person use and for explicitness in detail. This applies to obvious differences in cultural context (Taylor et al., 2017) and the cues' very linguistic nature. For instance, in the case of the much-mentioned diagnostic value of emotions, Hauch et al. (2015, p. 329) suggest that in order to arrive at a higher level of generalisability, eventually there must be further differentiation by type of emotion, such as expressed in different types of genres, a finding also repeated by Taylor et al. (2017), Adams and Jarvis (2006), and Hettler (2006). However, if further distinguished by linguistic criteria and discourse constraints, some findings seem to be applicable on a broader basis.

Suppose it is true that these linguistic markers or traces can provide access to the specific cognitive processes involved in language use indicated. It is assumed that these markers, to be interpretable, must 'register' as deviations from a default level of use: there must be a 'physical trace' (Hazard & Margot, 2014) identifiable by linguistic methods that may eventually be elevated to the status of evidence. Identifying a feature as 'deviating' from a default level is not normally available for the naive language user, but as a rule requires either a linguistic analysis or quantitative, corpus-based statistical analysis, or both, in order to be detected. This is where alternative methodological approaches are applicable in different data and corpus availability situations. Large corpora lend themselves to automated quantitative approaches, while, as is often the case in forensic contexts, small data sets must resort to more conventional approaches. For such an analysis to be carried out, there must be an input hypothesis, mostly based on previous studies, predicting some sort of deviation.

A first major methodological issue, antecedent to any practical application, is how to establish and validate the effect of above-mentioned content types beyond the pre-existence of some 'idea' of what could be a content type—a perfectly honourable core-scientific origin of ideas and hypotheses!—that can be a linguistic-surface epiphenomenon of lying as a sign of cognitive over-work.

The methodological gold standard for the establishment of the 'ground truth' (Chaski, 2013, p. 336f.) is the availability of undoubted facts, such as available in the study by Adams and Jarvis (2006), where 'statements were collected during the initial investigation and upon conclusion of the case these statements were made available for research' (p. 10). The previously recorded statements could then be checked against the facts established by the court's resolution, assuming that the judicial narrative did represent the actual physical experience. The propositions stated could then be evaluated against the facts. However, even this clear-sounding case with ground truths available is based on the assumption that any discrepancy between the facts and the facts asserted in the statement are cases of lies. The above-discussed issues relate to intentionality, the sources of memory knowledge, and what is uttered as the 'text' applies in the same way.

The bare fact of a discrepancy between what is uttered and what is externally a fact is too tenuous to alone warrant the assumption of a lie in every case even in this controlled situation. Consequently, conclusions about the diagnostic value of features have to be carefully assessed and systematised with other, unrelated studies. As a secondary source of ground truth is psychological assessments of the type discussed in Sect. 3.

4.2 Narrowing Down the Baseline

A second methodological issue is the default baseline from which an observed feature occurrence is supposed to be deviating. It is the nature of these markers that their diagnostic value resides in their character as deviating from some default norm. This default baseline of occurrence from which an utterance is considered deviating is a crucial methodological aspect of the linguistic diagnosis of lying. Saying that the number of first-person pronouns is lower and the number of third-person pronouns is higher implies the question: higher or lower than 'what', 'where', 'in what type of language use situation', 'by whom' and 'in what type of occasion'. A concrete case to be discussed in Sect. 6 is the German particle *halt*.

The assumption regarding the relativity basis operates on different levels of analysis:

1. A general frequency 'in language'—that is in all uses in languages.
2. In a given type of language and culture.
3. In a given genre—for example written statement by an accused person, in a cross exam, in a story.
4. In a given electronically available corpus (e.g. COCA), on the assumption that that corpus or section of a corpus is homogeneous concerning genres and medial subtypes.
5. Far from postulating the notion of an 'idiolect', different people have different personal linguistic habits or styles, which preceding psychological analysis aims to establish as a kind of individual language baseline.

There is, besides, a complex interaction between these five parameters. For instance, mastery of spoken and written genres may not be available in a person (Linde, 2015) abstractly as a matter of development of communicative competence or culture, or it may not be available in all situations as under pressure in a police interviewing situation or otherwise stressful situation as a victim, as likely all legal situations are. This means that a genre baseline—the linguistic make-up of a story, for instance—may not be operative as a calibration point for a deviation from normal language use. Furthermore, it is always a moot point to which extent a personal idiosyncrasy of usage (such as frequent uses of particles such as 'like') may override the 'rules' for language use in a genre.

As Taylor et al. (2017) have pointed out, we cannot assume that all traditionally investigated markers or cues work the same way across all cultures. Some of these markers are associated with, for instance, the use of the first-person category, cultural values such as collectivist or individualist societies: 'A culture x lie type x pronoun type interaction,…, confirmed significant cultural differences in the way participants changed their pronoun use when lying compared to when telling the truth' (Taylor et al., 2017, p. 7). The effect of cultural values underlying the use of content and linguistic forms used as markers must be borne in mind especially in major migratory processes as observed globally.

Besides, it has been shown that the subject of assertions themselves may influence the occurrence of markers: '..participants' affect-related language varied when they lied about opinions but not experiences' (Taylor et al., 2017, p. 10). Apart from the more individual factor of experience in lying or something like lying competence, the occurrence of '..emotive language during deception may have strategic rather than "leakage' roots"' (Taylor et al., 2017, p. 10).

4.3 Genre as Baseline Determinant

As implied in several places in the preceding discussion, a major factor potentially vitiating generalising statements about how lies could be read off surface structures is the genre. By way of a salient example, Adams and Jarvis (2006) investigate the genre of police written statements. This specific language production situation—a prompted written report—constrains the use of the 'classic' types of markers (cf. above) that can be investigated. On the other hand, it enables testing a marker that applies to this specific language use situation only, like a 'partitioning' of the text that includes a 'Prologue' that—much like the orientation section in a narrative—provides details that situate the main event. This introductory section's quantitative relationship to the main incident section was shown to be an indicator of veracity due to a 'delaying the discussion of the incident by instead focusing on previous actions' (Adams & Jarvis, 2006, p. 6). The variation in the ratio between the two sections provided one of the strongest parameters correlating with the ground truth that was independently established. While the details of this result can be interpreted in this particular case, and can also be interpretively linked to findings from other studies, it is also clear that the result of this study, as of the rare cases involving comparison to ground truth, is entirely specific to this particular genre of language use and therefore cannot be generalised to a statement.

As another illustrative case of the 'localness' of markers to the genre, the use of parameters is the positioning of 'then' in narrative texts, such as use as one of several parameters by Svartvik (1968) in his forensic analysis of the language of the then suspect who was later wrongfully sentenced to death. Although it is very tempting to do so, there is no way to establish a diagnostic equation between lying and 'I then + Verb'. Even if related languages like German have a similar propositionally identical pair of positional alternatives, it is clear that much language-specific varietal knowledge is required to identify the diagnostic value of the structure, such as what kind of author with which kind of education and genre competence and in which language medium, to name a few.

In addition to individual differences in communicative styles, cultural differences and strategic behaviour, this broader and general relativity of findings to specific genres is an obstacle to generalisable statements of the initially described type such that, temptingly, x categorically indicates truth and y indicates falsity. Even classic indicators often held to be more or less reliable across the board may be misleading: 'unique sensory detail' may be absent for various reasons (Adams & Jarvis, 2006, p. 16), possibly because this was not observed occasionally.

Therefore, the baselines, to the extent that they are based on statistically reliable data, are relative to a narrowly circumscribed set of data, as a rule to a genre, to a medium, to a very specific situation, that must be elevated and abstracted to the level of some type to be used as a baseline, which is—methodically speaking—an abstraction from individual cases. This abstraction process and the elevation to a point where it can be used as calibration rod is the methodological bane of the baseline's notion. This must be made explicit in both the analysis and in the presentation of the forensic report to the court of justice.

Naturally, it is easier to define linguistic properties the closer and more constrained the external situation is. A situation like insurance fraud in real or purported robbing cases in a tourist environment makes for pretty high predictability of linguistic lie behaviour. This specific situation has enabled a rather successful definition of linguistic markers, thereby considerably increasing the chances of a formal and computational definition with a set of linguistic features that is both pretty finite and formally identifiable by computer, such as a list of nouns, with a one: one relationship between form and function. Suppose genres can be defined at such a low level of generality (Giltrow & Stein, 2009, pp. 1–26) and the baselines are correspondingly definable in highly constrained and formally simple ways, in that case the chances for successful automatic identification of lie candidates are increased over the genres at a higher level of generality (Quijano-Sánchez et al., 2018). Besides, in cases like this, there is a large enough body of ground truth cases to establish a more reliable, if probabilistic, baseline. This is, however, not normally the case, and certainly not in the type of cases to be initially discussed below.

It is a characteristic of widely used hypotheses and baselines that the data are gleaned, not from realistic language occurrences, but experimental settings. The problems inherent in artificially constructed experimental data and their validity concerning what access they can provide to underlying cognitive processes, such as are involved in lying, are too well-known to require further rehearsing here (cf. Sect. 3 above). It is simply a very different thing to ask a person to tell a lie rather than producing a 'live' lie. The two acts of language use are too far apart in their nature for one to be able to supply valid conclusions as to the processes involved in the other. The situation is very different from, for example, comparing a live apartment description from an experimental set-up that investigates apartment descriptions.

Even the practice—current in psychological investigations—of having a witness produce a mock or fabricated story to access idiolectal linguistic practices as an element of personal baselines is problematic because the intention to delude—a key determinant of the use of a linguistic expression—is absent. Consequently, it is doubtful if a personality-ingrained idio-style of expression can be accessed. This is probably also true of such 'surface' phenomena such as the use of particles or particle-like expressions like *halt* in German or 'then' in English. The assumption is also problematic from a pragmatic point of view in that it is related to a view that ties qualities such as lying to surface elements and not to deeper cognitive processes. The situation concerning experimental data is aptly summed up by Picornell (2013):

> To date, the information we have regarding behavioural cues to deception has been largely obtained from laboratory-based experiments dealing with low-consequence lies and psychological perspectives as to how liars should

> behave when lying. Their success is difficult to quantify as no one has yet identified a single cue or set of cues that are consistently identified with deception. (p. 1)

To the extent that genres are involved in setting up baseline corpora, the issue is how subdifferential the genres must be. Setting up a genre 'narrative texts' is arguably too gross to capture important differences between different genres, let alone spoken and written narrative texts. It is a major challenge in preparing automatic corpus genres to set up a sufficiently subdifferential corpora body. For many, if not most cases of practical forensic work, pre-existing corpus data do simply not (yet?) exist to be practically and reliably applicable. Cases in point are the specific narratives discussed in Sect. 6 and the case of (false) confessions.

As a rule, automated corpora capture 'text-types', not 'genres'. Text types are aggregations of surface forms, while genres are notional categories tied to social, interactional and institutional activity types. Since 'text types' underdetermine genres, it is not possible in principle to gain 'automatic' access to genres, which is the locus where the lie is taking place as an event generated and co-created in cognitive worlds.

A corollary of tying the identification of lies to aggregations of surface forms ultimately presupposes a notion of a lie as hypostasised out of its individuated genre embedding and tied to surface expressions, as if in principle 'transportable' across genre contexts, and divorceable from its context of origin, an idea also inherent in Eades' notion of the ideologies of 'inconsistency' and of 'narrator authorship',—all based on the idea that linguistic-surface production can be analysed and interpreted as 'decontextualised evidence' (Eades, 2012, pp. 475–480) divorced from its 'interactional production' (Eades, 2012, p. 277). A live lie is part of a live context of use and, as such, derives its identity from membership in a genre, as are all manner of communicative acts (Georgakopoulou, 2020, p. 6). Consequently, it can most prominently be identified as a lie if it is analysed as close as possible to its original concrete genre embedded 'event' of creation, an approach that is more typical of a pragmatic-interactionist view.

5 A Case Study of Verbal Testimony

5.1 Telling a Story

Vrij et al. (2011), in their survey of approaches to non-verbal and verbal lie detection, summarise the situation as follows: 'nonverbal and verbal cues to deception are ordinarily faint and unreliable. This makes lie detection a difficult task, as there are no non-verbal or verbal cues that lie detectors can truly rely upon' (Vrij et al., 2011, p. 110f). Instead they 'encourage lie detectors to become actively engaged in exploiting truth tellers' and liars' different mental processes.' (Vrij et al., 2011, p. 111). This is what this section is trying to do in a very specific case.

In psychological investigations, the 'cognitive load' approach, such as described by Vrij (2015a), has already moved away from analysing 'text' in the sense of static symptoms of a communicational process that has taken place in the past to analyse the real-time process involved in producing utterances in ongoing communication and interpreting it in terms of 'leakage' of information about deceptive intentions. Besides, and related to the cultural issues earlier mentioned, such as related to the moral dimension, some factors are likely to be of considerable impact on the 'amount' or weight of work in terms of cognitive load, such as the gravity of the lie in terms of departure from the truth, the hurt inflicted or the detectability (Stratman, 2016, p. 9f).

To illustrate the difference between a 'surface' and a 'pragmatic interactionist' procedure looking at online cognitive processes, we will look at a notorious type of veracity issue in a case in which spoken testimony is often the only type of evidence available. This is intended to exemplify the direction in which a more fine-grained realistic definition of an ideal baseline of linguistic behaviour would ideally have to go. It radically enlarges the postulate by Hauch et al. (2015, p. 330), already referred to (Sect. 1) to add more 'semantic content', extending the domain of 'content'—that is verbal co-text and non-verbal context, to include knowledge elements that more recent advances in pragmatics have elaborated.

The type of case to be used as exemplification here are cases of child abuse—a type of case where the large majority of forensic analyses including language analysis, are applied for obvious reasons: it often enough is the only evidence available. The cases from which the following examples are drawn come from a German practice. They are part of full-scale statement validity assessments as described in Sect. 3. Following accusations of sexual assault by adults towards German-speaking girls aged 12–16, the girls were interviewed for several hours with various questioning techniques. After a considerable time (roughly 2 hours) of questioning, the girls were asked to tell a story of the relevant incident coherently without being interrupted by the interviewer except for short clarification questions, initiated by the well-known 'Now tell me what happened' formula. This section is preceded by an explicit request by the interviewer, at a much earlier point in the interview, to tell a fake, not experience-based story. The intention is to establish a personal, or idiolectal, story-telling baseline.

The story-telling section of the interview bears enough resemblance to a conversational story of the commonly known type with the well-known functional parts such as orientation, evaluation and others as discussed by Labov and Waletzky (1997). This type of short story also calls for analysis in terms of 'small stories' advocated by Georgakopoulou (2020). This latter type of analysis would lay another layer of 'meaning' of great interest to forensic analysis. This small story interpretation would produce another avenue of access to evaluating a witness but is beyond this paper's quantitative analysis.

The type of narrative to be initially discussed falls in the category described by Fobbe (2011, pp. 203–229) for its application in specific forensic contexts. Two aspects deserve special attention: the cases concern narratives far from any notion of 'literary' narratives but are more like everyday conversational narratives. The other aspect concerns that narrative competence is developmental: the individual story's interpretation needs to be seen against the baseline of the relative communicational maturity of the child or adolescent in terms of genre competence. In addition to the judicial context and its constraints in terms of knowledge and strategies (Fobbe, 2011, p. 207), these narratives are also heavily environed by developmental and further personal history constraints, such as a background of traumatisation.

As such types of narratives, they are characterised by specific cooperation constraints. In its asymmetrical power structure it is very different from a standard oral narrative. As the notion of intentions was invoked above (Sect. 1) to characterise lies, the situation in the type of narrative at hand presents a very specific situation better characterised as an 'uncooperative' situation (Jaszczolt, 2019, p. 21) where 'people often communicate in the context of diverging interests'. Where intentions have traditionally been seen, especially in the case of smaller utterance sizes, as the decisive instance of a judicial decision about lying or not, the diverging intentions of lying or truth telling as the highest-ranking intention in determining utterance content in the present type of narrative are constitutive of this genre in a judicial context, just as other narratives in the legal and judicial contexts (Heffer, 2018) have different constellations of prime determinants of the communicative structure. The complexity of this specific 'game' (Jaszczolt, 2019, p. 21) with its competing and diverging aims—in this case of a liar—can be hypothesised as manifesting itself, not in individual expressions, but discursive behaviour, and presupposes the interpretation of linguistic expressions in these terms, such as a tendency by a liar to discourage further inquiry for details or to engage in genre routines and refrain from shaping the narrative independent from the communicative needs of the partner at certain points. This communicative behaviour would then provide access to a realistic baseline, with departures inviting diagnostic interpretations.

It is important to note that the following discussion will not refer to the whole of the contextualising interview but only to that portion of the witness's narrative in character. By this we mean an orally presented story representing past own experience under personal emotional involvement. The essential difference to an 'account' of a past event is personal involvement and the concern with the 'participation' of the hearer in re-living a personal experience. The logical structure of a story is described in Kraft et al. (1977) in an information-flow structure that, as an especially relevant element in the present context of a discussion, includes the responsiveness of the online generation of the story in response to the monitoring of the cognitive activities of the hearer.

This online character of meaning-making has been emphasised by recent work in Pragmatics (Foolen, 2019, p. 43), which has been elaborated by recent work in cognitive, interactionally oriented pragmatics. The analysis presented in the following depends on this view of the process of an oral narrative. The purpose of the following discussion is not to demonstrate the final and definite resolution of 'credible or not' in the particular case at hand, but to illustrate some of the considerations that will have to be taken into account from a functional perspective in assessing whether a text is experience-based or not.

In the absence of more data about the concrete individual context and individual speech style, the tentative character of any interpretation must be emphasised, in addition to the fact that only an initial discussion of the linguistic issues can be offered here.

Characterising this type of genre as a narrative already involves a departure from the normal situation of a conversational narrative that tends not to be prompted in a kind of 'official' way in an asymmetrical situation but that arises more naturally in a conversational context. Already this special situatedness of narratives in the context of a specific domain (Heffer, 2018) makes for a restricted and modified interpretability of the text in terms of narrative categories of what has which functional, interactive meaning, and what has been, not said, but communicated—yet another clear pointer to the fact that the meaning of utterances is co-created by the participants in a genre, and its more general cultural relativity.

Therefore, there is no question of asymmetrical cooperative nature of co-creation in the type of embedded narrative in a formal interview session. The situation is doubly asymmetrical: in the 'natural', genre-inherent asymmetry in the turn-taking respect and the sense that there is a distinct power asymmetry between the witness and the interviewer. Besides, there are the conflicting aims of witness and interviewer: one side wants to hide or impart non-experience-based knowledge, the other is trying to elucidate that very fact. The latter two aspects make this version of the genre 'embedded narrative' a bad candidate for establishing a more general, non-individually restricted genre baseline.

5.2 Texts and Analysis

The following excerpts were audio-recorded and transcribed. The portions cited here were anonymised to the extent that the individuals concerned cannot be recognised. It should above all be mentioned that the following labelling of the sample texts as 'true' or 'untrue'—that is assessed as experience-based or not on the basis of the psychological interview—does not imply an apodictic verdict, and therefore the much-coveted definitive external ground truth. In most cases of this type with the interview as the only testimony, the ground truth may never be known. Besides, the results of the psychological interview session may point in a certain direction, on occasions distinctly. However, even in most cases where the interview results point to lived experience, a case is not often brought as the case's total picture does not yet warrant a successful trial in that direction. Above all, psychological testing results for experience-basedness invariably result in probabilities that are often not strong enough to serve as a basis for an indictment. Consequently, the classification of the following texts as experience-based or not is to be taken as the result of the overall assessment in the psychological session.

The best way to approach these texts is from a conversational-interactive point of view and see how linguistic expressions can be seen to be diagnostic in supporting the reconstruction of the interaction. This seems, at least at this stage of analysis in forming a hypothesis about accessing the cognitive process underlying experience-baseness or not, the preferred order of procedure in order not to accord to individual expressions a categorial or even categorical invariant diagnostic status, as has been misguidedly done in several studies of 'linguistic cues' such that, for instance, 'adverbs' would automatically be classed as indicative of experience-basedness or similar crude equations.

Text 1 True

- Interviewer: Dann sag mal.

Witness: <u>Also</u> ich war mit meiner Freundin X und zwei anderen Freunden, <u>also</u> Jungs- also <u>eigentlich</u> nicht meine Freunde, sondern ihre Freunde,

> die haben wir im Haus bei uns getroffen, die sind dann mit uns gefahren. Und, ähm, dann hab ich halt mit diesem Y auf WhatsApp, glaub ich, war das, geschrieben. Weil dieser Z war mal mit A zusammen und, ähm, diese A hat mir dann erzählt, ähm, er hätte ihr mal eine Kette geschenkt oder so und, äh, die wären verlobt, und dann hab ich halt Y angeschrieben darauf, ob das stimmt, und, äh, er meinte, nein. Und die hat mir halt noch ·n paar Sachen erzählt, dass halt, ähm, Y hatte mal ' ne Freundin und der hätte angeblich von der die Kette geklaut oder so und hätte ihr die dann geschenkt. Und dann hab ich mich mit dem getroffen an dem McDonalds, weil wir dann reden wollten darüber, weil ich auch von A's Seite aus mit ihm reden sollte. Weil er ja meinte, das würd' nicht stimmen mit der Kette oder dass er verlobt wär'.

After being prompted by the interviewer: *Dann sag mal* ('So, then, why don't you let us know what happened') the interviewee gives her version of events, which are preparatory to the event that the interview is targeting, and which itself is not represented in the passage, but only the development of the personal relationship she had with a male person. The passage is interesting as it gives an impression about what an experience-based story looks like, in contrast to others, to be discussed later.

The interviewee uses the particle *Also* ('so') to ratify the request to start telling part of a story and signals that she is prepared to share what and how she remembers. At the beginning of the story, the repeated use of *also* is to be interpreted as a signal of a collaborative attempt to create a focused cognitive space of shared knowledge. The first sentences have a clear orientational character. The repeated use of *also* signals that she is trying to give the details (marked by bold type) that she considers relevant to the hearer's understanding of her story. This is the overwhelming impression of the whole passage. What she relates is completely geared to the hearer's complete understanding of the situation. There is a clarification about the types of the friends, how she come to be with them, among other aspects. All this is information that 'any reasonable person' would be interested in hearing in this particular situation of having the role of a particular male person explained in the context of this interview. The story moves on at a slow pace and is interrupted by more orientational material: *Weil dieser Z war mal mit A zusammen.* ('Z had earlier gone out with A'). The further content of the passage relates only relatively little in terms of the narrative movement but frequently interrupts the storyline to give background material, the purpose of which being to make the hearer understand why the interviewee behaved as she did. For instance, she wants to clarify the charge that the male person had earlier stolen **a necklace** from his former girlfriend.

The point that matters here is that the passage is dominated by empathy with the comprehension of motivations and reasons from the interviewee's side. She interrupts the narrative flow several times and inserts information without surface connectors and with a main clause word order—for example *die haben wir im Haus bei uns getroffen*, ('these we have met in our house') which is to be taken as a switch to an orientational meta-mode. It is also typical that in one of these switches (*Weil dieser W war mal....zusammen. 'because this W once was together'*) *Weil* ('because') appears in a main clause SVO order—a phenomenon of 'epistemic' use of *weil*, which is really a meta-linguistic use: 'I am telling you this because...'. It shows the same concern of the author with the comprehension process on the side of the hearer. There are also several meta-remarks (z.B. *angeblich* ('purportedly') that comment overtly on the certainty or not of her memory. The witness is concerned and cares about the comprehension process and plausibility assumptions in her communication partner, monitors it and adds additional information independence of her empathy-guided estimate of the listener's comprehension.

This analysis can be taken to imply, in an interactionist view, that what is represented in the narrative not only reflects the content related but also portions with discoursal meta-work concerned with monitoring and securing comprehension. There is a genuine concern and a co-creative working with her communication partner, the interviewer. This type of effort and 'work' may indicate the rendering of experience-based memory content. The underlying hypothesis of the approach represented here is that, in a situation of lying, the witness is arguably more concerned with suggesting to the listener that she accept what has been said and does not engage in further asking back about details. Asking further questions about details is dispreferred by the lying hearer.

Text 2, Untrue

- Dann hat der mein Handy genommen, weil mein, also meine Mutter hat mehrmals angerufen und, ähm, diese X, weil ich schon ´n bisschen länger weg war. Und dann hat der mein Handy genommen und hat aufgelegt und es dann ausgemacht. Und, ähm, hinterher dann halt, also er hat dann mein—**ich weiß nicht mehr genau, wie das war**—auf jeden Fall hat der mein Handy dann danach hinterher, nachdem er das ausgemacht hat, **ich weiß nicht mehr genau**, der hat das irgendwo hingetan, **aber ich weiß nicht mehr genau**, wohin. Und, ähm, dann hat der halt noch mal versucht, meine Hand die ganze Zeit zu ihm zu ziehen. Und, ähm, hinterher hab ich dann mein Handy genommen und bin gegangen, also gerannt. Und dann hat, also hab ich mein Handy angemacht und, ähm, dann hat dieser, der hieß ***, der auch dabei war, also meine Freundin X war schon weg, weil die nach Hause musste, aber die meinten, die hätten mich gesucht oder so. Und, äh, dann hat, ähm, dieser, also ein Junge davon hieß ***, der hat mich dann angerufen und, ähm, hat gesagt, die würden da irgendwo mit der Polizei stehen, also an dieser Kneipe, und dann bin ich da hingegangen."

I: "Hm. Sonst noch irgendetwas, woran du dich erinnern kannst?"
Z: "Ähm. Mmh, nein." (schüttelt den Kopf)
I: "Du schüttelst den Kopf. Okay. Ähm, dann hab ich jetzt noch ´n paar Fragen zu."

Text 2, by contrast, contains several comments expressing uncertainty (three times 'can't remember', marked in bold type) or lack of knowledge, imprecision and hesitation features that seem to betray cognitive work originating from work to construct a story that is not experience-based. The content contains many unresolved uncertainty expressions, re-starts as in line 4–8: *Und, ähm,.. .., wohin*. The details offered later are not very specific, and their presentation is nowhere near the detail level offered in text 1. It may be significant that the passage contains eight hesitation markers (*Ähm, äh*), and several indications of not being able to supply more detail where it could be expected under experience-based assumptions. The contrast with text 1 is illuminating. In terms of syntax, text 2 is much less complex than text 1, where the frequent breaks with full SVO structures can be interpreted as the result of monitoring the hearer's comprehension and a realisation that at this point more adduction of relevant detail is called for. This is just one more example for the postulate mentioned in Nicklaus and Stein (2020, pp. 42–44) that a mere equation of 'hesitation', 'syntactic break', 'false starts' with lying is inadequate. What matters is a much more fine-grained, interactionally embedded categorisation and interpretation. We have tried to point to an important distinction in interactive terms: phenomena like those observed in text 1 are hearer-oriented, and the phenomena observed in text two are speaker-oriented. The linguistic phenomena identified for either type are arguably not in a 1:1 correspondence with the differences in interactive work, but they do provide clues to different types of 'work': cognitive work in 'creating' content that is not pre-existing and in a way neglects the hearer by supplying only the barest details to enable the hearer to accept some minimally coherent story versus work 'caused' by best serving the hearer with a satisfying story that he can integrate into her pre-existing knowledge, or, in relevance-theoretical phrasing, to derive most effortlessly cognitive benefits. It is this latter aspect that will be taken up later.

Text 2 is more smooth-running and more moving forward in narrative events and narrative clauses. A striking surface feature is the frequent occurrence of *und dann*, or simply *dann*, which signals the 'next event' in narrative terms in a temporal (and causal) sequence of events. The usage of *dann* as temporal conjunction roughly corresponds to English 'then' if sentence-initially introducing a new event in an ordered temporal sequence of events: *und, ähm, dann hat der halt nochmal versucht, meine Hand die ganze Zeit zu ihm zu ziehen*. ('then he tried to pull my hand towards him all the time'). But there is also a more particle-like[9] use of *dann* that is less focused on a specific temporal sequencing: *Und, ähm, hinterher hab ich dann mein Handy genommen…* ['and afterwards I took my cellphone…')—that is 'eventually', 'sometime later'. The following figures do not differentiate between the two but suffice it here to say that there are four clear cases of the particle type in both texts. All in all, there are thirteen instances of *dann* or *und dann*, with only six in text 1. Text 1 shows temporal *dann* in a skeletal fashion—only two purely temporal cases, but text 2 shows this element in a fast sequence that leaves little space for more questions. Interestingly, the next exchange with the interviewer is also shown: *Sonst noch irgendetwas, woran du dich erinnern kannst?* ('anything else you can remember?') „*Du schüttelst den Kopf. Okay. Ähm, dann hab ich jetzt noch ´n paar Fragen zu.*" ('You are shaking your head, so I have a couple of additional questions about your story'.)

Text 2 is also remarkable for containing a high number of expressions containing unspecific questions in places where more specific information would be expected to be volunteered, indicating lack of such knowledge. The whole passage from line 4 "Und,ähm, … wohin." is a five lines long expression of uncertainty and not knowing. Also, the rest of the passage is full of unspecific expressions like *oder so* ('or so'): There are also several *halt* and *also*, really strategies to tell the hearer to be content with what little unspecific information she can offer.

Text 3 Untrue

- Und, ähm, dann hab ich meiner Freundin meine Tasche gegeben, weil ich die nicht tragen wollte, und er meinte halt, dass wir, ähm, wenn wir da durch so ´n , durch so ´n Park, Wald—ich weiß nicht genau, was das war—laufen, dass wir dann halt, wenn wir da so ´ne Runde laufen, wieder da rauskommen. Und, ähm, dann sind wir gelaufen und dann haben wir geredet über *** und er hat mir das dann noch mal so erzählt, dass das nicht stimmen würde. Und, ähm, dann sind wir hinterher also so ´n Weg hochgelaufen, da war ´ne Bank da. Dann, ähm, sind wir da stehengeblieben, dann haben wir uns hingesetzt. Und dann hat der mich die ganze Zeit zu sich gezogen und meine Hand die ganze Zeit zu seinem Penis runtergezogen. Und dann hat der mich hinterher gegen so ´n, ich weiß nicht, was das war, gegen. Also da stand so ´n, so was wie, wo man, also da war so ´n Teil—man kann ja manchmal so (unverständlich [incomprehensible] 00:29:59) oder so irgendwo draufstellen. Also das war so ´n Stamm. Also ich kann das jetzt nicht erklären. Da stand, ähm, also da stand so was draufgeschrieben, also in so´n Stamm eingeritzt. Und, ähm, dann hat der, ist der halt aufgestanden und hat mich dagegen gedrückt und, äh, hat dann seine Hose runtergezogen. Und, äh, dann hat der das aber hinterher nicht mehr gemacht und dann hat der, ähm, sich wieder hingesetzt.

This type of production is one to which the effect of the 'cognitive load' hypothesis about processes going on in the speaker's mind would apply, whereas text 1 shows additional work geared to the hearer. It does not contain interactive 'work' geared to give more detail the speaker emphatically believes the hearer may at this point want. This text is ego-centred; the hearer is of no concern to the speaker.

For comparison purposes, consider text 3, where a similar range of features can be found, which are far from *so was, so'n..* ('there was like something like a stone'], several *halt* and *also*. Again, there is the impression of a fast-moving text with little specific information between the *und dann*—the impression is to get it over quick without being taken to task for more specific information. The speaker's only concern is the speaker; there is no 'work' oriented to the hearer, as in text 1.

In the light of the preceding, what does one make of text 4?

Text 4

- Z: "Ähm, ich warte auf *** draußen, dass die rauskommt. Nee, erst gehe ich zu *** runter und frag: ‚Kommst du mit nach draußen, mit mir spielen?' Und dann sagt ***: ‚Ja, warte, ich muss mich kurz noch waschen.' Ähm, dann geh ich nach unten und sag sie: ‚Ich warte dann unten auf dich.' Und sie sagt: ‚Okay.' Und dann warte ich da und dann, wenn sie rausgegangen ist, wo sie rausgekommen ist, da hab ich gefragt: ‚***, soll wir uns am Kiosk ein Eis holen?' Ähm, und dann, ich hatte ja für uns Geld mit nach unten gebracht, dann haben wir erst ihre Mama gefragt und meine, da haben die gesagt, ja. Und dann sind wir da so stehengeblieben an der Straße, dann kam so Männer und haben uns umzingelt und haben uns das Portemonnaie aus der Tasche geklaut. Und sind abgehauen. Und wir gehen dann sofort nach meiner Mama und nach ihrer Mama, ähm, um das zu sagen. Dann klären die das wieder und dann gehen sie zur Polizei mit uns."

Text 4 is a text produced on the prompt to tell a fabricated and untrue story to establish a baseline. There is a striking similarity between texts 2,

3 on the one hand, text 4, the fantasy, a not experience-based story that the witnesses were asked to construct to establish a kind of idio-baseline. What strikes the eye is the 'smooth' passage of the story with lots of passages that constitute narrative clauses introduced by 'then' ('dann'). Besides, there is a naked catenation of additive *und* clauses in passages in the second half of the text. The text looks like a stereotypical narrative text as far as the narrative-clause structure is concerned. This is also what the non-experience-based text No 2 looks like. Furthermore, all evaluative and orientational elements are missing. These texts (2, 3, and 4, the fake story) look more like an uninvolved 'account', as a police report would look like with its monotonous 'and then' scaffolding, than a story in the sense of a re-lived narrative that reflects emotional involvement.

The final example consists of two stretches from the same interview, with text 5a, an account of a factually true portion, and text 5b from the incriminated event that is the subject of investigation of a male person. The external evidence available points to the non-experience-based character of section 5b. This is a frequent situation: the whole interview may contain factual information, but the core story, the cause of the criminal inquiry, may not be true. On the lower level of an individual story, part of the story may be true, like a couple of external circumstances or even processes, and the rest a fantasy constructed around it. This is also reflected in the occurrence of expressions like *halt*, *also* and *dann*, as well as other types of especially adverb and particle use that are here discussed as examples. The 'functions' they have in the interactions, with syntactic expressions much understudied and underexploited in this context (Nicklaus & Stein, 2020), may also appear in portions in the discourse. This also applies to the last two texts to be cited here concerning the particle German particle 'halt' whose occurrence is marked in the texts:

Text 5a, True

- Z: "Ja, da war ich, äh, im Dezember 20** bis Januar 20**, da war ich, glaub ich, ´n paar Wochen nur, vier Wochen, weil es da Unstimmigkeiten mit der Therapeutin gab."

I: "Und wie sahen die aus?"

Z: "Äh, das war der Winter, wo es so unglaublich schön viel geschneit hat. Und ich bin, ähm, einen Tag krank gewesen und mir ging es halt gar nicht gut. Ich hatte angerufen, dass ich nicht komm′ und das, ja, wäre kein Problem. Und am nächsten Tag wollte ich dann mit der S-Bahn fahren—oder es war genau andersrum, ich bin mir jetzt grad nicht mehr ganz sicher. Ich bin einen Tag, wollte ich mit der S-Bahn fahren und ich brauchte ′ne Dreiviertelstunde bis zu dieser Klinik. Und hab dann für ′ne Strecke, die normalerweise zehn Minuten die S-Bahn braucht, hab ich schon ′ne Dreiviertelstunde gebraucht. Und hab dann angerufen, hab gesagt, das bringt heute nix, denn die Gleise sind alle total dicht, bis ich da bin, sind alle Gruppen vorbei. Und nachmittags hätte ich nur, ich glaub, Tanzen gehabt und, ähm, zu der Zeit sind sowieso alle Patienten immer früher abgehauen, auch wenn es eigentlich nicht Therapieplan war, aber es war gang und gäbe in der Klinik. Ja, und, ähm, als ich dann am nächsten Tag in der Klinik war, hat der Therapeut mir dann eröffnet, dass, äh, ja die Krankenkasse dann eine Verlängerung haben wollen würde, wenn ich denn eine bräuchte, und er das da abgelehnt hätte. Woraufhin ich dann total geschockt war, weil ich überhaupt nicht wusste, was los wäre. Und, äh, hatte dann mit Mitpatienten darüber geredet so: Ja, ich bin dann am *** weg, irgendwie so was, was er dann mitbekommen hatte und dann nachfragte, warum ich denn so was sagen würde. Wo ich dann auch meinte: ‚Ja, hatten Sie doch gesagt, dass keine Verlängerung beantragt wird', und dann meinte er, ja, er wäre nur sauer gewesen und das wäre so im Ei-, im Eifer gewesen, dass er über mein Verhalten erbost gewesen wäre, dass ich einfach nicht gekommen wäre und, äh, das hätte er dann zu Grund gegeben. Da hab ich gesagt: ‚Damit wäre dann die Therapeuten-/Patientenbeziehung komplett zerstört', und ich würd′ nicht mehr mit ihm reden wollen, sondern so was gehört da nicht hin."

Text 5b, Not True

(W=witness, I= Interviewer)

W: "Also ich hatte während der ersten Vernehmung ja, ähm, was gesagt, was dann, was ich nachher weggenommen habe."

I: “Mhm, genau.”

W: “Und, ähm, das hatte ich auch während der Vernehmung gesagt, dass, ähm, so die Situationen, äh, mit Hose ausziehen gab´s auch, die sind auch st-, also haben auch stattgefunden, aber ich kann mich an diesem einen Tag eben nicht dran erinnern, dass es da war und das passte halt einfach nicht zu dem, was ich mir, also von den Bildern, die hochgekommen sind, passte das nicht zu diesem Tag.”

I: “Aha, also, ähm, das war auch mit dem Herrn X,”

W: (fällt I. ins Wort) “Genau.”

I: “aber das war zu ´nem anderen Zeitpunkt.”

W: “…jedenfalls in *** noch nie gesehen. Öhm, ja, und, öhm, an dem Tag haben wir dann zwangsläufig auch geraucht, wieder. Denk´ ich, weil wir in *** waren. Öhm, und da lag ich halt irgendwann auf der Ecke dieser Bank. Und die Beine lagen- waren halt nicht mehr auf der Bank. So, mit meinem Unterleib relativ offen war. …….Öhm, ja das sind so Situationen, die noch relativ klar da sind…. Und, ja. Und er hat halt dabei immer, relativ klar immer, gesagt, solche Sachen,… Und, öhm, ja, also eigentlich, solche Sachen, viel auch, die man so typisch aus Pornos kennt…. Also solche, sich selbst anspornenden Sachen. Ja– das ist jetzt, glaub´ ich, erst mal so…”

It will be observed that the density of occurrence of *halt* in the non-experience-based text 5b (7 occurrences of *halt*, some of which had to be deleted for reasons of offensive content) contrasts with the much longer portion of text 5a, with only one, in which *halt* amounts to an appeal suggesting to the hearer ‘to not further explore the details of why I was not feeling well on that day, accept that I will not offer to add more detail, please cooperate and comply’. The same semantics applies to the uses in text 5b, where *halt* amounts to a request to the communicative partner to ‘simply accept’ and ‘do not further ask me to specify details’ in a situation when the otherwise natural mention of further details—an accepted indicator for truthfulness—would mean an embarrassment, as it would have to be fabricated (cf. below). In certain uses, it can be equivalent to English ‘well’—for example ‘well, he is that sort of a guy’.

A methodological remark is in place here. The interpretive discussion of an individual expression like *halt* must not argumentationally be misinterpreted. While any discussion of the argumentation value of *halt* must of necessity start from its function in a shared cognitive space in a concrete interaction, its argumentation value in adjudging truth or not must always be supported by parallel occurrences in different contexts and cases of the same genre type. The occurrence or non-occurrence in genres itself is a pointer towards a functional interpretation. The particle *halt*, just like the particle use of 'like'—and not like the use of 'like' in this very sentence—is unlikely to occur in a scientific article, not because it 'sounds' spoken, but because it has the gesture of 'don't ask me further', which is contrary to the attitudinal mode of a scientific text, as a locus for radical questioning that leaves no stone unturned. The register or genre distribution is then an effect of the function in discourse.

It should be added that text 5b contains a large number of expressions that express a lack of further specific details, either knowledge of such or unwillingness to offer such, like *solche Sachen* or *alle möglichen Sachen* ('such things' or 'all kinds of things') that would be essential information in such a legal context.

In addition to the fact that particles like *halt* are homonymous with other uses and, therefore, withstand access to automatic corpus analysis, their appearance has also to be measured against idiolectal regularities. Just as there are people who use particle 'like' in every second sentence, this also applies to *halt* in the German case. Therefore, a baseline-based interpretation must consider using that expression in that person's language use and story-telling competence (in such a legal context) in specific genres and not across the board. To an appreciable extent, this happens in the embedding interview context.

5.3 From Cognition to Syntax

This brief discussion was intended to highlight the difference between a formal and a functional approach to how lying is manifested in language production. A functional approach would ask to what extent a text (better: an utterance live-observed) would reflect the cognitive-interactional work involved in fabricating evidence. The baseline is then to be established on the level of the type of cognitive work manifested in linguistic choices, like the choice to use '*halt*' or to use 'epistemic *weil*' (Keller, 1995). The German conjunction can be used with normal subordinate sentence word order: 'weil ich nicht komme', with a clause-final position of the finite verb ('because I don't come') and in 'weil ich komme nicht', with the middle position of the finite verb. This latter usage has been termed 'epistemic *weil*'. The positional contrast does not exist in English. The use of this 'epistemic *weil*' as an indication of meta-discursive activity is to be distinguished from the use of a syntactically integrated '*weil*', for which it can be hypothesised that it indicates the search for constructing reasons for a course of action that is internally generated—that is when a subject needs to give a reason for a fabricated event or circumstance. Non-experience-based content needs the support of general assumptions in the shape of clichés. What an expression like '*halt*' does is invite the reader to see a statement as sufficiently supported by referring to such a general, unspecific type of shared cognitive content (Hettler, 2012, p. 62). In the same way, causative clauses, like the ones initiated by *weil*, tend to be used in non-experience-based context since they tend to be used '..wenn Schemawissen in einer Situation nicht mehr ausreicht.'[10] ('if schema knowledge is not enough in a specific situation') (Hettler, 2012, p. 64). So while the individual linguistic expression can never be categorically used as a 'proof' of lying, the co-occurrence of several, discursively motivated and explicable expressions can be seen as a linguistic indication—as a trace—that the narrative may not be experience-based. The same cognitive source condition, the absence of personal experience, can explain the occurrence and the empirical co-occurrence of such expressions as suppositions or indeterminacy. It is an interesting issue to investigate to which extent these expressions also occur in cases of 'false memory' and similar phenomena, which do not involve intentional deceit and therefore refer to a much different cognitive source situation.

If we look at the conversation as an online 'series of interactively made decisions', we have to locate the baseline in the nature of these decisions at different points in the online process. What is then 'interpretable' or potentially diagnostic is not the use of '*halt*' or 'then', but the intended communicative move at a given point in the discourse process—whether we conceive it as to be expected or deviating.

This process is highly constrained by what communicative and cognitive-interactive processes define the genre. Such an analysis crucially involves an interpretive-hermeneutic activity by the analyst. To what extent it will eventually be possible to identify formal markers that can serve as diagnostic cues will have to be shown by future research. For instance, the use of what has been termed 'epistemic *weil*' (Keller, 1995) as in the above text 1 could be more regularly indicative of interactionist meta-work of the type indicated here, as it gives a meta-reason why certain content was uttered. A presumptive regularity that could be part of a formal identification procedure would have to identify all cases of '*weil*' with SVO word order in this particular subtype of the narrative genre. Another eligible feature is the use of parentheses as in commas or brackets as meta-comment. What is absent in texts is as much of interest as what is observed. Space forbids the interpretive discussion of several other features in the texts cited, such as the variation between definite article and demonstrative determiner or the use of direct speech vs indirect speech, among other aspects.

The point to emphasise here is that linguistic access to the identification of lying in terms of deviations from baselines must be based on identifying highly context-restricted and individual regularities, arguably much more highly constrained than has been previously thought. It is not the case that all uses of '*weil*' are suspicious, but only uses of '*weil*' with SVO in genuine narratives, where they indicate meta-comment. The same applies to parentheses. As we argued in the case of insurance fraud, the closer constrained the context of occurrence, and the genre itself are, the higher the chances to identify linguistic markers that can be interpreted as indicative of fraud. The price to pay for narrowing down the genre (and personality) constraints in baseline definition amounts to giving up the advantages afforded by computational corpus analysis.

As the supply of empirical data for research is in most cases strongly constrained by legal obstacles, what is available for empirical research, for instance in the case of '*weil*' and parentheses, requires careful examination, as the transcriptive path from video-taped spoken materials to texts on paper or in pixels is characterised by the potential vitiating influence of normative and 'normalising' ideas about language, especially syntax, and especially what written language should be like, as this is more subject to ideologies about 'good' language than more undomesticated spoken language (cf. Sect. 3).

This observation arguably applies to forms that are more typical for spoken language, such as articles or other non-propositional items in danger of being weeded out in transcriptions, but which are highly indicative of the cognitive-interactive work of the type indicated here. Besides, word order departures from canonical word order like SVO in English and German (inversions, pre- postponing) need to be scanned, as they often contain discourse-structuring information that departs from canonical linearisation and that is likely to be of interest for the type of analysis indicated here. The fact of their presence is as interpretable as their absence—under the assumption that what we find or do not find in transcribed texts is not an artefact of editing.

It should finally be pointed out that the type of cognitive-interactive work discussed here as a discriminant of true and false narratives is different from the measurable types of psychological processes early advocated by Vrij et al. (2011): 'As we will argue in the present article, effective lie-detection interview techniques take advantage of the distinctive psychological processes of truth-tellers and liars, and obtaining insight into these processes is thus vital for developing effective lie-detection interview tools.' (p. 90). Our cognitive work notion here is a structural or logical, information-flow one, in principle unrelated to what is implied by psychological notions of cognitive processes that have a real-time dimension. This is also why cognitive load measurements are only indirectly related to the cognitive discourse processes postulated here. The psychological processes postulated are an epiphenomenon of the deeper cognitive work. Whether they predict an effect that is measurable as an effect of the cognitive load must be reserved for future study.

So there are, in principle, four levels of analysis involved that interact in complex ways:

1. A pragmatic-interactive theoretical construct of what goes on in the speaker's mind in a concrete situation as she tries to influence the contents of the hearer's cognition. This is where 'intentions' would have to be located.
2. A real-time view of measurable processes.
3. What is determined by No 1 is reflected in effects on choice and linearisation of linguistic-surface forms.

4. The effect of No 3 on the hearer's cognition, or the intended contextual effect in relevance-theoretical terms.

The approaches to lie detection from No 1 to 4 to access No 1 differ in at which point they try to tap into the information flow. Ultimately, they all involve interpretive processes that translate their analysis results—statistical or hermeneutic—to level 1. This is also the level that judicial processes refer to. To be sentenced for perjury does not mean being found guilty for using 'wrong words', but for an intention to try and trigger false contextual effects.

6 Conclusion: De-surfacing the Trace

Given the fundamental importance of establishing baselines in using linguistic evidence in the narrow sense of looking at smaller linguistic-surface units, the aim of this chapter was to point to the methodological issues attendant on explicitly defining such baselines. Previous research tended to define these deadlines in far too broad terms, to the extent they were considered at all. It is especially the notion of the genre in a more modern pragmatic sense, emphasising underlying cognitive and interactive processes that need to constrain any notion of baseline narrowly. Also, the baseline must be located, not in the distribution of a fixed set of surface 'cues', but in the co-constructive process of meaning-making and in the way expectations (baselines) are departed from in each discourse process. Such a view follows the line of research indicated by Carter (2014):

> The findings support a call to move away from explorations that identify, collect and use cues to deception as a way to predict and understand it. It suggests that a focus directed towards the influence of the questioner's talk on the deceiver's response would ultimately provide a more useful understanding of the manifestation of deception by reframing it as part of the interactional design rather than a collection of discrete cues drawn upon at the point of deception. (p. 137)

Many different linguistic forms may represent a given cognitive-interactive type of move in a given communicative process, with these forms interpretable only in this unique context. This implies that, in principle, it is impossible to assign fixed diagnostic functions to any given form *per se*, as the form will receive its function—for example to deflect the questioner's attention away from a touchy piece of content only in a communicative context. This, then, is the point where the linguistic 'trace', the equivalent to the 'physical trace' (Hazard & Margot, 2014) of criminal investigations by other forensic sciences, is to be located. It is only if it can be established that the linguistic phenomenon observed can be interpreted cognitively in the way adumbrated as a meaningful departure from a narrowly defined baseline. It can be elevated to linguistic evidence in the legal sense, not the physical occurrence itself in its temporal-spatial existence. This is an approach also advocated in principle by Picornell (2013) in her analysis of narratives: not as a static text, but as a process, where individual expressions are not cues as members of a static list but receive their interpretation, and their diagnostic interpretability, in a particular section of the progress of the discourse. 'Do linguistic cues to deception arise from "leakage", or are they the product of a deliberate linguistic strategy to control reader perception?' (Picornell, 2013, p. 8). The present chapter has opted for the latter strategy against the background of dissatisfaction with the former strategy and the questionable status of stand-alone expressions. It also takes account of the pragmatic embeddedness of meaning-making even in monologic discourse like narrating the personal version of a crime.

What may be diagnostic is then the attempt to de-focus a piece of circumstance or information, not a particular linguistic item. So, one of the take-home results for practical applications is to consider the relevance of fine-grained genre baseline. This is what Hauch et al. (2015, p. 330) refer to: '..linguistic cues to deception are sensitive to contextual factors..'. That this suggestion has not yet been followed in the face of expectations of fast results of the automatic analysis with its very obvious advantages explains the disappointing results of a survey of the computer's role in lie detection (Hauch et al., 2015, p. 330).

This 'de-surfacing' of the diagnostic cue notion may go further in some contexts and genres than in others. Above, for instance, we have argued that a certain type of expression, like particles, may 'standardly' have a place as a likely diagnostic feature in identifying suspicious structures in conversational genres. However, this does not mean that a particle-like '*halt*' is in itself a diagnostic cue, and invariably the same cue at that, but that the conversational meaning-making process in which it is employed is the suspect for cues leading to traces.

This approach needs to be invoked and further exploited in future research to more fully exploit its potential, even if this is at the cost of a decrease in formalisation and amenability to automatic analysis. A very narrowly defined context of use seems to be essential and often a methodological problem that is very hard to overcome in practice. Nevertheless, an awareness of the problem must attend on any use of baselines to produce results that can be used in legal contexts with a specified degree of confidence.

In the field of forensics, pragmatics has, up to now, been a rare bird. Language as evidence is a very obvious candidate for being analysed in terms of especially the newer orientations of pragmatics. That context in all its facets, embodied in the pragmatic concept of genre, is a basic assumption of the present contribution. While generally true for all constituent parts of all versions witness examinations, it is especially true for an embedded narrative that 'the setting creates the parameters for what story should be told and how' (Smith-Khan, 2017, p. 31). What Smith-Khan (2017) demonstrates for the very specific context of asylum applications is true with a vengeance for the high-stakes context of veracity evaluation. In a forensic situation veracity evaluation carries a very high weight. An awareness of the asymmetry of the situation and the mutual awareness and meta-awareness of the stark differences of goals is of paramount importance. The co-creational aspects of this genre need to be included in whatever further—badly necessary—study of discourse in such legal contexts. The study of narratives, and especially small narratives, and what people do with it and in it must be another primary concern for research in forensic linguistics (Georgakopoulou, 2020).

Notes

1. LIWC is the abbreviation for *Linguistic Inquiry and Word Count*, a tool to be used for scientific purpose; also see Chap. 5.
2. See Fobbe (In press), for a linguistically based criticism of the somewhat naive application of the category 'pronoun' in deception detection.
3. See the sentence of the *Bundesgerichtshof*, BGH 30.7.1999 1 StR 618/98.
4. Fitzpatrick et al. (2015, p. 32) translate as: 'Statement validity analysis'.
5. Vrij reports an average error rate of 30% in laboratory studies (Vrij, 2005, p. 32).
6. Steller and Köhnken (1989, p. 235) report that in 90 % of the by then known cases, the judge had followed the expert's evaluation. The courts' trust in the Content Criteria has recently been extensively criticised (Geipel, 2021, pp. 84–100).
7. Sporer et al. (2021, p. 25) conclude: '[…] both the CBCA and RM can be applied to different domains, with some criteria showing larger validities in some domains than others.'
8. Actually, the example consists of two sentences: 'I went to Sainsbury, to the "free from" section where I found the chocolate bar. It was 50p, and I paid with a £1 coin.'
9. The category of 'particles', as it is understood here refers to interactive discourse management only, such as pointing the hearer to types of shared knowledge, similar to expressions of stance (cf. Chap. 5 in this volume). This is only one aspect of the uses of particles, which are a homonymous category with several types of non-propositional functions. Cf. for German the entry for 'Abtönungspartikel' in Hentschel (2010). It should also be pointed out that the studies mentioned in Sect. 3 variously refer to types of expressions under the term 'particles' that are different from the class of expressions discussed here. For a comprehensive discussion of discourse markers cf. Heine et al. (2021) especially § 1.1, pp. 6–16 that explicitly discusses the metatextual functions and function as processing instructions for discourse.
10. „Die Verwendung von „halt" (Schwäbisch im Sinne von „eben") wird aus der Verwandtschaft zum negativen Merkmal Klischees …heraus als neues verbales Warnsignal abgeleitet. „Halt" und „eben"können nach der Operationalisierung des Merkmals Klischees …als Signalwort für eben dieses verstanden werden (z.B."..wie man das halt so macht,…" oder „…wie so eine Unfallstelle eben aussieht. Chaotisch und…") (Hettler, 2012, p. 66, also p. 189 for further examples).

References

Adams, S. H., & Jarvis, J. P. (2006). Indicators of veracity and deception in analysis of written statements made to police. Speech language and the law. *International Journal of Speech, Language & the Law, 13*, 1–22. https://doi.org/10.1558/sll.2006.13.1.1

Almela, A., Valencia-García, R., & Cantos, P. (2013). Seeing through deception: A computational approach to deceit detection in Spanish written communication. *LESLI, 1*, 3–12. https://doi.org/10.5195/lesli.2013.5

Arntzen, F., & Michaelis-Arntzen, E. (2011). *Psychologie der Zeugenaussage. System der Glaubwürdigkeitsmerkmale*. Beck.

Bogaard, G., Meijer, E. H., Vrij, A., & Merckelbach, H. (2016). Scientific Content Analysis (SCAN) cannot distinguish between truthful and fabricated accounts of a negative event. *Frontiers in Psychology, 7*, 1–7.

Carter, C. E. (2014). When is a lie not a lie? When it's divergent: Examining lies and deceptive responses in a police interview. *International Journal of Language and the Law/Linguagem e Direito, 1*(1), 122–140.

Chaski, C. (2013). Best practices and admissibility of forensic author identification. *Journal of Law and Policy, 21*(2). Brooklyn Law School.

Cooper, B. S., Hugues, F. H., & Yuille, J. C. (2014). Evaluating truthfulness: Interviewing and credibility assessment. In W. Bruinsma & S. Weisburd (Eds.), *Encyclopedia of criminology and criminal justice* (pp. 1413–1426). Springer. https://doi.org/10.1007/978-1-4614-5690-2

Douglis, A. (2018). Disentangling perjury and lying. *Yale Journal of Law & the Humanities, 29*(2), 339–374.

Eades, D. (2012). The social consequences of language ideologies in courtroom cross-examination. *Language in Society, 41*, 471–497. https://doi.org/10.1017/s0047404512000474

Ericsson, A., & Lacerda, F. (2007). Charlatanry in forensic speech science: A problem to be taken seriously. *International Journal of Speech, Language & the Law, 14*(2), 169–193. https://doi.org/10.1558/ijsll.2007.14.2.169

Fitzpatrick, E., Bachenko, J., & Fornaciari, T. (Eds.). (2015). *Automatic detection of verbal deception*. https://doi.org/10.2200/s00656ed1v01y201507hlt029

Fobbe, E. (2011). *Forensische Linguistik. Eine Einführung*. Narr.

Fobbe, E. (In press). Linguistik und psychologische Täuschungsforschung—zum Problem der verbalen Lügenindikatoren am Beispiel der Selbst-Referenz. In M. Meiler & M. Siefkes (Eds.), *Linguistische Methodenreflexion im Aufbruch. Beiträge zu einer aktuellen Diskussion im Schnittpunkt von*

Ethnographie und Digital Humanities, Multimodalität und Mixed Methods (Linguistik – Impulse & Tendenzen). De Gruyter.

Foolen, A. (2019). Quo vadis pragmatics? From adaptation to participatory sense-making. *Journal of Pragmatics, 145*, 39–46.

Geipel, A. (2021). *Beweisführung und Lügenerkennung vor Gericht*. Schöningh.

Georgakopoulou, A. (2020). Small stories research and narrative criminology: 'Plotting' an alliance. In M. Althoff, B. Dollinger, & H. Schmidt (Eds.), *Conflicting narratives of crime & punishment* (pp. 1–19). Palgrave Macmillan.

Giltrow, J., & Stein, D. (2009). *Genres in the Internet. Issues in the theory of genre*. Benjamins. https://doi.org/10.1075/pbns.188.01gil

Greuel, L. (2001). *Wirklichkeit, Erinnerung, Aussage*. Beltz.

Hardin, K. J. (2019). Linguistic approaches to lying and deception. In J. Meibauer (Ed.), *The Oxford handbook of lying* (pp. 56–70). Oxford University Press.

Hauch, V., Blandón-Gitlin, I., Masip, J., & Sporer, S. L. (2015). Are computers effective lie detectors? A meta-analysis of linguistic cues to deception. *Personality and Social Psychology Review, 19*(4), 307–342. https://doi.org/10.1177/1088868314556539 . pspr.sagepub.com

Hauch, V., Sporer, S., Masip, J., & Blandon-Gitlin, I. (2017). Can credibility criteria be assessed reliably? A meta-analysis of criteria-based content analysis. *Psychological Assessment, 29*(6), 819–834. https://doi.org/10.1037/pas0000426

Hazard, D., & Margot, P. (2014). Forensic science culture. In G. Bruinsma & D. Weisburd (Eds.), *Encyclopedia of criminology and criminal justice* (pp. 1782–1795). Springer. https://doi.org/10.1007/978-1-4614-5690-2_534

Heffer, C. (2018). Narrative practices and voice in court. In J. Visconti (Ed.), *Handbook of communication in the legal sphere* (pp. 256–284). deGruyter Mouton.

Heffer, C. (2020). *All bullshit and lies?: Insincerity, irresponsibility and the judgment of untruthfulness*. Oxford University Press.

Heine, B., Kaltenböck, G., Kuteva, T., & Long, H. (2021). *The rise of discourse markers*. CUP.

Hentschel, E. (Ed.). (2010). *Deutsche Grammatik*. de Gruyter.

Hettler, S. (2006). *Wahre und falsche Zeugenaussagen*. VDM Verlag Dr. Müller.

Hettler, S. (2012). *Wahre und falsche Zeugenaussagen. Evaluation von Zeugenaussagen mit unterschiedlichem Wahrheitsgehalt mittels erweitertem Kanon inhaltlicher Kennzeichen*. AV Akademikerverlag.

Horn, L. R. (2017). Telling it slant: Toward a taxonomy of deception. In J. Giltrow & D. Stein (Eds.), *The pragmatic turn in law. Inference and interpretation in legal discourse* (Mouton Series in Pragmatics) (pp. 23–55). De Gruyter/Mouton. https://doi.org/10.1515/9781501504723-002

Jaszczolt, K. (2019). Rethinking being Gricean: New challenges for metapragmatics. *Journal of Pragmatics, 145*, 15–24.

Johnson, M. K., & Raye, C. L. (1981). Reality monitoring. *Psychological Review, 88*(1), 67–85.

Keller, R. (1995). The epistemic 'weil'. In D. Stein & S. Wright (Eds.), *Subjectivity and subjectivation. Linguistic perspectives* (pp. 16–30). CUP.

Kleinberg, B., Arntz, A., & Verschuere, B. (2019). Being accurate about accuracy in verbal deception detection. *PLoS ONE, 14*(8), e0220228. https://doi.org/10.1371/journal.pone.0220228

Kraft, E., Nikolaus, K., & Quasthoff, U. (1977). Die Konstitution der konversationellen Erzählung. *Folia Linguistica, 11*(3–4), 287–337. https://doi.org/10.1515/flin.1977.11.3-4.287

Labov, W., & Waletzky, J. (1997). Narrative analysis: Oral versions of personal experience. *Journal of Narrative & Life History, 7*(1–4), 3–38. https://doi.org/10.1075/jnlh.7.02nar

Linde, C. (2015). Memory in narrative. In K. Tracy, C. Ilie, & T. Sandel (Eds.), *The international encyclopedia of language and social interaction*. Wiley. https://onlinelibrary.wiley.com/doi/full/10.1002/9781118611463.wbielsi121

Luke, T. J. (2019). Lessons from Pinocchio. Cues to deception may be highly exaggerated. *Perspectives on Psychological Science, 14*(4), 646–671. https://doi.org/10.1177/1745691619838258

Nahari, G., et al. (2019). 'Language of lies': Urgent issues and prospects in verbal lie detection research. *Legal and Criminological Psychology, 24*, 1–23. https://doi.org/10.1111/lcrp.12148

Newman, E., Steven, J., & Loftus, E. (2014). False memories. In G. Bruinsma & D. Weisburd (Eds.), *Encyclopedia of criminology and criminal justice* (pp. 1555–1563). Springer. https://doi.org/10.1007/978-1-4614-5690-2_534

Newman, M. L., Pennebaker, J. W., Berry, D. S., & Richards, J. M. (2003). Lying words: Predicting deception from linguistic styles. *Personality and Social Psychology Bulletin, 29*(5), 665–675. https://doi.org/10.1177/0146167203029005010

Nicklaus, M., & Stein, D. A. (2020). The role of linguistics in veracity evaluation. *International Journal of Language and Law, 9*, 23–47. https://www.languageandlaw.eu/jll/issue/view/9

Picornell, I. (2013). Analysing deception in written statements. *LESLI, 1*(1), 41–50.

Quijano-Sánchez, L., Liberatore, F., Camacho-Collados, J., & Camacho-Collados, M. (2018). Applying automatic text-based detection of deceptive language to police reports: Extracting behavioral patterns from a multi-step classification model to understand how we lie to the police. *Knowledge-Based Systems, 149*, 155–168. https://doi.org/10.1016/j.knosys.2018.03.010

Smith, N. (2001). *Reading between the lines: An evaluation of the Scientific Content Analysis technique (SCAN)* (Police Research Series, 135). Great Britain, Home Office, Policing and Reducing Crime Unit.

Smith-Khan, L. (2017). Telling stories: Credibility and the representation of social actors in Australian asylum appeals. *Discourse & Society, 28*(5), 512–534. https://doi.org/10.1177/0957926517710989

Sporer, S. (2004). 4. Reality monitoring and detection of deception. In P. A. Granhag & L. A. Stömwall (Eds.), *The detection of deception in forensic contexts* (pp. 64–102). Cambridge University Press.

Sporer, S., Manzanero, A. L., & Masip, J. (2021). Optimizing CBCA and RM research: Recommendations for analyzing and reporting data on content cues to deception. *Psychology, Crime and Law, 27*(1), 1–39. https://doi.org/10.1080/1068316X.2020.1757097

Steller, M. (1989). Recent developments in statement analysis. In J. C. Yuille (Ed.), *Credibility assessment: Proceedings of the NATO Advanced Study Institute on Credibility Assessment* (pp. 135–154). Maratea, Italy, 14–24 June 1988. Kluwer. https://doi.org/10.1007/978-94-015-7856-1_8

Steller, M., & Köhnken, G. (1989). Criteria-based statement analysis: Credibility assessment of children's statements in sexual abuse cases. In J. D. Raskin (Ed.), *Psychological methods for investigation and evidence* (pp. 217–245). Springer.

Stratman, J. (2016). *A forensic linguistic approach to legal disclosures*. Routledge.

Svartvik, J. (1968). *The Evans statements. A case for forensic linguistics*. Parts I and II. Almqvist & Wiksell.

Taylor, P. J., Larner, S., Conchie, S. M., & Menacere, T. (2017). Culture moderates changes in linguistic self-presentation and detail provision when deceiving others. *Royal Society Open Science, 4*, 1–20. https://doi.org/10.1098/rsos.170128

Undeutsch, U. (1967). Beurteilung der Glaubhaftigkeit von Aussagen. In U. Undeutsch (Ed.), *Forensische Psychologie. Handbuch der Psychologie, 11* (pp. 26–181). Verlag für Psychologie.

Verigin, B. L., Meijer, E. H., & Vrij, A. (2020). A within-statement baseline comparison for detecting lies. *Psychiatry, Psychology and Law*. https://www.tandfonline.com/doi/full/10.1080/13218719.2020.1767712 ; https://doi.org/10.1080/13218719.2020.1767712

Volbert, R., & Steller, M. (2014). Glaubhaftigkeit. In T. Bliesener, F. Lösel, & G. Köhnken (Eds.), *Lehrbuch der Rechtspsychologie* (pp. 391–407). Huber. https://doi.org/10.1016/b978-3-437-22902-2.00039-0

Vrij, A. (2005). Criteria-based content analysis: A qualitative review of the first 37 studies. *Psychology, Public Policy, and Law, 11*(1), 3–41. https://doi.org/10.1037/1076-8971.11.1.3

Vrij, A. (2008). *Detecting lies and deceit. Pitfalls and opportunities*. Wiley.

Vrij, A. (2015a). Cognitive approach to lie detection. In P. A. Granhag, A. Vrij, & B. Verschuere (Eds.), *Detecting deception: Current challenges and cognitive approaches* (pp. 207–227). Wiley-Blackwell.

Vrij, A. (2015b). Verbal lie detection tools: Statement validity analysis, reality monitoring, and scientific content analysis. In P. A. Granhag, A. Vrij, & B. Verschuere (Eds.), *Detecting deception: Current challenges and cognitive approaches* (pp. 3–35). https://doi.org/10.1002/9781118510001.ch1

Vrij, A., Fisher, R., & Blank, H. (2017). A cognitive approach to lie detection: A meta-analysis. *Legal and Criminological Psychology, 22*(1), 1–21. https://doi.org/10.1111/lcrp.12088

Vrij, A., Granhag, P. A., & Porter, S. (2011). Pitfalls and opportunities in nonverbal and verbal lie detection. *Psychological Science in the Public Interest, 11*(3), 89–121. https://doi.org/10.1177/1529100610390861

Vrij, A., Hope, L., & Fisher, R. (2014). Eliciting reliable information in investigative interviews. *Policy Insights from the Behavioral and Brain Sciences, 1*(1), 129–136. https://doi.org/10.1177/2372732214548592

Vrij, A., Mann, S., Leal, S., & Fisher, R. P. (2021). Combining verbal veracity assessment techniques to distinguish truth tellers from lie tellers. *The European Journal of Psychology Applied to Legal Context, 13*(1), 9–19. https://doi.org/10.5093/ejpalc2021a2

7

Authorship Identification

Eilika Fobbe

1 Introductory Definition of the Area of Inquiry

Authorship identification deals with the analysis of a person's language use and serves two different purposes. One is to analyse a person's language for text comparison to determine whether the questioned texts have joint authorship; the other is to create an author profile. According to Kniffka (2007, p. 83), the term identification itself is misleading because the method cannot identify a person from a group of suspects, let alone a group of unknown size, but it can prove a charge against a defendant or exonerate him. However, for larger amounts of text, the field of Automatic Authorship Investigation does attempt recognition of the identity of the author, as described in Chap. 8. Other related tasks are *author obfuscation* and *author imitation*. *Author obfuscation* examines whether the language use and writing skills an author displays are authentic. If they show linguistic inconsistencies, such as a nuanced lexis accompanied by various misspellings even of the basic vocabulary, this can indicate an author's attempt to deceive. While *author obfuscation* often

E. Fobbe (✉)
Bundeskriminalamt/Federal Criminal Police Office, Wiesbaden, Germany
e-mail: eilika.fobbe@bka.bund.de

V. Guillén-Nieto, D. Stein (eds.), *Language as Evidence*,
https://doi.org/10.1007/978-3-030-84330-4_7

serves the purpose of diverting the reader's attention away from the actual author, *author imitation* reflects the opposite strategy. By copying another person's use of language, known in literature as a 'pastiche', the author directs the reader's attention directly to someone, perhaps even someone known to the reader.

1.1 Authorship Profiling

An author profile is created on the assumption that the language of a text reflects its author's different social relations. Since the basis of an author profile is a written text, the analysis only includes those social categories that are known to be closely related to the acquisition of written language competence, such as educational background, regional origin, native-speaker competence, age, occupation, writing routines—which, for example, point to a profession requiring special writing skills, attitudes, or group memberships (Dern, 2009, pp. 64–66). The determination of gender and personality traits should be addressed, if at all, with caution, as gender has been found to be a poorly defined category (Nini, 2018) and psychological assessments should be left to psychologists, especially in a forensic context. The findings are used to categorise the anonymous author socio-biographically, thus helping the investigators narrow the group of possible suspects. For example, seemingly incorrect use of standard language may turn out to be specialist jargon, or wrong case inflexion may reflect an underlying dialectal influence. Therefore, a linguistic author profile is more of investigational than evidentiary value. Since linguistic analysis is more concerned with the author's linguistic choices than with content, it foregrounds such linguistic aspects which may be easily overlooked by linguistic laypersons.

1.2 Text Comparison

Text comparison works on the assumption that authors develop individual linguistic preferences and patterns of use in their communication with others by choosing from the range of language options available.

This individual language use—or style—can be identified, described and analysed in principle through its constituent features. Accordingly, texts by different authors often can be distinguished from one another, and texts by the same author attributed to him/her based on their linguistic features. Due to the properties of language itself and the very circumstances that enable or prevent individual language use, this level of distinctiveness sometimes may not exist. Thus, it is not always possible to assign texts to their corresponding authors.

2 The State of the Art, Theories and Controversies in the Area

2.1 Quantitative Versus Qualitative

The current debates fall into three different perspectives, at the intersection of which is forensic authorship analysis: (1) the discussion about proper methodology which relates to science per se; (2) concepts and theoretical assumptions coming mainly from linguistics; and (3) other arguments relating to the expert's role, questions of probative value, the evaluation of reports, and the corresponding theoretical framework. The discussions in this area point to the status of forensic linguistics as a forensic science. Accordingly, research also extends to these three areas, albeit to varying degrees.

In the case of linguistic authorship identification, automated authorship attribution, as it is done in the computer sciences, is both a challenge and an opportunity. On the one hand, computer-assisted and computer-driven methods show the potential for applying quantitative methods as presented in Chap. 8; on the other hand, this very fact asks for a differentiated consideration when adopting such methods into the forensic context and applying them to forensic data material.

There has always been consensus on the value of statistical analysis in forensic authorship identification: Statistical analysis confirms the reliability of the analysis independently, shows the significance of occurrences and, to quote Ishihara (2017), allows 'evaluating the probative values of particular quantitative measures' (p. 68). Positions vary on how both linguistic and statistical analysis should be combined and what limits apply to the latter. Both approaches claim to analyse a person's style. Either way, stylistic analysis draws on repeating features, interpreting both frequencies of occurrence and absences as signs of relevance. One crucial difference is the different conceptions of style that computational and linguistic methods have from a linguistic perspective. By looking at the different concepts of style researchers provide, one can deduce what they believe they can achieve with stylistic analyses—that is, what statements can be made about a text and its authorship. The other main difference concerns not the quantification of linguistic features but their definition. In the so-called quantitative or automated approach, which works with automated systems, the relevant features or features sets to be analysed are usually pre-defined or, if it is an unsupervised self-learning system, are defined by the system itself. When authorship identification works with unsupervised systems such as neural networks, it is even more necessary to explain the stylistic relevance of the selected linguistic features. Therefore, a current direction within authorship attribution in computer sciences seeks to translate computer-defined categories into human categorisations to facilitate their understanding—for example, Boenninghoff et al. (2019). Ideally, these computer-defined categories turn out to be linguistic categories that are also relevant for stylistic analysis.

A more relevant discussion for the field relates to linguistics as forensic science and Bayes' theorem as the adequate theoretical framework for forensic sciences in general. Only a few linguistic studies have favoured the likelihood-ratio approach so far, including Queralt (2018) and Ishihara (2014, 2017), who uses n-grams for text comparison analysis, as well as experimental studies by the BKA (Ehrhardt, 2018). Although Bayes' theorem is the mathematical way to work with conditional probabilities, the essential point here is that conditioning inference and reasoning are core parts of the scientist's work with empirical data. The concept is thus by no means limited to use with automated systems, but also explicitly encompasses the knowledge and experience of the scientist (Biedermann et al., 2017; ENFSI Guideline, 2015). Therefore, the lack of reference corpora for different linguistic features is not thought to be an obstacle to applying the concept itself. It is quite intriguing that, in (forensic) linguistics as part of the humanities, the close relationship to the philosophical foundations of the discussion has so far neither been generally recognised nor made fruitful for linguistics as a forensic science.

2.2 Concepts of Style

This chapter defines style with a functional and pragmatic framework (Brinker et al., 2018; Sandig, 2006). Style refers to how people express themselves linguistically in a given communicative situation depending on context, participants, topic, social role and the communicative goals they pursue. In forensic authorship identification, the focus of analysis is often mainly on the producer (the author) of the style. However, any concept or theory of style should include both the reader and the text because the text and its genre have a sustainable influence on the author's choices and the reader's expectations. As for the role of the recipient in identifying style, any concept should address how the recognition of style depends on the reader's stylistic knowledge (Spillner, 2009).

It is not surprising that although style is a fundamental concept in authorship identification, its definition together with its conceptual basis and analysis are far from uniform. The prevailing notion of style in forensic linguistics and linguistic stylistics is that of choice among linguistic elements known to the individual in a specific communicative situation. This notion presupposes existing variants the author can choose from and implies a difference between language use and style. If such variants do not exist, an author's language use cannot be considered style.

What determines a linguistic choice and how to explain it is defined differently. If we consider linguistic choice a type of habit and say that habits result from prior deliberate choices, then linguistic choice may be considered cognitive behaviour. By contrast, if we think of a person's linguistic behaviour as a social activity within a norm or deviating from a norm, then linguistic choice is called stylistic. Such differentiation may reflect different research backgrounds, but they are not the primary cause of the current methodological issues arising from the forensic application of stylistic analysis (Grant, 2021, p. 560). Both conceptualisations throw light to different aspects relating to how a person uses language and how people develop habits in correlation with what a specific norm allows.

From stylistic research, it is known that people usually vary in the way they use language and their stylistic relevant decisions compared to others and themselves. This characteristic makes 'style' be mostly about variation and less about uniformity or constancy. Linguistic variation of this kind—both inter-author and intra-author variation—is described in terms of similarity and typicality. It can occur in different forms to different degrees and can generate a very distinctive style in some cases, but a more generic style in others. It is this fundamental characteristic of style that poses an unsolvable dilemma to stylistic analysis per se. If authors are similar to themselves and dissimilar to others, then their intra-author variation is low, and their inter-author variation is high. This situation is the optimal situation to achieve good results in a forensic text comparison, whatever method is applied (Schmid et al., 2015, p. 124). However, the three remaining options are less satisfying. Firstly, authors can be similar to themselves and others, meaning that individual written style lacks distinctiveness. Alternatively, authors may also be neither similar to themselves nor others, and texts written by one author cannot be attributed to him correctly because of the lack of similarity. A third case involves authors which are not similar to themselves (high intra-author variation) but *are* similar to others (low inter-author variation), causing the texts of one author to be falsely attributed to one or more other authors. When comparing two author's styles, the term similarity refers to features both authors exhibit, while typicality addresses how common and widespread these linguistic features are in the relevant population of authors (Ehrhardt, 2018, p. 187). Low typicality describes an uncommon feature, such as the use of the German word *Kabel* ('cable', *neuter*) with the masculine article *der* instead of its neutral form *das*. High typicality, by contrast, would describe a widespread spelling error, such as writing the conjunction *dass* ('that') with a single *s*. Consequently, texts sharing only widespread errors can produce a very similar error distribution while originating from different sources. Lastly, it should be mentioned that the description of style by the parameters of typicality and similarity allows a direct use of likelihood ratios, see Jessen (2018) for voice comparison and for a more detailed explanation.

2.3 Feature Selection

Before starting with the linguistic analysis, the indicational value of the stylistic features employed should be cleared. One way is to define beforehand a set of features to be applied to the text which identify style as something that is only realised within that set, and which describe style as rather stable and unchanging. This idea is often favoured by approaches that claim that style is unique and distinctive, drawing parallels with fingerprinting and DNA analysis. Most prominent among the established features are (for various reasons) function words and token n-grams of varying length. As these features have proven particularly well-suited to distinguish between different authors, they are also used in the case study in Chap. 8. However, even if one agrees to a pre-defined set of features, a problem remains with the differentiation between language use and style. Studies favouring a quantitative approach often do not sufficiently consider how the usually applied feature sets acquired their stylistic value other than through statistical significance. In order to determine why they represent individual non-class characteristics—stylistic features—in contrast to commonly shared class characteristics of a language or dialect, one would have to explain what caused their appearance in the first place.

An alternative to pre-determining features is to extract them from the questioned texts, thus defining their relevance from scratch every time. This approach perceives style as something formed differently in various texts depending on the text function, context, and author's goals and, accordingly, it cannot be bound to a pre-defined set of features. We know from the long tradition of stylistic research that many features have been analysed—a comprehensive list is provided in McMenamin (1993). Hence the linguist will regard those linguistic features as potentially relevant in any new text and closely examine them. Both approaches work on the hypothesis that linguistic features which have proved relevant in the past will also be relevant in the future. The two views differ in that the first—which often is associated with the 'quantitative' or 'automated' approach—assumes that the pre-defined features have a given stylistic value, while for many of those who prefer the so-called qualitative approach, any feature is regarded as potential feature that may—or may not—acquire a stylistic value.

Following the latter view, the set of features applied is open in principle, and the definition of the stylistic features of a text does not precede the analysis but is part of it. While both perspectives consider the combinations of features relevant in determining an author's style, the functional-pragmatic approach would go further and seek to identify stylistic traits that evolve from combinations of features with similar functions across different linguistic levels (Sandig, 2006).

2.4 Idiolect

Nearly any study on authorship analysis discusses the concept of idiolect at some point. The term focuses on the individual whose language activity we can observe (Hockett, 1960). Any analysis of any written or spoken linguistic event is, in fact, the analysis of an individual's language at a given moment. However, one cannot understand the individual's language without referring to the language of others. According to Hazen (2006), some researchers, depending on their research focus, emphasise the relationship between idiolect and dialect/sociolect whereby both idiolect and dialect are considered abstractions derived from the analysis of many individuals' language. Other researchers argue that the idiolect exclusively refers to the individual part of a language. A major criticism of the applicability of the concept of idiolect is that it is not possible to describe any idiolect in full (Coulthard, 2004). These concerns are understandable only if idiolect is understood to include those linguistic choices which are potentially at the individual's disposal but which do not become evident, a definition given by Bloch (1948). To avoid these methodological problems and to label what is realised by an individual at a given time, Turell (2010) has suggested the compound term 'idiolectal style'.

However, even though linguistic choices are inherently individual, they do not necessarily lead to a distinctive use of language, as the term 'idiolectal style' may imply. Therefore, the term 'idiolect' should be used for those instances that refer to how the language system and the individual's language use relate. The term 'style', by contrast, refers primarily to how an individual uses language and not so much to the fact that it is the individual who uses language. If one wants to refer to linguistic aspects that appear to be genuine idiosyncrasies, then the expression 'individual style' should be preferred. Rather than idiolect, it is 'register' that is directly related to style because both terms refer to the concrete use of language in a communicative situation (Felder, 2016).

Some researchers point out that because it is the individual who uses language, this use is unique and should, therefore, in principle, be distinctive and identifiable from others only if enough data were available (Wright, 2013). Interestingly, these assumptions are most common not among linguists but rather among computer scientists (Fobbe, 2021). Even if one assumes with Coulthard (2013, pp. 446–447) that the individual combination of linguistic elements is unique in its entirety, this does not solve the dilemma of stylistics: individuals can share common choices of linguistic forms when communicating. Moreover, the assumption of uniqueness is not verifiable in a strict sense, and its axiomatic character shows its origins lie in philosophy instead of empiricism (Cole, 2009; Robertson et al., 2016).

3 Applied Methods and General Considerations

This section presents three established methods of analysis and explains the general procedure when analysing a forensic text. The three methods are error analysis, stylistic analysis and text-structure analysis, which is part of stylistic analysis but refers to cross-sentence phenomena at the text level.

Error analysis is very closely related to research on second language acquisition, and the taxonomies of error identification, description and evaluation from language acquisition have been adopted for the most part. An influential distinction introduced by Corder (1967) is between errors and mistakes: while errors reflect the subject's lack of linguistic knowledge, mistakes can be potentially corrected by learners. Another research question is how to assess a linguistic form as an error in terms of form appropriateness, its frequency of occurrence, and how much the error jeopardises successful communication (Kleppin, 2010). Equally relevant is the linguistic rule or norm to which a given linguistic form refers because the stricter the rule and the more prescriptive the norm, the more likely a violation will be considered an error. The interpretation of errors made by native speakers and second language learners differs because the conditions of the errors' occurrence may be different. Language transfer phenomena, for example, are most typical to non-native speakers.

Error analysis covers linguistic levels from punctuation to lexical errors and may also include stylistic phenomena related to word choice. If the author's writing competence is low, text analysis usually provides more clues related to errors than to style. By contrast, if the author's writing competence is high, stylistic analysis dominates the examination and error analysis may be backgrounded or even omitted. The stylistic analysis does not evaluate a person's use of language as correct or incorrect but as appropriate or inappropriate compared to linguistic norms and social conventions. The stylistic analysis begins with the text formatting and ends with content structure and intertextuality aspects. Text-structure analysis provides information on how the author approaches the communicative goal—for example, the strategy he uses. Furthermore, text-structure analysis looks at the text as an independent entity and examines how its pragmatic function is expressed by the underlying speech acts, how these acts are related to the content-structure arrangement, whether they are realised directly or indirectly and what linguistic means the author uses to express them. The analysis also looks for coherence, logical gaps in the content, implicatures, topic changes, repetitions and omissions. Text-structure, genre and text-type analyses are relevant because they help distinguish between the features that are class features and thereby, part of the text-type requirements, and those that are potentially individual features (Brinker et al., 2018).

Every analysis begins with a critical look at both the material and the client's question. The enquiry must include a linguistically answerable question and, if necessary, be rephrased. If the client asks for a text comparison, the enquiry has to reflect one of two hypotheses. The H0 (or Hp as the prosecution's hypothesis) will be that both texts have common authorship (were written by the same author or suspect), and the alternative H1 (or Hd as the defence's hypothesis) that the text in question was not written by the suspect but by someone else. How to answer these hypotheses is dealt with at the end of Sect. 4.

Furthermore, the material must be suitable for analysis. Unbalanced material will affect the results in two ways. If there is enough material, sufficient features can usually be extracted, but many variables will not appear in both texts/text groups if only limited data is available. Material of different text types can also influence the results, as text types require different stylistic choices, the variety of which can render texts no longer comparable. Texts should be legible printouts or copies; any third-party additions should be marked and recognisable. If questioned or anonymous material contains more than one text, each text has to be compared with every other text as a matter of principle. The client's statement that some texts are written by the same author is a strong indication but should not be taken for granted, as it cannot be ruled out that the texts come from different sources.

Each text is analysed separately, and its examination should always follow the same steps. In this respect, as McMenamin (2002, p. 120) points out, one ensures that one identifies variations that do not occur in both texts/text groups but only in one of them. Both error and style analysis start with text layout, spelling and punctuation, then deal with word order and formation, syntax and lexis. The analysis of each linguistic level should begin with identifying the features, followed by their description. Only then should explanations be given for their occurrence. Especially in error analysis, descriptions and interpretations of features are often conflated and thus pre-empt what the analysis should only later elaborate.

Even if identifying a feature seems easy, one must be aware that a prerequisite for identification is applying the same norms and rules by which the feature is later determined to be correct, stylistically relevant, insufficient or—as an error—false. Some features are very easy to identify because they refer to familiar concepts or categories—for example 'word' or 'sentence', but this does not necessarily make them 'objective features', as Ainsworth and Juola (2019, p. 1172) argue, unless we think of 'objective' as being intersubjectively valid. Linguistic categories such as 'sentence' have always caused definitional problems in linguistics and computational linguistics because they carry an inherent fuzziness that cannot be eliminated so easily. The analysis in Sect. 4 exemplifies that, for example, lack of punctuation can make it difficult to determine what counts as a sentence.

4 Case Study

The two texts analysed in this section are from a case of severe arson in a city in south-western Germany where an anonymous offender set several fires to stores.[1] He commented on the fires in anonymous e-mails to the state police threatening to continue the arson if the state police did not delete their internet pages. During the investigation, police linked a secured explosive device to an older case of burglary in which an extortion letter had been found at the crime scene. The police wanted a forensic linguist to determine whether the same author could have written the e-mails and the extortion letter. The material for comparison consisted of seven e-mails of about 100 to 250 words each. All e-mails were signed by the pseudonym *roter Kosar* ('Red Kosar'), and they all referred to the same events and earlier e-mails. The first e-mail sent to the police was of a more formal tone while the e-mails that followed grew more and more emotional and came closer to the extortion letter's register.

A first review of the material selected shows that both the first anonymous e-mail and the blackmail letter are very short (67 and 118 words). Therefore, the texts only allow a limited view of the language of their respective authors and the small amount of data only cautious conclusions. If a comparison of texts of this size were to indicate common or different authorship, the expert opinion would lower the statement's degree of probability accordingly. In practice, requests for very short texts may have to be declined due to these methodological limitations.[2]

4.1 The Extortion Letter

The original extortion letter can be read in Fig. 7.1 and its English translation in Fig. 7.2 below.

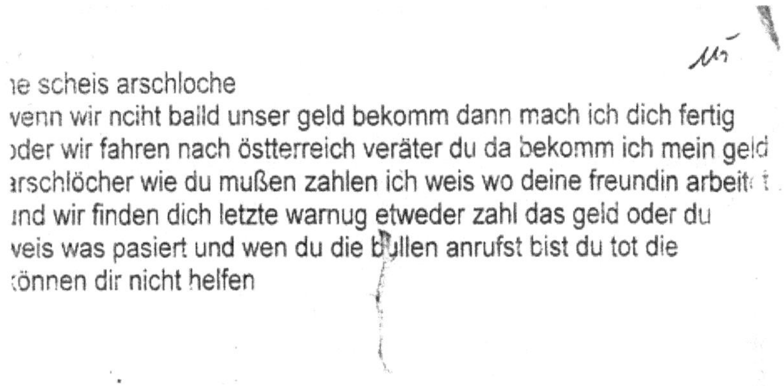
ıe scheis arschloche
venn wir nciht balld unser geld bekomm dann mach ich dich fertig
ɔder wir fahren nach östterreich veräter du da bekomm ich mein geld
ırschlöcher wie du mußen zahlen ich weis wo deine freundin arbeit
ınd wir finden dich letzte warnug etweder zahl das geld oder du
veis was pasiert und wen du die bullen anrufst bist du tot die
können dir nicht helfen

Fig. 7.1 The original extortion letter

1 Hey, fucking asshole,
2 if we don't get our money soon, I'm gonna finish you off
3 or we go to Austria, you traitor, I will get my money there.
4 Assholes like you have to pay. I know where your girlfriend works
5 and we'll find you. Last warning, either you pay the money or you
6 know what will happen, and if you call the cops, you're dead, they
7 can't help you.

Fig. 7.2 English Translation of the original extortion letter

The first part of the analysis comprises the errors found on different linguistic levels. The text contains many misspellings and shows an absence of punctuation. Furthermore, all nouns lack the capitalisation that German orthography demands. The remaining orthographical errors concentrate on the level of grapheme-phoneme-correspondences and show patterns in their distribution, as presented in Table 7.1.

In contrast to the various additions, permutations and omissions of graphemes, including the umlaut, the incorrect representations of the voiceless /s/ point to the application of spelling rules and, thereby, to linguistic knowledge. It is advisable to introduce as little additional information into the text as possible—i.e. we should not use punctuation marks other than commas and always consider alternatives for structuring the text. There are only two instances where a full stop insertion is necessary

Table 7.1 Error distribution

Error description		Word/correct spelling
Additions	inner, duplication	balld / bald ('soon') (2), östterreich / österreich ('Austria') (3)
	final	arschloche /arschloch ('asshole') (1)
Permutations	inner	nihct / nicht ('not') (2)
Omissions	inner, part of affix	ve[r]räter ('traitor') (3), warnu[n]g ('warning') (5), e[n]tweder ('either') (5)
	final	bekomm[en] ('get') (2), wen[n] ('if') (6), weis[t] ('you know') (6)
Substitutions	umlaut	mußen / müssen ('must') (4)
	voiceless /s/	pasiert / passiert ('happens') (6), scheis /scheiß ('shit') (1), weis / weiß ('I know') (4), mußen / müssen ('must') (4)

after *Geld* ('money') and *helfen* ('help'). Both the <ss> and the <ß> are written as <s>, but <ss> is written as <ß> also, while other representations of /s/ are correctly realised as <s>. One could describe this as the irregular application of graphemes that mark the /s/ voiceless under specific conditions. This is a known German orthography problem because it presupposes an understanding of what diphthongs and vowel quantity are. Many people do not learn to follow this rule correctly in school; hence misspellings of /s/ are frequent and expected.

In the next step, we turn to similar words that the author has spelt correctly to determine whether our author is consistent in his spelling. We can deduce the rules that the author knows and those that he does not know. For example, he knows that *Österreich* ('Austria') is written with an umlaut /ö/. Accordingly, the missing /ü/ in *mußen* ('must') is most likely a mistake. The same applies to all other spellings with a correct counterpart such as *nihct* and *nicht*, *wenn* and *wen* and *weis* and *bist*, the latter realising the inflectional morpheme {st} correctly. These findings make it plausible that omitted, permuted and added graphemes are most likely due to the author's typing and lack of spelling competence. As far as the realisations of /s/ are concerned, the author is no exception to other German writers here: he seems to know that there are several spelling rules but is uncertain about their exact content and application.

The next step is stylistic analysis. The present text has only three minor structuring elements: the line break after the salutation line and the connection between the end of the sentence and the end of the line (after *arbeitet* and *Geld*). The author's abandonment of punctuation affects the syntactic analysis of the letter and its interpretation. To enable the syntax analysis, we have to make additional assumptions, such as defining where each sentence ends. It is advisable to introduce as little additional information into the text as possible—that is, we should not use punctuation marks other than commas and always consider alternatives for structuring the text. There are only two instances where a full stop insertion is necessary after *Geld* ('money') and *helfen* ('help'). In the third instance (after *dich* 'you'), where a full stop seems reasonable, the author appeals to the reader once again with the words *Letzte Warnung* ('last warning').

The syntax of the letter is relatively simple. The text contains five separate main clauses and two types of hypotactic structures—a relative clause and a conditional clause, both occuring twice. The author uses the conjunctions *oder* ('or') and *und* ('and') to connect additional clauses, but these connections are relatively loose because the added clauses are syntactically independent.

The same applies to the sentence content because the conjunctions introduce new information that is only loosely linked to what is already known to the reader: In the first paragraph, the author talks about 'finishing off' the victim if he does not pay the money, but then the author defines an alternative possibility by saying that they would go to Austria. Similarly, in the second paragraph, the author claims to know where the victim's girlfriend works and then adds that they will find him, something one would not necessarily associate with the girlfriend's workplace. In the last paragraph, the conjunction *und* ('and') introduces new content as the author tells the victim not to call the police. The overall impression is that the author uses conjunctions to signal to the reader that there is more to say and keeps his story going.

Having analysed the syntax, we continue with the author's vocabulary and register. The language is colloquial standard German, containing pejorative expressions such as *fertigmachen* ('to finish off') and *Bullen* ('cops'). Both the lexis and the syntax are closely based on spoken language, which suits the communicative situation framing the text well. Blackmail letters represent a special form of private communication, although many blackmailers tend to adapt official templates. At the same time, the secrecy and informality of the communicative situation are often an encouragement for the perpetrator not to impose any restrictions on his choice of words.

The author's reference to himself changes between *ich* ('I') and *wir* ('we') which is also a typical feature of blackmail letters. Extortionists tend to present themselves as part of a (dangerous) group, but most authors cannot uphold that impression throughout the whole text. Dern (2009, p. 146) reports crime statistics that confirm that the average perpetrator acts alone, is male and middle-aged.

The text does not seem to be an initial letter because the author refers to the fact that the payment has still not been made and provides a last warning. This fact implies that other warnings have been given at some point before. Moreover, the author refers to shared knowledge several times, for instance, by accusing the victim of being a traitor or by mentioning the victim's girlfriend. Shared knowledge could also explain why the author does not specify the exact amount of money and why he refers to the money using the determiners *unser* ('our'), *mein* ('my') and *das* ('the') instead of the zero article. Using *ein* ('a') or the zero article combined with nouns, people can bring new discourse objects and topics that are unknown to the other participants into a discussion. Either the author named the sum in an earlier letter or the recipient knows it because he owes it to the author. The use of the possessive pronouns *mein* ('my') and *unser* ('our') supports this interpretation.

The exact sum of the money demanded is not specified, nor is the threat. The author threatens the reader to finish him off, face death and face the consequences ('you know what will happen'). These threats differ concerning concreteness; the meaning of the expression *fertigmachen*, translated here with 'to finish somebody off' can cover psychic pressure, bullying, and beating someone up, but it does not mean killing that person. The allusion of knowing what will happen leaves it to the recipient to come up with an explanation, and the expression *du bist tot* ('you're dead') describes the result but not the action preceding it. The threats refer to different scenarios and leave an impression of indeterminacy to the recipient. While syntax and lexis have provided first insights into the author's communicative strategy, an examination of the text and its communicative function as a whole may even provide more. If we think of the text as an instrument to master the communicative situation successfully, its design may reveal the author's linguistic strategies. From a pragmatic perspective, every text has a function. The function here is to appeal—that is, the author tries to make the reader do what he wants him to do. Research on blackmail letters by Brinker (2002) has identified some obligatory and optional so-called thematic patterns by which the content is structured and the basic speech acts of 'threat' and 'demand' are realised. While the 'demand for a specific action'—for example to pay money—and the threat—announcement of a counterreaction in case the demand is not fulfilled—for example the sum is not paid—are obligatory because they constitute the act of blackmailing, other aspects are optional but appear frequently. These aspects comprise—in Brinker's terms, five so-called thematic patterns: (1) 'handover procedures'—or ways of making contact, (2) 'attribution of responsibility', (3) 'assurance of determination', (4) 'request of compliance' and (5) the author's 'self-presentation' (cf. Fobbe, 2020).

The demand is repeated four times: once addressing the victim directly by *zahl das Geld* ('pay the money'), indirectly and in a general manner *arschlöcher wie du müssen zahlen* ('assholes like you must pay') and twice from the offender's perspective in *unser Geld bekommen/bekomm ich mein Geld* ('we get our money'/'I get my money'). The threat is also expressed in different ways. The reference to the girlfriend's workplace and the subsequent threat to find the victim represent the pattern of 'assurance of determination'. The pattern 'request of compliance' is realised by the warning not to call the police.

Despite the letter's briefness, several words appear twice in the letter: the insult *arschloch* ('asshole'), the payment *Geld* ('money') and receipt of the money, as expressed by *bekommen* ('to get'). These occurrences have their direct counterparts in the text pattern described above. Together they yield the dominant pattern of repetition which is a salient stylistic trait of this text. The lack of punctuation marks that would structure the text for both author and reader, combined with the vague references and the repetition gives the reader the impression of a rather spontaneous flow of thought that lacks structure and reflection.

4.2 The Comparison Text

The analysis of the comparison text undergoes the same steps. Firstly, the material is analysed for its errors and afterwards for its style. Again, we have to refrain from comparing our findings too early with the known text. Only when we have completed the analysis we can compare both. It is clear that we have the first findings in mind, but we must be aware of them and work on not being biased—that is, not to look only for elements that would support our hypothesis by matching the findings described earlier (Figs. 7.3 and 7.4).

The errors and mistakes are relating to the absence of punctuation, lack of capitalisations of nouns and several misspellings. The first categorisation of these errors shows the distribution depicted in Table 7.2.

Another four mistakes refer to word-formation and syntax. Although nominal compounds have to be written together or with a hyphen in German, the author writes *rlp polizei* ('rlp-police'), *polizei seite*, *polizei seiten* ('police page(s)') instead of *RLP-Polizei*, and *Polizeiseite(n)*. The syntactical error is a syntactical breach (or anacoluthon) in line 12 *als zeichen meiner das sie mich Ernst nehmen* ('as a sign of my that you take me seriously'), leaving the clause incomplete.

Stylistically, the letter's syntax is simple; it has six main clauses, two if-clauses, another two subordinate clauses with *dass* ('that'). Since German word order allows many variations, the author's syntactical decisions cannot be called incorrect, although they result in deviations from standard word order. Still they represent tendencies but, as they reflect systematic variation, are potentially significant (McMenamin, 2021, p. 552) and could develop an individualising character if more material were available. For example, the author keeps the phrasal expression *Brände legen* ('to set fires') apart, although according to German standard word order, the object *Brände* ('fires') is positioned close to the verb as in *werde ich in der Umgebung mehrere Brände legen* ('I will set several fires in the area') because of its phrasal expression character. Other cases of word order variations are *also sofort werden die Fahndungen gelöscht* ('So, immediately the APBs are to be deleted') instead of *die Fahndungen werden sofort gelöscht* ('The APBs are to be deleted immediately'), and the

die seite der rlp polizei wird sofort gelöscht
sollten sie dieser
auforderung nicht nachkommen werde ich mehrere brände in der umgebung klegen
dies hat zur folge das die ganzen
geschäfte und wohungen mit schweren schäden rechnen müssen ebenso werde ich brände in autos
garagen haäusern
und geschäften logen in ihrem
interesse loschen sie sofort die
polizei seiten
i#im besonderen die fahnden die
sollen sofort gelöscht werden wenn icht lege
ich brände als zeichen miner das sie mich ernst nehmen wird ich diese
woche eine ne brand legen und ich werde isie wieder anschreiben
also sofort werden die fahndunegn
gelöscht und die polizei seite
inherhalb von 24 stunden ansonsten haben sie die schäden zu verantworten
gezeichnet der
rote kosar

Fig. 7.3 The first anonymous e-mail

The rlp [Rhineland-Palatinate] police page will be deleted immediately
If you do not comply with this
request, I will set several fires in the area
As a result, all
stores and apartments will be severely damaged, and I will set fires in cars
garages, houses
and stores In your
interest you should immediately delete the
police pages
especially the APBs [all-points bulletins], which
should be deleted immediately, if not, I will set
fires as a sign of my that you take me seriously, I will set a fire this
week and I will write you again
So, immediately the APBs
are to be deleted and the police page
within 24 hours, otherwise you have to answer for the damages
signed the
red kosar

Fig. 7.4 The English translation

Table 7.2 Error distribution

Error description		Word/correct spelling
Additions	initial	klegen / legen ('set') (2) isie / Sie ('you' polite) (13)
	inner	haäusern / Häusern ('houses') (6)
	inner, combined with symbol	i#im /im ('in') (10)
	final, combined with blank	eine ne / einen ('a' acc.) (13)
Permutations	inner	fahndunegn / Fahndungen ('APBs') (14)
Omissions	initial	[n]icht ('not') (11)
	inner	m[e]iner ('my', gen.) (12)
	inner, part of affix	woh[n]ungen ('apartments') (5), au[f] forderung (3), fahnd[ung]en ('APBs') (10)
	final	wird[e] ('I will') (12)
Substitutions	inner	logen / legen ('set') (7), inherhalb / innerhalb ('within') (16), wird / werde ('I will') (12)
	inner, umlaut	loschen / löschen ('delete') (8)
	final, voiceless /s/	das / dass ('that', conj.) (4, 12)

positioning of the temporal adverbial phrase *innerhalb von 24 Stunden* ('within 24 hours') at the right end of the sentence.

At first sight, the author uses a neutral or even formal register. Instead of single verbs, he uses several prepositional phrases and noun phrases with nominalisations combined with a function verb. This use is typical of a professional domain and formal register, for example: *einer Aufforderung nachkommen* ('to comply with a request'), *Brände legen* ('to set fires'), *zur Folge haben* ('result in'), *mit schweren Schäden rechnen* ('to expect severe damages'). Other formal expressions are: *im Besonderen* ('especially'), *in Ihrem Interesse* ('in your interest'), *als Zeichen meiner* ('as a sign of my'), the verb *anschreiben* instead of neutral *schreiben* with dative ('write to somebody'), the use of *gezeichnet* ('signed') to sign a digital document and *Schäden zu verantworten haben* ('to have to answer for the damages'). A search of the web and two German online databases (Juris and Cosmas II) links this latter phrase to economics and law domains (especially liability law).[3]

Apart from the word choice, the syntax of the letter also points to a formal register. One instance is the use of *haben* ('have') in *haben Sie die Schäden zu verantworten* ('you have to answer for the damages'), the other is the use of the modal verb in *sollten Sie (nicht)* ('if you do (not)'/'should you fail to') for a conditional clause. A third structure typical of formal writing is the use of passive voice. This is particularly used in the author's demands to delete the police website: *sofort werden die x gelöscht* ('immediately the x's are to be deleted'), *sollen sofort gelöscht werden* ('should be deleted immediately'), *wird sofort gelöscht* ('will be deleted immediately').

A closer look to the text reveals that several colloquial expressions are also present in the letter. For instance, there is the use of *die* ('they') as a demonstrative pronoun, which is part of spoken German. Another example is the before-mentioned anacoluthon where the author fails to complete the more formal structure *als Zeichen meiner* ('as a sign of my') with the word *Entschlossenheit* ('determination'). Instead, the author starts anew with the more colloquial expression *ernst nehmen* ('to take somebody seriously') in line 12. Another two examples of spoken language are *und* ('and'), through which he adds new information to the paragraph, and the discourse particle *also* ('so'), which closes a topic or a conversation sequence. Furthermore, there is the use of *ganzen Geschäfte* ('all stores') with *ganz* meaning 'whole', which in written language should only be used when referring to uncountable nouns but not to countable nouns in which case *all* is the preferred option.

>The lexis analysis also yields the repetition of certain words and phrases such as *einen Brand/Brände legen* ('to set fire'), *Schäden* ('damages'), and *Geschäfte* ('stores'). This repetition is not arbitrary but instead intentional because it is closely linked to the thematic text patterns 'announcement of action' and 'attribution of responsibility'. As the reader can see, the arrangement of the text patterns follows a certain repetitive pattern. First, the author states the demand; second, the author anticipates the possibility that the victim will not follow his instructions, and threatens to set fires. The next sentence represents the optional thematic pattern of 'attribution of responsibility' and is closed by another threat or 'announcement of action' (Table 7.3).

Table 7.3 Thematic patterns of the letter's first section

Text	Thematic text pattern
die seite der rlp polizei wird sofort gelöscht ('The rlp [Rhineland-Palatinate] police page will be deleted immediately')	demand for action
sollten sie dieser auforderung nicht nachkommen ('If you do not comply with this request') werde ich mehrere brände in der umgebung klegen ('I will set several fires in the area')	indirect attribution of responsibility, announcement of action
dies hat zur folge das die ganzen geschäfte und wohungen mit schweren schäden rechnen müssen ('As a result, all stores and apartments will be severely damaged')	assurance of determination
ebenso werde ich brände in autos garagen haäusern und geschäften logen ('and I will set fires in cars, garages, houses and stores')	announcement of action

The same sequence of patterns can be found in the following paragraph (see Table 7.4). The author repeats both the demand for deleting the internet pages and his announcement of setting fires if the police do not comply. Then the author assures the victim of his determination by threatening again that he will set a fire and informs the reader of the letter about contacting him later.

In the third section, the author again states his demand and holds the victim responsible for potential damage. The text closes with a self-presentation in the form of a pseudonym. The author does not justify the crime, nor does he provide further details about himself (Table 7.5).

Table 7.4 Thematic patterns of the letter's second section

Text	Thematic text pattern
in ihrem interesse loschen sie sofort die polizei seiten i#im besonderen die fahnden die sollen sofort gelöscht werden ('In your interest, you should immediately delete the police pages especially the APBs, which should be deleted immediately')	demand for action
wenn icht lege ich brände ('if not, I will set fires')	indirect attribution of responsibility, announcement of action
als zeichen miner das sie mich ernst nehmen wird ich diese woche eine ne brand legen und ich werde isie wieder anschreiben ('as a sign of my that you take me seriously, I will set a fire this week and I will write you again')	assurance of determination, announcement of action, contact

Table 7.5 Thematic patterns of the letter's closing section

Text	Thematic text pattern
also sofort werden die fahndunegn gelöscht und die polizei seite inherhalb von 24 stunden ('So, immediately the APBs are to be deleted and the police page within 24 hours')	demand for action
ansonsten haben sie die schäden zu verantworten gezeichnet der rote kosar ('otherwise you have to answer for the damages, signed the red kosar')	attribution of responsibility, self-presentation

4.3 Findings and Discussion

4.3.1 Author Profiling

If the client is interested in knowing the author's social background, his attitudes or interests, then he may ask for an author profiling report. In the present case, an author profile is created on the anonymous arsonist based on his first e-mail for illustrative purposes. This e-mail is full of spelling mistakes but not grammatical or lexical mistakes that would reflect a non-native-speaker competence. Therefore, we can reasonably argue that the author is a native speaker of German. We further claim that the author has an average educational background and does not seem to have too much writing experience because he does not meet the stylistic requirements of a written standard language. However, he is familiar with expressions that belong to a professional domain and formal style. The wording of the expression *Schäden zu verantworten haben* ('to have to answer for damages') could indicate that he is somehow acquainted with liability law issues. His geographical origin cannot be determined, as the text provides no evidence of dialectal or regional vocabulary. However, the fact that he uses the abbreviation *rlp* for Rhineland-Palatinate and claims an interest in the state police pages point to a person who is, at least, familiar with the region. The recourse to formal expressions and the absence of any teenage language makes it more likely that the author is an adult.

As mentioned above, the findings from the analysis done point to categories that are closely related to the acquisition of writing competence. It should be noted that there are also attempts to determine these categories, including gender, through automated approaches. A major problem here is defining the relevant social categories via linguistic features and strongly context-dependent variables. Accordingly, in a recent study on the suitability of automated approaches, Nini (2018) advises 'focusing not on techniques but linguistic explanations, theories and knowledge, with particular attention to the forensic context' (p. 54).

Further reflections on the material may be considered hints that can support insights gleaned by other forensic disciplines participating in the investigation. As we can see, the author tends to repeat himself, and within his repetitions he focuses on his demand and setting fires. Nevertheless, there is a certain redundancy and inconsistency that cannot be explained by repetition alone. By mentioning the stores and apartments first, one thinks of them as the main targets. From a semantic and referential perspective, therefore, the houses mentioned afterwards seem redundant, because here the more specific (apartment, store) precedes the less specific (house) unless the author is thinking of houses as opposed to apartment buildings and stores. This assumption finds some support in the additional mention of stores in that sentence ('As a result, all stores and apartments will be severely damaged, and I will set fires in cars, garages houses and stores'). The author also speaks of setting fires in cars, but this would require him to be inside the car, which seems rather unlikely. Taken together, one can reasonably argue that the author's focus is mainly on the stores and less on other objects.

Another point is the author's demand itself. It is a very atypical demand, and it remains unclear what purpose it will serve. The same applies to the demand to delete the all-points bulletins, since these exist regardless of any online presence. Nevertheless, the author's communicative approach to the situation at hand takes the linguistic form he believes suitable. The atypical demand and repeated threat thus would seem to have a particular meaning. Even if this meaning cannot be determined linguistically, it can be presumed to exist since, according to Keller (2018, pp. 209–210), all communication is grounded on the rationality principle and is always meaningful. At this point, these linguistic observations may lead to relevant non-linguistic conclusions, support hypotheses of investigating officers or can independently substantiate their findings.

4.3.2 Text Comparison

A comparison of texts always refers to the constellations of errors and style markers, and the range of variation. While single markers may point to possible common authorship in the first place, their value must be proven based on the whole range of variations afterwards. The comparison of the identified types of errors in both texts shows corresponding types. Due to data sparseness, errors found in one text will likely have non-occurrences in the other, thus limiting the findings' comparability. Therefore, we look both for identical errors and identical types of errors, for instance, the different spellings of /s/. The misspelling of *dass* as *das* does not appear in the extortion letter, and the misspellings of <ss> and <ß> have no counterparts in the anonymous e-mail. However, here like there, the author displays uncertainty in the spelling rules of /s/. Therefore, the findings in the e-mail do not contradict those in the extortion letter.

The omitted, added or permuted letters refer only to the grapheme-phoneme-level in both texts, do not reflect grammatical errors, and cover identical or similar categories (ss/ß, umlaut, omissions in words with *-ung* and prefixes). It is of equal importance that other German orthography issues do not play a role in either text (e.g. *h* as a marker of vowel lengthening), and several words occur correctly written too. Consequently, we can state that both texts share similar error constellations whose origins can be explained accordingly. Finally, both letters share the absence of capitalisation of nouns and sentence-initial words.

An Internet query was conducted on misspellings of voiceless /s/ and missing umlaut to support the observations made empirically. The query showed that *weis* instead of *weiß* ('I know') is relatively common among writers, while the spellings *scheis* instead of *scheiß* ('shit') and *pasiert* instead of *passiert* ('happens') are significantly less frequent.[4] Furthermore, the phrases *hat zur Folge das* and *hat zur Folge dass* ('as a result') were searched on the Internet to determine the relative frequency of <das> instead of <dass>. A subsequent query in BKA's database of forensic texts yielded similar results: Only 176 of about 6200 texts had a consistent lower case. In this subset of 176 texts, 63 texts contained writings of *das* instead of *dass*, and in 24 of the 63 texts, spellings of <s> instead of <ss> were present. A final combined retrieval including umlaut only identified the texts in question and another text. In summary, although each of the errors occurs with varying frequency, the constellation of findings shows relatively low typicality and thus, indicates joint authorship. Another commonality to both letters is the lack of punctuation. As a result, both convey their message in a relatively unstructured way. The syntax of both letters is simple and contains only first-degree subordinate clauses.

There are differences in the vocabulary in terms of formality which result from the type of relationship between author and addressee in their respective communicative situations. While the blackmail letter leaves the reader with the impression that the author and victim are somehow familiar, the e-mail's addressee is not personally known to the author. The e-mail is directed to the police as an institution and contains some formal expressions but does not meet formal writing requirements. Both texts use words that belong to the spoken language; they also share the use of *und* ('and') to add a new aspect to the subject, a task which in written language is usually performed by adverbs.

The comparison of text patterns yields more similarities than differences. In both texts, the demand and the announced action are repeated several times, partly verbatim. Unlike in the blackmail letter, which offers different future actions, there is only one in the e-mail that the author describes again and again with the same words. These differences might point to the stage of planning the author had reached when writing the letter.

Taken together, it is the corresponding types of typos and mistakes, the joint lack of formal structure and content combined with repetition that speak for common authorship. The latter, text-structure-related features also reflect a similar strategic approach to a threatening scenario in both texts. The differences in lexis observed so far together with the non-occurrences of identical misspellings or conjunctions are caused by data sparseness and explained by the different communication partners and different contexts.

4.3.3 Evaluation of the Findings within the Framework of a Probability Scale

For several reasons, a statement on authorship based on a text comparison cannot be made categorically—yes versus no—but only in degrees of probability. Firstly, at least theoretically, one has to reckon with the fact that the text under scrutiny may have been written by someone else who has not provided any reference material. Thus, the text comparison works always under the premise of a so-called open set scenario. Secondly, the characteristics of language and style do not allow any identification in the strict sense based on linguistic features only, and thirdly, there are the requirements that originate from the expert's role.

Commonly used probability scales are ordinal scales with verbally expressed degrees—or levels. The probability scale applied here uses the following levels, starting with 'slightly high probability' as the lowest:[5]

with slightly high probability
with moderately high probability
with high probability
with very high probability
with exceedingly high probability

If the findings are inconclusive, pointing to neither direction, they are described by the term *non-liquet*.

Comparing the texts has revealed significant similarities in the range of variation at all linguistic levels and no significant dissimilarities. A significant dissimilarity would have been a higher level of spelling proficiency, the use of punctuation, a more complex sentence structure, and a message conveyed precisely with no redundancies. The limited size of the texts (67 and 118 words) and the non-occurrences of some variables result in a lower degree of probability, here phrased as 'with moderately high probability'.

In contrast to interval scales, whose intervals between levels are the same across the entire scale, the intervals of ordinal scales vary, and their interpretation, according to Nordgaard (2012, p. 5), 'often suffers from subjectivity', in the sense that, in theory, in two largely identical cases the attribution of the corresponding level could render different. However, these scales and their use in the law sciences, social sciences or the humanities cannot be compared directly to those applied in the natural sciences, for instance to physical or chemical matters. The applied scale levels here cannot be defined in terms of how many and which features should be present to support the expert's assessment, as the relevant characteristics and their variations only emerge from the analysis. Therefore, McMenamin's (2002, pp. 126–127) assessment criteria—such as 'few', 'some', 'substantial' similarities/dissimilarities; 'no limitations present'—can be taken as a reasonable tool for the elaboration of the conclusions.

Current probability scales often state the probability in words such as 'the same person likely wrote the texts'. Strictly speaking, this wording would be incompatible with an expert's role, since it draws evidentiary conclusions related to the case and not just to the evidence. As mentioned earlier, criticism of such formulations is part of a cross-disciplinary discussion about the appropriate theoretical framework to the forensic expert's work, namely on the deployment of Bayes' theorem and the use of likelihood ratios. A more appropriate formulation—as provided in the ENFSI Guideline—would thus refer to the hypotheses on the evidence alone and express the expert's degree of certainty about which one of the hypotheses being true given the evidence; or, in other words, to what extent (moderately, strongly, among other options) the evidence supports one of the hypotheses but not the other.

In the case discussed above the results of the linguistic text comparison corroborated the link between the arson and the burglary (where the extortion letter had been found). A subsequent search of the suspect's house identified several items the man had reported stolen at the burglary. He was an Austrian who had lived in the area for some years and was constantly in financial difficulties (Heinz, 2007b, p. 103).

5 Conclusions and Suggestions for further Research

This chapter aimed to introduce the reader to the topic of authorship identification from a qualitative perspective. After pointing out focal issues in the current debate, a case study explained the main qualitative methods in more detail. While errors and stylistic features are central to the analysis, pragmatic aspects such as text-structure analysis have not yet been generally integrated into the forensic analysis of texts. This area invites further research. Another desideratum is the suitable reference corpora. Although the World Wide Web has established itself as a reference corpus for forensic issues, there are still no corpora on error distribution in adult writers (for instance) and other writing style-related issues. To conclude with Robertson et al. (2016, pp. 180–181), more attention should also be paid to the role of scientific interpretation as such. Both as a scientific technique and as part of the theoretical framework, interpretation of evidence is fundamental to those who work as linguists in a forensic setting.

Notes

1. A detailed description of the investigation that includes all seven e-mails and the extortion letter is provided in Heinz (2007a, 2007b).
2. Due to space restrictions, the case analysis only includes the questioned text and the first e-mail. To keep the comparison authentic, the statement about the similarity of the error distribution shows the small amount of data, although there are exact equivalents in the other e-mails.
3. https://www.juris.de/, https://cosmas2.ids-mannheim.de/cosmas2-web/faces/home.xhtml. Juris is a legal database, and Cosmas II an annotated corpus of German newspapers, including digital content such as Wikipedia. The phrase mentioned appears in contexts where participants debate who is liable for the respective damage. These discussions do not exclusively refer to law issues in the strict sense but also politics, economy, and people generally in charge who can be held responsible for damages.
4. The results of the Internet search were: *scheis* 217,000 vs *scheiß* 6,610,000; *ich weis* 2,180,000 vs *ich weiß* 34,700,000; *pasiert* 174,000 vs *passiert* 67,800,000, and *hat zur folge das* 47,200 vs *hat zur folge dass* 10,200,000.
5. The English version of the scale is partly based on the translation given by Köller et al. (2004) and partly on the ENFSI Guideline's formulations.

References

Ainsworth, J., & Juola, P. (2019). Who wrote this?: Modern forensic authorship analysis a model for valid forensic science. *Washington University Law Review, 96*, 1161–1189. https://openscholarship.wustl.edu/law_lawreview/vol96/iss5/10

Biedermann, A., Bozza, S., Taroni, F., & Aitken, C. (2017). The meaning of justified subjectivism and its role in the reconciliation of recent disagreements over forensic probabilism. *Science & Justice, 57*, 80–85. https://doi.org/10.1016/j.scijus.2017.08.005

Bloch, B. (1948). A set of postulates for phonemic analysis. *Language, 24*(1), 3–46. https://doi.org/10.2307/410284

Boenninghoff, B., Hessler, S., Kolossa, D., & Nickel, R. M. (2019). *Explainable authorship verification in social media via attention-based similarity learning.* https://arxiv.org/pdf/1910.08144

Brinker, K. (2002). Textsortenbeschreibung auf handlungstheoretischer Grundlage (am Beispiel des Erpresserbriefs). In K. Adamzik (Ed.), *Textsorten: Texte—Diskurse—Interaktionsrollen. Analysen zur Kommunikation im öffentlichen Raum, 6* (pp. 41–59). Stauffenburg.

Brinker, K., Cölfgen, B., & Pappert, S. (2018). *Linguistische Textanalyse: Eine Einführung in Grundbegriffe und Methoden* (9th ed.). *Grundlagen der Germanistik, 29*. Erich Schmidt.

Cole, S. A. (2009). Forensics without uniqueness, conclusions without individualisation: The new epistemology of forensic identification. *Law, Probability and Risk, 8*, 233–255. https://doi.org/10.1093/lpr/mgp016

Corder, S. P. (1967). The significance of learner's errors. *International Review of Applied Linguistics, 4*, 161–170.

Coulthard, M. (2004). Author identification, idiolect, and linguistic uniqueness. *Applied Linguistics, 25*(4), 431–447. https://doi.org/10.1093/applin/25.4.431

Coulthard, M. (2013). On admissible linguistic evidence. *Journal of Law and Policy, 21*(2), 441–466. https://brooklynworks.brooklaw.edu/jlp/vol21/iss2/8

Dern, C. (2009). *Autorenerkennung: Theorie und Praxis der linguistischen Tatschreibenanalyse*. Boorberg.

Ehrhardt, S. (2018). Authorship attribution analysis. In M. Rathert & J. Visconti (Eds.), *Handbooks of applied linguistics [HAL]. Handbook of communication in the legal sphere, 14* (pp. 169–200). De Gruyter.

European Network of Forensic Science Institutes. (2015). ENFSI Guideline for evaluative reporting in forensic science: Strengthening the evaluation of forensic results across Europe. https://enfsi.eu/wp-content/uploads/2016/09/m1_guideline.pdf

Felder, E. (2016). *Einführung in die Varietätenlinguistik*. Wissenschaftliche Buchgesellschaft.

Fobbe, E. (2020). Text-linguistic analysis in forensic authorship attribution. *Journal of Language and Law, 9*, 93–114. https://doi.org/10.14762/jll.2020.093

Fobbe, E. (2021, in press). Stilkonzepte in computerbasierten Verfahren der Autorschaftsattribution im forensischen Kontext. In K. Luttermann & A. Busch (Eds.), *Rechtslinguistik: Recht und Sprache: Konstitutions- und*

Transferprozesse in nationaler und europäischer Dimension, 11 (pp. 229-251). LIT.

Grant, T. (2021). Text messaging forensics. In M. Coulthard, A. May, & R. Sousa-Silva (Eds.), *Routledge handbooks in applied linguistics. The Routledge handbook of forensic linguistics* (2nd ed., pp. 558–575). Routledge.

Hazen, K. (2006). Idiolect. In K. Brown (Ed.), *Encyclopedia of language & linguistics* (Vol. 5, 2nd ed., pp. 512–513). Elsevier.

Heinz, S. (2007a). Roter Kosar (Teil 1): eine nicht alltägliche Brandstiftungsserie mit ungewöhnlichem Hintergrund aus der persönlichen Sicht des Polizeiführers. *Die Kriminalpolizei, 25*(2), 59–63. https://www.kriminalpolizei.de/ausgaben/2007/juni/detailansicht-juni/artikel/roter-kosar-teil-1.html

Heinz, S. (2007b). Roter Kosar (Teil 2): eine nicht alltägliche Brandstiftungsserie mit ungewöhnlichem Hintergrund aus der persönlichen Sicht des Polizeiführers. *Die Kriminalpolizei, 25*(3), 100–104. https://www.kriminalpolizei.de/ausgaben/2007/detailansicht-2007/artikel/roter-kosar-teil-2.html

Hockett, C. F. (1960). *A course in modern linguistics*. Macmillan.

Ishihara, S. (2014). A likelihood ratio-based evaluation of strength of authorship attribution evidence in SMS message using N-grams. *The International Journal of Speech, Language and the Law: Forensic Linguistics, 21*(1), 21–50. https://doi.org/10.1558/ijsll.v21i1.23

Ishihara, S. (2017). Strength of forensic text comparison evidence from stylometric features: A multivariate likelihood ratio-based analysis. *The International Journal of Speech, Language and the Law: Forensic Linguistics, 24*(1), 67–98. https://doi.org/10.1016/j.forsciint.2017.06.040

Jessen, M. (2018). Forensic voice comparison. In M. Rathert & J. Visconti (Eds.), *Handbooks of applied linguistics [HAL]. Handbook of communication in the legal sphere, 14* (pp. 219–255). De Gruyter.

Keller, R. (2018). *Zeichentheorie: Eine pragmatische Theorie semiotischen Wissens* (2., durchgesehene Auflage). A. Francke Verlag. http://www.utb-studi-e-book.de/9783838548784

Kleppin, K. (2010). Formen und Funktionen von Fehleranalyse, -korrektur und -therapie. In H.-J. Krumm, C. Fandrych, B. Hufeisen, & C. Riemer (Eds.), *Handbücher zur Sprach- und Kommunikationswissenschaft. Deutsch als Fremd- und Zweitsprache. Ein internationales Handbuch* (pp. 1060–1072). De Gruyter.

Kniffka, H. (2007). *Working in language and law: A German perspective*. Palgrave Macmillan.

Köller, N., Nissen, K., Ries, M., & Sadorf, E. (2004). *Probabilistische Schlussfolgerungen in Schriftgutachten*. Luchterhand.

McMenamin, G. R. (1993). *Forensic stylistics. Forensic Science International, 58*. Elsevier.

McMenamin, G. R. (2002). *Forensic linguistics: Advances in forensic stylistics*. CRC Press. https://doi.org/10.1201/9781420041170

McMenamin, G. R. (2021). Forensic stylistics. In M. Coulthard, A. May, & R. Sousa-Silva (Eds.), *Routledge handbooks in applied linguistics. The Routledge handbook of forensic linguistics* (2nd ed., pp. 539–557). Routledge.

Nini, A. (2018). Developing forensic authorship profiling. *Language and Law/Linguagem e Direito, 5*(2), 38–58.

Nordgaard, A., Ansell, R., Drotz, W., & Jaeger, L. (2012). Scale of conclusions for the value of evidence. *Law, Probability and Risk, 11*, 1–24. https://doi.org/10.1093/lpr/mgr020

Queralt, S. (2018). The creation of base rate knowledge of linguistic variables and the implementation of likelihood ratios to authorship attribution in forensic text comparison. *Language and Law/Linguagem E Direito, 5*(2), 59–76.

Robertson, B., Vignaux, G. T., & Berger, C. E. H. (2016). *Interpreting evidence—Evaluating forensic science in the courtroom: Evaluating forensic science in the courtroom*. John Wiley & Sons. https://doi.org/10.1002/9781118492475

Sandig, B. (2006). *Textstilistik des Deutschen* (2nd ed.). De Gruyter. https://doi.org/10.1515/9783110911121

Schmid M. R., Iqbal, F., & Fung, B. C. M. (2015). E-Mail authorship attribution using customized associative classification. *Digital Investigation, 14*, 116–126. https://doi.org/10.1016/j.diin.2015.05.012

Spillner, B. (2009). Verfahren stilistischer Textanalyse. In U. Fix, A. Gardt, & J. Knape (Eds.), *Handbücher zur Sprach- und Kommunikationswissenschaft: Vol. 31.2. Rhetorik und Stilistik. Ein internationales Handbuch historischer und systematischer Forschung* (pp. 1739–1782). De Gruyter Mouton. https://doi.org/10.1515/9783110213713

Turell, M. T. (2010). The use of textual, grammatical and sociolinguistic evidence in a forensic text comparison. *The International Journal of Speech, Language and the Law: Forensic Linguistics, 17*(2), 211–251. https://doi.org/10.1558/ijsll.v17i2.211

Wright, D. (2013). Stylistic variation within genre conventions in the Enron e-mail corpus: Developing a text-sensitive methodology for authorship research. *The International Journal of Speech, Language and the Law: Forensic Linguistics, 20*(1), 45–75. https://doi.org/10.1558/ijsll.v20i1.45

8

Automatic Authorship Investigation

Hans van Halteren

1 Introduction

In authorship investigation tasks, we have one or more texts of unknown or disputed provenance and we want to determine specific *extralinguistic properties* purely based on the *linguistic properties* of these texts. The names of the various tasks are generally linked to the desired extralinguistic properties. Often, the desired property is the author's identity (*author identification*, *author recognition*) but this task comes in several guises. When there is a fixed (and generally small) set of potential candidates, determined through extralinguistic information, we speak of *author attribution*. In some studies, we are also allowed to pose that the text is not written by any of the suggested candidates; in many cases, this is wise, but it does complicate the task. When the complete set of candidates is in principle unknown, the task tends to focus on one specific candidate at a

H. van Halteren (✉)
Center for Language Studies (CLS), Radboud University Nijmegen,
Nijmegen, The Netherlands
e-mail: Hans.vanHalteren@ru.nl

V. Guillén-Nieto, D. Stein (eds.), *Language as Evidence*,
https://doi.org/10.1007/978-3-030-84330-4_8

time and tries to determine whether this candidate is or is not likely to have produced the text, in which case we speak of *author verification*. If the identity cannot be established at all and we try to determine only specific qualities of the author, such as gender, age, mother tongue, dialect or psychological characteristics, we speak of *author profiling*—described in more detail in Chap. 7. Other related tasks exist as well, such as determining whether a text was written by a single author—also discussed in Chap. 7—where fragments may have been inserted into a text by another author, or whether the author has attempted to hide their identity (*obfuscation*) or imitate another author (*imitation*). The same techniques as mentioned here can also be applied to other types of text classification, such as detecting fake news, but this falls outside the scope of this chapter. Note also that we deal exclusively here with written texts. If spoken material is present, the speech signal is probably a better indication of the author's characteristics (cf. Chap. 9) but the techniques presented here might be applied to provide additional evidence.

Whereas Chap. 7 focuses on qualitative analyses, here we turn to quantitative comparisons. The underlying idea is that we attempt to measure symptoms of each person's unique instantiation of any specific natural language (*idiolect*), which has evolved based on their unique personal experience with that language. These measurements should target those aspects of the text composition process that are subconscious and hence uncontrollably influenced by their idiolect, not those that are more consciously chosen. We should avoid aspects influenced by author-external factors such as conventions of a text genre or the topic at hand. Considering adversarial scenarios, we should avoid aspects that can be understood and manipulated by authors to obfuscate their authorship or imitate that of others. These deliberations quickly lead to analyses not so much in terms of what is and what is not used but more in terms of frequencies of use, which are much harder to grasp and manipulate by (human) authors. Therefore, the general approach to analysis is based on statistics of various text properties (*features*), which are used to estimate whether a text's statistics are more compatible with the known patterns of linguistic behaviour of Author X than with those of other authors. If we repeat this comparison over a sufficient number of features, we can assign a (relative) probability of X being the actual author.

If we assume that 'a sufficient number' will be large, automatic analysis is necessary and manual analysis is infeasible. However, even if we assume that lower numbers may suffice, automatic analysis is preferable as it guarantees consistency and hence replicability and the possibility to measure error rates. With manual analysis there is always the risk that different analysts come up with different analyses, potentially even leading to accusations of deliberately biasing the analysis to one outcome or another. Unfortunately, using an automatic approach with large numbers of features also has a disadvantage: it is often practically impossible to explain how the system arrived at its conclusions, even though this might be desirable in some circumstances.

2 The Foundations of Automatic Authorship Investigation

The execution of authorship investigation tasks is based on two foundations: measuring *features* and comparing the resulting lists (*vectors*) of measurements. This section discusses these foundations in detail, especially what types of features can be used.

2.1 Background

Before we can go into details, we should provide a background against which the discussion can be understood better. This background is partly historical (2.1.1), partly theoretical (2.1.2) and partly practical (2.1.3), the latter describing the data from which we will take most of the illustrative examples.

2.1.1 A Brief Look into the History

Authorship investigation has a long tradition, with venerable examples such as Lorenzo Valla exposing the Donatio Constantini as a fake (Valla, 1439/1440) and Wincenty Lutosławski's handbook (Lutosławski, 1890).

The beginning of automatic methods is generally linked to Mosteller and Wallace's work on the Federalist Papers (Mosteller & Wallace, 1964). However, systematic testing on texts with completely certain providence only starts towards the end of the twentieth century—for example Baayen et al. (1996). Thanks to the growth in all necessary components, being electronically readable texts, computing power and statistical techniques including machine learning, the field has developed enormously. It is impossible to describe all developments in this chapter, but there are good existing overview works such as those by Juola (2008) and Stamatatos (2009). Besides, the newest developments can be found in conference and workshop proceedings on related tasks, such as PAN at CLEF (cf. https://pan.webis.de/). As for application in court, either actual or potential, a good case is made by Ainsworth and Juola (2019), who describe various use cases and argue that modern automatic authorship attribution is in fact a good example of how forensic science should be organised.

2.1.2 Fundamental Considerations

The most fundamental notion for our methods is that not everybody uses their language in the same way, that everybody has an *idiolect*.[1] A natural language is not a fixed construct in which the content of a message implies a specific *linguistic form*—choice of words, phrases, pronunciation, among other aspects. A natural language is a wide collection of possible linguistic forms for almost every message component, from which we can choose and where the choice varies with our experience and preferences. These have evolved during a person's perception and production throughout their life, making them unique for that person. Furthermore, the preferences should be expressed qualitatively, what forms the person knows, and quantitatively, with what frequency the person uses each form.

The problem, of course, is that each message, such as a text, is not constructed randomly, purely built on those preferences. Various other factors are involved. The message has a meaning and intention, is about a specific topic, is aimed at a specific audience and embedded in a specific communicative situation. Furthermore, in particular circumstances, especially forensic circumstances, authors may want to attempt to hide their identity or pose as someone else by deliberately changing their chosen forms. All of these factors contribute to how a text is built. As we aim to discern just one factor, namely the author, we would have to control all others. However, this is practically impossible. Any author's available texts in any set of circumstances tend to be limited, and even more so in a forensic context. We can try to control as much as possible, such as working within a specific text type and general topic as is done in the exemplary case study in section 4, but we always need to remember that there will still be confounding factors.

Ideally, we would like to identify features that remain constant for authors in different circumstances. Again, proper datasets in which we could determine such features are not, to the best of our knowledge, available yet. A potential alternative is focusing on features that are less under conscious control. Content words, for instance, are chosen consciously and strongly influenced by topic and genre, and therefore should be worse markers for author identification. Good candidate features to tap into the subconscious behaviour might be counts of syntactic constructions or content independent measurements such as vocabulary richness measures. However, even these two features are still influenced by the confounding factors mentioned, although probably to a lesser extent.

Turning to more practical considerations, even if we identify good candidate features, we will also have to extract them from a text. Counting syntactic constructions implies doing syntactic analysis, either automatically—consistent but not necessarily correct—or manually—probably less consistent and probably more but still not necessarily fully correct. An alternative is to rely on 'shadows', a term first referred to by Baayen et al. (1996). Instead of counting syntactic constructions, we count corresponding function words, such as in Mosteller and Wallace's study (Mosteller & Wallace, 1964). Going a step further, we count character sequences as shadows of the linguistic units they form part of. An extreme use of shadows is falling back on measuring the behaviour of compression algorithms on texts by the same or different authors—as we see in Benedetto et al. (2002).[2] Such knowledge-poor approaches often work surprisingly well, as the underlying (knowledge-rich) features may be able to cast a strong and measurable shadow. Still, there are also enough unintended false shadows that our goal may be thwarted. As an example, in an investigation of dialect use in Twitter for the Dutch province of Limburg (van Halteren et al., 2018), a strong knowledge-rich marker was the alternation between two variants of the first person singular nominative pronoun ('I'): the standard 'ik' or the dialectal 'ich'. When we attempted to use character trigrams instead of tokens (as even tokenisation is sometimes difficult in tweets), we found that our measurements were seriously influenced by the fact that the trigram 'ich' is part of the name of the province's capital, 'Maastricht'. If shadows are to work, a very large set of features is needed, in which such false shadows lose the ability to do real damage, and even then, any explanatory value may be compromised by their presence.

Another problem with measurability is frequency. Overall measurements like vocabulary richness, or the presence of the word 'that' or a noun phrase are never problematic. Nevertheless, the rarer a feature becomes, the more difficult it will be to assign a value to it for every text, especially if the texts are very short, as they might well be in a forensic context. For this reason, it appears best to focus on features that can be measured for all or at least for a significant part of the texts (which may, by the way, vary per text type). On the other hand, idiosyncratic features may well be very useful (Daelemans et al., 1999). Just as with the shadows, their use should not be ignored, but only as long as there are very many of them and none has an inordinately large influence on the final decision.

2.1.3 Example Data

Apart from the occasional example from existing research, all examples in this chapter are based on 2231 texts from the British National Corpus (BNC XML Edition; BNC Consortium, 2007). All of them are written texts of at least 5000 words. They have been processed by the Stanford CoreNLP system (Manning et al., 2014), from which the POS tagging, constituency analysis and dependency analysis were used to extract features. The system is not perfect in its analysis, but the system output has been used directly, as manual postprocessing is prohibitive for this amount of text (2.5 million words in total). There was automatic post-processing, though, in that a more complete, lexicalised and differently structured constituency structure was created, more similar to the trees used in the TOSCA Project (Aarts et al., 1998).

Further sources for feature extraction were a list of about 750,000 words with their IDF[3] values calculated on all 4049 written texts in the BNC, used for IDF-related features, and the Scowl 70 list (cf. http://wordlist.aspell.net/scowl-readme/) for determining the level of out-of-vocabulary (OOV) words. We also defined several groups of words that might indicate authorship in fictional prose, namely reporting verbs and several types of adverbs, and created lists for each.

Within the BNC texts, special attention will be given to the 49 texts published by Mills & Boon (henceforth M&B), a publisher specialising in Romance Fiction. The restriction to this specific set of texts is an attempt to control for text type and general topic, and hence to have a clearer measurement of author-related language use preferences. Within the M&B texts, the author of each text is known and there is one author with three texts, three with two, and forty with only one text. Our running example will focus on verification of authorship by Stephanie Howard, the author of three texts in our set, as we will do with complete systems in Section 4.

As the texts are of variable length, which might influence our experiments, we took samples of 2000 words.[4] 2000 is a compromise between the realistic size in many forensic contexts, and the necessary size to measure many interesting features and reliable identification. For all 2231 texts, we drew 10 random samples, with the sampling unit being a sentence (according to the annotation in the BNC itself). For the 49 M&B texts, for more detailed analysis and training for machine learning methods, we drew 200 random samples instead of 10.

It is clear that using only English examples is not optimal, as other languages might well show other effects. On the other hand, there is insufficient space in this chapter for a wider examination and there is the added advantage that all readers will be able to follow the examples.

2.2 Features

The basis of our statistical comparisons is provided by measurements on the various texts in the investigation. In our terminology, we are measuring *features*, which we then line up in a *feature vector* for each sample, or rather we line up the *feature values*, being the outcome(s) of the measurements. Depending on which features we use, there may be *missing values* in the sense that some positions in a vector may not be filled—for example because a feature did not (or could not) occur in a text. Our vector comparison will have to take this into account.

In principle, features can be anything that can be (reliably) measured. It is possible, and probably sensible, to borrow features from existing research, but intuitions that as yet unused features might be useful and are measurable, these intuitions should be followed up and the features included. In an earlier publication (van Halteren et al., 2005), the collection of possible features was compared to the mapping of the genome, which was at that time being industriously pursued, leading to the term *stylome*. This analogy is still valid and a more extensive mapping of the stylome still seems a good idea. However, we have to accept that it is open-ended and can never be mapped fully. Still, the following section provides a glimpse into such a mapping.

2.2.1 Anatomy of a Feature

Let us first list what properties a feature has that are important for the task at hand. As an example, we use the relative frequencies of two word forms, 'the' and 'suddenly', in the text sample, that is the number of occurrences of 'the' (or 'suddenly') divided by the number of all tokens in the text (as given by CoreNLP). The top row in Fig. 8.1 shows the distributions of these frequencies over our 22,310 general BNC text samples. As expected, every sample contains the word 'the', so all frequencies are higher than zero, but 'suddenly' is rarer and most counts are zero.

Using 2000 words per sample is at the low end of what we need, as can be seen in rows two to four in Fig. 8.1. Each row shows the measured frequencies of 'the' and 'suddenly' in 200 samples randomly selected from

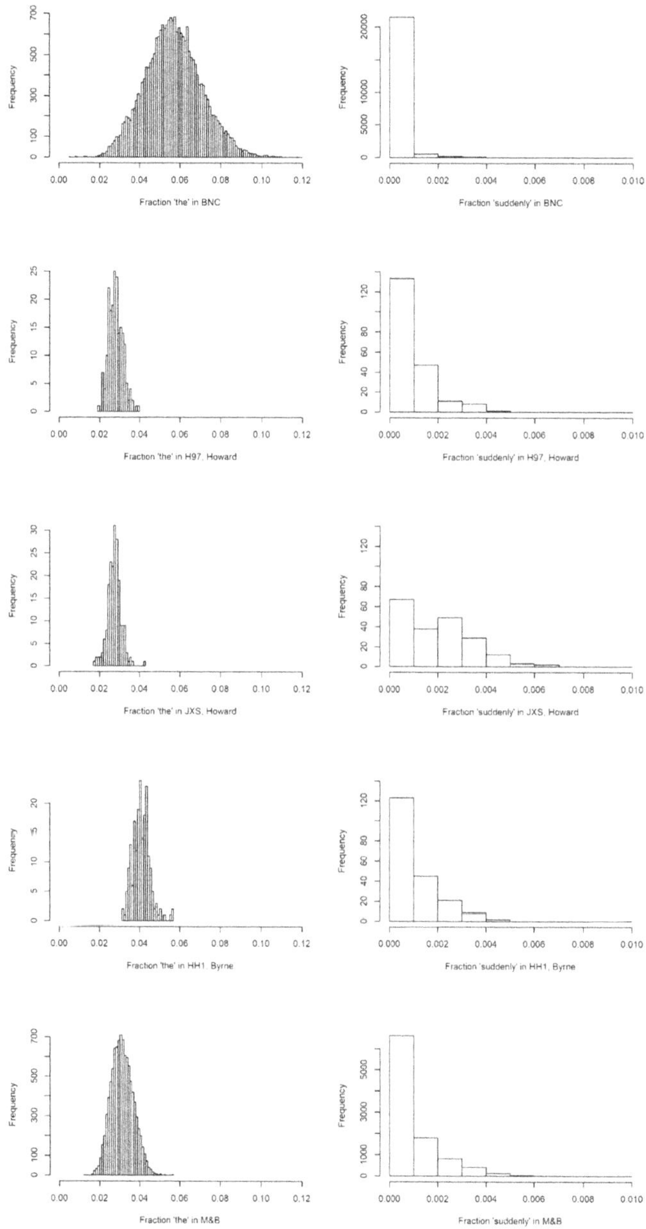

Fig. 8.1 Histograms for the frequency counts of 'the' and 'suddenly' in various subsets of text samples

an M&B book, each sample having 2000 words. Even when taken from the same book, the measurements show substantial variation. With larger samples, this variation should decrease, but we always need to consider that our feature values will be affected by noise, another reason to use more rather than fewer features in the analysis. Furthermore, the rarer a feature is, the stronger this variation affects our judgement. For even rarer features than 'suddenly', we will measure only one present (*hapax legomenon*) or zero (absent). These may still be useful but have to be handled with care—that is we need to check how the chosen vector comparison method copes with these.

Once we know that a feature can be measured reliably enough, we have to determine whether it is useful in distinguishing between authors. This depends on two characteristics. First of all, it is advantageous if an author is constant between texts. The second and third rows from the top in Fig. 8.1 show the measurements for M&B books by Stephanie Howard; the distribution is almost equal for 'the', but very different for 'suddenly'. Secondly, texts by alternative authors should preferably show different values. Examining the fourth row in Fig. 8.1, for an M&B book by Julia Byrne, we see nicely deviating figures for 'the', but conflicting outcomes for 'suddenly'. For normally distributed features, like the frequency of 'the', we could formalise such impressions by looking at the difference in means and the size of the standard deviations, but for—the various types of—non-normal distributions different measures should be used. An overly simplified but always applicable measure is the amount of overlap. If we pose a baseline classifier that determines its opinion on shared authorship of two books by checking whether a specific feature's values for one book's samples have values in or outside the observed range for the other book's samples, we can use the accuracy of this classifier as a kind of distinguishing power.[5] If we take this Overlap Classifier Success Rate (OCSR) for verification of Howard within M&B, then we get a score of 0.27 for 'the', which can be very roughly interpreted as 27% verification accuracy based on the frequency of 'the' alone. Byrne's book turns out to be the most different from Howard's within M&B; all others are closer and sometimes even indistinguishable. The OCSR for 'suddenly' is almost the same, 0.26. It is important to note that the OCSR is merely an indication, as we use much more refined classifiers in reality.

If our task is verification, and we are searching for useful features to distinguish the author in question, we will typically compare to average behaviour. Comparing to all BNC samples (top histogram in Fig. 8.1), we may conclude that Howard's use of 'the' is much lower than normal. However, at this point we have to check for possible confounding factors. A clear one here is the genre: the bottom row of Fig. 8.1 shows the measurements for all samples from the 49 M&B books. As you can see, the genre in general underuses 'the'. Even within the genre, Howard is still on the low side, but much less remarkably so than with regard to all texts in the BNC.

Another characteristic is related not to individual features but rather to pairs (or larger groups). We refer to their mutual correlation. In our example, the measurements for the word form 'the', the lemma 'the' and definite noun phrases will be strongly correlated and possibly even the same (depending on the exact setup and quality of the feature extraction). Some vector comparison methods will be hampered by correlated features. So, either such methods should be avoided or the number of features have to be reduced, for example, by selecting one feature from each correlated group. However, determining the level of correlation for all pairs is not straightforward for the enormous number of features we extract in the first place. Furthermore, the correlation is often not 100% and the differences might well hold information, so the best option is use of a system which is robust against correlation.

More in general, which of any of the described feature characteristics is important for feature selection or exclusion depends on the comparison method. The behaviour of candidate systems with the various candidate feature classes should therefore be carefully tested, using samples with known provenance.

As for the final selection of features for the classification, we advise using as much information as possible and letting the system decide what is useful. As yet, this position cannot be fully sustained. Extracting all features described in the next sections from the BNC data leads to about 25 million features for M&B and even about 40 million for the larger set. Most, if not all, current systems would still be overwhelmed by such an amount. We therefore decided to apply three reductions. First, only the features that were observed in at least 5% of the samples were retained.

Then, features with hardly any or even no variation ($\sigma/\mu<0.01$) were removed. Finally, features were merged if they showed exactly the same distribution, which means that they represented different views of the same underlying feature—for example the word 'suddenly' and the lemma 'suddenly'. These reductions left about 200,000 features. Some statistics per type of feature, including their usefulness as expressed in terms of OCSR are shown in Table 8.1. We will refer to these in the sections below.

2.2.2 Absolute Counts

The class of features most often used, at least after it became possible to process large numbers of features, is simply the count of various linguistic units in the complete sample. Note that, even though the header here says 'absolute', these counts should always be corrected for the sample size. Here, we used the fraction, but common are also the counts per thousand or million words. Again, we have to be aware that this works fine for common features and large texts, but that very low counts like one or two may now be recalculated to different values, for example one occurrence in a 900-word text becomes 0.0011, while one occurrence in a 1000-word text becomes 0.0010. This means that using fractions may be misleading as to the real equalities and differences in frequency for rare words. This may be another reason to exclude such idiosyncratic features, but an alternative would be special treatment in comparison.

What counts can be extracted depends on the availability of linguistic analysis tools—or human resources for annotation. When no tools are available, we can still count character n-grams.[6] Even unigrams already have power, as they include, for instance, punctuation and—in social media—emoji. Character bigrams and trigrams represent shadows of function words and morphology; longer n-grams represent shadows of longer words and token n-grams. Still, character n-grams should be used only if the linguistic alternatives are unavailable. As mere shadows, they may be misleading, and they are also more affected by the—more consciously chosen—content words, as well as more sensitive to biases. We do, however, include them here, as we are evaluating options; for the

Table 8.1 Statistics for various feature types in BNC measurements

Feature Type	Total number	Number with OCSR≥0.1	Best OCSR within type	Example feature with best OCSR within type
CC-ABS	12	10	0.6855	CC_SPA_<NEWLINE>_ABS
CC-REL	9	7	0.6651	CC_SPA_<NEWLINE>_RCC
CG1-ABS	87	53	0.7014	CG1_._ABS
CG2-ABS	1557	255	0.6470	CG2_.'_ABS
CG3-ABS	6662	575	0.6470	CG3_.'<SPACE>_ABS
CG4-ABS	14304	728	0.6413	CG4_,<SPACE>an_ABS
CG5-ABS	15969	681	0.6627	CG5_<SPACE>Then_ABS
CG6-ABS	13674	527	0.6375	CG6_,<SPACE>and<SPACE>_ABS
WR-ABS	5870	354	0.6900	WF_._ABS
WV-ABS	2788	174	0.6907	WFV_.._ABS
WGR-ABS	350	30	0.5512	WGL_GrpVrepx_smile_ABS
WGR-REL	321	36	0.5377	WGL_GrpVrepx_smile_RWG
WGV-ABS	311	20	0.4948	WGFV_GrpVrepx_smiledvbd_ABS
T1-ABS	6056	396	0.6903	T1_P_._ABS
T1V-ABS	5728	386	0.6903	T1V_P_._ABS
T2-ABS	11407	532	0.6980	T2_WP_,_CC_ABS
T2V-ABS	12828	564	0.6980	T2V_WP_,,_CC_ABS
T3-ABS	22558	682	0.6532	T3_WPW_._"_<END>_ABS
T3V-ABS	29983	750	0.6532	T3V_WPW_.._"_<END>_ABS
TM2-ABS	1129	15	0.2996	TM2_<START>_<MSK>_he_ABS
TM3-ABS	933	11	0.2534	TM3_in_<MSK>_of_the_ABS
SNN-ABS	29396	1268	0.8264	SFCF_UTT_S_SU_ABS
SNN-REL	13996	1211	0.7020	SFCFC_UTT_S_NOFUpunc_"_RSFC
SNL-ABS	16064	814	0.6904	SCFCW_ROOT_NOFUpunc_._._ABS
SNL-REL	14358	1748	0.5642	SCW_._!_RSC
SNV-ABS	16863	733	0.6904	SCFCWV_ROOT_NOFUpunc_._.._ABS
SRN-ABS	2065	83	0.7918	SRFC_ROOT_UTT_S_NOFUpunc_._ABS
SRN-REL	1817	104	0.6024	SRFC_ROOT_UTT_S_NOFUpunc_._RSC
MGEN	18	16	0.6970	M_MSLEN
MRCH	615	158	0.5111	M_ENT50_SRFC_SC_ROOT
OVERALL	**195099**	**10642**	**0.8264**	**SFCF_UTT_S_SU_ABS**

running example, we used character n-grams with n up to six. Their numbers are shown in Table 8.1, under CG1 to CG6. The total number increases with length, but this is counteracted at higher lengths by the 5% threshold. Only a small percentage is distinguishing, with most power residing in punctuation and function words. The CC type also concerns punctuation, namely choice of spacing, quotes and hyphens. Here, this is fully controlled by the BNC encoding, but as this encoding has one sentence per line, Howard's generally short sentences show as the presence of more newline characters than texts by other authors.[7]

The simplest analysis is tokenisation, splitting the texts into tokens and possibly sentences. This opens up the option of token n-grams. Typically, unigrams, bigrams and trigrams, but longer n-grams can be included, especially when they are frequent—for example terms and fixed expressions. If we have access to morpho-syntactic analysis, the word forms in the n-grams can be replaced by POS[8] tags, lemmas or corresponding predefined word groups. If we have access to IDF measurements, we can also replace a form by its IDF range—for example low, middle or high. Combining IDF with POS, we can also mask content words in an attempt to block content-related biases and produce masked n-grams. Here, we used all token n-gram combinations, with n up to three. Individual tokens and membership of word groups are present in Table 8.1 in the W-types. Relatively few tokens reach the 5% threshold and 5% to 10% of these are useful. We see the same features coming back in slight variations as the highest scoring in their subtype, namely the period (short sentences) and the verb 'smiled'. The numbers are higher for the uni-, bi- and trigrams (T1, T2, T3), and here too, punctuation scores best in all subtypes. We also see that more features are kept for the version with masking (T1V, T2V, T3V). The masked skip-grams (TM) appear to be hardly ever very useful here, possibly because we have an in-genre task.

Finding useful combinations of non-adjacent tokens becomes possible when we have a dependency analysis: now we can build syntactic n-grams—we can build features stating that two (or more) tokens are in a specific syntactic relation. However, we did not use these for the running example, but rather derived features from a constituency analysis. This lets us build syntactic n-grams of constituents. Unigrams of nodes in the analysis tree represent the presence of specific constructions, bigrams immediate dominance, trigrams immediate dominance and linear precedence. Larger n-grams are possible but here too, we have to decide what still brings enough added value. We do include the full composition of each constituent in terms of the immediately dependent nodes (the so-called *rewrite*). At each node we can include information about what kind of constituent it is (*category*), what its function in the mother node is (*function*), additional syntactic information (*attributes* such as number or tense) and the lexical content, typically the headword. Which of these components are possible depends largely on the available analysis system: CoreNLP provides both constituency and dependency and allows the extraction (with the aid of some postprocessing) of categories, functions and headwords.[9] As Table 8.1 depicts, relatively many syntactic n-grams (SN) and rewrites (SR) are useful, especially those without lexicalisation (SNN). The frequency of sentential utterances with a subject (UTT_S_SU) provides the overall highest OCSR (not implying that Howard uses more subjects, but rather fewer other sentence components). With lexicalised features, punctuation is again most prominent.

Further analysis may allow the addition of more features. However, we are now approaching semantics and text structure, which are probably more under conscious control. Also, such further analysis is as yet not as advanced as syntactic analysis and much less available. New options do come up in specialised fields. As an example, for historical or artistic texts we want to include features like patterns of end or internal rhyme, metre and alliteration.

2.2.3 Relative Counts and Alternations

Although absolute counts are the easiest to determine, they are not always optimal. If we measure how many determiners there are within noun phrases, this is influenced by the number of noun phrases there are in the first place. Our measurement is not pure. Instead, we should divide the number of determiners in noun phrases by the number of noun phrases, leading to *relative counts*.

Another relative count is based on *alternations*, such as the dative alternation ('I gave John a book' versus 'I gave a book to John'). The dative alternation would need a good syntactic analysis, but there are also lexical alternations such as between synonyms—as used by, for example, Koppel et al. (2006). There are even alternations at the character level, such as the various existing quotation marks, hyphens and brackets. Some alternations may, in principle, be open-ended, such as all the possible ways to form a noun phrase, which theoretically can contain any number of post-modifiers. In practice, rare subdivisions behave like rare words and will not lead to insurmountable problems.

The problem with relative counts is that the total count within which something is relative must be high enough for a proper estimate. In the experiments for this chapter, we required the total count in a sample to be at least ten. This means that, when the total count is less than ten, we will have a missing value in our feature value vector, but this is preferable over an unreliable measurement. However, the presence of missing values forces us to use a method that can deal with them.

For verification of Howard's authorship, we used relative counts within POS tags, word groups, various syntactic n-grams and rewrites. The relative counts are shown in Table 8.1 as '-REL'. All in all, they seem to be less effective here in the higher ranges than the absolute ones, but there are more of them showing an OCSR over 0.1.

2.2.4 Basic Variation

Overall frequency is just one aspect of the use of a linguistic unit. Equally interesting is its variation throughout the text or sample. If we know the sentence boundaries, we can take various measurements at the sentence level and calculate the mean and standard deviation (or, if we prefer, the coefficient of variation, CV = σ/μ).

Typical measurements to measure variation for are sentence length, word length, the fractions of function and content words, various IDF levels, out-of-vocabulary words (with in-vocabulary determined by some selected word list), and punctuation, all of which were used for the current task. As Table 8.1 shows that all 18 used features (listed under the header 'MGEN') are always present and 16 of them are useful (the other two being alliteration and the standard deviation of the fraction of content words per sentence). As mentioned earlier, sentence length is a very valuable marker for Howard and comes up here as well.

2.2.5 Richness Measures

Another traditional indicator of authorship is vocabulary richness: we do not measure what words are used exactly, but how varied they are. In theory, this gives us insight into how many words the author knows, which should differ between many author pairs and thereby, may enable us to distinguish one author from others.

The best-known of the vocabulary richness measures compares the number of different words in a sample (*V*) to the total number of words in the sample (*N*), simply by taking the *type-token ratio* (*TTR*) V/N. Many such measures have been proposed, an investigation of which is presented by Tweedie and Baayen (1998). The other traditional measure is the fraction of *hapax legomena* (words occurring only once) in the sample, and sometimes even *hapax dilegomena* (twice).

Inspired by information theory, we can also measure the *entropy* of the word frequency distribution. This gives a more detailed picture of the use of the various frequencies in that it looks beyond the mere number of different options by considering how often each of the options is used.[10] A similar evaluation of how often options are used is inspired by Zipf's Law, which claims an exponential distribution for word frequencies. Given a word frequency distribution, we can measure the area between the actual distribution curve and the corresponding theoretical curve according to Zipf—a number we dubbed *non-Zipfiness.*

The fact that all the referred measures have been described in terms of word frequencies is purely historical. This is how they were first applied. However, they can also be applied to all possible ways to build a syntactic constituent—for example noun phrase structure.

There is, however, a fundamental problem with richness measures. They are dependent on the sample size. As samples get larger, the entropy goes up and the other richness measures go down, converging to some asymptote which would be the 'real' measurement for the author but which is hardly ever attained. There have been attempts to correct for this—for example Covington and McFall (2010)—but they were never fully successful. The easiest solution is to keep the size constant, which works well enough for the word counts in the 2000-word samples used here. However, it is more restricting for the relative counts within constituent types. There, we would have to aim for the common minimum total, which is likely to destroy valuable information.

For the running example, we used all four richness measurements for vocabulary, word choices within each group, and syntactic rewrites, all at the size levels 10, 20, 50, 100, 200, 500, 1000, as far as present in the various samples. Table 8.1 shows that 615 such features occur in at least 5% of the samples and about 25% of these have some power in distinguishing between authors. This power is highest for the entropy of rewrites of the utterance as a whole in terms of functions and categories, as measured on 50 utterances, which is relatively low for Howard. If we investigate what this means, we find that a large majority of Howard's utterances consists of a sentence followed by a period, whereas other authors show much more variety here.

2.2.6 Further Options

The preceding sections listed the most important traditional features. However, as already said, anything that can be reliably counted is a potential feature. The fact that it is not yet in the mapped stylome is irrelevant. If something might be distinguishing within the domain in question, there should be an attempt to measure it and to include it as one or more features. Many systems can work with very large numbers of features and such features can be added without problems. For less forgiving systems, the included features have to be selected for each individual task. In all cases, it has to be tested whether the chosen combination of feature set and system functions well for texts of known provenance.

2.3 Feature Vector Comparison

Once feature vectors have been extracted from all texts relevant for the investigation, including background corpus texts, the task is to figure out whether each feature vector is compatible with each candidate author's behaviour as observed in their known texts. An exact probability would be best, but this is usually not possible. Seeing how the samples have been collected, how many different features of various types are used and how they interact, and how a comparison score is determined, the desired probability estimate is usually replaced by a much harder to interpret score, which is mostly useful in deciding that Author A is more or less likely than Author B. At this point one could try to score many texts and derive probabilities of specific scores, but this again is hampered by the unavailability of sufficient numbers of texts comparable to the disputed texts.

For the actual comparison we can take our pick from a multitude of statistical and machine learning approaches. Any system is useful as long as it can relate the given classes to the similarities or differences in the corresponding vectors. Again, we refer to overview articles and current literature for an impression of what is in vogue at the moment. There are, however, some points to keep in mind. First of all, we need to check whether a potential method can cope with the large number of features. For instance, Linear Discriminant Analysis (LDA) on the statistical side and Decision Trees on the machine learning side tend to get confused if there are very many features, at least in their original form. We should therefore either avoid these methods or apply some form of *dimensionality reduction* to our data, such as Principal Component Analysis (PCA).

Furthermore, some methods work best if the various feature measurements are regular in specific ways. For instance, with PCA and k-nearest neighbour (kNN), it tends to be useful to *centering*—that is moving the mean to zero—and/or *scaling*—that is normalising the range over all features, often to [0,1] or [-1,1]. When the features are mutually exclusive and we want to measure the similarity of their distribution, it may be useful to apply *L2 normalisation*, that is all numbers are divided by the length of the vector so that the normalised vector's length is one. In general, the data processing advice for the selected learning method should be followed. This is equally true for the final point of attention, being the effect of unbalanced data. Especially with forensic problems, we will have much fewer examples of the author in question than of all the other authors. Many learning methods are lured into just assigning all cases to the negative class, as this already provides a high-quality score. If the chosen method has this problem, we can apply *upsampling*—that is positive cases are repeated—or *downsampling*—that is a sample is taken from the negative cases—to get equal amounts for each class.

2.4 Deep Learning

In recent years, 'big data' tasks are being more and more solved with the so-called *deep learning* approach. It is based on neural network methods, which were first developed in the twentieth century—for example *multilayer perceptrons*—but it applies these on a much larger scale. In a traditional network, an input vector was provided to a first level of 'neurons', after which the input values would be multiplied by *weights* and added as inputs to nodes in a *hidden layer*, where some *thresholding function* would keep only strong values. The same would be done from the hidden layer to the *output layer*, where results could be read off. On the basis of training data, the system would automatically learn the optimal weights and thresholding parameters. This was just one of many machine learning techniques and was in no way special.

Now, however, computing power has grown and the neural architecture can be supported by parallel processing in graphical processors (GPUs). New techniques have been developed, using many hidden layers instead of one or two, applying specific types of special layers, remembering information between the steps in processing sequences, and even learning where to look in the available information at any point. Combining the new techniques with enormous data sets has led to revolutions in many fields, such as image processing. A full description of all this is out of scope for this chapter and would probably be obsolete shortly.

Deep learning has also started to make its mark on natural language tasks, such as speech recognition and translation. Authorship investigations too are attempted with deep learning techniques. A full description is also beyond the scope of this chapter, but a recent overview is given by Ma et al. (2020).

The reason to set the deep learning approach apart is that the traditional separation into feature extraction and feature vector comparison is being dropped. For most tasks, the most popular approach is an end-to-end one. In authorship tasks, the text would be input as it is and the system would try to learn what is needed to distinguish between authors. We could view the bottom part of the layered network as feature extraction and the top as classification, but in fact these two parts are learned together and the learning process for the classification also influences what elements of the text are inspected. This integration makes it very hard, maybe even impossible, to determine fully what text properties are being used and to which degree. We may eventually get better results with deep learning than with previous methods, but can no longer explain what sets an author apart. Especially, we may be unable to discover whether the system is really learning the author's language use or merely confounding factors.

3 Methodology

In the previous section, we described the toolbox that is available for authorship studies. Here we take you through the individual steps of an actual investigation and show how this toolbox can be applied, and where our general deliberations lead to action. In this, we focus on the general methodology rather than propagating specific systems or techniques. Any 'best' choices vary greatly per task and, especially in such a fast-developing field, over time. Basic methodology, however, should remain rather constant.

3.1 Data Collection

When embarking on an authorship study, there is only one certainty: we have one or more text samples for which we need to determine some information related to authorship. What we can determine, even theoretically, depends on what other text samples are available or can be made available. Identity cannot be established if we have no other text samples by the suggested author(s). Attribution within a fixed group is impossible unless we have undisputed text samples from each of the candidates. Profiling is only possible if we have text samples known to be from the various profiling classes. Therefore, it is crucial that we collect such text samples or, if this is a hired job, to have the hiring party provide such text samples. If the samples are unavailable, we can only state that the investigation is cannot be done due to a lack of text samples.

In practice, we should collect as much text data as we can that could be relevant to the task. Furthermore, our chances of success will improve if our additional text samples are as similar as possible to the samples under investigation. Once in possession of the samples, we have to check for any biases. For example when profiling for gender, we should check that samples for both classes show an equal distribution for other factors, such as age, regional background and text type. Biases could also be caused by less apparent factors, such as editorial interference for published works, use of text processing software such as spelling correction, or even the type of input device such as speech recognition. If the background samples are taken from standard corpora, we have to make sure that text preprocessing for the corpora was not introducing regularities that were not in the original texts.

To determine—and show—how effective our analysis is, we will also have to collect one or more other sets of text samples that mirror the actual case set as much as possible. Obviously, for these mirror sets, we need the full knowledge of who wrote what. If the sets are similar enough, error rate measurements on the material of known provenance should give an acceptable approximation of the error rate on the disputed material. However, note that constructing mirror sets tends to be quite difficult in a forensic environment. We can increase the usefulness of our mirror data by techniques like *cross-validation* or *bootstrapping*—reusing the same data in other configurations. We have to beware, though, that this reuse does not lead to a misestimate of analysis effectiveness because there is too much repetition or because the various repetitions influence each other.

3.2 Data Preparation

Once all text samples are present, we can decide on subsampling the samples we have. The size of the subsamples obviously depends on the full sizes we have available, but also on the amount of text needed for proper processing. As a result, this step is necessarily linked to system selection, as the system determines the needs. Once the size is selected, we can start the creation of the subsamples for actual processing. Random samples give a better impression of the language use than contiguous samples (van Halteren, 2019), but contiguous samples might be better if the disputed text is very small, as we get a better picture of the intra-author variation. In both cases, at least full sentences have to be sampled, so that we do not lose syntactic information.

We can then progress to feature extraction, possibly adding features that may be of significance to the particular investigation. For the extraction, we may need to apply pre-processing such as syntactic analysis. It is advisable here to do overall checks that all samples were indeed processed and no error messages were given, and spot checks to see if the pre-processing is doing for the texts what we think it should be doing. If anything goes wrong here, it will introduce new biases which will confound the later analysis. Another potential source of biases is manual annotation. Some types of annotation cannot be done (fully) automatically. An option is to replace or enhance this, involving human annotators. However, a very clear annotation protocol and manual is needed if we want an acceptable consistency level. For consistency, and hence avoiding bias, and for replicability, it may well be better to use automatic annotation only and accept a certain level of error as the price for full consistency.

3.3 System Selection and Evaluation

The next step is the selection of a classification system. Over time, all of us tend to develop some preferences here, which have shown to do well, but we should always check whether the selection of systems is also doing well on this particular case. Furthermore, we should regularly check if newer methods might do better. For testing new methods, we can use the constructed mirror sets.

Depending on the chosen system, specific pre-processing may need to be applied. Also, depending on the specific data, the settings of the system may need to be adjusted. Some understanding of both text types and systems is useful here, but many systems can be used without extensive knowledge. Knowing more tends to lead to higher quality analysis, but this does not matter if no knowledge still leads to a sufficiently good analysis.

Similarly, some postprocessing may be needed. The system might be good at calculating scores but bad at selecting a threshold. Sometimes, we may need a (relative) probability rather than a score. We should be very careful that we do not use information about the disputed texts for any system settings. Such *information leaks* could invalidate the results.

Once the whole pipeline has been set up, we first apply it to the mirror sets and then measure how well the system is doing. Standard measures for authorship studies are False Reject Rate (FRR)—that is which percentage of samples by the actual author was not recognised, and False Accept Rate (FAR)—that is which percentage of samples by other authors was erroneously recognised. The chosen threshold influences these two percentages, a higher threshold giving lower FAR but higher FRR. Single measurements can be derived in the form of the Equal Error Rate (EER), which chooses a threshold so that EER=FAR=FRR, or the area under the curve when plotting FRR and FAR (or rather their inverses) against each other, giving an overview of the whole threshold range. More measures are used, such as true/false positive/negative rate; specificity and sensitivity; precision, recall and F_1-score. In principle, they are all interrelated. The best choice for a specific investigation is mostly determined by the exact field of study and the current task.

Apart from these measurements, we should also try to inspect which features are being used in recognising authors. It may well be that we missed a bias and the system is capitalising on that bias rather than on authorship. If we do spot a bias, we will have to try to improve our data sets or try to adjust the feature set in order to reduce the effect of the bias. Note that the latter is actually quite difficult as there may be unpredictable bias effects.

After applying test runs for various systems, we need to determine whether the recognition quality is high enough. We might still gain some quality by combining the opinions of the better working systems. If the quality is unacceptable, we have to report this and should not apply the system to the actual case data. If acceptable, we document our testing activities and outcomes, and progress to the next step.

3.4 System Application

Having determined that our selected system(s) can perform the given task acceptably well, we can progress to applying the system to the text samples of unknown provenance, following the exact same steps as those taken in the successful test.

Again, we should not accept the outcome at face value. We check that the scores or probabilities are compatible with the ranges seen in the system tests. If scores are remarkably high or low, we need to double-check for differences in the application of the system or in the data itself. We also check which distinguishing features are being found, if at all possible, again in order to determine that it is authorship that is being measured and nothing else. Especially in a forensic setting, where stakes might be high, a certain degree of paranoia is needed here.

3.5 Interpretation and Reporting

Once we are satisfied that we measured what we wanted to measure, we can report our results. Depending on the situation, we may be able to report the scores themselves or we may be forced to convert them to probabilities or possibly an odds ratio—how much more likely is one hypothesis than another. If hired, we need to check with the employer what exactly is needed. In fact, this should be done much earlier in the process, as the desired measurement may influence the system choice. In actually determining the probabilities, we can make use of our mirror set tests. They should have given us a large base of outcomes connected to positive and negative examples, from which we can determine what the probability is of the outcome we got with the case samples.

We should also include in the report, or at least in an appendix, a full log of our activities in all the steps outlined above. Only this will allow the reader to judge whether the investigation was executed properly and, in case of doubt, enable others to replicate it. In specific circumstances, the report may be enhanced with visualisations, such as showing where the outcome is placed in the ranges for positive and negative examples, or placing some measurement of the disputed text in a two-dimensional graph in relation to all other known (and possibly also unknown) texts. We should be aware, though, that such visualisations may also be used to mislead the viewer, as a selection of features used in the visualisation may hide contradictory information in other features.

4 Deep Learning to the Test

As an example of research on authorship, we tested the effectiveness of various methods and feature sets on a specific text collection. Note that this collection takes the place of the mirror sets that we advocated above, but that it does not actually mirror the text set in a real forensic case. Our main research question is whether the selected methods are useful for author verification when we have a text collection of medium size, being several dozen book-length texts. Secondary questions are a) whether there are substantial differences between the chosen methods, b) whether the system quality improves or degrades when we include rare features in our feature set and c) whether end-to-end deep learning is already a viable competitor for more traditional author recognition methods.

In order to measure and compare the effectiveness of the various systems, we trained and tested them on our dataset and investigated the scores assigned to unseen (during training) samples, from books by both the target author and other authors. To be exact, we will compare an end-to-end deep learning system (Bönninghoff et al., 2019) with 12 combinations of a separate feature extraction system and a separate vector comparison system. For feature extraction we use a traditional feature set, as described in Section 2, but at four levels of feature set size. For vector comparison we use two traditional systems and one neural network system.

4.1 Experimental Data and Task

As stressed above, we should strive to avoid any biases in our data, so that we can assume that the systems are indeed discovering author-related language use features. In this investigation, we do this by selecting only texts from a single text type and genre, namely romance fiction books published by the British publisher Mills & Boon in the 1990s, as present in the British National Corpus. All needed text files and general pre-processing are described in section 2.1.3.

4.2 Data Preparation

We took the extracted features (as described in sections 2.2.2 to 2.2.5) and normalised them to over- and underuse scores, based on the values of each feature for all 22,310 samples from the larger BNC selection. We used a non-parametric mapping: overuse is expressed as the fraction of samples in the higher half of the collection which had a lower value than the value in question; underuse—expressed as a negative number—similarly used the lower half and higher value. The extreme measurements thus turn into (almost) 1 and -1, the modal measurement into 0. As 0 expresses absence of special behaviour, we also mapped missing values to 0, interpreting them as the absence of confirmed observations of special behaviour. This pre-processing also means scaling and centering are no longer needed.

The extracted features were used at four levels. In all cases, only features were included which occurred in at least 5% of the 9800 M&B samples and which had a coefficient of variation of at least 0.01. This led to a total of 186,390 features, which formed the largest feature set. We also used a variant with only the masked features—that is those without explicit reference to topical or rare words—which amounted to 110,363 features. The smallest set included only those 1475 features which occurred in all 22,310 BNC samples used in the original feature set construction. A further intermediate level contained 15,000 features, which more or less corresponds to presence in 2/3 of the samples.

The derived data were split into training and test sets. Each of the three training sets included samples from two of the three Howard books, with the third book in the corresponding test set. The remaining 46 books were also split into three portions (of size 15, 15, 16), with repeating authors kept in the same portion, so that again two-thirds can be used for training and one-third for testing. From these three splits for the Howard books and three splits for the other books, we could build nine combinations and each system was tested on all nine.

4.3 System Descriptions

For the separate vector comparison, we used one traditional machine learning method, one statistical method and one neural network method.[11]The machine learning method was one that was known to yield good results in previous research, being support vector regression (SVR), as present in the libsvm package (Chang & Lin, 2011). We did not tune the hyperparameters but selected ones that performed adequately in earlier authorship research, namely ν-SVR with ν=0.3, c=32, γ=1/number_of_features and ε=1/512. We also weighted the positive cases with a factor of 15, as the training set contained about 15 times more negative cases than positive ones.

From the statistically inspired toolbox, we chose to use Principal Component Analysis (PCA) to select the 500 first principal components, to which we then applied Linear Discriminant Analysis (LDA) for final classification. The implementation was that in the SciKit Learn package (Pedregosa et al., 2011). We used the default settings, which according to the documentation include centering, but not scaling.

Next, we used a neural network system, namely torch.nn.Sequential from the PyTorch package (Paszke et al., 2019). We opted for a traditional three-layer architecture, with a hidden layer of 500 nodes, unbiased linear connections between the layers, an Adam optimiser working with the sum of MSEloss, a learning rate of 0.005 and 1000 epochs. As the random initialisation of weights may influence results, we repeated each run 10 times and took the average scores to use in the final classification.

As a representative of state-of-the-art deep learning systems, we selected the AdHominem system (Bönninghoff et al., 2019), which came to our attention by taking first place in the PAN Author Verification contest at CLEF 2020 (Bönninghoff et al., 2020). [12] Originally, this was designed for a slightly different task, namely deciding if two input text samples were written by the same author. The samples are both transformed into a numerical vector (an *embedding*), and these vectors are then taken as the basis for classification. What sets the system apart from what we saw above is that feature extraction is learned together with classification, as already stated, and that the two strings are jointly embedded, using a so-called Siamese network, thus enhancing the ability to discover markers for author identity. We have to note that the used embeddings here are rather small (word 20 dimensions, sentence 10, document 10) and are already conglomerates of observed text features, another difference between this system and what we are used to. For the current experiment, the system was used by providing only sample pairs including one known Howard sample. As the system was designed for smaller text sizes, all samples were split into five portions. For assigning a score to a test sample, all five portions were considered and scored with regard to ten different Howard comparison samples, after which the various scores were combined by taking the geometric mean (actually the arithmetic mean of the logarithms of the scores). It turned out that verification quality fluctuated strongly during the learning process. In reaction to this, we decided not to select a single point in the learning, but to use the average score over a longer period. Also, we repeated the whole learning process three times and again averaged the scores for the individual samples. A final postprocessing step was an attempt to make the scores for the nine split combinations (see 4.2) comparable, by taking z-scores based on the sample scores which are lower than the modal value.[13]

4.4 Evaluation

Table 8.2 shows the results of classification systems. At the top of each cell, you find FRR/FAR//SEP—that is false reject rate, false accept rate and the separation level of the two histograms. Below the score, we show the actual histograms of classification scores for all samples, on the left the non-Howard samples in grey, on the right the Howard samples in black. The histograms look like normal distributions, allowing us to represent the distance between positive and negative cases with the listed *separation* measure: SEP = $|\mu_1 - \mu_2| / (\sigma_1 + \sigma_2)$. This acts as a kind of Z-score for separation; once over 2 the distributions are practically non-overlapping. As the number of features goes up, the SEP increases. PCA-LDA appears to do a bit better, but this may be caused by its preference to produce numbers very close to 0 or 1. In fact, we had to take the $\log_{10}$

Table 8.2 Quality measurements for various systems for verification of Howard within M&B

System Features	PCA-LDA (log_{10})	SVR	NN
Traditional In all Samples 1,475	0.007/0.006//2.9 	0.003/0.002//2.8 	0.006/0.007//2.8
Traditional In ~2/3 of samples 15,000	0/0.0003//4.1 	0/0//3.9 	0.001/0.001//4.1 
Traditional, masked In 5% of samples ~110,000	0/0//5.1 	0/0//4.5 	0/0//4.5 
Traditional In 5% of samples ~180,000	0/0//5.6 	0/0//4.7 	0/0//4.8 
AdHominem	0.007/0.006//2.8 		

of the actual output values to produce a more informative graph. The preference is still visible in the strong peak at 1, which leads to a low standard deviation and increased SEP.

Although the separation increases, this fact does not imply that there will be no false rejects or accepts. While lagging in SEP, SVR already produces a zero error rate at 15,000 features; the others need more. The performance with just 1475 features, focusing on very frequent features alone, is also impressive, but none of the classifiers manages to avoid making errors.

The AdHominem system does not quite reach an EER of 0, but of approximately 0.007, putting it at the level of PCA-LDA and NN with 1475 features.

4.5 Conclusion

It would seem that our main research question has a positive answer. All selected methods are able to distinguish quite well between samples from Howard's books and samples from other authors' books. For the traditional methods, given access to the largest feature sets, separation of the two classes is even perfect. Assuming sufficiently similar texts, the systems could claim certainty in their classification. However, in forensic cases, separation is likely to be less perfect and we would have to derive probabilities corresponding to the various scores by real mirror set tests.

The differences between the three chosen traditional systems are minor rather than substantial. Given enough data, the three systems reach perfect classification. The addition of rare features leads to an improvement of the classification quality. In fact, all three methods need the rare features to reach perfection on this dataset.

Deep learning, at least in this incarnation, is not quite yet reaching the quality of the traditional methods. It is comparable to the traditional systems using the smallest feature set. It would seem that the amount of data we have available in this specific experiment is insufficient for proper—and, as mentioned, reproducible—learning with this system (Bönninghoff, personal communication). Still, given the low number of network nodes and the fact that it was designed for other data, this is already impressive. However, the problem dealt with here is still quite 'big' relative to many forensic cases and it is as yet unclear if deep learning will ever reach the desired quality for real 'small data' problems, even though they are known to do quite well at 'big data' ones.

5 Conclusions

All things considered, we can say that, under the right circumstances, authorship can be determined quite well automatically (Section 4). Furthermore, various strategies, both traditional and deep learning, produce good to very good results. However, before moving on to further conclusions, we should stress the fact that the systems above have never been applied in an actual court case. Any conclusions therefore reflect scientific investigation rather than practical experience. This is not to say that we would not like to put all this to a real test, but the right circumstances have not presented themselves as yet.

In fact, we may have to conclude that too often, the circumstances are not right at all. There may not be enough data, or data exists but is not available for legal or other reasons, authors may not be consistently using a consciously chosen style, or disputed and undisputed texts may be of a (very) different nature. Consequently, for a proper investigation, we must test the effectiveness of our systems under the circumstances that we are facing in the investigation at hand. Hopefully, we can draw on existing corpora or data sets for this test, but otherwise we have to create our own. Section 3 outlines what needs to be done, using the elements described in Section 2.

In order to support further development of effective authorship investigation, we have several tasks ahead of us. The most important, in our view, is the creation of proper background corpora to draw on, especially including authentic forensic texts (or at least realistic imitations) and texts from the same author but in different text types. Once we have these texts, we can proceed to map and extend the known stylome, including measurements of feature effectiveness in various text types and across text type boundaries. Furthermore, these corpora will enable us to develop further techniques, including deep learning ones, and monitor the applicability of developments in other fields that might be relevant for our work, such as linguistic analysis and machine learning.

Once data and techniques have been developed, we should recognise that not everyone is best served with just a methodology, but many potential users would prefer a standard system. We should investigate if such systems are possible, at least for a subset of forensic authorship tasks. A major choice here is whether such systems should be set up as black boxes. An advantage of the black box would be that, if data would never be seen by humans, but only by (pre-vetted) fully automated software, we might be allowed to use data which is currently ruled inaccessible. However, we fear (not out of mere prejudice but on the basis of experience with various datasets over the years) that, just like inconsistency and bias are the pitfall for manual methods, uncontrolled application of badly understood black boxes is likely to produce invalid results with some regularity. In any real application, we suggest that our boxes be made transparent, and should come with extensive explanations and instructions on how they should be monitored, thus keeping alive all the checkpoints listed above, at the proper levels of paranoia.

In the development of our arsenal, we should also consider what the 'client' wants. What level of error rate will be acceptable? Will our proven expertise be enough and will our probability estimates be accepted, or will we be challenged to explain our findings? If the latter, what kind of explanation would be acceptable? We can try to explain what the system does, but this becomes more and more problematic. We can also show visualisations or give text examples, but these might be more misleading than explanatory, as they are always simplified representations of a more complex reality. Furthermore, the most modern systems yield better recognition quality, but they are also more removed from the underlying data, so that explanations are much harder to find.

Looking at what we are currently accomplishing and are hopefully about to accomplish, our final conclusion must be that, in this field, we are living in interesting times, where our potential is continuously increasing, but where we will have to work hard to fulfil and properly apply that potential.

Notes

1. The concept of idiolect is discussed more extensively in Chap. 7.
2. Compression methods such as ZIP operate by replacing repeated character sequences by pointers to the previous use of those sequences. If two authors have preferences for different language use, and therefore different character sequences, compression will work better on single author texts than on mixed author texts.
3. IDF stands for *Inverse Document Frequency*: The log of the number of documents with the word divided by the number of all documents. Words occurring everywhere, like function words, have very low IDF, but rare and topic-specific tokens have high IDF.
4. In the XML version of the BNC, sentences are split into sentences. We removed the markers but used the sentence split to create 200 text samples of between 1950 and 2050 words. This was done by including full sentences until size 2000 was reached; in case size was over 2050, we removed the last included sentence and checked that size was at least 1950; if not, the current sample was deleted.
5. Looking at this from the perspective of correctly marked cases, the *true accept rate (TAR)* is the fraction of samples from a Howard book in the test set that have features values in the range of the current training book by Howard. The *true reject rate (TRR)*, is the fraction of samples for a non-Howard book in the test set that have features values outside that range. Similar to the calculation of the *F-score* for *precision* and *recall*, we calculate the OCSR as (2·TAR·TRR)/(TAR+TRR).
6. N-gram is the term for n items adjacent in the text, typically n characters or n tokens, for example the word 'character' contains the 4-gram 'ract'. N is often kept low, and there are separate terms for 1-gram ('unigram'), 2-gram ('bigram') and 3-gram ('trigram').
7. A newline character (10 in ASCII and UNICODE) indicates to the computer that the text should be continued on a new line.
8. POS stands for Part Of Speech. A POS tag contains morpho-syntactic properties of a token (in its current context). Apart from the major word class, such as Noun or Preposition, it may contain additional information, such as number or tense.
9. Stanford CoreNLP is just one of many options to obtain an automatic syntactic analysis. Some well-known alternatives are NLTK (Bird et al., 2009) and SpaCy (Honnibal & Montani, 2017).

10. For the computationally minded, the formula for entropy is $H(X) = -\Sigma_i P(x_i)\log(P(x_i))$.
11. This section contains many technical details that are of little interest to the reader without experience in computational linguistics and machine learning. However, they are of vital importance for researchers who want to replicate the analysis.
12. We would like to thank Benedikt Bönninghoff for providing us with useful assistance in using his software and adapting its functioning to our specific data and task.
13. In principle, we can see that all distributions are bimodal. Nevertheless, using this fact in the alignment would mean an unfair comparison, as we would use the knowledge about the number of positive test samples present. Assuming that we mostly have negative samples, we can use the leftmost mode as reference, and then use only the samples with even lower values to estimate a 'standard deviation' for calculating the z-score.

References

Aarts, J., van Halteren, H., & Oostdijk, N. (1998). The linguistic annotation of corpora: The TOSCA analysis system. *International Journal of Corpus Linguistics, 3*(2), 189–210.

Ainsworth, J., & Juola, P. (2019). Who wrote this?: Modern forensic authorship analysis as a model for valid forensic science. *Washington University Law Review, 9*(5), 1161–1189.

Baayen, F. H., van Halteren, H., & Tweedie, F. (1996). Outside the cave of shadows: Using syntactic annotation to enhance authorship attribution. *Literary and Linguistic Computing, 11*(3), 121–132.

Bird, S., Klein, E., & Loper, E. (2009). *Natural language processing with Python*. O'Reilly Media Inc..

Benedetto, D., Caglioti, E., & Loreto, V. (2002). Language trees and zipping. *Physical Review Letters, 88*(4), 048702.

BNC Consortium. (2007). *The British national corpus, v3 (BNC XML Edition)*. Distributed by Bodleian Libraries, University of Oxford, on behalf of the BNC Consortium.

Bönninghoff, B., Nickel, R. M., Zeiler, S., & Kolossa, D. (2019). Similarity Learning for Authorship Verification in Social Media. In 2019 IEEE International Conference on Acoustics, Speech and Signal Processing:

Proceedings: May 12-17, 2019, Brighton Conference Centre, Brighton, United Kingdom. IEEE. 2457-2461. Retrieved from https://doi.org/10.1109/ICASSP.2019.8683405

Bönninghoff, B., Rupp, J., Nickel, R.M., & Kolossa, D. (2020). Deep Bayes factor scoring for authorship verification. Notebook for PAN at CLEF 2020. In CLEF 2020 Labs and Workshops, Notebook Papers. CEUR-WS.org. Retrieved from http://ceur-ws.org/Vol-2696/paper_151.pdf

Chang, C.-C., & Lin, C. J. (2011). LIBSVM: A library for support vector machines. *ACM Transactions on Intelligent Systems and Technology, 2*(27), 1–27.

Covington, M. A., & McFall, J. D. (2010). Cutting the Gordian knot: The Moving-average type–token ratio (MATTR). *Journal of Quantitative Linguistics, 17*(2), 94–100.

Daelemans, W., Van Den Bosch, A., & Zavrel, J. (1999). Forgetting exceptions is harmful in language learning. *Machine Learning, 34*(1-3), 11–41.

Honnibal, M., & Montani, I. (2017). *spaCy 2: Natural language understanding with Bloom embeddings, convolutional neural networks and incremental parsing.*

Juola, P. (2008). Authorship attribution. *Foundations and Trends® in Information Retrieval, 1*(3), 233–334.

Koppel, M., Akiva, N., & Dagan, I. (2006). Feature instability as a criterion for selecting potential style markers. *Journal of the American Society for Information Science and Technology, 57*(11), 1519–1525.

Lutosławski, W. (1890). Principes de stylométrie. *Revue des études grecques, 41*, 61–81.

Ma, W., Liu, R., Wang, L., & Vosoughi, S. (2020). Towards improved model design for authorship identification: A survey on writing style understanding. Retrieved from arXiv:2009.14445

Manning, C. D., Surdeanu, M., Bauer, J., Finkel, J., Bethard, S.J., & McClosky, D. (2014). The Stanford CoreNLP natural language processing toolkit. *Proceedings of the 52nd Annual Meeting of the Association for Computational Linguistics: System Demonstrations*. Association for Computational Linguistics. 55-60. Retrieved from https://www.aclweb.org/anthology/P14-5010

Mosteller, F., & Wallace, D. L. (1964). *Inference and disputed authorship: The Federalist*. Addison-Wesley.

Paszke, A., Gross, S., Massa, F., Lerer, A., Bradbury, J., Chanan, G., Killeen, T., Lin, Z., Gimelshein, N., Antiga, L., Desmaison, A., Kopf, A., Yang, E., DeVito, Z., Raison, M., Tejani, A., Chilamkurthy, S., Steiner, B., Fang, L., Bai, J., & Chintala, S. (2019). PyTorch: An imperative style, high-performance deep learning library. In H. Wallach, H. Larochelle,

A. Beygelzimer, F. d'Alché-Buc, E. Fox, & R. Garnett (Eds.). (2019). *Advances in Neural Information Processing Systems, 32,* 8024-8035.

Pedregosa, F., Varoquaux, G., Gramfort, A., Michel, V., Thirion, B., Grisel, O., Blondel, M., Prettenhofer, P., Weiss, R., Dubourg, V., Vanderplas, J., Passos, A., Cournapeau, D., Brucher, M., Perrot, M., & Duchesnay, E. (2011). Scikit-learn: Machine learning in Python. *Journal of Machine Learning Research, 12*, 2825–2830.

Stamatatos, E. (2009). A survey of modern authorship attribution methods. *Journal of the American Society for Information Science and Technology, 60*(3), 538–556.

Tweedie, F., & Baayen, R. H. (1998). How variable may a constant be? Measures of lexical richness in perspective. *Computers and the Humanities, 32*, 323–352.

Valla, L. (1439-1440). *De falso credita et ementita Constantini Donatione declamatio*. Retrieved from https://history.hanover.edu/texts/vallatc.html

van Halteren, H. (2019). Benchmarking author recognition systems for forensic application. *Linguistic Evidence in Security, Law and Intelligence (LESLI) Journal, 3*. Retrieved from http://www.lesli-journal.org/ojs/index.php/lesli/article/view/20

van Halteren, H., Baayen, R. H., Tweedie, F. J., Haverkort, M., & Neijt, A. (2005). New machine learning methods demonstrate the existence of a human stylome. *Journal of Quantitative Linguistics, 12*(1), 65–77.

van Halteren, H., van Hout, R., & Roumans, R. (2018). Tweet geography. Tweet based mapping of dialect features in Dutch Limburg. *Computational Linguistics in the Netherlands Journal, 8*, 138–162. Retrieved from https://clinjournal.org/clinj/article/view/84

9

Speaker Identification

Gea de Jong-Lendle

1 Introduction

Both authorship and speaker identification have in common that they belong to fields—that is, text analysis and forensic phonetics,[1] that are relatively young, with forensic phonetics being the older of the two disciplines. What is the meaning of forensic phonetics, and what are the typical tasks, apart from speaker identification, that forensic phoneticians are asked to do? 'Forensic' describes the use of scientific knowledge and methodology in the investigation and establishment of facts in a legal context. 'Phonetics' is the scientific study of speech sounds. Phoneticians study the production and transmission of sounds and how these are perceived (Crystal, 2010; Kohler, 1977, p. 25). Whereas forensic text analysts study written documents, the primary object of investigation for a forensic phonetician is the audio signal or the voice. In that sense, forensic phonetics can be understood as one of the applied phonetic sciences

G. de Jong-Lendle (✉)
Philipps-University of Marburg, Marburg, Germany
e-mail: dejong@staff.uni-marburg.de

V. Guillén-Nieto, D. Stein (eds.), *Language as Evidence*,
https://doi.org/10.1007/978-3-030-84330-4_9

that deals with sound aspects that are relevant to the justice system. Despite most of the casework having some connection with the judicature, a small portion of requests may come from clients outside. For example, a private request may come from a client who wants to know whether it is indeed his wife speaking on a particular recording. A firm may ask 'What is said between 1:02–1:04 min. of the recording of the annual meeting on date X?' A journalist needs to know whether the person speaking on the recording is politician X, football player Y or Prince Z. Needless to say, before a request is accepted, a number of issues relating to, for example, expertise, quality of the materials, urgency, significance, finances, ethics or personal interest is considered.

Identifying speakers is what people do, mostly subconsciously, on a day-to-day basis. When we are working in the office and we hear the footsteps of a colleague coming closer, we may subconsciously try to guess which of our colleagues could produce such a sound. The moment the person starts speaking to us, we identify the speaker as the friendly security man from downstairs. We also identify the neighbour speaking to her daughter outside in the garden as the loud lady from number 13.

The type of speaker identification described in this chapter is carried out by forensic phoneticians. They auditorily and acoustically analyse voices, usually unfamiliar to them, using phonetic expertise combined with sophisticated software especially designed to analyse speech and sound.

Speaker identification should not be confused with speaker verification, which is used in telephone banking or access control of high-security buildings. In speaker verification, the task is to verify a claimed identity. It is therefore far less complicated for a number of reasons: (1) it is highly unlikely that the employee who wants to enter the building is trying to disguise his/her voice, (2) the speaker is cooperative, generously providing samples as he wants to be recognised, (3) the total number of possible speakers, also called the 'speaker set' is limited, for instance, to the number of employees working in the building, (4) the text is predefined and (5) the recording is of high quality. In speaker identification, however, entirely different conditions apply: (1) voice disguise may be attempted, (2) the speaker is usually non-cooperative, (3) the speaker set is extremely large, (4) the text is spontaneous and freely chosen and (5) the recording is usually of poor quality.

In everyday life people also find speaker verification easier than identification: matching the voice of a caller with the name on the display of the telephone is easier than guessing the name of a caller, whose ID is suppressed and who starts the conversation with 'Hi, it's me'. On the other hand, if it concerns a high-quality recording of a very familiar voice, recognition may be fast: an EEG study carried out in Marburg showed that German listeners produced a neural response indicating recognition within 0.5 seconds for the voice of Angela Merkel (Rinke et al., 2021).

2 What Does a Forensic Phonetician Do?

In the early sixties, the work of forensic phoneticians was primarily devoted to speaker identification (French, 1994). Since then, we have seen a diversification of tasks. At present, forensic phonetic areas comprise speaker identification/comparison, audio transcription and audio enhancement. Other less common tasks are speaker profiling, audio authentication and voice line-ups. A description of each task is provided in Table 9.1. The exact distribution of task types may vary somewhat depending on whether a particular forensic team or expert has special expertise or a specific tool. An example of such a tool would be the microscope especially designed to vizualise magnetic patterns on audiotapes (see Boss, Gfroerer, & Neoustroev, 2003) or the dialect information system at the Research Centre of the Deutscher Sprach Atlas at the University of Marburg described in 5.2.1 (Schmidt, J. E., Herrgen, J., Kehrein, R., & Lameli, A., 2008).

3 The Beginning of Forensic Phonetics

In many countries, forensic phonetics started with an important criminal case in which the investigative police team, usually under public or political pressure, decided to explore new ways, like involving a linguist. The following sections will provide some examples of past cases that have had an influence on how the use of forensic phonetics expertise was viewed within the justice system.

Table 9.1 Description of the main tasks in forensic phonetics

	Forensic phonetics tasks	
1	Speaker comparison	The analysis and comparison, by ear and specialised sound- and audio software, of two recorded speech samples. The disputed sample is the speech of an unknown perpetrator—for example, the voice in the background of an emergency call or the bank robber shouting on a security camera recording. The reference sample is the speech of a suspect—for example, in a police interview, on a surveillance recording or in a recorded phone call. The phonetic analysis aims to evaluate the degree of consistency between the samples and, when consistent, the distinctiveness of the different features analysed.
2	Speaker profile	A speaker profile is requested for intelligence purposes and consists, if possible, of a description of speaker features to limit the number of possible suspects. These features may include the gender of the person, an estimation of his/her age, dialect, foreign accent, idiosyncrasies or even level of education or profession based on the sociolect or jargon used by the speaker.
3	Audio transcription	Producing a detailed description of the content of a recording including not only speech but also non-verbal material like crying, barking, doors closing, beeps of an answering machine, car engine noise, gunfire, among other things. The transcript can serve two purposes: (1) to assist in forensic investigations: surveillance recordings may exist from a car that was used to transport drugs, or a Black Box recording is recovered from a crashed plane, (2) to be used as incriminating evidence in a court of justice—for example, the defendant may mention the transfer of money on a disputed tape.
4	Audio enhancement	The quality of a recording can be degraded by noise and distortion resulting from inadequate equipment and recording methods or the acoustic environment in which it was produced. Transmission problems are frequent in the case of mobile telephone recordings. The intelligibility of a recording can be enhanced by applying digital frequency filters and using high-quality equipment. In the first stage, specialised software is employed to analyse the spectral characteristics of the signal. Based on this analysis, filters are constructed to reduce the intensity of particular frequencies—for example in the case of disturbing noise like mains hum, wind or ventilator, and hence improve the intelligibility of the recording.

(*continued*)

Table 9.1 (continued)

Forensic phonetics tasks	
5 Audio authentication	Examining whether, or not, the recording is authentic. Authentication analysis may also include assessing how the recording was made and which equipment was used.
6 Voice line-ups	Assisting the police in the construction of a fair voice line-up, also called a 'voice identification parade'. This procedure is applied when a witness has heard the voice but has not seen the speaker's face, and a recording of the criminal does not exist.

3.1 United Kingdom: The Kray Brothers

In Chap. 5 of Baldwin and French (1990, pp. 92–101), Baldwin describes how his first case was part of an intensive campaign in the 1960s by the London Police against two gangsters, the notorious Kray twins Ronnie and Reggie, who were dominating the underworld in London at the time. The police had successfully persuaded an associate of the Krays to cooperate and aid in securing the arrest of as many of his former colleagues as possible, in return for a reduced sentence. It so happened that this associate had to undergo an operation that provided the police with the opportunity to place surveillance equipment in his hospital room. The associate was instructed to invite any member of the Kray circle to visit him and engage them in conversations that could be incriminating. The speaker to compare was one of these visitors. Although the solicitor looked for a 'voiceprint' expert (Baldwin & French, 1990, p. 95), the London Police found Baldwin and a phonetics colleague willing to investigate the tape recordings after it was explained that there is no such thing as a 'voiceprint'.

3.2 United Kingdom: The 'Yorkshire Ripper'

Another case was Peter Sutcliffe, a serial killer, who had murdered at least 13 women and injured another seven mainly in the Leeds, Bradford, Huddersfield and Manchester area in Yorkshire between 1975 and 1980.

Between 1978 and 1979, the police and the *Daily Mirror* newspaper received several letters signed 'Jack the Ripper' and a recording, taunting the authorities for their unsuccessful investigation:

> I'm Jack, I see you are still having no luck catching me. I have the greatest respect for you, George, but, Lord, you are no nearer catching me now than four years ago when I started. I reckon your boys are letting you down George, they can't be much good, can they? The only time they came near catching me was a few months back in Chapeltown when I was disturbed. Even then it was a uniformed copper, not a detective. I warned you in March that I'd strike again. Sorry it wasn't Bradford, I did promise you that, but I couldn't get there. I'm not quite sure when I'll strike again, but it will be definitely sometime this year, maybe September or October, even sooner if I get the chance. I'm not sure where. Maybe Manchester, I like it there, there's plenty of them knocking about. (Ellis, 1994, p. 197)

In the press, the murderer subsequently became known as the 'Yorkshire Ripper'. Stanley Ellis and Jack Windsor Lewis, both academics from the University of Leeds, were asked to assist by identifying the speaker's dialect on the recording. Ellis had been the principal fieldworker for the 'Survey of English Dialects' (see Orton & Halliday, 1962; Orton et al., 1978) and was known for his expertise on British dialects. Both phoneticians identified the accent as coming from the Sunderland area, Sunderland being an industrial coastal town in County Durham (Ellis, 1994, p. 198). As Ellis was asked if he could be more specific on the speaker's origin, the decision was made that Ellis should visit the Sunderland area to meet the locals. Escorted by a constable, who knew the area and equipped with two tape recorders, Ellis (1994) started recording the people he met: 'We moved further inland to the small village of Castletown, and in a pub there, we met a retired man whose segmental pronunciations, intonation patterns, rhythm and tempo closely resembled those of the questioned speaker' (p. 202). Ellis reported that he believed the man on the tape had been brought up in the Southwick or Castletown area. Lewis (Ellis, 1994, pp. 207–216) also analysed the letters for linguistic markers. Based on the (incorrect) assumption that the content of the sent items contained details of the murders that were not known to the public (French et al., 2006, p. 255), the police took the view that the author/speaker had to be the murderer. The investigation was subsequently moved around 120 km up north from the Leeds-Manchester area, where the murders had been committed, to the Sunderland area. However, Ellis and Lewis warned the police that their claim might be incorrect. Several details of the case could, in fact, be read in public newspapers and, therefore, anyone who had followed the published articles on the case could have written these letters. Rob Rohrer, a reporter from the *New Statesman*, also confirmed that neither the recording nor the letters contained knowledge of the crimes that were not publicly available (Ellis, 1994, p. 204). In other words, the author/speaker could be a hoaxer. If this was true, the investigation should focus again on the area where the victims were killed.

3.2.1 The Arrest of Peter Sutcliffe

On 2 January 1981, the police in Sheffield came across Peter Sutcliffe, a lorry driver from Bradford. He was stopped and questioned for driving with false number plates. As the officers suspected that Sutcliffe could have something to do with the murders, he was sent to West Yorkshire Police for further questioning. He confessed being the perpetrator, saying that the voice of God had sent him on a mission to kill prostitutes. In that same year, Sutcliffe was convicted and sentenced to life imprisonment. In the meantime, the hoaxer's identity was still unknown, despite recordings of his voice having been broadcasted on the local radio.

3.2.2 The Arrest of the Hoaxer John Samuel Humble

In 2005, however, a man called John Samuel Humble was identified as a suspect in a 'cold hit': his DNA, stored in the UK national database of DNA, came up as a match with the DNA from one of the hoax letters. He was subsequently convicted for the hoax and sentenced to eight years in prison (French et al., 2006). What was Humble's geographical origin? He came from an area within one mile from Castletown, one of the areas that Ellis had mentioned in his report. The 'Yorkshire Ripper' case was the first one in which linguists played such an important role.

They provided a speaker profile, speaker comparison, enhanced recordings, and the text and handwriting reports.

3.3 Germany: Die Rote Armee Fraktion

In Germany, the RAF-case led to the first forensic phonetician joining the Bundeskriminalamt (BKA) as an expert in 1980. Up until this point, the BKA had merely focused on automatic speaker identification systems. This technology, however, had not shown to be effective in the case of telephone recordings.[2] As a consequence, the prosecution had difficulty providing the evidence that their suspects had been involved. They subsequently decided to have the audio analysis carried out by phoneticians. A number of them were involved in the notorious case against the alleged kidnappers and murder of Hans Martin Schleyer. The kidnappers demanded the release of the 'first generation' RAF- members, who had been sentenced to life in prison in 1977. The victim that was chosen was a successful economic official and was president of the German employers and industries associations at the time. Nevertheless, he was also known for his uncompromising attitude towards industrial protests and for his SS-involvement in the past. Despite the increasing pressure on the government, chancellor Helmut Schmidt decided against negotiations and declined their demands. Schleyer was killed on day 43 of his kidnapping after the kidnappers received the news that their comrades had committed suicide in their prison cells.

The involvement of linguists was crucial in the long and complicated trial that followed. In his book Künzel reported how he used spectrographic analysis to compare, among other features, the lisp of an anonymous caller with the lisp of an alleged kidnapper and RAF-member (1987, p. 65, p. 71). Realising how useful a phonetician's expertise can be for the analysis of disputed audio-material, the authorities created the first position for such a linguist: Hermann Künzel became the first officially appointed phonetician at the BKA.

3.4 Netherlands: The Kidnapping of Gerrit-Jan Heijn

In the Netherlands in 1987, businessman Gerrit-Jan Heijn was kidnapped. During the investigation the police decided to turn to the public for help. In this case it was the frustration about the lack of useful tips that was the main motivation for creating a position for a forensic phonetician at the national forensic laboratory in Rijswijk (Broeders, 1993, p. 239). The first phonetician to fill this position was Anton Broeders. Mr. Heijn, one of the top managers of Ahold and grandson of Albert Heijn, founder of the famous supermarket chain, was kidnapped on 9 September 1987. Three days later, the family received a letter stating that Mr. Heijn has been kidnapped. Between 17 September and 30 September, the family received a package containing his car key, a tape with his voice and at a later point, a letter demanding 7.7 million Dutch Guilders and diamonds. After several requests from the family for a sign of life, they received another tape, and on 16 October, a used film tube with Heijn's cut off finger. Three days later, another tape followed together with a letter of instructions for transferring the ransom money. Despite not having received a sign of life or having established contact by phone with the victim, the family decided to pay the money.

The planned delivery at the Hotel Okura in Amsterdam, however, failed. A later attempt to deliver the first half of the money succeeded. In December, the Haarlem police finally decided to include the public in their search for the kidnapper. The police played the part of the telephone conversation that the kidnapper had had with the receptionist of the Okura Hotel in 'Opsporing Verzocht', the Dutch version of 'Crimewatch', 'Aktenzeichen XY' or 'America's most wanted' (shown in a TV broadcast by Huys & Krabbé, 2019) (Table 9.2).

Furthermore, the police distributed posters and offered 1 million guilders for a relevant clue. The police subsequently received 12,000 reactions, none of these being relevant. At this point in time they decided to involve a linguist; this person was asked to construct a speaker profile to reduce the number of possible suspects (Broeders, 1993, p. 230). On 6 April, the kidnapper, Ferdi Elsas, was arrested; it had been noticed that someone had paid with a 250 guilder note belonging to the ransom

Table 9.2 Transcript of the phone call of kidnapper Ferdi Elsas with the receptionist of the Okura Hotel played in a Documentary by Huys and Krabbé in 2019

Speaker	Transcript
Receptionist	Hotel Okura, Goedenavond
Elsas	Mag ik de heer Rosa van u?
Receptionist	Hoe spelt u de naam, meneer?
Elsas	R, O, S, A.
Receptionist	R, O, S, A, moment alstublieft
Elsas	Hij moet, hij moet bij u op de receptie zitten
Receptionist	Hij moet bij ons aan de receptie zitten?
Elsas	Ja
Receptionist	Pardon, dat begrijp ik niet helemaal
Elsas	Hij is bij de receptie bij u
Receptionist	Nou, ik zie'm niet meneer. Waar zou hij moeten zijn?
Elsas	Bij de receptie
Receptionist	Bij de receptie? Ja, ik zie'm niet. Ik weet niet, over wie het gaat, wat voo-, wat is het voor iemand? Een gast?
Elsas	Nee
Receptionist	Meneer, wat is het voor persoon?
Elsas	Een man
Receptionist	Een man, en waarom, waarom zou hij bij de receptie zijn?

money in a liquor store in north-Amsterdam, a few kilometres away from where Elsas lived in Landsmeer. The kidnapper turned out to be a 46-year-old engineer, married with children, in need of money.

In a later interview, Elsas admitted having watched the kidnapping case with his wife and daughter when it was reported in 'Opsporing Verzocht', the Dutch version of Crimewatch. Surprisingly, neither his wife nor his daughter recognised Elsas' voice. One reason could be due to the difference in voice quality; recordings played to the public often stem from telephone communication and as a result the listener is confronted with a signal with a limited frequency bandwidth. Frequencies below 350Hz and above 3200Hz—that is 3400Hz or more in the case of digital telephony—are not transmitted, cutting off important frequencies that contribute to voice quality. Another reason is pointed out by Broeders (1993, p. 231) who argues that in our daily lives, we may be dealing with speaker verification more than identification. We expect to hear the voice of our husband, hearing him coming downstairs. When he speaks, our assumption is confirmed. When we receive a phone call, the caller usually identifies him/herself. We hear the voice and conclude that it matches the person calling. In 'Opsporing Verzocht', one does not usually expect to hear the voice of the spouse. Under these unusual circumstances, Mrs Elsas did not recognise her husband as the caller of the Okura Hotel.

3.5 United States: The Lindbergh Case

When we discuss landmark cases that led to the establishment of the field of forensic phonetics, the name of Frances McGehee should be mentioned. She was not a linguist but a psychologist whose interests were voice identification and earwitness testimony. She had wondered about the fact that in the famous case of the State v. Hauptmann in 1935, a positive speaker identification with a retention interval of almost three years, had been admitted in court and given enough weight to persuade the jurors to convict the accused. It concerned the kidnapping and murder of the baby of Charles Lindbergh in 1932 and the conviction of Bruno Richard Hauptmann, who received the death penalty. The case received worldwide attention. However, the verdict and the fairness of the methods applied remain controversial even up until this day. Despite the seemingly strong case against Hauptmann at the time of the trial, soon after, investigators criticised the way the investigation and the trial had been conducted and the evidence obtained.

3.5.1 Who Was Lindbergh, and Who Was Hauptmann?

On 21 May 1927, Charles Lindbergh was the first pilot who managed to cross the Atlantic flying solo from New York to Paris. In the two years before, six well-known aviators had lost their lives trying to do the same thing. The 25-year-old unknown Air-Mail pilot became an international hero overnight (see Berg, 1998; Bryson, 2013; and Lindbergh, 1953 for detailed reports). A few years later, in 1932, his son was kidnapped, and the body found a few months later. The nation was in shock. After an exhausting search with the investigators being under enormous public and political pressure, a suspect was found two years later in the person of Richard Bruno Hauptmann, an immigrant from Germany. He fitted a large number of criteria the most important being that he owned ransom money. When he used the money to pay at a petrol station, his licence plate was noted. Although he had always claimed to be innocent, he was sentenced to death (State v. Hauptmann, Atlantic Rep, 1935), and electrocuted on 3 April, 1936. Hauptmann always claimed that the money was given to him by a good friend of his, Isidor Fisch, who wanted to visit his family in Germany (Hauptmann, 1935, p. 176). Before leaving, Fisch gave Mr. Hauptmann a package to store in a safe and dry place. At the time, he assumed that the package contained personal letters and pictures but was unaware of its content. In 1934, Hauptmann was informed that Fisch had died of tuberculosis in Germany. When Hauptmann accidentally discovered that the package contained money, he decided to use it, as his friend owed him money (Hauptmann, 1935, p. 181). The case was never solved. Hauptmann never confessed, Fisch had died and a third suspect had committed suicide. On at least two occasions, Hauptmann could have been persuaded to confess. First, the prosecutor Wilentz and the governor Hoffman had offered to request the Court of Pardons to change his death sentence to life in prison in exchange for Hauptmann's official confession. Hauptmann rejected the offer (Dantz & Oehl, 2014, p. 38). Second, the newspaper *Hearst Papers* had offered Hauptmann $100.000 to be paid into a fund for his son, if they were allowed to publish a detailed account of the crime after his death. He also refused this offer. In the last weeks before his electrocution, Hauptmann wrote a long letter to his mother in the form of a biography and called it 'Mutter ich bin unschuldig' ('Mother I am innocent'). This manuscript detailed his childhood until the events leading to his conviction. In addition, he wrote a letter to the governor, the priest and correction officers. He wrote to the latter:

> Ich bin überzeugt, dass ihre Leiden, ihre Qual größer sein wird als meine. Meine wird sofort vorbei sein. Ihre wird solange andauern, wie das Leben selbst dauert. (Dantz & Oehl, 2014, p. 219). (Eng. translation: I am convinced that your suffering, your torment will be greater than mine. Mine will be over soon. Yours will last as long as life itself lasts.)

Paul Ebert, a book press firm in Kamenz, the birthplace of Hauptmann, tried to have it published. Some earlier version had already been distributed. However, Hitler and Göring, head commander of the German air forces, decided at the time to make the publication of the autobiography illegal. Specifically, Göring had established a good relationship with his aviator-friend Lindbergh and they judged the publication to be potentially uncomfortable for the Lindberghs. It took 70 years for the autobiography to appear again. In 2014, an early copy was republished by Dantz, the Mayor of Kamenz, and Oehl, an investigative journalist. Two years before, Spiegel-TV had produced a documentary about the case 'Kamenz und das Lindbergh Baby' (Seelmann-Eggebert, 2012).

It was reported that witnesses confessed that they had been paid to testify. Secondly, one officer admitted that Lindbergh had seen and heard Hauptmann two days after he was arrested and that Lindbergh had admitted that he could not perform the voice identification. At the trial, Lindbergh testified nevertheless. In addition, it was discovered that Dr. Condon, the negotiator in the case, had told the police, on several occasions, that Hauptmann was not the kidnapper he had met on two occasions. Hauptmann was heavier, had different eyes, different hair, among other differences. Also, the handwriting expert, Albert Osborn, concluded that Hauptmann could not have written the ransom notes. However, once he knew that part of the ransom money had been found in Hauptmann's house, he changed his mind. Another major concern was the fact that Lindbergh had only heard the voice briefly on two occasions. First, over the telephone straight after the kidnapping—an old-style telephone with poor fidelity (Hollien, 1990, p. 195) and second, while sitting in a car, at a distance of approximately ninety metres from the place where the money exchange was going to take place. On that occasion, Lindbergh only heard the words 'Hey, doctor! Over here, over here' (Solan & Tiersma, 2003, p. 373). In other words, the amount of speech Lindbergh had heard from the kidnapper was rather limited and heard under poor conditions.

Hauptmann's widow, Anna Hauptmann, always claimed her husband's innocence. With the help of Robert Bryan, a human-rights lawyer, she fought for his name to be cleared until she died at the age of 94. In 1986, the investigation breakthrough came in a court procedure in San

Francisco. Mrs. Hauptmann and other witnesses were allowed to give a detailed account of the circumstances or report incorrect court procedures at the time of the trial. As a result, the Court of Historical Review and Appeals ordered their colleagues in New Jersey to form a committee to re-investigate the case, and consider the possibility of a rehabilitation process. However, such a process has not happened and Hauptmann still counts as the officially charged kidnapper and murderer of the Lindbergh baby. Lawyers, reporters and investigators involved in attempting to have the case reopened saw the case as an argument against the death penalty (Bryan, 1991; Dantz & Oehl, 2014).[3] In the meantime, it has been recognised that speaker identifications by untrained witnesses are prone to error (Bricker & Pruzansky, 1966; Hollien, 2002; Rose, 2002; Solan & Tiersma, 2005; Yarmey, 1995, 2007). A considerable amount of research was carried out over the 1980s and 1990s, on the basis of which procedures for earwitness line-ups were established (Broeders & Rietveld, 1995; Clifford, 1980; Künzel, 1990; de Jong, 1998; de Jong-Lendle et al., 2015; Nolan, 2003; Rietveld & Broeders, 1991; and Solan & Tiersma, 2003).

3.5.2 Critical Discoveries

McGehee was the first researcher focusing on earwitness memory. Until that time, witness research had mainly focused on investigating eyewitness memory (Sporer, 1982, cited in Yarmey et al., 2008). McGehee's research findings were published in her doctoral dissertation at Johns Hopkins University in 1936, and McGehee (1937, 1944). The main question McGehee tried to answer was how well unfamiliar voices are recognised after a considerable interval of time has elapsed since its first occurrence. She used the following procedure to answer this question: 740 listeners divided into 15 subgroups listened to an unfamiliar adult reading a short passage from behind a screen. As she wanted to test their unintentional—also called 'incidental'—memory, the listeners were not explicitly told to remember the voice. Subsequently, the listeners' recognition memory was tested at various time intervals. The recognition task consisted of selecting the voice they had heard from a line-up of the target and four distractor voices or foils. Using the same setup, McGehee also investigated the effects of gender, ethnicity, voice disguise and several voices initially heard on recognition memory. In a subsequent study, McGehee (1944) investigated: (1) whether recordings can be used instead of live voices, (2) why some voices are recognised better than others, (3) whether training in music or speech makes a difference, (4) whether physical characteristics like age, height and weight, personality or profession can be derived from the voice. Her findings showed that for the first week, recognition scores were slightly above 80%. However, as shown in Fig. 9.1 below, after a two-week retention interval, scores dropped progressively—that is 69% (after two weeks), 51% (after three weeks), 35% (after two months), 13% (after five months).

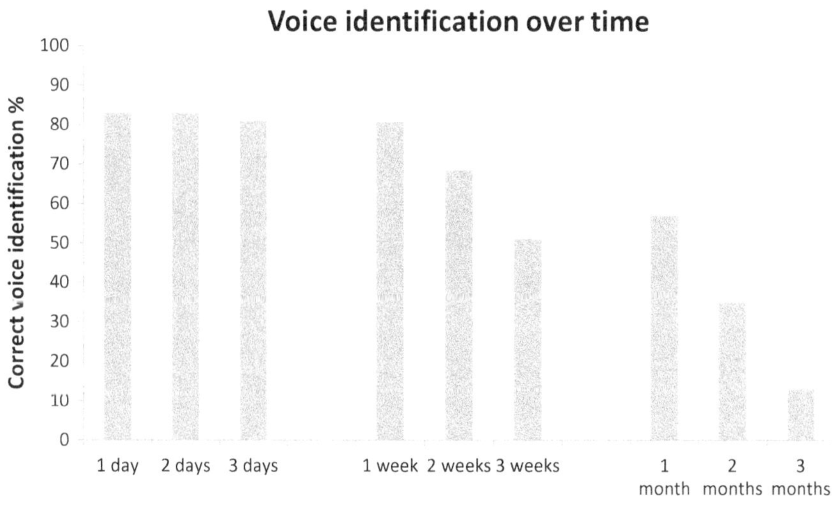

Fig. 9.1 Voice identification scores for different retention intervals based on the values reported by McGehee (1937)

3.5.3 Methodological Flaws but a Clear Message

In later articles, researchers recognised McGehee as the first earwitness researcher and pioneer of the field but also pointed out that her research design had certain flaws: a single person was used as the reader in most conditions, and the same group was assigned to more than one condition (Wells & Loftus, 1984; Thompson, 1985; Yarmey et al., 2008). As a result, the findings reported in McGehee's work cannot be generalised. However, her research can still be considered the first of its kind, and it showed a clear warning nevertheless: voice memory is less reliable than previously assumed and hence, this research area demands further investigation. McGehee died in 2004 at the age of 92. Since her first publication in 1937 the area of forensic phonetics developed rather quickly and it now profits from a solid research base, enabling scientists to find answers and improve forensic methods.

4 Methodologies

Over time new forensic analysis techniques were developed and methods and guidelines based on these new techniques were established in the forensic community. In the next section the main methods listed in Table 9.3 will be described.

4.1 The Auditory Method

The auditory method is probably most associated with John Baldwin, who provided a detailed description of this method in his book (Baldwin & French, 1990) and used the method for a number of years successfully in the court of law. Advocates of this method claim that speaker identification can be done by listening only. In Baldwin's view, the human ear and brain are uniquely equipped to interpret chaotic variability in speech; they can filter out what is not relevant and, by doing so, enable accurate description and comparison. Although he did not object to the combined auditory/acoustic approach, he claimed that the auditory method

Table 9.3 Speaker identification methods used over time

Methods of speaker identification	Description
1. Auditory Method	Comparing speakers through careful listening and a detailed phonetic analysis of the segmental features using the International Phonetic Alphabet (IPA) and supra-segmental features such as intonation by auditory reference to the notes of a musical scale (Baldwin & French 1990, p. 37). The main focus of the method is the speaker's dialect, voice quality and intonation patterns.
2. Voiceprint method	Comparing speakers solely through the analysis of spectrograms. Spectrograms are considered to be like a 'voiceprint', as unique as a fingerprint.
3. Auditory-Acoustic Method	Combining the descriptive findings from the auditory analysis with the quantitative findings of the acoustic analysis. If possible, adding estimations of specificity of features based on population statistics (e.g. Mean F0).
4. Automatic method	Automatic Speaker Recognition (ASR) software is used in surveillance and criminal investigations by police forces and intelligence agencies, often as a screening tool. The degree of similarity between samples is expressed as a likelihood ratio and calculated based on statistical models of speech-based features extracted automatically.
5. Auditory-Acoustic & Automatic Method	In addition to auditory and acoustic measurements, having the disputed and the reference recording being compared by an automatic system. As the automatic comparison can only be reliably applied, when a number of requirements are fulfilled (e.g. quality, duration, matching recording conditions) the combined method can at present only be applied in a limited amount of cases.

can stand alone, whereas the acoustic approach cannot. A critical review of the book and the method followed in 1991 by Francis Nolan. He argued that in addition acoustic analysis is necessary; the human hearing system is able to reduce or ignore information in the signal that is crucial for identification. This information can be recovered by acoustic analysis only. One example he described is the phenomenon of 'formant integration', where two different formants lying near each other are perceived as one formant (Nolan, 1991, p. 487). A spectrogram could prove the fact that two formants are present.

It was the case against Anthony O'Doherty that officially put an end to the evidentiary use of speaker comparison evidence based on auditory analysis only. Mr Doherty was convicted in 1997 of aggravated burglary and causing grievous bodily harm with intent, and sentenced to 12 years imprisonment, which he appealed. In the court of appeal, the defence expert Francis Nolan argued that the acoustic evidence showed that Mr. O'Doherty's voice was incompatible with that heard in the emergency call. Furthermore, using the same argument as in his 1991 paper, he argued that whereas auditory analysis can confirm whether or not, an accent and voice quality are the same, only objective acoustic analysis can show differences that the hearing system has learnt to ignore—for example differences in the shape and size of the mouth. The appeal was successful. In addition, the court officially stated that from then on auditory analysis should be complemented by acoustic analysis, which includes formant analysis (R. v. Anthony O'Doherty, 2002).

Nowadays, in the time of sophisticated speech analysis freeware like PRAAT (Boersma & Weenink, 2018) or Audacity, and the availability of a large number of acoustic phonetics courses at the university, it may be hard to imagine that this auditory method was ever seriously applied. However, this way of thinking has to be understood against the background of the intense voiceprint debate, which had reached its climax not long before. Second, at the time, speech analysis devices were expensive and the use of the auditory-only method was not uncommon. Whereas the auditory method was mainly a British problem, in the United States it was the voiceprint method that became problematic (French, 1994, p. 170).

4.2 The Voiceprint Method

In the late thirties, engineers from Bell Telephone in New Jersey worked on a special type of technology that consisted of making speech visible. One of these sound-spectrography devices was called Sonagraph—a sound analyser that could display a sound in a time-frequency-amplitude plot. The original motivation for this technique was to study speech production and measurement and also help deaf people to improve their speech. During World War II, however, the US-Government explored the technology for military purposes. It remains unclear what exactly happened in the years during the war, as these studies were classified. However, based on Bush, Conant and Pratt's report (1946, p. 35)[4] that became declassified in 1960, it is known that one of the goals was to analyse scrambled speech from intercepted communication, arguing that it is easier to detect a cryptographic coding strategy from a picture than from an audio recording.[5] The spectrograph technology may have served another purpose as well: the identification of speakers. In 1944, two engineers, Grey and Kopp, published an indoor report entitled 'Voiceprint Identification'. They used the term 'voiceprint' referring to a spectrogram as a way to capture someone's voice in a printed format in analogy with the fingerprint (Grey & Kopp, 1944). Two publications followed making the invention public to the rest of the world. In 1945, Potter published his article 'Visible patterns of speech' in the *Science Journal*, and a more detailed account was provided in a book by Potter, Kopp and Green in 1947.

Some years later, in 1960, the New York City Police Department received a number of calls containing bomb threats against some major airlines. The case led to a renewed interest in 'voiceprints'. The FBI requested assistance from Bell Labs in the identification of the individuals making the telephone calls. Physicist Lawrence G. Kersta, who was familiar with the spectrograph studies, was given the task to carry out speaker identification. Soon after, in 1962, Kersta published a paper called 'Voice identification' in which he claimed that speakers could be uniquely identified using spectrographic images. In addition, he described how some experiments based on voiceprint matching produced minimal error rates below 3%. Only four years later in 1966, the Michigan State Police created a voice identification unit under the direction of Lieutenant Ernest Nash, whom Kersta had trained. In 1971, the *International Association of Voice Identification* was founded. Several courts started to admit the voiceprint technique as evidence. In a short time, the method had gained popularity amongst certain forensic practitioners and police forces. This development prompted the *Acoustical Society of America* to set up the Technical Committee on Speech Communications', consisting of six respected members of the society, to evaluate Kersta's studies. In their report published in 1970, known as the Bolt Report, Kersta's findings were not supported but heavily criticised for several reasons: (1) the voiceprint method was never explained and could, therefore, not be repeated, (2) heterogeneous samples of voices were used—for example, different accents, different ages, among other elements that could explain the spectrographic differences, (3) a closed design was used so that subjects merely selected the best match, even though in forensic circumstances an open set is applicable in the majority of cases and (4) the method was lacking standardised decision criteria for judging whether two spectrograms matched, making the decision process highly subjective (Bolt et al., 1970; Stotland & Brown, 1978). In 1972, Tosi, Oyer and Nash in response to the criticism expressed in the Bolt Report reported the results of a two-year project: low error rates below 0.51% were found for closed set designs using words spoken in isolation; the error rate for open trials using non-contemporary spectrograms and words spoken in a random context was over 18%; 6.4% were false identification errors and 11.8% were false elimination errors (Tosi et al., 1972). A response to the Tosi article by the Bolt Committee followed in 1973, criticising the lack of decision criteria again and pointing out a considerable disagreement among different panels of observers as to what constitutes a match when given the same task (Bolt et al., 1973; Stotland & Brown, 1978). In the meantime, the voiceprint controversy was moved into the court, where the Frye Ruling was subsequently put to the test. The Frye Ruling states that a new method is admissible when it is shown to be generally accepted as a reliable method within the particular field to which it belongs (Frye v. United States, 1923). The voiceprint discussion raised some questions regarding this ruling: (1) How many scientists are required to fulfil the 'generally accepted' requirement? (2) How can a new method be qualified as 'generally accepted'? (3) How do we handle the problem of conflicting opinions within the same field? See Anonymous (1998) for a detailed report from a legal perspective. In the meantime, several studies were carried out to test the reliability of the voiceprint method, all of these producing error rates much higher than those reported by Kersta (1962) and Tosi et al. (1972). When testing disguised voices, Hollien and McGlone (1976) found a 75% error rate and Reich et al. (1976) reported between 50%–78% error rates. Rothman (1977) tested the voiceprint method

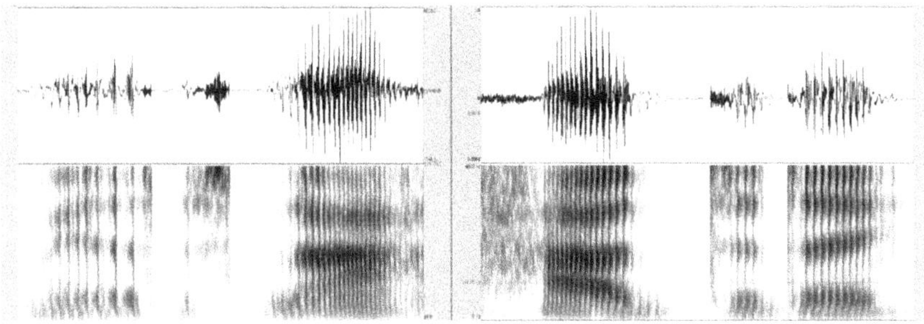

Fig. 9.2 The *same* (creaky) male speaker reading 'had today' in the left recording with a rising F0 ('uptalk'), in the right with a final fall. The speaker is SSBE-speaker nr. 37 from the DyViS database (Nolan et al., 2009)

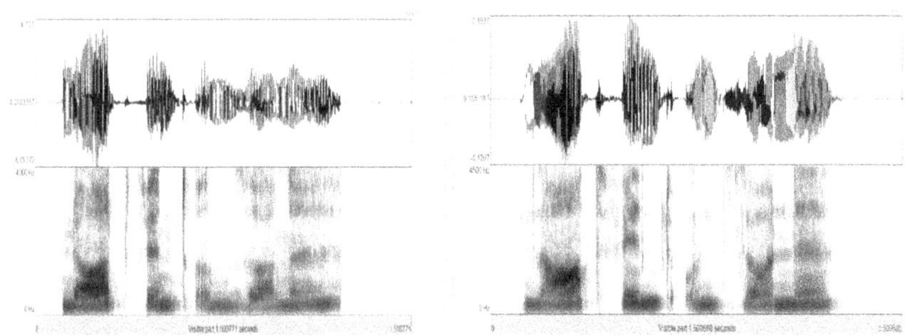

Fig. 9.3 Two *different* female speakers, German students at the university of Marburg, with the same accent and a similar voice quality (left, slightly breathier towards the end) reading 'Nordwind und Sonne'

using sound-alikes and non-contemporary samples and found error rates ranging between 61% and 94%.

The spectrogram pairs above are some examples that show where the voiceprint method could go wrong. It is noteworthy that these are high-quality samples recorded in a sound-proof booth—poor quality recordings may be even more problematic (Figs. 9.2 and 9.3).

The controversy about the voiceprint method has not been solved; however, based on the high error rates reported in a large number of studies, the majority of the relevant scientific community members believe that the method is not reliable or scientific enough to be used in investigations or in court. In 2007 the *International Association for Forensic Phonetics and Acoustics* (IAFPA) passed the resolution that the association dissociates itself from the voiceprint method; the approach is considered to be without scientific foundation and should not be used in forensic casework.[6] The method has not completely disappeared and is most probably still in use in certain areas of the world. In 2002 voiceprint evidence was used in an Australian court (Rose, 2002). Poza and Begault (2005) claimed that the method has improved and that it could provide reliable data in legal situations. Schwartz (2006) explained that the voiceprint problem in the US is twofold. First, the accreditation of crime labs is usually based on standards defined by official working groups. Typically, these groups consist of audio engineers without a linguistic background. The entire process is managed exclusively by the FBI who are still using voiceprints for investigative use. Second, the methods of private voiceprint examiners are less regulated. Even now, companies in the US are still offering voice identification services based on aural and spectrographic analysis.[7] Apart from being associated with an unreliable method, the term 'voiceprint' is problematic for another reason: It suggests that there is a unique print that can distinguish individuals as much as a 'fingerprint' can.[8]

A final word on the voiceprint method and the use of spectrograms: What was criticised was the voiceprint method, reducing speaker comparison to a highly subjective pattern-matching task, and the analysts who performed it, engineers lacking any background knowledge in linguistics. Spectrography itself was still seen as a useful tool in forensic phonetics. It shows valuable features such as formants and other speaker-specific resonances and voice quality features, e.g. creak and breathiness (cf. Nolan, 1997, p. 763).

4.3 The Auditory-Acoustic Method

The auditory-acoustic methods combines the descriptive findings from the auditory analysis with the quantitative findings of the acoustic analysis. A detailed description of this method can be found in Sect. 5.

4.4 The Automatic Method

At the beginning of the 1990s and in the years following, the use of Automatic Speech Recognition systems (hereinafter ASR) for forensic speaker identification was seen rather critically by IAFPA members. This had a reason: at the time, the technology was often used by engineers, who reported their findings as evidence in a trial without their recordings being subjected to a detailed linguistic analysis. The conclusions were ASR-based only. This strategy changed over time and, judging by the increasing number of IAFPA-conference contributions on ASR methods in the past years, the automatic comparison of speakers is gaining acceptance as an additional tool in forensic speaker analysis.

The ASR method involves the following stages: first, the expert chooses from the available recording selections that he/she deems suitable for the automatic analysis. Subsequently, acoustic characteristics are automatically extracted. Typical features are Mel Frequency Cepstral Coefficients, Linear Prediction Cepstral Coefficients, formant frequencies, F0, intensity, duration and N-grams (Drygajlo et al., 2015). The parameter distributions for both the disputed and the reference speaker are transformed into a mathematical model. The system subsequently compares these two models and compares the disputed model with a set of models from a reference population of other ideally very similar speakers stored in the system. The output of the comparison is the likelihood ratio (LR) indicating the strength of the evidence. The LR is best explained as the ratio of the probability of the evidence in favour and against the hypothesis. The difference between (forensic) ASR and semi-ASR systems lies at the feature extraction level; specifically, in the latter this process involves human intervention.

ASR can be quite successful in discriminating between speakers when the samples were recorded under controlled conditions. However, samples that do not match in terms of the speaker characteristics—for example health, emotions, speaking style—or in terms of technical and environmental circumstances—for example, microphones, recording device, background noise—can be potentially problematic. Mismatched conditions can be solved to a certain extent—for example, by the removal of background noise or selections with emotional speech. There are obvious advantages to ASR systems. For example, the minimally subjective component during the analysis and the interpretation, the speed at which they operate (French & Stevens, 2013), the fact that different languages can be analysed (the system mainly judges resonance features) and the fact that results are expressed in LRs. The latter is considered to be a logically correct way of reporting results in court cases (Evett, 1998; Robertson & Vignaux, 1995). Some important disadvantages are: (1) useful information is ignored or not used—for example, lexical information, voice-onset-time and the articulation of particular sounds; (2) the system only works with recordings having a reasonably good Signal-to-Noise ratio. However, the problem is that noisy recordings are the standard in forensic casework. In this respect, Harrison and French (2010) reported that in a study involving 767 recordings from past cases, 80% of the recordings would have to be rejected or thoroughly re-edited before being suitable for automatic analysis; (3) the end-user does not usually know the mathematical calculations on which the result is based; (4) the system may not have the reference population that is needed or the appropriate population may be difficult to define. The use of non-matching populations has been criticised (Hughes & Foulkes, 2014, p. 5; Morrison et al., 2012); (5) most systems can be quite expensive and even require expensive training; and (6) some users may be tempted to base their report conclusions on the outcome of the ASR system only, possibly due to the absence of linguist colleagues who can analyse and interpret the data or due to pressure from the management.

Another concern or limitation is expressed in French and Stevens (2013, pp. 189–190). In their view, ASR-technology primarily examines supra-laryngeal vocal tract resonance features.[9] These features are defined by the speaker's anatomy and by regionally defined articulatory settings. Studies on the anatomic features of the vocal tract have shown, however, that little variation exists between speakers of the same gender, age and racial background. For example Xue and Hao (2006) reported minimal standard deviations between 0.54 and 1.33 cm for 20 subjects per racial group for the parameters of oral length, pharyngeal length and total vocal tract length calculated for White American, African American and Chinese men. These minimal inter-speaker differences in addition to the plasticity of the vocal tract (Nolan, 1983) make the authors conclude that:

> Given that ASR systems work exclusively on analysis of this output, it leads to a performance limitation that is unlikely to be surmounted simply by further technical development of ASR software. (French & Stevens, 2013, p. 189)

4.5 The Auditory-Acoustic and Automatic Method

The automatic method can be applied in combination with the auditory-acoustic approach, as long as the following requirements are satisfied: (1) the quality is reasonably good, (2) the duration is long enough, 15–60 seconds are reported depending on the system used, (3) the recording background of the samples under comparison is similar, (4) the speaking modes match in terms of style and emotional status and (5) the comparison is calculated against a reference population matching the speakers. Due to future technological developments, these requirements may change over time; however, at present this applies to approximately 10%–20% of the cases. Nevertheless, automatic approaches can still be useful in the investigative process, e.g. as a screening tool when large numbers of calls are involved; as a backup estimate when language/accent disguise is attempted;[10] and assisting the phonetician in the foil speakers selection process for a voice parade (Gerlach et al., 2020).

5 The Auditory-Acoustic Method in Speaker Comparison

As the auditory-acoustic method is currently considered the method that is most reliable in the majority of casework, this section is devoted to this type of analysis. Short examples are used to demonstrate how the analysis is done. Synonyms used for this method are phonetic-acoustic, auditory-acoustic or auditive-instrumental. The first detailed description of this method was provided by Künzel (1987) in his 'Sprecher-Erkennung: Grundzüge forensischer Sprachverarbeitung' and a summary provided by the same author in 2003. The main principle is that a detailed linguistic analysis is carried out of all speaker-specific features found in the recording by a forensic linguist/phonetician. These features are extracted from three different areas: voice, language and speaking manner. The extraction process consists of two stages: (1) features extracted auditorily (subjective) and (2) objectively quantified by acoustic measurements. In Table 9.4 several useful parameters are listed for analysis in casework. It should be noted that in forensic analysis not all of these parameters may

Table 9.4 An overview of the speaker characteristics analysed in the auditory-acoustic method

Voice	
Pitch	Measured in F0 (mean, mode, median, sentence-final fall)
Intonation/Melody	Measured in F0-range, F0-SD or F0-Varco
Voice quality	Auditorily categorised using VQ description schemes (e.g. Laver framework, RBH-scales) Measured as vocal fold vibration patterns as jitter (F0 variability) or shimmer (intensity variability) or Harmonics-to-Noise-Ratio VQ-measurements only apply to high-quality recordings (rare)
Language	
Dialect	Type and degree (measured as the total number of deviations from the standard language)
Foreign accent	Type and degree (measured as the total number of deviations from the standard language)
Sociolect	Language variety spoken by a particular social group, like the jargon associated with a particular profession or teenager speech associated with an age group
Idiolect	An idiolect is a language variation that characterises a particular individual
Speaking manner	
Articulation and speaking rate	Total number of syllables per second as syllable rate (or articulation rate, when pauses are subtracted)
Pausing behaviour	Number, duration, type (e.g. silent pause or filled pause or combination of both)
Phonetic Quality (timbre) of filled pauses	Formant distribution of the vowel in fillers like 'uh' or 'uhm'
Breathing behaviour	Frequency, duration, spectrum of in-exhalations
Rhythm	Timely distribution of accents
Pathological features	Pathological characteristics are highly specific, e.g. a lisp resulting in extra strong resonances in certain areas of the spectrum

be acoustically quantified. Apart from a number of standard measurements in the report, the expert usually selects additional parameters based on their discrimination potential. Parameters with a low specificity for that case may be left undiscussed—for example, breathing patterns or rhythm.

5.1 Voice

5.1.1 Fundamental Frequency

Whether a person is speaking with a high or low voice can be measured by calculating the mean F0 in Hertz—that is cycles per second—over a stretch of speech.[11] It is a direct measure of the number of times the vocal folds are completing an opening and closing cycle. The approximate mean F0 for German men is 115Hz and 219Hz for women (Künzel, 1987). An advantage of the F0 mean is the fact that this measure can be compared with other studies, as most studies report the F0 mean. However, this measure is highly influenced by extreme F0 values that can be found in laughter or highly emotional speech. It is, therefore, important to carefully edit the sample beforehand. Another advantage is that most population statistics for F0 are based on the mean. From such a distribution curve (Hudson et al., 2007; Künzel, 1987; Lindh, 2006), it is possible to derive the specificity of a particular value. The mode is a measure less sensitive to extreme values. Another value that is rather stable is the F0 of the sentence-final fall (de Jong et al., 2005) even with raised intensity levels.

The standard deviation from the mean F0 would be an indication of how lively or monotonous the person is speaking. However, both Künzel (1987) and Kraayeveld (1997) indicate that F0 variation should be expressed as a variation coefficient, as F0–SD is also dependent on the mean F0; it increases as the mean F0 of the speaker increases. The 'varko' is calculated as 100 * (F0-SD/F0-Mean). A male speaker with a Varko of 11% or lower speaks fairly monotonous. Speakers with a Varko above 23% speak lively. Average is a Varko between 15% and 19% (Jessen et al., 2005).

It is important to note that the mean value of F0 increases when the intensity of the speaker increases (Jessen et al., 2005). It is therefore common to find a higher mean F0 in disputed criminal recordings, where the speaker may speak louder, compared to reference recordings in which the speaker is being interviewed in a police station or is having a relaxed conversation with his partner on the phone.

5.1.2 Voice Quality

Voice quality, in the broader sense of the term, is defined by both laryngeal features and supra-laryngeal features. It depends on the vibration patterns of the vocal folds and on the resonances of the vocal tract. For example, vocal folds that vibrate irregularly may give the speaker a hoarse voice. Incomplete closure, on the other hand, may make the voice sound breathy. A creaky voice can be caused by very low pulmonic air pressure resulting in a low and slightly irregular vibration rate. A voice may sound hyponasal when the nasal cavity is blocked, for example, due to a cold. Although voice quality is an important feature in forensic reports, and although phoneticians are well-equipped with the detailed classification framework of Laver (1980) and the transcription VoQS system designed by Ball et al. (1995), none of these frameworks have been systematically used in the past. Some of the reasons may be the complexity of Laver's classification, a lack of training, the poor quality of the recording (Nolan, 2005), and high inter-rater reliability (Kreiman & Gerrat, 2011). Over the last 15 years, however, efforts have been made to enable a qualified voice quality assessment as part of the forensic analysis again. For an excellent introduction including the proposal for a simplified VQ scheme, see Köster and Köster (2004). Training schemes have shown to improve inter-rater agreement (Köster, Jessen, Khairi, & Eckert 2007; San Segundo et al., 2019). The RBH classification[12] of Nawka and Anders (1996) has been successfully used in Germany as a classification and diagnostics tool for voice pathology. As their publication includes a CD with useful samples, it can be recommended for training and calibration purposes. The publication by Eckert and Laver (1994) includes audio samples from a non-pathological perspective. A project on 'Population statistics on voice quality' was recently completed in Brandenburg: voice quality for 215 male speakers between 18 and 45y. was judged by four experts (see also Kluge et al., 2018).

As far as recording quality is concerned, when the quality of the samples is unusually good, the acoustic measurements considered to be associated to voice quality like jitter, shimmer and Harmonics-To-Noise-Ratio (HNR) can be attempted. On the other hand, when the quality of the recording is poor and/or very different in type between the samples, the expert should be careful, as for example reverberation can have a strong effect. In such cases, it may be impossible to make a VQ judgement or conduct VQ measurements.[13]

5.2 Language

The most important tool here are analytic ears and IPA-transcription training. The first international phonetic alphabet was created in 1888. The alphabet has undergone a number of revisions during its history, including some major ones codified by the IPA Kiel Convention (1989). Since then, the IPA-Chart has stayed fairly stable and the changes applied are only minor.

As can be seen in Table 9.4, the basic principle of language analysis in casework is to use an officially known standard variety as the reference and to describe the deviations from this reference language found in the sample. Different types of language variety are dialect (or other versions that are region-based), foreign accent, sociolect and idiolect.

5.2.1 Dialect and the REDE-System

A dialect may take the form of a small number of dialectal features in the otherwise fairly standard variety to a large number of deviations from the standard language in a traditional dialect. In the case of a speaker profile, a detailed feature analysis may give the phonetician an idea of the region, where the speaker spent their youth, or where the foreign speaker may have learnt their German. The Deutsche-Sprach-Atlas in Marburg is particularly fortunate to have inherited the old dialect maps of Georg Wenker (1852–1911), a linguist who collected dialectal information from

Table 9.5 A phonetic analysis of a German speaker saying the words 'stand', 'have' and 'are'

Variable	Standard German variant	Non-standard variant
stehen (inf.) *'to stand'*	ʃteːən	ʃtɪː
haben (1st pl) *'we have'*	haːbən	huː
sind (1st pl) *'we are'*	zɪnt	za͡e

approximately 40,000 different places in Germany. The Wenker database was incorporated into a dialectological Information System called REDE (www.regionalsprache.de) together with another 30 linguistic databases on German dialects and a few other neighbouring languages like Dutch and Frisian.

In the following example, a small demonstration is given about the potential of a dialectal information system. In this case, the analysed speaker exhibited several dialectal features. These are shown in Table 9.5.

When these three dialectal features were imported in the REDE-System, the following 100x100km region was defined based on the area that all filtered selections shared (Fig. 9.4).

5.2.2 Foreign Accents

In a past speaker profiling case the criminal was part of a well-organised call-centre: callers would contact their victims who had responded to a too-good-to-be-true job-advertisement. The purpose of the call was to explain the new job and collect their personal banking details to arrange for 'their salary to be paid'. The caller was fluent in German but exhibited a strong East-European accent. Based on a detailed phonetic analysis, it was assumed that the caller´s native language was Russian. Here are a few examples of the phonetic features found:

1. The vowels in stressed syllables, short in standard-German, are produced long—for example *niiischt* for 'nicht'. This was also found for the first component of diphthongs in stressed syllables—for example *Paaaula* for 'Paula'.

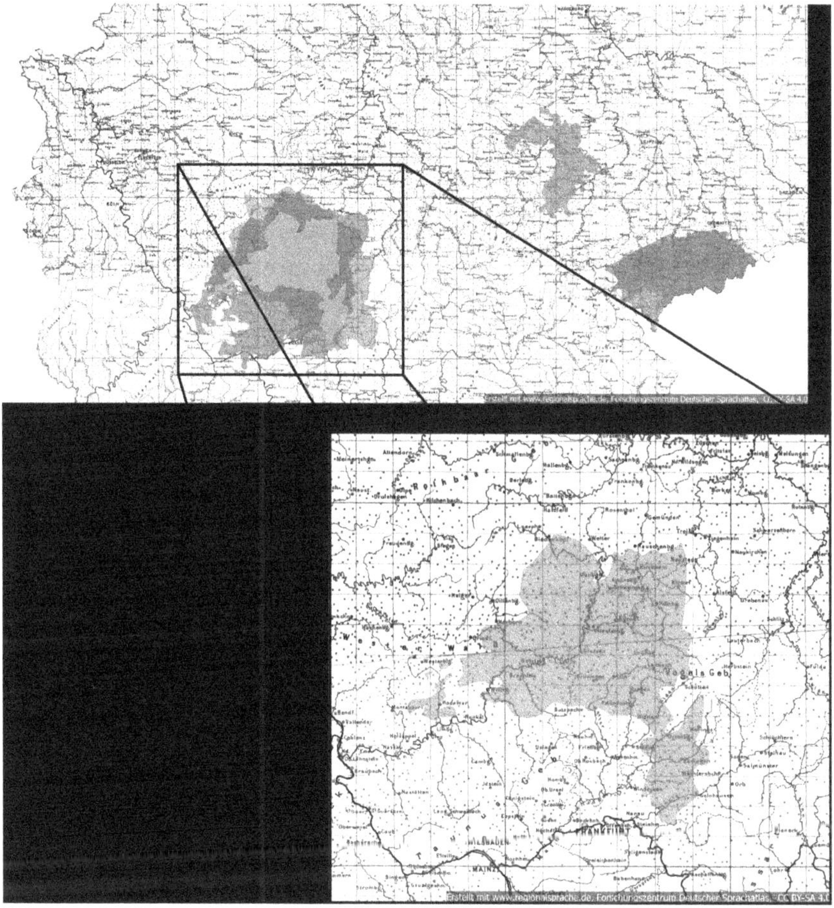

Fig. 9.4 The region defined by REDE, based on the pronunciation of the words 'stand', 'have' and 'are' (Kehrein, 2021)

2. Apical realisation of the r-sound in the coda—for example, in Theodor; uvular productions like [ʁ] are rare.
3. Voiceless plosives are produced without aspiration—for example, in Paula.
4. The German velar nasal /ŋ/, which is not present in the inventory of the Russian, is produced incorrectly as [ŋk] or [ŋg].

5. Regressive voice assimilation in Lu<u>d</u>(wig).
6. The [ɡ, s, k, l, f] are palatalised (= secondary articulation).
7. The German vowel /ɔ/ is produced as [a] in unstressed syllables in *M<u>a</u>ment, D<u>a</u>kument, <u>A</u>ktober* instead of Moment, Dokument and Oktober. This feature is common in Russian.

Another phenomenon was noticed: the speaker produced different sounds for the word-initial /g/. In the German word *geantwortet,* it was produced as a palatalised voiced velar fricative [ɣʲ] and in the word *gut* as an (unaspirated) voiceless velar plosive [k]. The pronunciation of /b, d/ in word-initial position was unmarked. It was suspected that the speaker could be speaking a variety of Russian spoken in the south-west of Russia or in East-Ukraine: here the [g] does not exist. The /g/ is pronounced as a voiced velar or glottal fricative (in allophonic variation). The [k] in *gut* was considered his incorrect interpretation of the German [ɡ̊]; in standard-German the sounds [b d g z ʒ] are slightly devoiced word-initially. As it turned out later, the caller came from Rostow am Don, a city in the south-west of Russia and close to the East-Ukrainian border.[14]

5.2.3 Sociolect and Idiolect

The sociolect concerns the variety that is typical for a social group. This could be an age group (e.g. 'teenager-talk') or it may involve the jargon related to a particular profession. In Germany, a new variety has developed in the last 20 years called 'Kiez-Deutsch'. Although its origin is in Berlin-Kreuzberg, it is now spoken by young people with and without a migrant background, in multicultural urban regions all over Germany. It is a mix of a number of foreign language features implemented in German (Dirim & Auer, 2004). The sentence 'Lassen wir mal am Moritzplatz aus dem Bus steigen' is reduced to 'Lassma Moritzplatz aussteigen' (Wiese, 2012).

An idiolect is a language variation that is characteristic for an individual speaker (Hazen, 2006; Jessen, 2012, pp. 176–177; Künzel, 1987, p. 87). In a speaker-profiling case, the suspect, a detective selling confidential information from a police database to his criminal clients, exhibited features that are typical for a London accent together with segmental and supra-segmental features—for example, intonation—from the lowlands area of Scotland. This fairly specific combination of features can be considered his idiolect.

5.3 Speaking Manner

5.3.1 Articulation and Speaking Rate

In normal spontaneous speech, sounds are articulated between 50% and 60% of the time. In the remaining part of the time, pauses occur for planning and breathing (Goldman-Eisler, 1968). People vary in their speaking and articulation rates. These rates can, therefore, be useful parameters to measure in speaker identification (Künzel, 1997). The difference between both types of rates is that articulation rate (hereinafter AR) is measured without pauses, while the speaking rate (SR) is measured including the pauses. As a result, the AR is a measure of pure articulation speed and has shown to have a smaller intra-speaker variability than the speaking rate.[15] The following case involved a young speaker with an exceptionally high articulation rate.

A woman called the emergency services and reported a burglary in a small village. The police arrived at the scene and did not find any evidence of a burglary having taken place. At the same time, a group of men were trying to break into some ATM-machines in a town 15 km away. At a later point in time, drawing on the traces left at the scene, the investigators found the men responsible. As it turned out, the leader of the group had a 23-year-old girlfriend, who sounded quite similar to the caller in the disputed emergency call and exhibited an equally high articulation rate. In addition, a caller in another emergency call relating to a 'crash-and-grab' theft shared a number of features with both speakers as well. The police requested a speaker comparison analysis comparing the caller in each of the emergency calls with the reference recording of the suspected girlfriend.

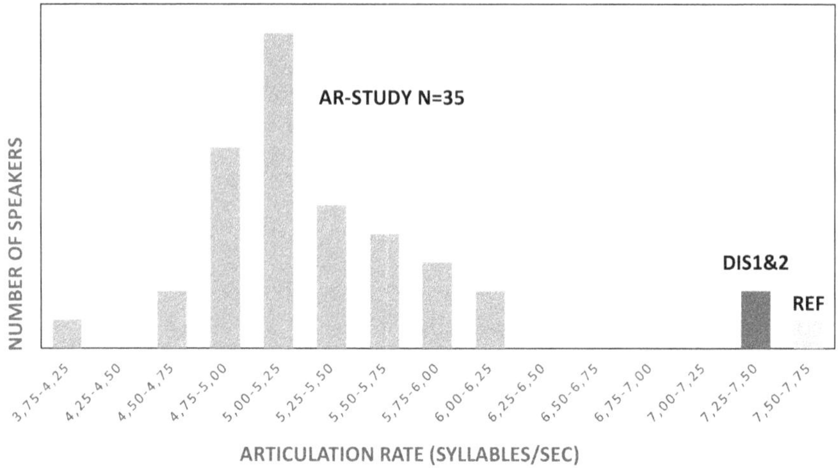

Fig. 9.5 Articulation rate distribution (syll./s) for 35 female German speakers (20–25y.) speaking spontaneous compared with the AR rates found for the two emergency calls and the reference recording. Calculations are based on a minimum of 15 Memory Stretches per person (Mean 24,4 MS) using the measuring method described in Jessen (2007). Study carried out at the University of Marburg to provide background data for a forensic case involving a 23-year woman exhibiting an extremely high articulation rate above 7 syll./s.

Using the AR measuring method described in Jessen (2007), it was found out that the caller in emergency call 1 exhibited extremely high AR rates between 4.2–8.8 syll./s with a mean of 7.3 syll./s. The woman in the second call exhibited rates that were equally high between 6.2–9.0 syll./s, mean 7.4 syll./s. The reference recordings showed AR rates between 5.2–8.7 syll./s. with a mean of 7.6 syll./s. In the absence of AR population data for young women, the investigators decided that a small study testing the AR-rate in spontaneous speech for 35 female speakers (20–25y.) should be carried out. Despite the fact that the case recordings were most probably produced under more stressfull conditions compared to the laboratory conditions, the results showed that the rates found in the disputed and reference material are quite specific indeed (Fig. 9.5).

In this study, the AR rates were calculated with the help of PRAAT, as this software contains some useful functions. The recordings were divided in memory stretches using first the annotate>to Textgrid (silences) function in PRAAT. The boundaries were subsequently corrected when necessary. In case too many silences were counted in the resulting textgrid, the 'Min. Silent interval' was increased to 0.25s or more.

5.3.2 Pausing Behaviour

It was shown that this parameter is a valuable speaking manner measure, as speakers tend to organise and produce their thinking and breathing pauses differently. Useful literature on this topic includes Clark and Fox Tree (2002), Corley and Stewart (2008), Jessen (2012) and Künzel (1987).

5.3.3 Breathing Behaviour

Breathing patterns[16] are not necessarily measured, unless the speaker shows an unusual pattern. In case the inhalations are more frequent than usual and exhibit audible friction noise due to poor health, spectral measurements may be useful.

5.3.4 Rhythm

Languages differ in their temporal patterns. When listening to Spanish in comparison to English, one notices that the former shows a much faster staccato-type rhythm pattern than the latter. According to Pike (1945) and Abercrombie (1967) the rhythm of languages is either stress-timed rhythm or syllable-timed. In a stress-timed language like English and German, the metrical foot plays an important role in the rhythmical organisation, whereas in a syllable-timed languages like Spanish and French it is the syllable (Laver, 1994). Different forensic scientists have tried to construct a timing measure to quantify rhythm patterns and study their intra-speaker variability. The percentage of a syllable that is vocalic, indicated as %V, was introduced as a temporal measure by Ramus et al. (1999). Dellwo (2006) and Dellwo et al. (2015) showed that this measure and its derivatives may be forensically useful. Other researchers studying the temporal domain of speech are Johnson and Hollien (1984), who showed that timing information derived from the amplitude envelope is speaker specific even when disguise is attempted. McDougall (2004, 2006) found that temporal features derived from the dynamics of formant frequencies vary between speakers.

5.3.5 Pathology

In the case of a suspected pathology, it is useful to consult a clinical linguist. Despite the fact that most phoneticians are able to produce an accurate description of the person's speech, it may still be useful to consult the expert. Knowing the cause, stability, durational aspects of the pathology, occurrence and factors having an effect on the severity of the pathology, allows the forensic expert to interpret the findings correctly.

In a past case the person being investigated happened to be a detective. In the UK, it is standard practice that police interviews are recorded. Therefore, a large number of interview tapes existed with the suspect as an interviewer. At first, the detective seemed to be a perfectly fluent speaker. However, after listening to some minutes of the recorded interviews, it turned out that at certain times his speech briefly became rather disfluent, shown by interruptions and sound or syllable repetitions. This was particularly noticeable when the detective had to read something and was not able to circumvent a particularly difficult stop sound by choosing a less sensitive word. His mild stutter could have gone unnoticed, if there had not been such an abundance of reference speech. Fortunately, the disputed sample had a fair amount of speech and contained disfluencies. Other case reports of speakers with disfluent speech are found in Baldwin and French (1990, pp. 50–56) and Künzel (1987, p. 94). Whereas Van Riper (1973) states that the disfluency pattern of a person that stutters is highly unique, other researchers report a large variability within the same person depending on the speaking situation. In a case study by Martin, de Jong-Lendle, Kehrein & Duckworth (2021), the speech of three speakers, who were being treated for disfluency, was recorded in three different conditions: (1) describing a happy memory as part of a therapy session, (2) a casual conversation with a close friend or relative and (3) a serious interview with an unfamiliar person of authority conducted as a video conference call. These conditions were chosen on the basis of the patients' judgements regarding speaking condition and dysfluency severity. It was found that the level of perceived stress correlates with the number of disfluencies and that within-speaker variation in terms of disfluency frequency can be high. For speaker B, the disfluency score for the stressful condition—that is the interview—was six times as high as for the phone call (see Fig. 9.6). Speaker C found the therapy session the least stressful, whereas subject A and B showed the lowest rates for their phone call condition.

The feature of disfluency for normally fluent adults was studied by McDougall and Duckworth (2017). They reported that speakers demonstrated extensive speaker-specific differences in their fluency profiles both in terms of the types of disfluency features they employed and their rate of occurrence.

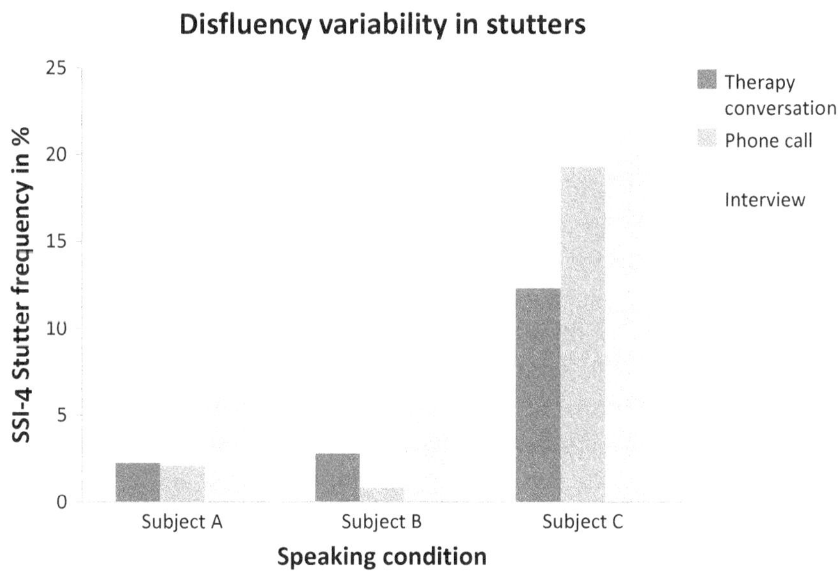

Fig. 9.6 The SSI-4 stutter frequency for 3 stutter patients in 3 different speaking conditions. The calculations were based on the Stuttering Severity Instrument for Adults and Children (SSI-4), see Riley (2009)

In casework, it is not uncommon to come across speakers exhibiting some form of a pathology. As these types of features are highly specific, their presence drastically reduces the size of the set of possible speakers. For example 5% of the population stutter (or did so in early childhood). Persistent developmental stuttering in adults occurs in approx. 1% of the adult population, predominantly in male speakers (Ptok et al., 2006; Yairi & Ambrose, 1999, 2013).

5.4 Age Estimation

Age estimation[17] is one of the tasks carried out routinely by forensic phoneticians, especially in profiling cases. Studies on age estimation from the face reported a six-year deviation (Amilon et al., 2007; Voelkle et al., 2012). How good are experts in guessing a speaker's age based on his/her voice? Studies have shown that our age estimation abilities are limited. In fact, so limited that several authors have suggested that in forensic reports broad descriptions like young, middle aged, senior are more appropriate (Braun & Rietveld, 1995; Cerrato et al., 2000).

Generally, accuracy of voice assessment decreases with speaker's age, the judgements for children and adolescents being most accurate (Hughes & Rhodes, 2010; Huntley et al., 1987; Moyse, 2014). Estimates between 5 and 10y. deviation are reported for adult voices and good-quality recordings (Braun, 1996; Braun & Cerrato, 1999; Neiman & Applegate, 1990; Shipp & Hollien, 1969; Shipp et al., 1992). For telephone-transmitted samples Braun reported approx. 12y. deviation, whereas Cerrato et al. (2000) studying different age groups reported 4–14y. Concerning the effect of the listener's age, it is shown that older listeners tend to overestimate speaker age, while young listeners tend to underestimate it (Braun, 1996; Cerrato et al., 2000; Huntley et al., 1987; Shipp & Hollien, 1969). Listeners' confidence judgments have been shown to be unreliable. In a study by Skoog Waller (2021), a correlation close to zero was found between confidence and accuracy.

The most important cues for age estimation are voice quality and articulation rate (Braun & Rietveld, 1995; Harnsberger et al., 2008, 2010). Mean F0 seems an additional cue, however, articulation rate exhibits a far stronger correlation (Shipp et al., 1992). As poor health related to vocal tract seems to increase the estimate, Braun and Rietveld (1995) concluded that perception may be geared to biological age rather than chronological age.

Non-familiarity with the language of the speaker seems a factor for a wrong age estimation too: Nagao (2006) showed that estimates were poorer for English judging Japanese samples and vice versa. On the other hand, Rodrigues and Nagao (2010) showed that even an Arabic accent reduces the accuracy for American English listeners. The latter study may indicate that age estimation also has an anatomical component.

6 Transcription

As mentioned earlier, audio transcription is one of the more frequent requests a forensic phonetician receives. It involves producing a detailed (orthographic) description of the content of a recording in order to assist in an ongoing investigation or to serve as evidence in court. The request often includes the attribution of speakers to utterances. The transcript contains anything that can be identified with a certain level of confidence and encompasses not only speech but also non-verbal material. The fact that someone is locking a door may be important in the case of a sexual delict. The repetitive noise of windscreen wipers indicates that the speaker is calling from a car. The purpose may be investigative (assisting the police in their attempt to uncover the facts in an alleged crime). If their investigation is successful, the transcript may or may not become part of a subsequent trial. When a transcript is required for evidentiary purposes, its status is a different one. Despite never being able to provide a precise account of the content of a recording, here the reliability of the transcript is crucial. According to Fraser (2014), ideally the transcript should be (re)-transcribed by an independent professional transcriber.

6.1 Factors Influencing the Quality of the Transcript

The quality of the recording is not the only factor influencing the quality of the transcript. It helps to have a listener familiar with the language, accent or jargon spoken by the speaker being transcribed. In addition, good-quality equipment (headphones, sound cards, audio equipment, among other devices) is essential. Before transcribing, it is worth ensuring that the recording received is authentic.

6.2 Enhancement Tools in Audacity

Proper tape enhancement is better left to the audio professionals. Secondly, speaker comparison should be carried out using the original recording, as any filter application means a 'distortion' of the original signal. However, in case a transcription is required, transcribing a long recording with a disturbing level of extraneous noise can be tiring and may cause hearing damage. Based on a general observation, 1 minute of recording may easily take around 20 minutes to transcribe, depending on the quality. In other words, it is worth trying to reduce disturbing noise beforehand. There are a few easy tricks that help. For example, in Audacity, the noise reduction function lets you establish a noise profile. The first step is to select a few seconds of a selection without speech and obtain a noise profile. Audacity can now reduce the background noise with the resulting profile by applying the profile to the entire recording. With the noise reduction setting (dB), it is possible to adjust the level of reduction. The Graphic EQ (Equalizer) allows the user to amplify/reduce particular frequencies by a set of sliders. Dragging the sliders up or down increases or decreases the volume by a maximum of 20dB. The FLATTEN-Option sets all frequencies back to 0—this means no frequencies have their intensity level modified. The PREVIEW feature is extremely useful, as it plays a short preview of what the audio would sound like if the effect is applied with the current settings without making actual changes to the original. The length of this preview can be modified under Edit>Preferences>Playback. It is important to note that your slider settings may result in particular selections being amplified beyond the clipping level if the slider is set too high. As a result, unwanted distortion effects may arise.

6.3 The Possibilities and Limitations of Enhancement

In terms of enhancement, what is possible? Often the expectations are unrealistically high, and, in most cases, improvements are limited. The best advice is to ensure wherever possible that recordings are produced in good quality in the first place. Most difficult are recordings in which the signal itself is distorted in some way. One possible cause is a recording level set too high which results in the clipping of a signal: for example instead of having the complete round sine wave, the top and bottom are cut off resulting in a harsh distortion. This is particularly true in the digital domain, digital audio which is clipped creates a particularly unpleasant sound which can obscure all the sound one may wish to reveal. Nowadays sound recording devices are often equipped with automatic limiters—for example Automatic Gain Control in a dictating device. The main problem with these automatic limiters is the fact that the slow recovery time of these devices can cause speech to disappear, for example immediately after a door has been slammed.

Reverberation caused by sounds being reflected from hard surfaces can also obscure sounds that are of interest. Whereas this phenomenon is natural and adds a sense of space, it can reduce speech intelligibility: whereas a 0.8s reverberation time may be perceived as comfortable without affecting intelligibility too much, 2 or 3s may result in complex interactions occurring between the direct and reflected wavefronts masking speech syllables by causing them to overlap.

Sounds that are recorded indirectly or with the microphone accidentally being covered by something can sound muffled due to the subsequent loss of high frequencies. A common problem are recordings that are made at a low intensity level. In such case the signal of interest is at a similar level to the inherent system and background noise. As a result no amount of amplification will reveal the wanted signal, as all the material (speech and noise) will be amplified to the same level. Sounds recorded with a reduced bit depth can also sound noisy. Ideally sounds are recorded with a bit depth of at least 16 Bit per sample. When sounds are not distorted, but rather masked by other sounds, enhancement may be possible to a certain degree. Disturbing sounds that are predictable and regular, for example in the case of mains electrical hum, can often be removed. Unwanted sounds that are unpredictable and contain frequencies in the speech range, like music or speech from irrelevant speakers, cause a real challenge. Fortunately, a complete removal may actually not be needed: often a reduction of the intensity of the disturbing sounds may prove enough to improve the intelligibility.

It is important to be aware that particular types of distortion may have an effect on what we hear. The telephone bandwidth, for example, cuts off frequencies that are crucial to distinguish fricatives with important information in the higher frequency ranges like the [s] or the [f]. These sounds are easily confused in telephonic recordings. Another problem are sounds that are briefly interrupted due to transmission problems; the sudden cut in the signal may give the impression of a glottal stop or a plosive. Adding our special cognitive skill of being able to fill in missing sounds guided by our expectations on the one hand and the confirmation provided by the acoustic signal on the other (Samuel, 1981; Warren, 1970) and we 'hear' a very different word. It is therefore useful to have a group of transcribers, preferably with different backgrounds and expertise. Changing headphones may also provide a different perceptive experience. For useful overviews of transcription and/or enhancement see Hollien (1990, pp. 127–159), Broeders (1992) and Fraser (2003, 2014). For an overview of the different technical problems regarding audio-recordings see Jessen (2012, pp. 8–13). A detailed account of the problems associated with the Global System Mobile Communication (GSM) technology used in mobile phones is provided by Guillemin and Watson (2009).

6.4 Transcription Coding Format

There are many ways in which a phonetician can present his/her transcript. However, the coding structure below has stood the test of time for several reasons: (1) the coding is intuitive, minimal and easy to understand, (2) the content remains readable, (3) the time information and the line numbers are particularly useful for other analysts or law professionals involved in the case or court and (4) the format, perhaps with minor adaptations, is used in several countries in Europe (Table 9.6).

The following transcript is a demonstration of the coding structure described in Table 9.3. It shows the conversation of two booksellers selling illegal books in their pop-up bookstall. Their ware was provided by a network of acquaintances who stole these books, often in large quantities, from local book shops. Their business was quite successful. However, MV1 had just been visited by a detective who was not interested in buying.

Table 9.6 An example of a transcription coding format

Transcription conventions	
MV1	First male voice identified
FV2	Second female voice identified
MV*	Male voice that could not be attributed
MV5?	Fifth male voice attributed with a low degree of confidence
~~MV1~~	First male voice can be excluded for this utterance
FV-C1	First female customer
*	Voice (male or female) that could not be attributed
( )	Speech material transcribed with a low degree of confidence
(( ))	Speech material transcribed with yet a lower degree of confidence
(the/this)	Alternative candidate words
{INDISTINCT}	Speech that cannot be transcribed
(- -)	Unidentified syllables
'**He** did it'	Marked stress in terms of intonation or intensity
'So he …'	Incomplete utterance
'd-, does he'	Dysfluency
{MUSIC}	Non-speech sound
[MV2:Yeah]	Speaker MV2 interrupting another speaker, for example: MV1 Nice bloke [MV2: yeah], isn't he?
...what I mean.'	Overlapping speech

Table 9.7 An example of a transcript using the transcription code format described in Table 9.6

Transcription of File 'LPSS 563 location 3.mp3'			
Nr.	Time (mm:ss)	Speaker	Transcription
1	01:23	MV1	He started asking a few questions here. Where do you get the books from, and all that... (Now) why's he (say/saying) that?
2	01:31		(-) (weird) (-)
3	01:33	MV2	Well (-) yeah, a new law can restart a case. He- he can make his own nick, regardless of ((your involvement)). He can make his own, own conclusion.
4	01:36	MV1	Where did you get the books from? I said I buy them. He wasn't really interested in the books. He was {INDISTINCT} ((street trade/street trading)). I don't really want to pack up. I. it's not my. I don't- I think it's all a load of bollocks. What do you think?
5	01:40	MV2	It's up to you (really) (-).
6	01:42	MV1	Eh?
7	01:45	MV2	If they do come, he- he- he- he [MV1: What?] could seize the gear. I mean if they come back, I mean, they will have you {INDISTINCT}.
8	01:46	FV-C1	How much are your children's books?
9	01:47	MV1	Three fifty.
10	01:50	FV-C1	Three fifty.
11	01:54	MV1	He's caused me a lot of aggro now he has, <u>that bloke</u>.
12	01:57	MV2?	<u>(- -) leave</u> 'em here.
13	02:01	MV1	I've got Billy coming along as well ((with all this)).

During the conversation, a female customer visited the stall. As can be seen in the transcript below, this woman is coded as 'FV-C1'. Like this customer passing by (or a bartender serving drinks heard in surveillance recording), speakers who are not part of the case can be coded differently to make them stand out as regular speakers not part of the investigation. In this case, 'FV-C1' stands for 'female voice—customer 1'. In the case of a larger time gap between two utterances of the same speaker, a new text-box is created—for example between utterances 1 and 2 (Table 9.7).

The speakers in the disputed recording are coded as MV1 and MV2 as their identity is unknown. In case speaker comparison is required, they will subsequently be compared to reference speakers.

6.5 Transcription Using PRAAT

The software programme PRAAT has features that are extremely useful for the purposes of transcription. The function TIER>Add interval tier creates a transcription textbox parallel to the speech sample. Selecting and pressing Ctrl-1 will add two boundaries on the first tier. In the transcription box right at the top, text can be added. Ctrl-2 will add boundaries to the second tier, and so on. As shown in Fig. 9.7 several different tiers can be added, each with its own name. This process is particularly useful in cases where transcription needs to take place on different levels. In one particular case, the police requested a transcript of a telephone call. They were interested in the speech of the caller and the announcements of the different tram stations heard in the background. The woman travelling was suspected of having murdered an elderly lady. The police assumed that she had used the tram to flee from the crime scene. As she had cleverly managed to delete the location data from her mobile, her route had to be reconstructed using the station announcements in the background. In addition, we were asked if the recording contained the sirens of a police car at any point. These were heard right after the announcement of the station close to the crime scene.

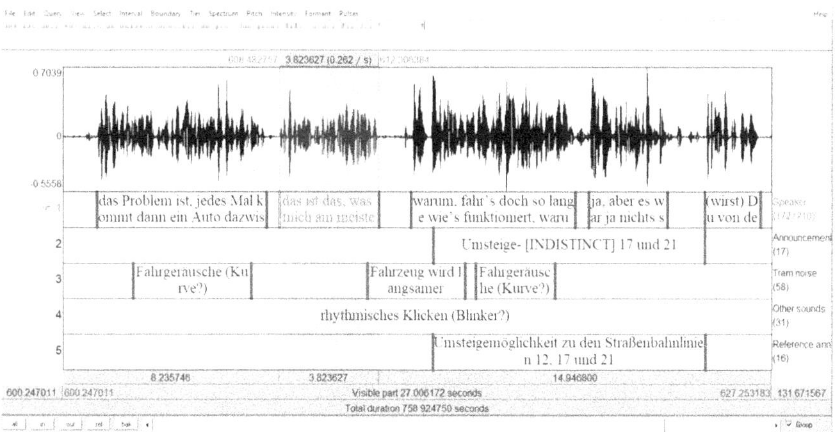

Fig. 9.7 An example of a transcript with different levels using PRAAT TextGrids

Figure 9.7 shows how, in this case, the speaker is transcribed on tier 1. The next tier is reserved for the station announcements. Tier 3 describes the different mechanical sounds of the tram, like stopping, accelerating, hitting a curve or doors opening and closing. Tier 4 contains all other sounds like the rhythmic sound of a blinker or sirens. Tier 5 shows the transcript of the reference recordings produced for all tram lines relevant to the case (Fig. 9.7).

The information of each tier can be extracted and exported in a text file using TIER> Extract entire selected tier. This function produces a new object in the PRAAT-objects listing called Textgrid Speaker. Using TABULATE>List produces a listing with the transcript and the time information associated with each utterance. This information can now be imported in the transcription depicted in Table 9.7.

7 Reporting the Results

The scientist's detailed shades-of-grey-perspective is a different one from the detective's black-and-white or yes-or-no perspective. Section 4 of the IAFPA Code of Practice is particularly devoted to reporting the analysis results and states that (1) reports should be scientifically accurate but still formulated in such a way that they can be understood by non-specialists; (2) in the case conclusions are presented on a scale, this scale should be shown in the report and (3) evidence limitations should be explained in the report, in the court of justice, and in other communications.

As in forensic text analysis, handwriting analysis, fibre analysis, footwear marks, the exact framework of reporting is still a matter of debate. A universal framework has not yet been established and a variety of formats are currently in use. In the past decades, it was standard to use some form of verbal expression like 'The speaker in recording X is fairly likely to be the speaker in recording Y'. However, since the late 1980s, a number of authors have pointed out that this way of formulating the forensic report conclusions is logically incorrect (Champod & Meuwly, 2000; Evett, 1991; Robertson & Vignaux, 1995; Thompson & Schumann, 1987). The main problem concerns what is known as the 'Prosecutor's

Fallacy'—this term was first used by Thompson and Schumann (1987) and is also known as the 'Fallacy of the transposed conditional'. In case speaker X happens to share a large number of features with speaker Y, the conclusion 'Speaker X is highly likely speaker Y' is misleading: Speaker X is as likely to be speaker Y as any other person from the small group of speakers that share the same characteristics. In a paper given at IAFPA in 2011, Michael Jessen demonstrated, why this way of reporting is logically incorrect: he described a scenario based on a real case in which, at the end of the investigation, suddenly the brother of the suspect turned up having many features in common with the disputed speaker. A second comparison was conducted; the brother appeared to share even more features with the criminal speaker than the suspect. The case lead to an absurd situation: If the expert wanted to be consistent, he had to conclude that it was highly likely that both subjects were the disputed speaker in the criminal recording (Jessen, 2011). It is, therefore, astonishing that this verbal likelihood scale has survived for so long. In 2011, 40% of the practising forensic speech scientists were still using it (Gold & French, 2011). In Bayesian terms the problem is known as the expert reporting the prior odds, although in reality he/she cannot know the prior odds (Rose, 2002, p. 63).[18]

However, judging by the number of guidelines or proposals that have recently appeared on this topic (ENFSI, 2015; NFI, 2016; French, 2017), it seems that over the years we have reached a far better understanding of the problem. The frameworks proposed are all attempts to avoid reaching conclusions that are logically incorrect and attempts to give both the prosecution and the defence hypotheses the same weight. In the case of a positive result, the conclusion may now be formulated as: 'the probability of obtaining these results is (much) greater under a same-speaker hypothesis than under a different-speaker hypothesis' or an adapted version of it. A negative conclusion may sound like: 'the probability of obtaining these results is (much) greater under a different-speaker hypothesis than under a same-speaker hypothesis' (French, 2017, p. 9). Such formulations correctly leave the final decision regarding the suspect's guilt to the court (Aitken, 1995, p. 4).

8 Conclusion

Owing to a small group of pioneers, phonetics became an established field within forensics. Over the years it has developed at an astonishing pace. The establishment of the International Association for Forensic Phonetics and Acoustics (IAFPA) was surely the main catalyser for the field of forensic phonetics and we can be grateful for the efforts the founding members made to provide future generations with official structures like an association, a conference and a journal, that enable the exchange of ideas and methods. At present, the field is a very different one: The association counts over 100 members from almost 30 different countries. Forensic institutes have grown from one phonetician to a small team, often including audio and IT-experts. A survey by Morrison et al. (2016) conducted in the 190-member countries of INTERPOL showed that worldwide almost half of the law enforcement agencies have the capacity to analyse voice recordings. Other associations such as Forensic Speech and Audio Analysis Working Group of the European Network of Forensic Science Institutes (ENFSI), Praxis-workshops and summer schools were established. The archive of the journal *International Journal of Speech, Language and the Law* lists a total of 55 different issues starting in 1994. Linguistics students with an interest can now receive a solid background and training as part of an MA or PhD degree.

This chapter opened with a brief history of the field of forensic phonetics. The methods used in the past were explained and critically discussed. The main focus of the chapter, however, was on providing a detailed description of the auditive-acoustic approach. This method was illustrated using anonymised examples from real casework.

I have tried to provide the reader with the most essential aspects of forensic phonetics. In short, research has shown that speech is highly variable (Nolan, 2001). This variability is caused by (a) the flexibility and condition of the speech organs—for example, stress, cold, among other possibilities—and (b) the language—for example, style, dialect, and articulation precision. Second, it is important to note that poor recording quality, short sample durations, mismatching speaking conditions, lack of particular expertise, among other elements may cause serious limitations to the analysis or even render a comparison or transcript impossible. For this reason, a conviction should not occur based on voice evidence alone. Third, in the majority of cases the set of possible speakers must be considered an open set consisting of a large number of members. Even if two samples have a large number of features in common, there still may be a considerable number of speakers sharing the exact same set. The size of this set is determined by the specificity of the features. Another relevant aspect to bear in mind is the fact that auditory analysis may reveal features that acoustic analysis cannot and vice versa. Automatic methods are clearly a useful tool in particular forensic situations when, for example, good-quality recordings are available or in cases where a large numbers of recordings are available and a screening tool is required. Finally, the probability of the findings should be considered under the different-speaker hypothesis and under the same-speaker hypothesis, both hypotheses carrying the same weight.

Are speakers unique? Speakers can only be considered unique once proven that there is no overlap between the individual speaker areas that each person can cover based on the considerable number of speaker parameters and the associated degrees of freedom. One can imagine that in the case of an unusual pathology in addition to some other highly specific features, this may be true for a small number of speakers. However, for most speakers, we have not reached that point yet, partially due to the fact that most forensic recordings only provide us with a derivative of the speaker's real voice. On the other hand, in the case of speaker comparison demonstrating that two speakers are not the same or reducing the number of possible speakers can still be extremely important from a forensic point of view. In sum, when all the above is considered, the field of forensic phonetics and acoustics can make a useful contribution in forensic investigations and in the court of law.

Acknowledgments I am grateful to the editors for comments on an earlier draft of this article. Any errors remain my own.

Notes

1. The novice reader of forensic phonetics may find the following introductory books useful: Jessen (2012), Künzel (1987), and Hollien (1990, 2002). A more advance research is represented by the works of Nolan (1983) and Rose (2002). Overview articles include: Braun (2012), Eriksson (2012), French (1994), French and Stevens (2013), Foulkes and French (2012), Gfroerer (2006), Hollien et al. (2014), Jessen (2008, 2010), Künzel (2003), Morrison (2010), Nolan (1991, 1997), and Watt (2010).
2. Personal communication 25.03.2021.
3. A detailed account of the case and its context can be found in de Jong-Lendle (2016).
4. The chapters in the Bush et al. report 'Cryptographic tools and methods' (pp. 48–61) and 'The sound spectrograph' (pp. 61–99) give an account of these decoding efforts.
5. See also: https://griffonagedotcom.wordpress.com/2018/07/26/the-secret-military-origins-of-the-sound-spectrograph/.
6. The IAFPA Voiceprint Resolution is also made available on their site: https://www.iafpa.net/the-association/resolutions/.
7. For an example of a US firm offering aural/spectrographic voice identification, please go to https://www.owenforensicservices.com/voice-identification-the-aural-spectrographic-method/.
8. In contrast with the highly variable voice, a person's DNA and fingerprints do not change over time and are highly specific. The author is aware of the fact that the analysis and interpretation of these patterns can still lead to erroneous results in the case of unclear fingerprints—for example, in 2004, the FBI identified an innocent person as the bomber in the Madrid train bombing case (Stacey, 2004). See Dror (2015) for examiner's bias; Lander (1989) and Thompson (1995) for faint DNA-bands that allow different interpretations as occurred in the Castro case. An excellent study explaining the significance of this case with regard to the Frye ruling is Mnookin (2007). For a detailed explanation on intra-speaker variability, see Nolan (1997, pp. 749–753).
9. Useful introductions can be found in Drygajlo et al. (2015), Jessen (2008), and Rose (2002).
10. In the case, an intruder with an unusual talent for languages managed a convincing disguise in an emergency call, imitating a foreign accent in

German. He later confessed to the call. The effectiveness of the automatic approach in this case is currently being explored.

11. For a review on fundamental frequency, see Jessen (2012, Chap. 3) and Braun (1995).
12. RBH is the abbreviation of the German words 'Rauigkeit', 'Behauchtheit' and 'Heiserkeit' (translated as rough, breathy and hoarse), nasality not being part of the RBH classification.
13. For a detailed review on the potential of the Laver framework for forensic phonetics, the limitations of voice quality judgements and the forensic value of formant measurements, see Nolan (2005).
14. Despite the fact that the fricative pronunciation of the /g/ is the non-prestige variant, it obviously does not prevent anyone from having a career: another person being known for his /g/ was former president Gorbatschow.
15. For a discussion on this topic, see Jessen (2007; 2012, pp. 133–145). Furthermore, a detailed account of the perception of articulation rate is included in Schubert and Sendlmeier's work (2005), and also in Pfitzinger (2001) who compares syllable and phone rate.
16. For breathing patterns, see Grosjean and Collins (1979), Trouvain (2014), Trouvain, Fauth and Möbius (2016).
17. For a review on age estimation (from faces) and voices, see Moyse (2014).
18. For a detailed explanation of the problem, see Robertson and Vignaux (1995), and Rose (2002, pp. 55–79).

References

Abercrombie, D. (1967). *Elements of general phonetics*. Edinburgh University Press.

Aitken, C. C. G. (1995). *Statistics and the evaluation of evidence for forensic scientists*. John Wiley & Sons.

Amilon, K., Van de Weijer, J., & Schötz, S. (2007). The impact of visual and auditory cues in age estimation. In C. Müller (Ed.), *Speaker classification II. Lectures notes in artificial intelligence* (pp. 10–21). Springer.

Anonymous. (1998). The voiceprint dilemma: Should voices be seen and not heard? *Maryland Law Review, 35*(2), 267–296.

Baldwin, J., & French, F. (1990). *Forensic phonetics*. Pinter.

Ball, M. J., Esling, J., & Dickson, C. (1995). The VoQS system for the transcription of voice quality. *Journal of the International Phonetic Association, 25*(2), 71–80. https://doi.org/10.1017/S0025100300005181

Berg, A. S. (1998). *Charles Lindbergh—Ein Idol des 20. Jahrhunderts*. Karl Blessing Verlag.

Boersma, P., & Weenink, D. (2018). Praat. Doing phonetics by computer. http://www.fon.hum.uva.nl/praat/

Bolt, R. H., Cooper, F. S., David, E. E., Jr., Denes, P. B., Pickett, J. M., & Stevens, K. N. (1970). Speaker identification by speech spectrograms: A scientists' view of its reliability for legal purposes. *Journal of the Acoustical Society of America, 47*, 597–612.

Bolt, R. H., Cooper, F. S., David, E. E., Jr., Denes, P. B., Pickett, J. M., & Stevens, K. N. (1973). Speaker identification by speech spectrograms: Some further observations. *Journal of the Acoustical Society of America, 54*, 531–534.

Boss, D., Gfroerer, S., & Neoustroev, N. (2003). A new tool for the visualization of magnetic features on audiotapes. *The International Journal of Speech, Language and the Law—Forensic Linguistics, 10*(2), 255–276. https://doi.org/10.1558/sll.2003.10.2.255

Braun, A. (1995). Fundamental frequency – How speaker-specific is it? In A. Braun & J.-P. Köster (Eds.), *Studies in forensic phonetics* (pp. 9–23). WVT.

Braun, A. (1996). Age estimation by different listener groups. *Forensic Linguistics, 3*, 65–73.

Braun, A. (2012). Forensische Sprach- und Signalverarbeitung. In J. Bockemühl (Ed.), *Handbuch des Fachanwalts Strafrecht* (pp. 1644–1666). Carl Heymanns Verlag.

Braun, A., & Cerrato, L. (1999). Estimating speaker age across languages. In *Proceedings of the International Conference of Phonetic Sciences* (pp. 1369–1372). San Francisco, USA.

Braun, A., & Rietveld, T. (1995). The influence of smoking habits on perceived age. In K. Elenius & P. Branderud (Eds.), *Proceedings of the 13th International Congress of Phonetic Sciences* (pp. 294–297). Stockholm.

Bricker, P. D., & Pruzansky, S. (1966). Effects of stimulus content and duration on talker identification. *Journal of the Acoustical Society of America, 40*, 1441–1449.

Broeders, A. P. A. (1992). Verstaanbaarheidsverbetering – Het forensisch onderzoek van audio-opnamen (IV). *Modus, 2*, 42–43.

Broeders, A. P. A. (1993). De stem als bewijsmateriaal: Forensisch spraakonderzoek 1. *Onze Taal, 62*(10), 230–231.

Broeders, A. P. A., & Rietveld, A. (1995). Speaker identification by earwitnesses. *Studies in Forensic Phonetics*, 24–40.

Bryan, R. (1991). The execution of the innocent. *NYU Review of Law and Social Change, 18*, 33.

Bryson, B. (2013). *One summer: America 1927*. Transworld Publishers.

Bush, V., Conant, J. B., Pratt, H., & National Defense Research Committee & Columbia University, Division of War Research. (1946). *Speech and facsimile scrambling and decoding—Summary Technical Report of Divisions 13*. Office of Scientific Research and Development, National Defense Research Committee. https://archive.org/details/speechfacsimiles03unit?view=theater

Cerrato, L., Falcone, M., & Paoloni, A. (2000). Subjective age estimation of telephonic voices. *Speech Communication, 31*(2–3), 107–112. https://doi.org/10.1016/S0167-6393(99)00071-0

Champod, C., & Meuwly, D. (2000). The inference of identity in forensic speaker recognition. *Speech Communication, 31*, 193–203.

Clark, H., & Fox Tree, J. E. (2002). Tree using uh and um in spontaneous speaking. *Cognition, 84*, 73–111.

Clifford, B. R. (1980). Voice identification by human listeners: On earwitness reliability. *Law and Human Behavior, 4*, 373–394.

Corley, M., & Stewart, O. W. (2008). Hesitation disfluencies in spontaneous speech: The meaning of um. *Language and Linguistics Compass, 2*, 589–602.

Crystal, D. (2010). *The Cambridge encyclopedia of language*. Cambridge University Press.

Dantz, R., & Oehl, F. (2014). *Jahrhundert-Verbrechen—Bruno Richard Hauptmann und die Entführung des Lindbergh-Babys*. Saxophon Verlag.

de Jong, G. (1998). *Earwitness characteristics and speaker identification accuracy*. Unpublished doctoral thesis, University of Florida, USA.

de Jong, G., House, J., Cook, N., & Young, A. (2005). *The speaker discriminating power of the final fall: Spontaneous speech*. Presented at IAFPA, Marrakech.

de Jong-Lendle, G. (2016). Der Strafprozess des Jahrhunderts—Die Geschichte eines Piloten, eines deutschen Immigranten, einer skeptischen Wissenschaftlerin und des Beginns der forensischen Phonetik. *Literaturkritik.de, 2016*(8).

de Jong-Lendle, G., Nolan, F., McDougall, K., & Hudson, T. (2015). Voice lineups: A practical guide. *Proceedings of the 17th ICPhS*, August, Glasgow, UK.

Dellwo, V. (2006). Rhythm and speech rate: A variation coefficient for deltaC. In P. Karnowski & I. Szigeti (Eds.), *Language and language-processing* (pp. 231–241). Peter Lang.

Dellwo, V., Leemann, A., & Kolly, M. J. (2015). Rhythmic variability between speakers: Articulatory, prosodic, and linguistic factors. *The Journal of the Acoustical Society of America, 137*(1513). https://doi.org/10.1121/1.4906837

Dirim, I., & Auer, P. (2004). *Türkisch sprechen nicht nur die Türken*. De Gruyter. https://doi.org/10.1515/9783110919790

Dror, I. E. (2015). Cognitive neuroscience in forensic science: Understanding and utilizing the human element. *Philosophical Transactions of the Royal Society of London. Series B, Biological Sciences, 370*(1674), 2014025. https://doi.org/10.1098/rstb.2014.0255

Drygajlo, A., Jessen, M., Gfroere, S., Wagner, I., Vermeulen, J., & Niemi, T. (2015). *Methodological guidelines for best practice in forensic semiautomatic and automatic speaker recognition*. European Network of Forensic Science Institutes.

Eckert, H., & Laver, J. (1994). *Menschen und Ihre Stimmen*. Weinheim.

Ellis, S. (1994). The Yorkshire Ripper enquiry: Part I. *Forensic Linguistics: The International Journal of Speech, Language and the Law, 1*(2), 197–206.

Eriksson, A. (2012). Aural/acoustic vs. automatic methods in forensic phonetic case work. In A. Neustein & H. Patil (Eds.), *Forensic speaker recognition. Law enforcement and counter-terrorism* (pp. 41–69). Springer.

European Network of Forensic Science Institutes. (2015). *ENFSI guideline for evaluative reporting in forensic science*. Retrieved from https://enfsi.eu/wp-content/uploads/2016/09/m1_guideline.pdf

Evett, I. W. (1998). Towards a uniform framework for reporting opinions in forensic science casework. *Science & Justice, 38*(3), 198–202. https://doi.org/10.1016/S1355-0306(98)72105-7

Foulkes, P., & French, P. (2012). Forensic speaker comparison: A linguistic-acoustic perspective. In L. M. Solan & P. M. Tiersma (Eds.), *Oxford handbook of language and law* (pp. 557–572). Oxford University Press.

Fraser, H. (2003). Issues in transcription: Factors affecting the reliability of transcripts as evidence in legal cases. *Forensic Linguistics, 10*(2), 203–226.

Fraser, H. (2014). Transcription of indistinct forensic recordings. *Language and Law, 1*(2), 5–21.

French, P. (1994). An overview of forensic phonetics with particular reference to speaker identification. *Forensic Linguistics, 1*, 169–181.

French, P. (2017). A developmental history of forensic speaker comparison in the UK. *English Phonetics*, 271–286.

French, P., Harrison, P., & Lewis, J. W. (2006). R v John Samuel Humble: The Yorkshire Ripper Hoaxer trial. *International Journal of Speech Language and the Law, 13*(2), 967.https://doi.org/10.1558/ijsll.2006.13.2.255

French, P., & Stevens, L. (2013). Forensic speech Science. In R. A. Knight & M. Jones (Eds.), *The Bloomsbury companion to phonetics* (pp. 183–197). Continuum. https://doi.org/10.5040/9781472541895.ch-012

Frye v. United States. (1923). 293 F. 1013 (D.C. Cir. 1923), Court of Appeals of the District of Columbia.

Gerlach, L., McDougall, K., Kelly, F., Alexander, A., & Nolan, F. (2020). Exploring the relationship between voice similarity estimates by listeners and by an automatic speaker recognition system incorporating phonetic features. *Speech Communication, 124*, 85–95. https://doi.org/10.1016/j.specom.2020.08.003

Gfroerer, S. (2006). Sprechererkennung und Tonträgerauswertung. In G. Widmaier (Ed.), *Müncher Anwaltshandbuch Strafverteidigung* (pp. 2005–2526). C.H. Beck.

Gold, E., & French, P. (2011). International practices in forensic speaker comparison. *International Journal of Speech Language and the Law, 18*. https://doi.org/10.1558/ijsll.v18i2.293

Goldman-Eisler, F. (1968). *Psycholinguistics: Experiments in spontaneous speech*. Academic.

Grey, G., & Kopp, G. A. (1944). Voiceprint identification. *Bell Telephone Laboratories Report*, 1–14.

Grosjean, F., & Collins, M. (1979). Breathing, pausing and reading. *Phonetica, 36*(2), 98–114.

Guillemin, B., & Watson, C. (2009). Impact of the GSM mobile phone network on the speech signal – Some preliminary findings. *International Journal of Speech Language and The Law, 15*(2). https://doi.org/10.1558/ijsll.v15i2.193

Harnsberger, J. D., Brown, W. S., Shrivastav, R., & Rothman, H. (2010). Noise and tremor in the perception of vocal aging in males. *Journal of Voice, 24*(5), 523–530. https://doi.org/10.1016/j.jvoice.2009.01.003

Harnsberger, J. D., Shrivastav, R., Brown, W. S., Rothman, H., & Hollien, H. (2008). Speaking rate and fundamental frequency as speech cues to perceived age. *Journal of Voice, 22*(1), 58–69. https://doi.org/10.1016/j.jvoice.2006.07.004

Hauptmann, B. R. (1935). Die Lebenserinnerungen von Bruno Richard Hauptmann. In R. Dantz & F. Oehl (Eds.), *Jahrhundertverbrechen-Bruno Richard Hauptmann und die Entführung des Lindbergh-Babys* (pp. 53–203). Saxophon Verlag.

Hazen, K. (2006). Idiolect. In K. Brown (Ed.), *Encyclopedia of language & linguistics* (Vol. 5, 2nd ed.). Elsevier.

Hollien, H. (1990). *The acoustics of crime*. Springe.

Hollien, H. (2002). *Forensic voice identification*. Academic.

Hollien, H., Huntley-Bahr, R., & Harnsberger, J. D. (2014). Issues in forensic voice. *Journal of Voice, 28*(2), 170–184.

Hollien, H., & McGlone, R. E. (1976). The effect of disguise on 'voiceprint' identification. *Journal of Criminal Defense, 2*, 117–130.

Hudson, T., de Jong, G., McDougall, K., Harrison, P., & Nolan, F. (2007). F0 statistics for 100 young male speakers of Standard Southern British English. In J. Trouvain (Ed.), *Proceedings of the 16th International Congress of Phonetic Sciences* (pp. 1809–1812). Saarbrücken, Germany.

Hughes, S. M., & Rhodes, B. C. (2010). Making age assessments based on voice: The impact of the reproductive viability of the speaker. *Journal of Social, Evolutionary, and Cultural Psychology, 4*(4), 290–304. https://doi.org/10.1037/h0099282

Hughes, V., & Foulkes, P. (2014). The relevant population in forensic voice comparison: Effects of varying delimitations of social class and age. *Speech Communication, 66*. https://doi.org/10.1016/j.specom.2014.10.006

Huntley, R., Hollien, H., & Shipp, T. (1987). Influences of listener characteristics on perceived age estimations. *Journal of Voice, 1*(1), 49–52. https://doi.org/10.1016/S0892-1997(87)80024-3

Huys, T., & Krabbé, T. (Producers). (2019, November 18). *De schrijver, de moordenaar en zijn vrouw*, [Television broadcast]. : BNNVARA.

Jessen, M. (2007). Forensic reference data on articulation rate in German. *Science & Justice: Journal of the Forensic Science Society, 47*(2), 50–67.

Jessen, M. (2008). Forensic phonetics. *Language and Linguistics Compass, 2*, 671–711.

Jessen, M. (2010). The forensic phonetician: Forensic speaker identification by experts. In M. Coulthard & A. Johnson (Eds.), *The Routledge handbook of forensic linguistics* (pp. 378–394). Routledge.

Jessen, M. (2011). *Conclusions on voice comparison evidence in Germany and a challenging case*.

Jessen, M. (2012). *Phonetische und linguistische Prinzipien des forensischen Stimmenvergleichs*. LINCOM.

Jessen, M., Koster, O., & Gfroerer, S. (2005). Influence of vocal effort on average and variability of fundamental frequency. *The International Journal of Speech, Language and the Law, 12*(2), 174–213. https://doi.org/10.1558/sll.2005.12.2.174

Johnson, C., & Hollien, H. (1984). Speaker identification utilizing selected temporal speech features. *Journal of Phonetics, 12*, 319–326.

Kehrein, R. (2021, Juli 1). Wo kommt die/der denn her? Dialektkarten für das Speakerprofiling. *Sprachspuren – Berichte aus dem Deutschen Sprach Atlas*. Retrieved from https://www.sprachspuren.de/author/roland-kehrein/

Kersta, L. G. (1962). Voiceprint identification. *Nature, 196*, 1253–1257.

Kluge, K., Müller M., Dubielzig, C., Meinerz C., & Masthoff, H. (2018). *Distribution of voice quality features in German. Preliminary results*. Poster presentation of the Conference of the International Association for Forensic Phonetics and Acoustics. Huddersfield, UK.

Kohler, K. J. (1977). *Einführung in der Phonetik des Deutschen*. Erich Schmidt Verlag.

Köster, O., Jessen, M., Khairi, F., & Eckert, H. (2007). *Auditory-perceuptual identification of voice quality by expert and non-expert listeners*.

Köster, O., & Köster, J.-P. (2004). The auditory-perceptual evaluation of voice quality in forensic speaker recognition. *The Phonetician, 89*, 9–37.

Kraayeveld, H. (1997). *Idiosyncrasy in prosody. Speaker and speaker group identification in Dutch using melodic and temporal information*. Doctoral thesis, Katholieke Universiteit Nijmegen, The Netherlands. Retrieved from https://core.ac.uk/download/pdf/43592901.pdf

Kreiman, J., & Gerrat, B. (2011). Comparing two methods for reducing variability in voice quality measurements. *Journal of Speech Language and Hearing Research, 54*, 803–812.

Künzel, H. J. (1987). *Sprechererkennung: Grundzüge forensischer Sprachverarbeitung*. Heidelberg: Kriminalistik Verlag.

Künzel, H. J. (1990). *Phonetische Untersuchungen zur Sprechererkennung durch linguistisch naive Personen, Zeitschrift für Dialektologie und Linguistik, 69*. Steiner Verlag.

Künzel, H. J. (1997). Some general phonetic and forensic aspects of speaking tempo. *Forensic Linguistics, 4*, 48–83.

Künzel, H. J. (2003). Die forensische Sprachverarbeitung. Ein Überblick über den gegenwärtigen Stand. *Kriminalistik, 57*, 676–684.

Lander, E. S. (1989). DNA fingerprinting on trial. *Nature, 339*(6225), 501–505. https://doi.org/10.1038/339501a0
Laver, J. (1980). *The phonetic description of voice quality*. Cambridge University Press.
Laver, J. (1994). *Principles of phonetics*. Cambridge University Press.
Lindbergh, C. A. (1953). *The spirit of St. Louis*. Scribner.
Lindh, J. (2006). Preliminary descriptive F0-statistics for young male speakers. *Lund University Working Papers, 52*, 89–92.
Martin, S., de Jong-Lendle, G., Duckworth, M., & Kehrein, R. (2021). *The variability of stuttering: A forensic phonetic study*. Poster presented at the IAFPA conference in Marburg, August.
McDougall, K. (2004). Speaker-specific formant dynamics: An experiment on Australian English /aI/. *The International Journal of Speech, Language and the Law, 11*(1), 103–130. https://doi.org/10.1558/sll.2004.11.1.103
McDougall, K. (2006). Dynamic features of speech and the characterisation of speakers: Towards a new approach using formant frequencies. *The International Journal of Speech, Language and the Law, 13*, 89–126.
McDougall, K., & Duckworth, M. (2017). Profiling fluency: An analysis of individual variation in disfluencies in adult males. *Speech Communication, 95*, 16–27. https://doi.org/10.1016/j.specom.2017.10.001
McGehee, F. (1937). The reliability of the identification of the human voice. *Journal of General Psychology, 17*, 249–271.
McGehee, F. (1944). An experimental study of voice recognition. *Journal of General Psychology, 31*, 53–65.
Mnookin, J. L. (2007). People V. Castro: Challenging the forensic use of DNA evidence. *Journal of Scholarly Perspectives, 3*(1). https://escholarship.org/uc/item/362776cz
Morrison, G., Sahito, F., Jardine, G., Djokic, D., Clavet, S., Berghs, S., & Dorny, C. (2016). INTERPOL survey of the use of speaker identification by law enforcement agencies. *Forensic Science International, 263*, 92–100. https://doi.org/10.1016/j.forsciint.2016.03.044
Morrison, G. S. (2010). Forensic voice comparison. In I. Freckelton, & H. Selby (Eds.), *Expert evidence* (pp. 1–106). Thomson Reuters.
Morrison, G. S., Ochoa, F., & Tharmarajah, T. (2012). *Database selection for forensic voice comparison*. Proceedings of Odyssey 2012: The Language and Speaker Recognition Workshop.
Moyse, E. (2014). Age estimation from faces and voices: A review. *Psychologica Belgica, 54*(3), 255–265. https://doi.org/10.5334/pb.aq

Nagao, K. (2006). *Cross-language study of age perception.* Unpublished doctoral thesis, Indiana University, USA.

Nawka, T., & Anders, L. C. (1996). *Die auditive Bewertung heiserer Stimmen nach dem RBH-System.*

Nederlands Forensisch Instituut. (2016). *Vakbijlage – vergelijkend spraakonderzoek.* Retrieved from https://www.forensischinstituut.nl/publicaties/publicaties/2020/02/03/vakbijlage-vergelijkend-spraakonderzoek

Nederlands Forensisch Instituut. (2017). *De reeks waarschijnlijkheidstermen van het NFI en het Bayesiaanse model voor interpretatie van bewijs.* Vakbijlage (Versie 2.2 mei 2017).

Neiman, G. S., & Applegate, J. A. (1990). Accuracy of listener judgments of perceived age relative to chronological age in adults. *Folia Phoniatrica et Logopaedica, 42*(6), 327–330. https://doi.org/10.1159/000266090

Nolan, F. (1983). *The phonetic bases of speaker recognition.* Cambridge University Press.

Nolan, F. (1991). Forensic phonetics. *Journal of Linguistics, 27*, 483–493.

Nolan, F. (1997). Speaker recognition and forensic phonetics. In W. Hardcastle, & J. Laver (Eds.), *The handbook of phonetic sciences* (pp. 744–767). Blackwell.

Nolan, F. (2001). Speaker identification evidence: Its forms, limitation, and roles. In *Proceedings of the Conference on Law and Language: Prospects and Retrospect* (pp. 1–19). Levi, Finnland.

Nolan, F. (2003). A recent voice parade. *The International Journal of Speech, Language and the Law—Forensic Linguistics, 10*(2), 277–291. https://doi.org/10.1558/sll.2003.10.2.277

Nolan, F. (2005). Forensic speaker identification and the phonetic description of voice quality. In W. J. Hardcastle, & J. Mackenzie Beck (Eds.), *A figure of speech* (pp. 385–413). Routledge.

Nolan, F., McDougall, K., De Jong, G., & Hudson, T. (2009). The DyViS database: Style-controlled recordings of 100 homogeneous speakers for forensic phonetic research. *International Journal of Speech Language and the Law, 16*(1), 31–57. https://doi.org/10.1558/ijsll.v16i1.31

Orton, H., & Halliday, W. J. (Eds.). (1962). *Survey of English dialects basic material: Vol. 1, The six northern counties and the Isle of Man.* E. J. Arnold.

Orton, H., Sanderson, S., & Widdowson, J. (Eds.). (1978). *The linguistic atlas of England.* Croom Helm.

Pfitzinger, H. R. (2001). Phonetische Analyse der Sprechgeschwindigkeit. *Forschungsberichte des Instituts für Phonetik und sprachliche Kommunikation, 38*, 117–264.

Pike, K. L. (1945). *The intonation of American English*. University of Michigan Press.

Potter, R. (1945). Visible patterns of sound. *Science, 102*(2654), 463–470. http://www.jstor.org/stable/1673144

Potter, R., Kopp, K., & Green, H. (1947). *Visible speech* (Bell telephone laboratories series). D. Van Nostrand Company.

Poza, F., & Begault, D., & (2005). Voice identification and elimination using aural-spectrographic protocols. *Proceedings of the Audio Engineering Society Conference*, Denver, USA.

Ptok, M., Natke, U., & Oertle, H. M. (2006). The management of stammering. *Deutsches Arzteblatt, 103*, 1216–1221.

R. v. Anthony O'Doherty. (2002). Court of appeal in Northern Ireland. Ref: NICB3173.

Ramus, F., Nespor, M., & Mehler, J. (1999). Correlates of linguistic rhythm in the speech signal. *Cognition, 73*, 265–292.

Reich, A. R., Moll, K. L., & Curtis, J. F. (1976). Effects of selected vocal disguises upon spectrographic speaker identification. *Journal of the Acoustical Society of America, 60*, 919–925.

Rietveld, A. C. M., & Broeders, A. P. A. (1991). Testing the fairness of voice parades: The similarity criterion. In *Proceedings of the International Congress of Phonetic Sciences* (pp. 46–49). Aix-en-Provence, France.

Riley, G. (2009). *The stuttering severity instrument for adults and children (SSI-4)* (4th ed.). PRO-ED.

Rinke, P., Beier, K., Kaul, R., Schmidt, T., Scharinger, M., & DeJong-Lendle, G. (2021). Neurophysiological evidences for automatic speaker recognition: Neural correlates of voice familiarity. In *Talk Presented at the International Association for Forensic Phonetics and Acoustics Annual Conference*, Marburg, Germany.

Robertson, B., & Vignaux, G. A. (1995). *Interpreting evidence*. Wiley.

Rodrigues, P., & Nagao, K. (2010). Effects of listener experience with foreign accent on perception of accentedness and speaker age. *The Journal of the Acoustical Society of America, 127*(3), 1956. https://doi.org/10.1121/1.3384968

Rose, P. (2002). *Forensic speaker identification*. Taylor & Francis.

Rothman, H. B. (1977). Perceptual (aural) and spectrographic identification of talkers with similar-sounding voices. In *Proceedings of the International Conference on Crime Countermeasures* (pp. 37–42). Oxford, UK.

Samuel, A. G. (1981). The role of bottom-up confirmation in the phonemic restoration illusion. *Journal of Experimental Psychology: Human Perception and Performance, 7*(5), 1124–1131. https://doi.org/10.1037/0096-1523.7.5.1124

San Segundo, E., Foulkes, P., French, P., Harrison, P., Hughes, V., & Kavanagh, C. (2019). The use of the vocal profile analysis for speaker characterization: Methodological proposals. *Journal of the International Phonetic Association, 49*(3), 353–380. https://doi.org/10.1017/S0025100318000130

Schmidt, J. E., Herrgen, J., Kehrein, R., & Lameli, A. (Eds.) (2008). *Regionalsprache.de (REDE). Forschungsplattform zu den modernen Regionalsprachen des Deutschen.* Retrieved from https://regionalsprache.de

Schubert, A., & Sendlmeier, W. (2005). Was kennzeichnet einen guten Nachrichtensprecher im Hörfunk? Eine perzeptive und akustische Analyse von Stimme und Sprechweise. In W. Sendlmeier (Ed.), *Sprechwirkung – Sprechstile in Funk und ernsehen* (pp. 13–69). Logos.

Schwartz, R. (2006). Voiceprints in the United States – Why they won't go away. In J. Lindh, & A. Erikson (Eds.) *Proceedings of the International Association of Forensic Phonetics and Acoustics Conference*, Sweden.

Seelmann-Eggebert, K. (Producer). (2012, 7th March). *Kamenz und das Lindbergh Baby* [Television broadcast]. Hamburg, Germany: Spiegel TV.

Shipp, T., & Hollien, H. (1969). Perception of the aging male voice. *Journal of Speech and Hearing Research, 12*, 703–710.

Shipp, T., Qi, Y., Huntley, R., & Hollien, H. (1992). Acoustic and temporal correlates of perceived age. *Journal of Voice, 6*, 211–216.

Skoog Waller, S. (2021). Accuracy and confidence in estimation of speaker age. *International Journal of Speech Language and The Law, 27*, 2. https://doi.org/10.1558/ijsll.39700

Solan, L. M., & Tiersma, P. M. (2003). Hearing voices: Speaker identification in court. *Hastings Law Journal, 54*, 373–435.

Solan, L. M., & Tiersma, P. M. (2005). *Speaking of crime: The language of criminal justice*. University of Chicago Press.

Sporer, S. L. (1982). A brief history of the psychology of testimony. *Current Psychological Reviews, 2*, 323–340.

Stacey, R. B. (2004). Report on the erroneous fingerprint individualization in the Madrid train bombing case. *The Journal of Forensic Identification, 54*(6), 706–718.

State v. Hauptmann, Atlantic Rep. (1935). 180, 809-829.

Stotland, D. M., & Brown, G. O. (1978). Voiceprints. *Dalhousie Law Journal, 4*(3), 708–738.

Thompson, C. (1985). Voice identification: Speaker identifiability and a correction of the record regarding sex effects. *Human Learning, 4*, 19–27.
Thompson, W. C. (1995). Subjective interpretation, laboratory error and the value of forensic DNA evidence: Three case studies. In B. S. Weir (Ed.), *Human identification: The use of DNA markers* (Contemporary issues in genetics and evolution (CIGE)) (Vol. 4, pp. 153–168). Springer. https://doi.org/10.1007/978-0-306-46851-3_17
Thompson, W. C., & Schumann, E. L. (1987). Interpretation of statistical evidence in criminal trials. *Law and Human Behavior, 11*, 167–187. https://doi.org/10.1007/BF01044641
Tosi, O., Oyer, H., & Nash, E. (1972). Latest developments in voice identification. Abstract. *Journal of the Acoustical Society of America, 51*, 132.
Trouvain, J. (2014). Laughing, breathing clicking—The prosody of nonverbal vocalisations. In N. Campbell, D. Gibbon, & D. J. Hirst (Eds.), *Proceedings of the 7th International Conference on Speech Prosody (SP7)* (pp. 598–602). Trinity College.
Trouvain, J., Fauth, C., & Möbius, B. (2016). Breath and non-breath pauses in fluent and disfluent phases of German and French L1 and L2 Read Speech. *Proceedings of the 8th Conference on Speech Prosody*. Boston.
Van Riper, C. (1973). *The treatment of stuttering*. Prentice Hall.
Voelkle, M. C., Ebner, N. C., Lindenberger, U., & Riediger, M. (2012). Let me guess how old you are: Effects of age, gender, and facial expression on perceptions of age. *Psychology and Aging, 27*(2), 265–277. https://doi.org/10.1037/a0025065
Warren, R. M. (1970). Perceptual restoration of missing speech sounds. *Science*, 392–393.
Watt, D. (2010). The identification of the individual through speech. In C. Llamas, & D. Watt (Eds.), *Language and identities* (pp. 76–85). Edinburgh University Press.
Wells, G. L., & Loftus, E. F. (1984). Eyewitness research: Then and now. In G. L. Wells & E. F. Loftus (Eds.), *Eyewitness testimony: Psychological perspectives* (pp. 1–11). New York.
Wiese, H. (2012). *Kiezdeutsch. Ein neuer Dialekt entsteht*. C. H. Beck.
Xue, A., & Hao, J. G. (2006). Normative standards for vocal tract dimensions by race as measured by acoustic pharyngometry. *Journal of Voice, 20*, 391–400.
Yairi, E., & Ambrose, N. (1999). Early childhood stuttering I: Persistency and recovery rates. *Journal of Speech, Language, and Hearing Research, 42*, 1097–1012.

Yairi, E., & Ambrose, N. (2013). Epidemiology of stuttering: 21st century advances. *Journal of Fluency Disorders, 38*, 66–87.

Yarmey, A. D. (1995). Earwitness speaker identification. *Psychology, Public Policy, and Law, 1*, 792–816.

Yarmey, A. D. (2007). The psychology of speaker identification and earwitness memory. In R. C. L. Lindsay, D. F. Ross, J. D. Read, & M. Toglia (Eds.), *Handbook of eyewitness psychology: Memory for people, 2* (pp. 101–136). Erlbaum.

Yarmey, A. D., Yarmey, M. J., & Todd, L. (2008). Frances McGehee (1912–2004): The first earwitness researcher. *Perceptual and Motor Skills, 106*(2), 387–394. https://doi.org/10.2466/pms.106.2.387-394

10

Plagiarism Detection: Methodological Approaches

Victoria Guillén-Nieto

1 Introduction

Plagiarism detection is an area of expertise of forensic linguistics that investigates suspicious text similarity. The expert linguist examines texts to gather evidence as to the relationship of dependence or independence between the suspicious pair of texts (Butters, 2008, 2012; Coulthard et al., 2010; Guillén-Nieto, 2020b; Sousa-Silva, 2014, 2015; Turell, 2004, 2008; Woolls, 2010, 2012). Chaski (2013) refers to this area of expertise as 'intertextuality, or the relationship between texts':

> Forensic linguistics provides answers to four categories of inquiry in investigative and legal settings: (i) identification of author, language, or speaker; (ii) intertextuality, or the relationship between texts; (iii) text-typing or classification of text types such as threats, suicide notes, or predatory chat; and (iv) linguistic profiling to assess the author's dialect, native language, age, gender, and educational level. (p. 333)

V. Guillén-Nieto (✉)
Departamento de Filología Inglesa, University of Alicante, Alicante, Spain
e-mail: victoria.guillen@ua.es

V. Guillén-Nieto, D. Stein (eds.), *Language as Evidence*,
https://doi.org/10.1007/978-3-030-84330-4_10

However, one may reasonably argue that the usage of the term 'intertextuality' may be equivocal in a forensic context because it certainly overlaps with the literary term 'intertextuality' coined by Kristeva (1980), which refers to a different concept. While it is true that both literary critics and forensic linguists are interested in analysing the relationship between texts, their purposes are distinctively different. In what follows, we will try to clarify the different purposes that literary critics and forensic linguists pursue when looking at the relationship between texts.

As explained by Kristeva (1980), 'intertexuality' refers to the idea that creating a text is inevitably linked to earlier sources. Similarly, Bakhtin (1981) uses the term 'heteroglossia' to refer to the dialogue established between a text and other prior texts. Furthermore, Bazerman (2004) illustrates the concept of 'intertextuality' by depicting the writer's work as immersed in a 'sea of texts':

> We create our texts out of the sea of former texts that surround us, the sea of language we live in. And we understand the texts of others within that same sea. Sometimes as writers, we want to point to where we got those words from and sometimes we don't. Sometimes as readers, we consciously recognise where the words and ways of using those words come from, and at other times the origin just provides an unconsciously sensed undercurrent. And sometimes, the words are so mixed and dispersed within the sea that they can no longer be associated with a particular time, place, group, or writer. Nonetheless, the sea of words always surrounds every text. (pp. 83–84 in Chatterjee-Padmanabhen, 2014, p. A–103)

By depicting the writer's work as immersed in a sea of texts, Bazerman highlights the complex process of transformation and adaptation of earlier works to create a new text. Love (2002) also argues that authors do not really create in any literal sense, but instead produce texts through such complex processes of adaptation and transformation. In Coulthard and Johnson's view (2007), 'intertextuality' draws on the assumption that the competent reader will immediately recognise the unacknowledged text borrowing because words carry with them a history of texts or social contexts in which words have been used before. From the stance of literary critics, 'intertextuality' does not necessarily imply that the writer intends to conceal the matching relation between the text she authors and earlier texts, but instead that she wants to make the matching visible for purposes of triggering off new meanings and literary effects through a creative process of adaptation and recontextualisation. Therefore, one can reasonably argue that the term 'intertextuality' refers, in effect, to a generative, imaginative and creative process of new texts and meaning.

By contrast, the concept of plagiarism relates to an uncreative, unimaginative process resulting in deception and fraud (Eggington, 2008). We argue that the true plagiarist intends to conceal the matching relation between the text she authors and earlier texts. Plagiarism may then occur when one makes an unacknowledged use of the work of another, or when one claims attribution for a work she did not write, or when someone uses one's previous work without duly acknowledging it ('self-plagiarism'), or even when one uses another writer's words to write her writing ('ghostwriting') (Foltýnek et al., 2019).

Although we have seen that the terms 'intertextuality' and 'plagiarism' refer to different concepts, it is true that the notion of 'intertextuality' has provided a theoretical framework for plagiarism (Chatterjee-Padmanabhen, 2014) within which there seem to be differing views. According to Pennycook (1994, 1996), since all language learning involves a process of borrowing others' words, we should not have dogmatic views about where one should draw the line between acceptable and unacceptable textual borrowings. On the other hand, Turell (2008) claims that some plagiarists may try to protect themselves under the protective mantle of 'intertextuality' to avoid accountability for plagiarism charges.

In sum, we hope to have demonstrated along these introductory lines that the term 'plagiarism detection' is more accurate than that of 'intertextuality' to name the expert area of forensic linguistics that investigates text similarity. We will now move on to consider the different types of plagiarism.

As stated by Kraus (2016), when we use the term 'plagiarism detection', we can refer to two broad types: 'literal plagiarism' and 'intelligent plagiarism'. Each of these two types of plagiarism can be further divided into other subtypes. On the one hand, 'literal plagiarism' can involve either verbatim or modified text copies. On the other hand, 'intelligent plagiarism' can relate to text manipulation, translation and idea adoption. Foltýnek et al. (2019) offer a classification of plagiarism forms according to their level of obfuscation: (1) characters-preserving plagiarism (literal plagiarism), (2) syntax-preserving plagiarism (synonym substitution), (3) idea-preserving plagiarism (borrowing concepts and ideas) and (4) ghostwriting.

The chapter is structured as follows. We begin by clarifying the difference between plagiarism and copyright infringement. Then, the chapter provides a literature review of plagiarism detection addressing forensic linguistic analysis' big challenges. Furthermore, the chapter discusses the latest research in computer-based methods and their implementation in automated plagiarism detection systems. Subsequently, the chapter points to the essential complementary role that qualitative linguistic analysis plays in plagiarism detection and draws attention to the relevance of context analysis in plagiarism cases. Lastly, the chapter provides the reader with a detailed step-by-step analysis of a live case of plagiarism between translators.

2 Plagiarism and Copyright Infringement

Plagiarism and copyright infringement are two sides of the same coin because plagiarism may be an instance of copyright violation, and a copyright violation may be an instance of plagiarism. Although the concepts of plagiarism and copyright infringement may seem to overlap at first sight, they denote, in effect, two distinctively different wrongful acts. Green (2002) summarises the essential difference between plagiarism and copyright infringement in these words: 'Copyright Law protects a primarily economic interest that a copyright owner has in her work…, whereas the rule against plagiarism protects a personal, or moral, interest' (p. 202). In the following sections, we will look at plagiarism in terms of the intellectual property rights it may violate.

2.1 Plagiarism as a Violation of the Moral Rights of the Author

Within the legal framework of European law, plagiarism is seen as a violation of the European doctrine of moral rights (Green, 2002). In essence, according to this doctrine, the moral rights of a writer are three:

1. The right to preserve the integrity of the work. This right allows the author to object to any distortion, modification or alteration that may be prejudicial to her social prestige or to her legitimate interests.
2. The right to disclosure the work. This right allows the writer to decide whether her work is to be made available to the public and, if so, in what form.
3. The right to claim attribution of the work. This right ensures that a writer has the right to be identified as the author of any work she has created.[1]

Plagiarism is then an offence against the moral rights of the author of an earlier work.[2] The plagiarist may be accused of academic fraud and violation of the workplace honour code. This accusation may cause devastating effects on her academic status, social prestige and professional career. In many common law jurisdictions, plagiarism is neither a crime nor a civil tort, but instead an issue that is subject to moral condemnation (Butters, 2012). By contrast, in some civil law jurisdictions such as the case of Spain, plagiarism is a crime by law (art. 270 of the *Criminal Code—Organic Act 10/1995*); the plagiarised author would be eligible for compensation for both material and moral damages (arts. 138 and 140 of the *Intellectual Property Act 1/1996*).

2.2 Plagiarism as a Violation of the Legal Rights of the Copyright Owner

Plagiarism can also be a copyright infringement—an infringement of a set of exclusive rights granted to the copyright owner. However, copyright infringement can only happen if the source work is copyrighted and protected by copyright law. Copyright implies one enforceable limitation[3] to the general public's freedom of speech concerning a wide variety of creative productions, legally termed 'intellectual property', including literary, artistic and scientific works. These exclusive rights granted to copyright owners are justified as a means of both protecting and promoting the creation of literary, artistic and scientific works (Butters, 2012). Under the *Copyright, Designs and Patents Act 1988* in the UK, a common law jurisdiction, the rights covered include: (a) to copy the work, (b) to issue copies of the work to the public, (c) to rent or lend the work to the public, (d) to perform, show or play the work in public, (e) to communicate the work to the public and (f) to adapt the work. These exclusive rights are not absolute but subject to limitations that are transnational in scope due to several international treaties.[4] For instance, copyright is limited in time—for most countries, the set time for the copyright of literary works is neither less than fifty years nor more than one hundred years after the author's death. Another limitation to copyright is what is known as 'fair use' or 'fair dealing'. These restrictions apply to permissible acts without infringing copyrighted material, such as, for example, private research, copies for educational purposes, news reporting, parody, among other possibilities.

Plagiarism is copyright infringement when, for instance, someone copies or adapts a source work without the permission of the copyright owner. In such cases, plagiarism is an offence against the copyright owner's legal rights, who may, or may not, be the author. Interestingly enough, copyright infringement can still occur even if the source author or copyright owner is cited. In both common law and civil law jurisdictions, copyright infringement is actionable by the copyright owner and can be punished in a court of justice for prejudices caused by copyright infringement. It should be noted that in practice, copyright infringement is only subject to criminal prosecution in extreme cases, specifically if the plagiarism is intended for purposes of commercial advantage or private financial gain—for example, cases of piracy and counterfeiting.

3 State of the Art in Plagiarism Detection

Upon reviewing the literature on plagiarism detection, we observe that the academic debate focuses on three main problems: (1) the undervaluation of scientific linguistic expertise in the courts of justice, (2) the admissibility of scientific evidence in the courts of justice and (3) the evaluation of text similarity. In the next subsections, we will look at each of these problems in turn in further detail.

3.1 The Undervaluation of Scientific Linguistic Expertise in the Courts of Justice

As early as 1988, Rieber and Stewart (1990), acting under the New York Academy of Sciences' sponsorship, organised a workshop on the language scientist's role as an expert in the legal setting. The workshop pointed to the fact that the legal profession had been underutilising the contribution of language scientists in court cases if compared to the involvement of forensic scientists of other behavioural sciences such as forensic psychologists and psychiatrists, as shown in the following quote:

> Given the pervasive nature of language-related issues in the law, it would seem the legal profession has underutilised scientific expertise in that domain compared, for example, to such other behavioural sciences as psychology and psychiatry. If so, one wonders why this has been the case. Ironically, an answer might lie in the law. (Rieber & Stewart, 1990, p. 2)

Many legal practitioners mistakenly think that judges have sufficient linguistic knowledge to analyse linguistic expression and meaning in scientific terms simply because they have competence in the language they use as a vehicle for professional communication. It is important to note that having linguistic competence and intuitive abilities is not by any means equivalent to having the necessary scientific linguistic knowledge and expertise to deal with evidence given in language, unless the judge also has expert knowledge of phonology and phonetics, syntax, semantics, pragmatics, discourse analysis, sociolinguistics, psycholinguistics, computational linguistics, among other disciplines, as well as training in qualitative and quantitative methods of linguistic analysis.

Although twenty years have already gone by since Rieber and Stewart (1990) tried to draw legal practitioners' attention to the convenience of calling upon expert linguists, the truth is that the situation has not changed much over the years. When this book is written, forensic linguistics is still an unknown forensic science for many legal practitioners, and continues being the Cinderella of behavioural sciences in the courts of justice. Many linguists have raised their voices to criticise the inexplicable discrimination the expert linguist bears in the legal setting. Turell (2008), for instance, claims that in civil law jurisdictions such as the case of Spain, expert witnesses are rarely called upon in plagiarism cases.[5] Butters (2012) points to the fact that ordinary jurors in US courts of justice tend to believe that they are competent to make their judgments regarding text similarity and that evaluating the degree of similarity between two documents is well within the judge's competence. Butters (2012) further argues that the language scientist has a 'real and legitimate jurisprudential value to offer to the courts' (p. 473) because her role is to aid the judge and jury in interpreting linguistic facts in ways that non-experts cannot do on their own. In the same vein, Guillén-Nieto also draws attention to the role of the linguist as an expert witness in trade mark conflicts (2011), plagiarism detection (2020b), and in cases involving language crimes such as defamation (2020a) and sexual harassment (2021). Moreover, Nicklaus and Stein (2020) recommend collaboration between forensic psychologists and linguists in statement veracity evaluation.

Despite the low involvement of expert linguists in court cases, the assistance of an expert linguist may be called upon by the court—or by any of the contending parties in some civil law jurisdictions such as Spain—on different stages of the court proceedings. The expert linguist may be requested to either support preliminary proceedings at the investigatory phase or evaluate the evidence given in language for court proceedings.

3.2 The Admissibility of Scientific Evidence in a Law Court

Since the admission of unreliable scientific evidence may result in tragic miscarriages of justice, on both sides of the Atlantic law courts have raised the question of admissibility of scientific evidence and established standards to secure that forensic reports meet scientific principles (Ainsworth & Juola, 2019; Chaski, 2013; Coulthard & Johnson, 2007; Ehrhardt, 2018; Turell, 2008). For example, in US law, the legal standards are the Frye standard (1923)[6] and the Daubert standard (1993)[7] (see Chap. 3 of this volume). These legal standards help a trial judge make a preliminary assessment of whether an expert's scientific testimony is based on a methodology that is scientifically valid and can be properly applied to the case at issue. In the following, we look at each of these standards in turn in detail.

The Frye test or general acceptance test determines the admissibility of scientific evidence. This standard comes from Frye v. United States, 293 F. 1013 (D.C. Cir. 1923). To meet the Frye standard scientific evidence must be interpreted by the law court as 'generally accepted' by a meaningful segment of the associated scientific community. The necessary scientific foundation applies to procedures, principles or techniques presented in a court case proceedings.

The Daubert test comes from Daubert v. Merrell Dow Pharmaceuticals (1993). This standard provides a rule of evidence regarding expert testimony's admissibility during federal legal proceedings in the US. The guidelines for admitting scientific expert testimony are summarised as follows:

1. The judge is the gatekeeper. The task of assuring that the expert's testimony truly proceeds from scientific knowledge rests on the trial judge.
2. Relevance and reliability. This guideline requires the trial judge to ensure that the expert testimony is relevant and rests on a reliable foundation.

3. A conclusion will qualify as science-based knowledge if the proponent can demonstrate that it is the product of sound scientific methodology based on standard scientific practice.

Furthermore, there are some definitional factors in determining whether the criteria under the legal standards are met. For example, the expert's theory or technique is generally accepted in the scientific community; it has been subjected to peer review and publication and can be and has been tested, and the known or potential error rate is acceptable.

In civil law jurisdictions, court admissibility is also ruled, but the legal standards may be less accurately defined than in US law. As a way of example, let us take the case of Spanish civil law. There the expert's testimony is governed by the *Civil Procedure Act 1/2000* (LEC), art. 124–128 and 335–352[8] and the *Criminal Act* (LECrim)—*Royal Legislative Decree 1882*, arts. 456–485, 661–663 and 723–725).[9] Although Spanish civil law stresses the evaluative report's scientific quality, it does not provide any explicit legal standards for court admissibility of scientific evidence because this is at the discretion of the trial judge and is based on the principle of 'good reasoning' (*sana crítica*) (*Civil Procedure Act 1/2000* (LEC), art. 348) (see Chap. 4 of this volume). In practice, the lack of clearly defined legal standards by which court admissibility of scientific evidence may be assessed objectively can be quite problematic. Over the last few years, scientific testimony has been, in effect, a controversial topic of heated debate in expert circles in Spain. According to De Luca et al. (2013), implementing the Daubert standard could help resolve problems concerning the present regulation of the expert's testimony, especially the controversial issue of court admissibility of scientific evidence based on the principle of 'good reasoning'.

According to Ainsworth and Juola (2019), the fundamental criterion for the admission of forensic evidence should be whether the methodology generates valid and reliable results. Furthermore, the mentioned authors draw attention to the ways in which the administration of justice can benefit from using validity testing because it can assist judges in making improved admissibility decisions and weigh evidence more appropriately.

3.3 The Evaluation of Text Similarity

In close connection with the admissibility of scientific evidence in a law court, there is a discussion on the assessment of text similarity and subsequent evaluation of the results in an expert opinion (Ehrhardt, 2018). Among the linguists who have addressed the challenges assessing text similarity poses to plagiarism detection practice are Shuy (2008) and Coulthard et al. (2010). These linguists seem to share similar views on the three issues that the expert linguist must deal with when evaluating text similarity in plagiarism cases: (1) the amount of supposedly plagiarised material, (2) the degree of formal similarity between the earlier work and the questioned work—that is, the language scientist would have to assess whether the questioned text is a verbatim copy (word-by-word copy) or a transformed copy of the reference text and (3) the independent originality of the reference text and the questioned text both from each other and from generally accepted knowledge or format.

Delving into the issue of the amount of supposedly plagiarised material, Woolls (2012) claims that it is possible to identify the amount of shared vocabulary ('similarity threshold level') with the assistance of plagiarism detection systems when the texts are of roughly the same length and on the same topic; however, he argues that the evaluation of text similarity can become a much more complex task when the text length of the comparison texts is unbalanced. In the same work, Woolls points to the need to evaluate text similarity on the grounds of text length. For instance, if the whole of an already existing work consisting of ten sentences were copied into a new work of one hundred sentences, this would only represent ten per cent similarity if expressed from the perspective of the latter, when the author has, in effect, borrowed one hundred per cent of the earlier work. Similarly, if ten sentences from a document of one thousand sentences were copied into a document of one hundred sentences, the borrowing would represent ten per cent if expressed from the perspective of the new work, and only one per cent if expressed from the perspective of the earlier work. Furthermore, Woolls (2012) explains that if the questioned text introduces some lexical and grammatical transformation, the percentage of shared vocabulary with the reference text will be lower than if it includes copy-and-pasted material from the reference text.

It is noteworthy that when investigating plagiarism, apart from the score of similarity threshold, the language scientist must analyse the similarities found in common between the questioned text and the reference text, and make decisions about whether they are significant or unremarkable. Guillén-Nieto (2020b) argues that 'plagiarism detection, whether including copyright infringement or not, is a complex, multi-layered task going beyond and above the discovery of copied text of an earlier original work (the reference text) into a new one (the questioned text)'(p. 106). Moreover, Guillén-Nieto proposes in the same work a list of ten questions as useful guidance for evaluating text similarity and thereby, discerning between real cases of plagiarism and those that are not:

1. Is the reference text a copyrighted work?
2. Has a substantial amount of original text been copied?
3. Does the reference text contain original ideas?
4. Could the borrowing fit in the category of 'fair use' or 'fair deal'?
5. Did the suspect have permission to copy original ideas or a substantial amount of text from earlier work?
6. Does the borrowing in the questioned text embrace the whole or only a part of the reference text?
7. Is the borrowing direct (verbatim) or indirect (modified)?
8. Is the borrowing evident or hidden?
9. Is the borrowing intended or unintended?
10. Are the comparison texts sufficiently different and distinguishable?

The evaluation of findings is a critical issue in an expert opinion. The language scientist must choose an evaluative framework within which to express her opinion. To this end, the expert may use either a probability scale-based approach or a likelihood-ratio-based approach. (*ENFSI Guideline for Evaluative Reporting in Forensic Science*, Willis et al., 2015, p. 6). On the one hand, the probability scale-approach measures the probability of a hypothesis given the evidence: 'It is highly probable that the questioned text copied a substantial amount of original material from the reference text'. On the other hand, the likelihood-ratio-based approach measures the strength of support the findings provide to discriminate between propositions of interest: The findings provide moderately strong support for the proposition that the question text copied a substantial amount of original material from the reference text than for the proposition that the reference text did not copy a substantial amount of original material from the reference text. The main difference between the two approaches of evaluating evidence is that the first approach addresses the probability of a hypothesis given the evidence. By contrast, the second approach addresses the evidence given the hypotheses (Ehrhardt, 2018). Whereas the use of the likelihood-ratio-based approach is most convenient for evaluating population-level data, its application presents a dilemma for qualitative forensic linguistics because of the lack of data required for the calculation of likelihood-ratios. Thus, even if the *ENFSI Guideline for Evaluative Reporting in Forensic Science* recommends using the likelihood-ratio-based approach, the use of probability scales may be a more convenient option for qualitative forensic linguistic analysis.

4 Plagiarism Detection Frameworks

In the past, the discovery of unacknowledged material believed to come from earlier work was the domain of informed readers. Since the 1990s, plagiarism detection has been mainly software-assisted because the task of gathering the evidence for the assembly of a case can be performed electronically and much faster than if it were performed manually (Woolls, 2012). In essence, there are three different approaches for the general performance of a plagiarism detection system: (1) 'extrinsic' (2) 'intrinsic' and (3) 'cross-lingual' (Kraus, 2016) to which we will refer in the following.

4.1 Extrinsic Plagiarism Detection

The task of extrinsic plagiarism detection is to compare a questioned document against a source document or documents contained in a database or available on the Internet for purposes of identifying matches between the comparison texts (Lukashenko et al., 2007; Potthast et al., 2010). Extrinsic plagiarism detection searches for matches based on various linguistic features: (a) lexical features (n-grams or word grams), (b) syntactical features (chunks, parts of speech(PoS) and sentences), (c) semantic features (synonyms and antonyms), (d) structural features (text-types) and (e) stylometric features (word length average, sentence length average, paragraph length average, type/token ratio, frequencies of words, among others).

The success of web plagiarism detection tools lies in the fact that the plagiarist needs to reproduce full sentences from the source text to preserve text cohesion (Coulthard et al., 2010). To identify potentially plagiarised sections of a document, if the source text is available on the Internet, a search for a suspicious word sequence between six or eight identical words would automatically return a sentence match that may be a candidate for plagiarism (Coulthard & Johnson, 2007). Although extrinsic plagiarism detection performs well in identifying copied, or even slightly modified, material, it assumes a closed world: 'a reference collection must be given against which a plagiarised document can be compared. However, if the plagiarised passages stem from a book that is not available in digital form, they cannot be detected.' (Meyer zu Eissen & Stein, 2006, p. 565)

Some well-known examples of automated plagiarism detection systems using extrinsic plagiarism detection methods are *Turnitin*—the questioned text is compared against potential reference documents that are stored electronically in *Turnitin*'s database or available on the Internet—and *CopyCatch Gold* v2—a questioned text is compared against a reference text. (Woolls, 2002)

4.2 Intrinsic Plagiarism Detection

According to Stein et al. (2011), intrinsic plagiarism detection and authorship verification are closely related. In both cases, the analyst is given a single document (there is no reference corpus), and she must deal with the problem of finding the suspicious sections by identifying irregularities or inconsistencies in the author's writing style within the same document. For instance, the irregularities can be identified, looking at differing stylometric features (Meyer zu Eissen & Stein, 2006) and character-gram profiles (Stamatatos, 2009; van Dam, 2013).

4.3 Cross-Language Plagiarism Detection

As its name suggests, cross-language plagiarism detection attempts to detect plagiarism across different languages (Franco-Salvador et al., 2013; Sousa-Silva, 2014). Within this framework, plagiarists typically use translation as a mask to hide the plagiarism of ideas (Turell, 2008). It is common practice that the plagiarist will translate a source work and publish it as an original work in another language.

5 Computer-Based Plagiarism Detection Methods and Systems

Although a comprehensive literature review[10] on automated plagiarism detection is beyond the scope of this chapter, we point to the latest research developments in the field. First, we will briefly refer to the research on computer-based methods to detect literal plagiarism forms—that is, verbatim or including slight modification: lexical-based detection methods and syntax-based detection methods. On the one hand, lexical-based detection methods exclusively consider the characters and words in a text to assess text similarity. These methods can be further divided into three subtypes: (a) n-gram comparisons, (b) vector space models and (c) querying search engines. On the other hand, syntax-based detection methods analyse text similarity on the grounds of sentence structure. These methods employ PoS (parts of speech) tagging to determine the syntactic structure of the comparison sentences. Although the mentioned methods work well in literal forms of plagiarism detection, they fail to detect plagiarism once there is a departure from copy-and-pasted passages from a source document (Coulthard et al., 2010; Woolls, 2010, 2012).

After 2012 there has been a dramatic turn in the field of computer-based methods to plagiarism detection. Researchers are currently interested in identifying strongly obfuscated forms of plagiarism. As a result, the latest methods are mostly semantics-based (Hage et al., 2010; Hussain & Suryani, 2015; Mikolov et al., 2013; Turney & Pantel, 2010) and idea-based (Gipp, 2014; Meuschke et al., 2017). As its name suggests, semantics-based detection methods compare the meaning of sentences, paragraphs or documents. These methods hypothesise that the semantic similarity of two units derives from their occurrence in similar contexts. Within this broad category of semantics-based methods, one can further distinguish several approaches resistant to synonym replacements and syntactic changes that can assess the semantic similarity of texts using diverse techniques. In their state of the art on semantics-based methods, Foltýnek et al. (2019) provide a full analysis of the approaches listed below:

1. *Latent-semantic analysis* computes semantic similarity by comparing the underlying semantic structure of texts.
2. *Explicit semantic analysis* represents a text topic in a high-dimensional vector space of semantic concepts.
3. *Information retrieval-based semantic similarity* computes semantic similarity by modelling a questioned document as a set of words and employs a Web search engine to obtain a set of relevant documents for each word in the set.
4. *Word embeddings* compute semantic similarity by analysing the words that surround the term in question instead of the term occurrences in each document. The basic idea is that terms appearing in proximity to a given term are more characteristic of the term's semantic concept than more distant words.
5. *Word alignment* computes semantic similarity on the grounds of words that are marked as related. The semantic similarity of two words is typically retrieved from an external database like WordNet.
6. *Cross-language alignment-based similarity analysis* (CL-ASA) is a variation of the word alignment approach for cross-language semantic analysis. The approach uses a parallel corpus to assess the semantic similarity between the words in a suspicious document and the words in a potential source text. The sum of the translation probabilities

yields the total probability that the questioned document is a translation of the source text.

7. *Knowledge graph analysis* (KGA) computes semantic similarity by representing a text as a graph. The graph nodes indicate relations between the concepts—the relations are extracted from corpora such as WordNet or BabelNet. Through the application of this technique, the analyst can obtain a semantic similarity score for documents. This approach can also work with multilingual corpora to detect cross-language plagiarism, especially when the source text is translated literally.
8. *Universal networking language* deals with semantic similarity by constructing a dependency graph for each sentence in the source document and the questioned document and compares their lexical, syntactic and semantic similarity separately.
9. *Semantic role labelling* (SRL) (Osman et al., 2012) determines the semantic roles of terms in a sentence and the relations between the terms—that is 'who' did 'what' to 'whom', 'where' and 'when'—to extract arguments from sentences and assess their semantic similarity.

Apart from semantics-based methods, the new trends in research on automated plagiarism detection point to creating idea-based methods that complement detection methods analysing lexical, syntactic and semantic text similarity in cases of strongly obfuscated plagiarism. Idea-based detection methods assess semantic and structural text similarity by analysing non-textual content elements such as in-text citations (Meuschke et al., 2015), mathematical content (Meuschke et al., 2017) and graphical content (Franco-Salvador et al., 2013), which are language independent and contain rich semantic information. These approaches can be even combined in a meta-system for purposes of achieving better results in the task of intelligent plagiarism detection.

From the literature review of Foltýnek et al. (2019), one can draw some relevant conclusions. First, over the period the mentioned authors review (2013–2018) the field of computer-based methods has seen major advances regarding the automated detection of intelligent plagiarism. These significant advances are mostly due to improved semantics-based detection methods and the investigation of language-independent features—for example, in-text citations, graphical content and mathematical content—for idea-based detection methods. Second, because each method has both strengths and weaknesses, integrating several detection methods tends to outperform approaches based on a single method. Third, using machine learning to determine the best-performing combination of detection methods in each case is a promising area of research. Lastly, the datasets used for the comparative evaluation of plagiarism detection methods and systems should be improved because they mostly contain artificially created monolingual academic plagiarism instances, which are not suitable for cross-language plagiarism or idea-based methods.[11] The fact that the above-mentioned computer-based methods for plagiarism detection have not been tested in live cases of plagiarism in academic and professional domains challenges the effectiveness of such methods beyond controlled laboratory practice. There is also the added difficulty of compiling a corpus of live cases of plagiarism because of the confidential nature of the documents subject to analysis.

Research in developing plagiarism detection methods is typically applied to the creation of plagiarism detection systems. Some well-known examples of commercial external plagiarism detection systems are, for instance, *CopyCatch Gold* v2 (Woolls, 2002), iThenticate,[12] PlagScan,[13] Turnitin[14] and UNICHEK.[15] On the other hand, there are also free plagiarism detection webs such as Article Checker,[16] Copyscape[17] and software such as Antiplagiarist,[18] Dupli Checker,[19] Plagium[20] and Viper.[21] Since suppliers of plagiarism detection systems rarely publish information on the detection methods they employ, it is hard to know the impact of plagiarism detection research on tools design. Forensic linguists are naturally interested in using automated plagiarism detection systems because these can assist to detect text similarity. Plagiarism detection systems, which are mostly web-based, typically report on the similarity between a suspicious document and other sources, and highlight the parts of the suspicious document that likely originate from another source and which source. The source can be found provided that this is on the Internet, in a database, or available for comparison. However, it is important to note that the expert linguist must analyse the reported similarity because plagiarism detection systems do not perform this task.

Plagiarism detection systems have both strengths and weaknesses. On the one hand, the strengths come from the number of texts that can be processed consistently and fast together with the strong visual presentation of text similarity that a system may provide. On the other hand, the weaknesses come from the complexity of identifying text similarity. It is a well-known fact that the effectiveness of plagiarism detection systems diminishes once there is a departure from copy-and-pasted passages from earlier work. This failure is due to the inherent difficulty of creating plagiarism detection systems to identify the similarities between portions of texts after having experienced grammatical and lexical transformation. As Coulthard et al. (2010) argue, a central problem challenging the efficiency of plagiarism detection systems is that the plagiarist will rewrite the text that she has borrowed from an earlier work to avoid detection. More specifically, Woolls (2012) points to two difficulties hindering the efficiency of plagiarism systems: 'language flexibility'—words can change their form—and 'fuzziness'—words can be deleted, inserted or change their position. In such cases, unlike a human reader, a computer system, unless it implements semantics-based or idea-based plagiarism detection methods, would miss the semantic or idea match between the comparison texts if their wording is not exactly or almost the same.

6 Linguistic-Based Methods to Plagiarism Detection

As abovesaid, plagiarism detection systems can report on text similarity that helps determine, especially in literal plagiarism cases, whether a suspicious document has borrowed a substantial amount of text from an unacknowledged source document. However, it is important to note that currently, plagiarism detection systems cannot analyse text similarity qualitatively. This type of analysis is left to the informed reader or the expert linguist who will have to decide on which linguistic tools are the most appropriate in each case. Among the linguistic tools the expert linguist can employ are graphemics, morphology, lexicology, syntax, semantics, text analysis, discourse analysis and pragmatics.

Language-based methods to plagiarism detection are essentially two: (a) form-based and (b) integrated (Guillén-Nieto, 2020b). Whereas form-based methods consist of examining text similarities at a word, sentence, and text levels of linguistic analysis, integrated methods also analyse the context in which text similarity must be understood and interpreted appropriately. In such a broader pragmatic perspective, the focus of analysis is shifted from the analysis of the formal aspects of the documents compared to the analysis of the appropriateness of language use and discourse in the communicative situation in which the case is embedded. In Guillén-Nieto (2020b), the author, upon analysing a court case of presumed plagiarism between lawyers, claims the relevance of context in plagiarism detection and proposes van Dijk's (2015) 'context model' for purposes of analysing the communicative situation where a suspicious case of plagiarism must be understood. Such a model comprises several functional categories such as the physical setting, the participants involved, the social action, the goals and current knowledge.

In the remainder of this chapter, we will present a case of allegedly copyright-infringing material, and provide an example of the methodological procedure the expert linguist may follow in elaborating the expert opinion.

7 Case Study

The case study is based on a suspicious case of plagiarism between Spanish translators of Oscar Wilde's tale *The Nightingale and the Rose* (1888). Plagiarism between translators was analysed in depth by Turell (2008) who revisited a case that was decided as copyright plagiarism by the Supreme Court of Spain—Judgement 1268—in 1993. The case concerned two Spanish translations of Shakespeare's play *Julius Caesar*. Turell discusses the qualitative linguistic analysis done by the expert linguist, a Professor in English Literature, and demonstrates how such analysis could have been complemented with the quantitative data yielded by the plagiarism detection system *CopyCatch Gold* v2 (Woolls, 2002).

7.1 Purpose

In this case, the expert linguist could be asked by the prosecutor or by the court of justice to determine if the questioned translation[22] (QT) borrowed a substantial amount of original text from Gómez de la Serna's earlier translation (the reference translation or RT).

7.2 Hypotheses

According to the *ENFSI Guideline for Evaluative Reporting in Forensic Science* (Willis et al., 2015), the evaluative report should meet the requirement of 'balance'. Specifically, the findings should be evaluated, given at least one pair of propositions. Whereas one of the propositions is based on one party's account of the events—that is the null hypothesis, the other proposition is based upon an opposing party's account of the events—that is the alternative hypothesis.

In the case under examination, the evaluative report analyses two propositions:

1. The null hypothesis (the defendant's account of the events): We predict that there is no relationship of dependence between the questioned translation (QT) and the reference translation (RT)—that is, QT was written independently from RT.
2. The alternative hypothesis (the prosecutor's account of the events): We predict that there is a relationship of dependence between the questioned translation (QT) and the reference translation (RT)—that is, QT was not written independently from RT.

7.3 Questions

The evaluative report asks several questions that the expert linguist must reply to ensure that she will be able to stand cross-examination in a court trial:

1. Is the reference text a copyrighted work?
2. Has a substantial amount of original text been copied from the reference translation (RT) into the questioned translation (QT)?
3. Does the reference translation contain original ideas?
4. Could the borrowing fit in the category of 'fair use' or 'fair deal'?
5. Did the suspect have permission to copy original ideas or a substantial amount of text from the reference translation (RT)?
6. Does the borrowing in the questioned translation embrace the whole or only a part of the reference translation?
7. Is the borrowing direct (verbatim) or indirect (modified)?
8. Is the borrowing evident or hidden?
9. Is the borrowing intended or unintended?
10. Are the comparison translations sufficiently different and distinguishable?

7.4 Description of the Sample Documents

The expert linguist is provided with the suspicious pair of translations of Oscar Wilde's tale *The Nightingale and the Rose* (1888). These are shown in Table 10.1.

Next, the expert linguist compiles another two distractor translations to see how similarities between the questioned translation and Gómez de la Serna's compare with similarities between: (1) the questioned translation and each of the two distractor translations, (2) the reference translation and each of the two distractor translations and (3) the two distractor translations. The expert linguist selects the distractor translations by their date of publication. One of the distractor translations was the first known Spanish translation of Oscar Wilde's *The Nightingale and the Rose*

Table 10.1 Suspicious pair of Spanish translations of Oscar Wilde's *The Nightingale and the Rose* (1888)

Suspicious pair of translations	Date of publication	Type of audience	Artwork
Gómez de la Serna: Reference translation (RT)	1943 [1920]	Refined audience	No
Questioned translation (QT)	2003	Children audience	Yes

Table 10.2 Distractor Spanish translations of Oscar Wilde's *The Nightingale and the Rose* (1888)

Distractor translations	Date of publication	Type of audience	Artwork
Baeza: Translation 1 (T1)	1980 [1917]	General educated audience	No
Montes: Translation 2 (T2)	1988	General educated audience	No

published three years before Gómez de la Serna's, and the second distractor translation was published much later than Gómez de la Serna. Both distractors translations were published before the questioned translation. The distractor translations are shown in Table 10.2.

On including the distractor translations in the analysis, the expert linguist aims at performing multiple comparisons between the four translations in order to test whether the suspicious pair of translations—QT and RT—scores higher than the other pairs of translations on four separate tests performed with *CopyCatch Gold* v2 whose purpose is to identify and compare four objective characteristics: (1) similarity threshold, (2) shared vocabulary more than once between the comparison translations, (3) vocabulary only once in each translation and shared once between the translations and (4) vocabulary that is only in one translation of the two compared. In this way, the expert linguist can determine whether QT borrowed a substantial amount of original text from RT or, on the contrary, all translations are likely to share a substantial amount of overlapping vocabulary simply because they derive from the same source text. The validity of the method employed by the expert linguist can be tested because the analysis can be repeated by the expert linguist and replicated by other expert linguists to check if the results are accurate.

7.5 Tools

Since the case under examination involves the analysis of translations, it is expected that the type of plagiarism one may find, if there is such, is literal, including either verbatim or modified copied text. The expert linguist turns to *CopyCatch Gold* v2 (Woolls, 2002) because this system can detect literal plagiarism by comparing two available documents and calculating the proportion of words and sentences held in common between them.

The initial screen of *CopyCatch Gold* v2 is divided into two main boxes. In each one, the linguist can do basic working operations, such as Select Work Files, Select Comparison Files, CopyCatch, Compare with Work Files, Clear Work files and Clear Comparison Files. It is important to stress that the linguist must compile the comparison texts beforehand. The initial screen also shows other relevant buttons like Language, which allows the user to load a stop-list of functional words together with specific content words considered functional for particular subjects; Help, which provides a user-friendly manual in English; Similarity Threshold, whose function is to restrict the number of pairs on show by setting the threshold for text similarity.

Before analysing the texts, the expert linguist using *CopyCatch Gold* v2 must perform certain tasks. These are:

1. Set the Similarity Threshold limit. The Similarity Threshold is typically set at 50 per cent for works that are topic-related and at 70 per cent for derivative works, such as translations (Turell, 2008).
2. Add to the Spanish stop-list[23] the system contains specific content words that are likely to be shared between the comparison translations—for example, patronymics, place names, human characters, non-human characters and other essential content words that are likely to be shared between the texts.
3. Load the stop-list to the system by clicking on the Language button.
4. Select the comparison files.
5. Click on the Copycatch button to search for matches between the comparison texts—that is QT-RT, QT-T1 and QT-T2; RT-T1 and RT-T2; and T1-T2

When searching for similarities between the texts compared, *CopyCatch Gold* v2 can do the following tasks automatically:

1. Calculate the similarity threshold score between the texts compared.

2. Detect and measure the vocabulary and sentences shared more than once between the texts compared.
3. Detect and measure the vocabulary and sentences present only once in each separate text and shared only once between them (hapax legomena).
4. Detect and measure the vocabulary that is only in one text and not in the other.
5. Provide lists of both content word and function word frequencies.
6. Calculate percentages.

The tool *TextWorks* (Gil et al., 2004) is also employed to run a stylometric analysis of the four comparison translations. The stylometric variables studied are: (1) different words, (2) type/token ratio, (3) average word length, (4) number of sentences, (5) average sentence length, (6) number of paragraphs and (7) average paragraph length.

7.6 Procedure

The analysis begins by analysing the context framing the case, which is essential to understand and interpret the data adequately (Guillén-Nieto, 2020b). Then, a quantitative analysis is performed with the assistance of *CopyCatch Gold* v2. The expert linguist runs separate analyses to identify and compare four objective variables: (1) similarity threshold, (2) shared vocabulary more than once between the two comparison translations, (3) vocabulary that is only once in each of the two comparison translations and shared only once between them—hapax legomena and (4) vocabulary that is only in one of the comparison translations. For each analysis, the expert linguist draws the similarities between the four comparison translations. Upon analysing the results, the questioned translation (QT) could be a plausible candidate for plagiarism, if this translation were the top match against Gómez de la Serna's (RT). Since four independent tests are performed, the expert linguist is able to provide an empirically tested error rate for her methodology (for the expert's commitment to science, see Chap. 2 of this volume).

Next the quantitative analysis is complemented with the analysis of eight stylometric variables: (1) running words, (2) different words, (3) type/token ratio, (4) average word length, (5) number of sentences, (6) average sentence length, (7) number of paragraphs and (8) average paragraph length.

Subsequently, a qualitative linguistic analysis is performed for purposes of analysing the originality of each of the comparison translations. To confirm how common or rare certain terms used in the comparison translations are, two databases of natural language are consulted. CREA[24]—the database of Spanish today (1975–)—and CORDE[25]—the database of diachronic Spanish (1974). Consulting databases of natural language is not only a useful technique in assessing the rarity of certain terms found in the comparison translations (Turell, 2004, 2008), but also provides objective reasons to confirm, or not, the rarity of such terms. (Ainsworth & Juola, 2019).

Lastly, for the elaboration of the conclusions of the expert opinion, the expert linguist uses a probability scale-based approach that measures the probability of a hypothesis given the evidence.

7.7 Findings and Discussion

7.7.1 Context

As mentioned earlier, the analysis of the communicative situation framing the case involves several contextual elements such as the participants, the social action, the goals and current knowledge. To begin with, the participants of the communicative situation are Oscar Wilde—the author of *The Happy Prince and Other Tales* (1888) in which *The Nightingale and the Rose* is included—and four Spanish translators of Wilde's tale: Ricardo Baeza, Julio Gómez de la Serna, Catalina Montes and the suspect translator.

The Nightingale and the Rose must be understood in Victorian England in which the industrial revolution resulted in radical social transformation. As each of Wilde's works, *The Nightingale and the Rose* is full of originality, wit and brilliant expression. The tale is structured in the shape of a parable in which the nightingale's sacrifice symbolises altruism and, according to Gamini Fonseka (2020), also reflects Wilde himself sacrificing his freedom for the love of his male lover against social standards and Victorian law.

The first translation of Wilde's *The Happy Prince and Other Tales* (1888) was, in effect, Baeza's (1980 [1917]), shortly followed by Gómez de la Serna's (1943 [1920]), the reference translation in the case. These two translations were close in time to the original work's aesthetic literary movement. Subsequently, other translations were published, such as Montes' (1988) and much later, in the beginning of the twenty-first century, the questioned translation (2003).

The edition of Gómez de la Serna's translation the expert linguist has in her hands is from 1943; it is a leather hardback edition aimed at a refined audience capable of appreciating Wilde's literary creativity and brilliant lyrical prose. By contrast, the suspect translation (2003) is a paperback edition aimed at a children audience in their first school years. Perhaps, for this reason, the edition contains large beautiful illustrations accompanying short texts written in large font. The editions of the other two translations the expert linguist analyses—that is, Baeza's and Montes'— are both paperback editions addressing a general educated audience.

Literary translation refers to translating creative poetry and prose into other languages. This type of translation involves social action due to its contribution to communication and understanding between nations, cultures, groups and individuals. Literary translation is harder than other types of translation. The difficulty lies in the balance to remain true to the source text while writing a unique text that tries to recreate equivalent effects in the target language. The translator knows that the author of the original work has chosen a particular word, expression or sentence for very specific stylistic reasons. Therefore, it is under the translator's responsibility that the lexical and syntactic choices of the original work are rightfully delivered in the target language.

The legal framework in which the case must be judged is Spanish civil law. According to the *Intellectual Property Act 1/1996*, translations and adaptations are derivative works and thereby, 'the subject of intellectual property, without prejudice to the copyright in the original work.' (Title

II. Rightholder, Subject Matter and Content. Chapter II, art. 2). A translation is a derivative work because it derives from a work that has already been copyrighted. So, the new work arises—or derives—from the source work. Legally, only the copyright owner—that is, the creator of the underlying work or someone the creator has given the copyright to, has the right to authorise the derivative work. In our case, both Baeza's translation (1980 [1917]) and Gómez de la Serna's translation (1943 [1920]) had to be authorised by the copyright holder of Oscar Wilde's *The Happy Prince and Other Tales* because when these first two translations were published in Spain, seventy years had not yet passed since the death of Oscar Wilde in 1900. Because the other Spanish translations were published in 1988 and 2003, authorisation from the copyright holder of the original work was not needed.

Given that a translation derives from original work, its scope of protection is only applicable to the translation itself, its structure, the syntax and the lexical choices. On the contrary, place names and patronymics are not protected by copyright law because these elements belong to the original copyrighted work. It should be pointed out that whereas the source work and the subsequent translations deriving from it are sufficiently different and distinguishable, all the translations are categorised as the same type of derivative work. This fact brings in the requirement of originality in derivative works such as translations and adaptations. In other words, each new translation or adaptation must be a creative variation on the earlier translations or adaptations. Otherwise, a translation or adaptation may damage an earlier translator's moral rights and incur copyright infringement. The four Spanish translations under analysis were published as independent translations; therefore, none of them is supposed to adapt an earlier translation. More specifically, if the questioned translation (2003) were an adaptation of Gómez de la Serna's (1943 [1920]), it should have obtained permission and paid the copyright holder of Gómez de la Serna's translation because when it was published, only twenty years had passed since the death of Gómez de la Serna in 1983.

The results from the analysis of the contextual elements framing the case help us to reply to four of the ten questions raised on the onset. First, the reference translation is copyrighted work because it is a derivative work under Spanish Copyright law. Second, in the case the suspect translation has borrowed original ideas or a substantial amount of text from the reference translation, the borrowing could not fit in the category of 'fair use' or 'fair deal' because it does not meet any of the limitations provided in the *Intellectual Property Act 1/1996* (Title III. Chapter II. Limitations). These include, among others, provisional reproductions and private copy (art. 31), quotations and summaries (art. 32), articles on topical subjects (art. 33) and parodies (art. 39). Third, in the case the suspicious translation has copied original ideas or a substantial amount of text from the reference translation, the borrowing could not be considered unintended because unacknowledged borrowing of a substantial amount of original text from an earlier translation into a new one is a deliberate act intended to procure fame, social prestige and economic advantage to the plagiarist. Fourth, there is no evidence that the suspect was granted permission from the copyright holder of the reference translation to copy a substantial amount of original text into the questioned text.

7.7.2 Quantitative Analysis

As explained earlier, for the quantitative analysis we resort to *CopyCatch Gold* v2 (Woolls, 2002). Before comparing the translations, to avoid over matching, a number of content words that are likely to be shared by the comparison translations were added to the Stop-list provided by the system. Specifically, the content words added were: names of the human characters ('joven', 'estudiante', 'hija', and 'chambelán') and non-human characters ('ruiseñor', 'lagartija', 'mariposa' and 'rosal'); names of plants and flowers ('rosas', 'rosa, 'encina', 'jacinto', and 'campanillas'); names of colours ('roja', 'rojas', 'blancas' and 'amarillas'); names of (semi) precious stones ('ópalos', 'marfil', 'perla', 'esmeraldas', 'oro', 'rubí' and 'coral'); names relating to music ('música', 'arpa', 'violín', and 'canción'); names of stars ('luna', 'sol', and 'estrellas'); names of body parts and fluids ('corazón', 'pecho', 'sangre'); names of birds ('palomas'); names relating to science ('libro', 'filosofía', 'metafísica', 'lógica', and 'leer'); and names of emotional states ('enamorado').

The expert linguist performed four separate quantitative tests with *CopyCatch Gold* v2: (a) similarity threshold, (b) vocabulary shared more than once between the translations, (c) vocabulary that appears only once in both translations and is shared once between them (hapax legomena) and (d) vocabulary that is only in one translation. What follows is the presentation of the findings of the four tests.

Similarity Threshold

As earlier mentioned, the similarity threshold is a parameter that measures text similarity. Any percentage exceeding the similarity threshold set at 70 per cent—which is the maximum percentage established for text similarity between translations, as suggested by Turell (2004, 2008)—will indicate a substantial amount of text copied from one translation into another. As shown in Fig. 10.1 below, since the texts compared are all translations of the same source text, their similarity threshold scores are, in all cases, very high. However, the only pair exceeding 70 per cent is the suspect pair of translations reaching 79 per cent. This high

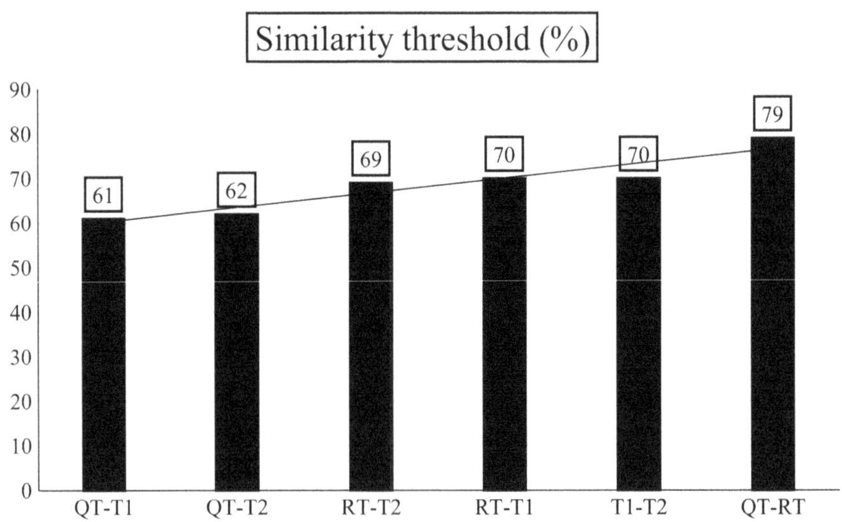

Fig. 10.1 Similarity threshold comparisons

percentage evidences that the suspect pair has more passages in common than when any of the other non-suspicious pairs of translations are compared. In this case, the 'directionality' (Turell, 2008) of the borrowing is clear because Gómez de la Serna first published his translation in 1920, while the questioned translation was published in 2003.

Shared Vocabulary more than once

This parameter shows the percentage of vocabulary that is shared more than once between the non-suspicious and suspicious translations. The higher the percentage of shared vocabulary more than once between the texts, the more likely it is that the texts have not been written independently from each other. The data yielded by *CopyCatch Gold* is shown in Figs. 10.2 and 10.3.

As Fig. 10.2 depicts the proportions of shared vocabulary more than once reach their highest scores in the suspicious pair of translations: QT (51 per cent)-RT (46 per cent) against the scores of the other two pairs: QT (40 per cent)-T1 (43 per cent) and QT (42 per cent)-T2 (44 per cent). Furthermore, Fig. 10.3 below shows that the scores for the proportions of shared vocabulary more than once between the non-suspicious pairs of translations are in all cases below the proportion of the suspicious pair: RT (44 per cent)-T1 (46 per cent), RT (48 per cent)-T2 (46 per cent), and T1 (48 per cent)-T2 (49 per cent).

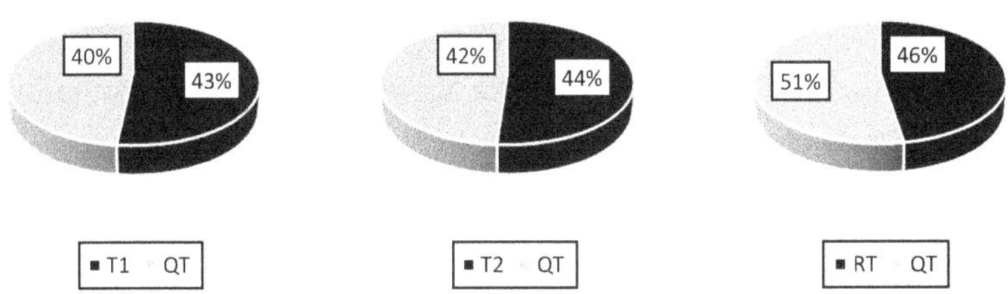

Fig. 10.2 Shared vocabulary more than once comparisons (1)

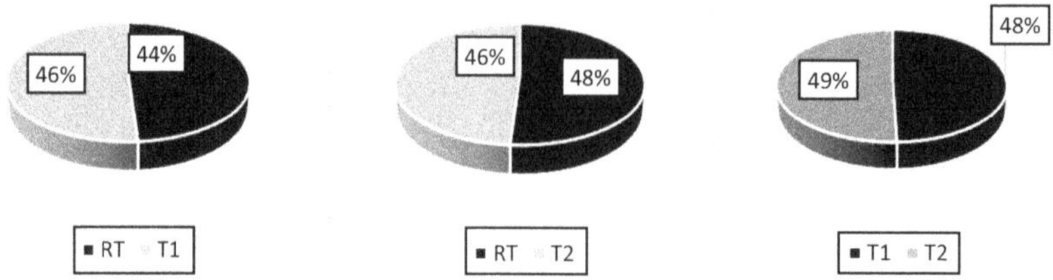

Fig. 10.3 Shared vocabulary more than once comparisons (2)

Hapax legomena

The analysis of hapax legomena is useful for plagiarism detection purposes because, as Woolls (2010) explains, 'comparing the word lists of two independently produced documents on the same subject will normally show a great deal of difference in the words which occur only once or twice' (p. 585). Since hapax legomena are thought to be idiolectal features of the author, the vocabulary only once in both texts and shared once between them can be considered an indicator of a strong relationship between the texts.

As shown in Fig. 10.4 below the highest number of hapax legomena corresponds to the suspicious pair of translations—that is, Gómez de la Serna's translation (RT) and the questioned translation (QT). These two translations have 284 unique content words and 31 unique functional words in common. The rest of the pairs of translations show lower scores, especially as content words are concerned. It is noteworthy that when the questioned translation (QT) is compared to Baeza's (T1) and Montes' (T2) respectively, there are 116 unique words less in common than when the questioned translation (QT) is compared to Gómez de la Serna's (RT).

Vocabulary that is only in One Translation

Another parameter *CopyCatch Gold* v2 automatically analyses is the vocabulary that is only in one of the translations compared. The results are depicted in Fig. 10.5.

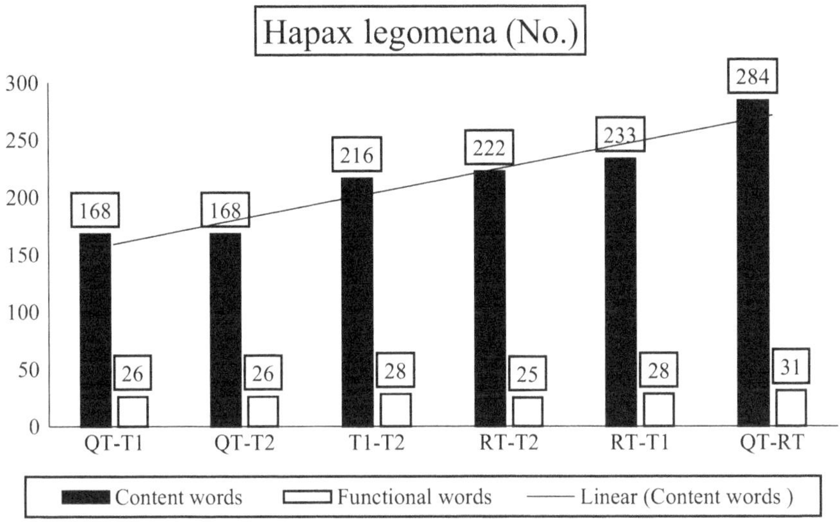

Fig. 10.4 Hapax legomena comparisons

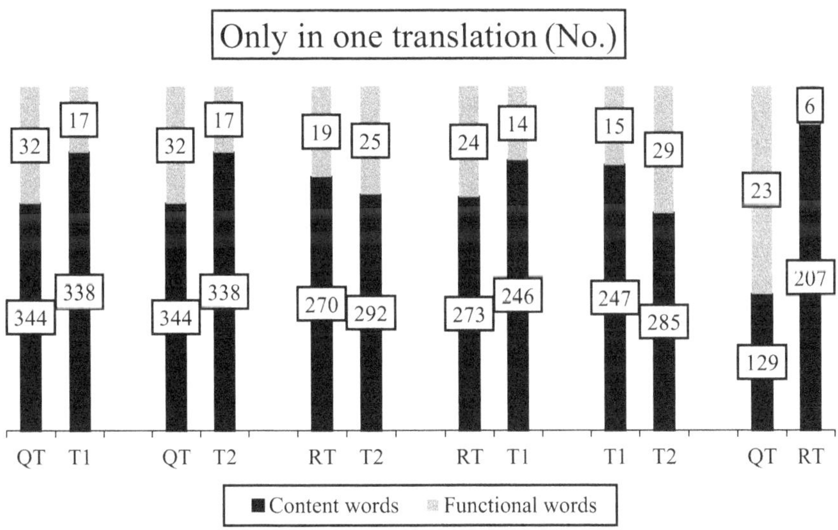

Fig. 10.5 Vocabulary that is only in one translation

As depicted in Fig. 10.5, the suspicious pair of translations is the one that exhibits the largest difference in unique content and functional words not shared between the two. Whereas Gómez de la Serna's translation has 207 content words and 6 functional words, the questioned translation has 129 content words and 23 functional words. There is a difference in the number of both content words and functional words—that is, the questioned translation (QT) has 78 fewer unique content words and 17 more functional words.

From the quantitative data yielded by *CopyCatch Gold* v2, we can draw the following partial conclusions. First, the suspicious pair of translations is the only one reaching 79 per cent score and thus, exceeding the similarity threshold set at 70 per cent for derivative works. Second, Gómez de la Serna's is the translation with which the questioned translation exhibits the largest proportion of shared vocabulary more than once—QT (51 per cent)-RT (46 per cent), and the highest number of shared hapax legomena (284 content words and 31 functional words). On the other hand, as for the vocabulary that is only in one text and not in the other, the questioned translation has the lowest number of unique vocabulary (129 words) when compared to Gómez de la Serna's (207 words). The four independent tests ran with *CopyCatch Gold* v2 point to the questioned translation as a plausible candidate for having borrowed a substantial amount of text from Gómez de la Serna's. Therefore, the error rate of the method employed is 0 per cent. In conclusion, the quantitative analysis results support the alternative hypothesis—the prosecutor's account of the event, which predicts that there is a relationship of dependence between the questioned translation (QT) and Gómez de la Serna's (RT).

Apart from providing essential quantitative data, *CopyCatch Gold* v2, as other plagiarism detection systems also do, can help the expert linguist to assemble the suspicious fragments for the case much faster than if she had to do it manually. The system also provides a visual display of the text matches in red; however, it leaves the evaluative analysis of such matches to the language scientist.

The quantitative analysis is complemented with a stylometric analysis performed with *TextWorks* (Gil et al., 2004). The results are shown in Table 10.3.

Table 10.3 Stylometric analysis

Texts	No. running words	No. different words	Average word length (%)	No. sentences	Average sentence length (%)	No. paragraphs	Average paragraph length (%)
RT	2165	709	6.1	124	17.5	78	1.6
QT	**2017**	**654**	**5.8**	**127**	**15.9**	**84**	**1.5**
T1	2189	672	5.9	120	18.2	73	1.6
T2	2378	694	5.8	114	20.9	67	1.7

Table 10.3 displays the results of the stylometric analysis. The questioned translation is the shortest text (2017 words) and has the lowest score in different words (654), average sentence length (15.9 words) and average paragraph length (1.5 sentences). But it has the largest number of sentences (127) and paragraphs (84). These stylometric differences are in concordance with a kids edition. In other words, the questioned translation contains artwork, large font, short paragraphs, short sentences and less vocabulary richness because it addresses a children audience.

7.7.3 Qualitative Linguistic Analysis

Qualitative linguistic analysis is complementary to quantitative analysis because it can help determine whether the borrowing is direct or indirect, evident or hidden, among other aspects. Furthermore, this type of analysis can help the expert linguist find out whether the substantial amount of copied text is, in effect, original or uncreative. It is unlikely that someone untrained in linguistics would spot specific text characteristics pointing to originality, hence the relevance of the professional assistance of an expert linguist to the court of justice.

The expert linguist consults the databases CREA and CORDE from the Spanish Royal Academy to provide quantitative assertions about certain terms used in Gómez de la Serna's translation (RT) and their originality. The analysis performed by the expert linguist is based on linguistic facts that can be 'established repeatedly, reproducibly, and accurately by superficial examination by any competent reader' (Ainsworth & Juola, 2019, p. 1172). Due to space constraints, the qualitative linguistic analysis is illustrated through two representative examples of Wilde's elegant lyric prose. The selected examples are chosen because of their richness in rhetorical figures. Therefore, both examples are supposed to challenge the translator's creativity to rightfully convey into Spanish the stylistic effects the Irish writer originally engendered in English. In each example, we provide the source text and compare the four Spanish translations.

The first example is a fragment from the dramatic opening of *The Nightingale and the Rose*. The student expresses his sorrow over the lack of a red rose that would win the Professor's daughter's love for him.

Example 1

'The musicians will sit in their gallery,' said the young Student, 'and play upon their stringed instruments, and my love will dance to the sound of the harp and the violin. She will dance so lightly that her feet will not touch the floor, and the courtiers in their gay dresses will throng round her. But with me she will not dance, for I have no red rose to give her'; and he flung himself down on the grass, and buried his face in his hands, and wept (Wilde, 1888).

Table 10.4 Spanish translations comparison

Baeza (1980 [1917]) (T1)	Gómez de la Serna (1943 [1920]) (RT)
Los músicos se sentarán en la galería —decía el Estudiante—, y tocarán en sus instrumentos, y mi amor bailará al son del arpa y del violín. Bailará tan levemente, que sus pies no tocarán el suelo, y los cortesanos, con sus trajes vistosos, harán corro en torno de ella. Pero conmigo no bailará, porque no tengo rosa roja que darle.Y se arrojó sobre la hierba y, escondiendo su rostro entre las manos, lloró.	Los músicos estarán en su estrado—decía el joven estudiante—. Tocarán sus instrumentos, y mi adorada bailará a los sones del arpa y del violín. Bailará tan vaporosamente que sus pies no tocarán el suelo, y los cortesanos, con sus alegres atavíos, la rodearán solícitos. Pero conmigo no bailará, porque no tengo rosa roja que darle. Y dejándose caer en el césped escondió su cara en sus manos y lloró.

(*continued*)

Table 10.4 (continued)

Montes (1988) (T2)	QT (2003)
Los músicos estarán sentados en su **estrado** —dijo el joven estudiante—, y tocarán sus instrumentos de cuerda y mi amada danzará al son del arpa y del violín. Danzará tan ligera que sus pies no rozarán el suelo, y los caballeros de la corte, con sus trajes alegres, estarán todos rodeándola. Pero conmigo no bailará, pues no tengo una rosa roja para darle. Y se arrojó sobre la hierba, y ocultó el rostro entre las manos y lloró.	Los músicos estarán en su estrado — decía el joven estudiante —. Tocarán sus instrumentos, y mi **amada** bailará a los sones del arpa y del violín. Bailará tan vaporosamente que su **pie** no **tocará** el suelo, y los cortesanos, con sus alegres atavíos, la rodearán solícitos; **pero** conmigo no bailará porque no tengo **rosas rojas**. Y dejándose caer **sobre** el césped, **hundía** la cara en sus manos y **lloraba**.

In Example 1, Wilde provides visual ('The musicians will sit in their gallery'), auditory ('and play upon their stringed instruments', 'the sound of the harp and the violin'), kinetic ('my love will dance', 'with me she will not dance', 'he flung himself down on the grass'), and tactile ('her feet will not touch the floor') imagery to create the atmosphere of delight and pleasure the Student imagines. In the first sentence, an external narrator's voice verbalises, through direct speech, the Student's desires and aspirations. When writing a text, the author must carefully select the linguistic forms to convey the intended meaning and stylistic effects to the audience. Since word for word translation from English into Spanish or vice versa does not work, the translator is challenged to recreate the original work by carefully selecting the best possible linguistic choices for each word, nominal group, phrase and sentence. Table 10.4 above depicts the four Spanish translations of Wilde's source text under comparison. As shown in Table 10.4, Baeza (1980 [1917]), the first Spanish translator of Wilde's tale, uses mostly a word for word translation method but makes interesting lexical choices to convey equivalent aesthetic effects in Spanish. For example, Baeza translates 'the courtiers in their gay dresses will throng round her' as 'los cortesanos, con sus trajes vistosos, harán corro en torno de ella'.

Gómez de la Serna turns to a freer translation seeking to create equivalent effects in Spanish: 'los cortesanos, con sus alegres atavíos, la rodearán solícitos'. The lexical choices convey an erudite tone that best suits a refined audience avid for the intellectual enjoyment of Wilde's literary work. At this point we would like to draw the reader's attention to the term 'atavíos', which was classified as hapax legomena by *CopyCatch Gold* v2. It is noteworthy that for a Spanish native speaker, the term 'atavíos' sounds rare in current Spanish. For this reason, the term is looked up in CREA—the database of Spanish today (1975–)—and CORDE—the database of diachronic Spanish (1974). These are the results: While there are 33 instances of the term 'atavíos' in 22 documents (1.5 ratio) in CREA, there are 543 instances in 247 documents (2.1 ratio) in CORDE, many of the documents even being from the fifteenth and sixteenth centuries. We can then reasonably argue that the term 'atavíos' can be considered a rare term in Spanish today because it is an archaic diction.

Moreover, Gómez de la Serna proposes some interesting solutions to convey Wilde's visual imagery in his work. It is particularly original how the translator depicts the lightness of the young girl's dance comparing it to vapour—'Bailará tan vaporosamente que sus pies no tocarán el suelo'. This original comparison beautifully recreates a dreamy-like atmosphere in the Spanish translation. Gómez de la Serna also employs a sentence structure change strategy. Specifically, he changes the first sentence's syntactic structure by replacing the comma with a full stop. In this way, the translator first introduces the setting framing the scene and after projects the student's dreams on it.

Montes, on her side, turns to literal translation but offers clever lexical choices too. As a whole, the translation is more similar to Baeza's than it is to Gómez de la Serna's but it is evident that she borrows the original term 'estrado' for the translation of 'gallery' from the latter.

Upon comparing the translation of Gómez de la Serna (RT) with the question translation (QT), it is obvious that this is a literal copy of the former, including very few modifications—highlighted in bold type in the text. It is important to note that the translator has made a pragmatic mistake because the copied text includes all the sophisticated lexical choices of Gómez de la Serna—for example, 'estrado' ('gallery'), 'bailará tan vaporosamente' ('dance so lightly'), 'rodearán solícitos' ('throng round') which are likely to be unintelligible to the children audience QT addresses. The copied text also includes the archaic term 'atavíos'. As earlier mentioned, the presence of this term (hapax legomena) in the questioned translation points to the strong relationship of dependence between the suspicious pair of translations.

Furthermore, on looking at the few modifications the translator of QT has made, one can see that while some of them are insignificant such as the preposition 'en' instead of 'sobre', or the use of the progressive verb tense 'lloraba' instead of the non-progressive one 'lloró', others can be considered inadequate for various reasons. First, the substitution of the singular number in the nominal group 'rosa roja' for the plural number ('rosas rojas') makes the red rose—that is even highlighted in the title of the tale—*The Nightingale and the Rose*—lose its singularity as a symbol of true love. Second, the substitution of the plural number of the common noun 'pies' ('feet') for the singular number —'pie' ('foot')—sounds weird. According to the *Diccionario de la lengua española*, 'no poner alguien los pies en el suelo' is a verb phrase that conveys the idea that someone moves very lightly. The verb phrase requires the common noun in plural number ('pies'/'feet') instead of singular number ('pie'/'foot'). Otherwise, the reader may get the wrong impression that the young girl only dances with one foot or, even worse, that she is single-footed.

The second example depicts the birth of the red rose that blossoms with the nightingale's blood. The nightingale self-sacrifices to win the love of the Professor's daughter for the Student. As in Example 1, this new excerpt is rich in visual imagery in the shape of personifications, metaphors, similes and stylistic repetition that engender elegant beauty in the source text.

Example 2

And on the top-most spray of the Rose-tree there blossomed a marvellous rose, petal following petal, as song followed song. Pale was it, at first, as the mist that hangs over the river, pale, as the feet of the morning, and silver as the wings of the dawn. As the shadow of a rose in a mirror of silver, as the shadow of a rose in a water-pool, so was the rose that blossomed on the top-most spray of the Tree (Wilde, 1888).

In Example 2, we observe that while Baeza and Montes mostly resort to literal translation and a careful lexical selection to convey equivalent stylistic effects in the target language, Gómez de la Serna's vocabulary is more singular, as illustrated in Table 10.5.

Table 10.5 Spanish translations comparison

Baeza (1980 [1917]) (T1)	Gómez de la Serna (1943 [1920]) (RT)
Y en la rama más alta del rosal floreció una rosa maravillosa, pétalo tras pétalo, como canción tras canción. Pálida era al principio, como la bruma que fluctúa sobre el río; pálida como los pies de la montaña, y plateada como las alas de la aurora. Como el reflejo de una rosa en un espejo de plata, como el reflejo de una rosa en una balsa de agua, así era la rosa que floreció en la rama más alta del rosal.	Y sobre la rama más alta del rosal floreció una rosa maravillosa, pétalo por pétalo, canción tras canción. Primero era pálida como la bruma que flota sobre el río, pálida como los pies de la mañana y argentada como las alas de la aurora. La rosa que florecía sobre la rama más alta del rosal parecía el reflejo de una rosa en un espejo de plata, el reflejo de una rosa en una laguna.
Montes (1988) (T2)	QT (2003)
Y en la rama más alta del rosal floreció una rosa admirable, pétalo a pétalo, a medida que una canción seguía a otra canción. Pálida era al principio, como la bruma suspendida sobre el río; pálida como los pies de la mañana, y de plata, como las alas de la aurora. Como la sombra de una rosa en un espejo de plata, como la sombra de una rosa en el estanque, así era la rosa que florecía en la rama más alta del rosal.	Sobre la rama más alta del rosal floreció una rosa maravillosa, pétalo **tras** pétalo, canción tras canción. Primero era pálida como la bruma que flota sobre el río, pálida como los pies de la mañana y argentada como las alas de la aurora. La rosa que florecía sobre la rama más alta del rosal, parecía **la sombra** de una rosa en un espejo de plata, **la sombra** de la rosa en un **lago**.

As Table 10.5 shows, Gómez de la Serna translates 'silver' as 'argentada' instead of 'plateada'. As in the case of 'atavíos', the term 'argentada' was also classified as hapax legomena by *CopyCatch Gold* v2. For a Spanish native speaker, the term 'argentada' also sounds rare in Spanish today. To confirm its singularity, the term is looked up in both CREA and CORDE. CREA yields 4 instances in 4 documents (1 ratio), while CORDE gives 543 instances in 247 documents (2.1 ratio), many of which are from the fifteenth and sixteenth centuries. Therefore, these quantitative data support the idea that 'argentada' is a rare term in current Spanish because it is an archaic diction. Furthermore, Gómez de la Serna introduces an interesting change in the sentence. If we take a narrower look at the translation of the last sentence:

> As the shadow of a rose in a mirror of silver, as the shadow of a rose in a water-pool, so was the rose that blossomed on the topmost spray of the Tree.

we observe that it contains a simile. The simile consists of a tenor or subject—'the rose that blossomed on the top-most spray of the Tree'—and a double vehicle or comparison used to describe the tenor—'the shadow of a rose in a mirror of silver, the shadow of a rose in a water-pool'. Interestingly enough, whereas Wilde writes the double vehicle first and the tenor second, Gómez de la Serna recreates the simile by reversing the position of the two parts of the simile—that is, he writes the tenor first and the two vehicles second, and even substitutes the literal translation of 'shadow' ('sombra') for 'reflejo' ('reflexion').

> La rosa que florecía sobre la rama más alta del rosal parecía el reflejo de una rosa en un espejo de plata, el reflejo de una rosa en una laguna.

Upon analysing the questioned translation, one can see that this is a literal copy of Gómez de la Serna's, including very few modifications—highlighted in bold type in the text. It should also be pointed out that the copied text from Gómez de la Serna's into the questioned translation includes erudite vocabulary that is likely to be unintelligible to the children audience the questioned translation is intended. The presence of the term 'argentada' (hapax legomena) evidences, once more, the strong relationship of dependence between the questioned translation and Gómez de la Serna's.

Findings from the qualitative linguistic analysis help us demonstrate with linguistic facts that a translation can be original and creative. In the case under study, whereas Gómez de la Serna's translation is original in structure, lexical choices and syntax, the questioned translation is uncreative because it is basically a literal copy of Gómez de la Serna's. Other signals of unacknowledged copied text are the semantic and pragmatic mistakes found, as well as unjustified omissions—the questioned translation is 183 words shorter than Gómez de la Serna's.

Table 10.6 Inductive probability scale

Grade	Probability
5	It is very likely that the questioned translation borrowed a substantial amount of original text from the reference translation
4	It is likely that the questioned translation borrowed a substantial amount of original text from the reference translation
3	Inconclusive
2	It is unlikely that the questioned translation borrowed a substantial amount of original text from the reference translation
1	It is very unlikely that the questioned translation borrowed a substantial amount of original text from the reference translation

7.7.4 Expert Opinion

After analysing the findings, the expert linguist must elaborate on the conclusions of the evaluative report. Because of the lack of data required for the calculation of likelihood-ratios, the expert linguist is likely to resort to the probability scale-approach that measures the probability of a hypothesis given the evidence—for example, 'It is likely that the questioned text copied a substantial amount of original material from the reference text'. As shown in Table 10.6 above the scale the linguist uses consists of five grades.

The conclusions that can be drawn from the multi-layered analysis performed in the case are as follows:

1. The questioned translation copied a substantial amount of copyrighted text from Gómez de la Serna's earlier translation. The quantitative analysis performed with *CopyCatch Gold* v2 yields a similarity threshold score of 79 per cent, which exceeds the 70 per cent set for derivative works. Furthermore, Gómez de la Serna's translation is the only one with which QT exhibits the largest shared vocabulary more than once (51 per cent) and the highest number of hapax legomena (284 content words and 31 functional words). QT is also the translation with the lowest number of unique vocabulary (129 words) compared to Gómez de la Serna's (207 words).

2. The questioned translation borrowed original text from Gómez de la Serna's earlier translation. Findings from the qualitative linguistic analysis show that Gómez de la Serna's translation can be qualified as original and creative for its structure, lexical choices and syntax. The questioned translation contains literal plagiarism—verbatim or slightly modified copied text—of Gómez de la Serna's earlier translation.
3. Both the quantitative and the qualitative results support the alternative hypothesis that predicts that the questioned translation has not been written independently from Gómez de la Serna's earlier translation.

The expert linguist concludes that it is very likely that the questioned translation borrowed a substantial amount of original text from Gómez de la Serna's earlier translation. Grade: 5.

It is important to stress that the expert linguist's job is not to judge the case but instead to aid legal practitioners in interpreting linguistic facts in many ways that non-experts cannot do on their own. However, it is up to the triers of fact to decide whether, or not, an expert opinion is relevant for the court decision.

8 Conclusions

This chapter was devoted to plagiarism detection, an expert area of forensic linguistics that analyses suspicious text similarity. Plagiarism, whether involving copyright infringement or not, relates to an uncreative process resulting in deception that may take different shapes: making an unacknowledged use of the work of another, claiming attribution of an original text one did not write, using one's previous work without duly acknowledging it ('self-plagiarism') or even using another writer's words to write one's work ('ghostwriting').

The chapter has drawn attention to the importance of understanding the context framing the plagiarism case. The expert linguist is not a lawyer but cannot ignore the legal framework where the case must be understood. In US law, what matters is copyright infringement; plagiarism is neither a crime nor a civil tort but an issue subject to moral condemnation. By contrast, in civil law, the law also provides for the violation of the moral rights of the author of an earlier work. Furthermore, in some civil law jurisdictions, as in the case of Spanish civil law, plagiarism is considered a crime.

There seems to be general consensus about the fact that expert opinion must rest on a reliable scientific foundation and provide validity measurements that can help to improve the administration of justice. According to the recommendations of the *ENFSI Guideline for Evaluative Reporting in Forensic Science* (2015), the expert opinion must be grounded in statistics such as the likelihood-ratio. Although it is necessary to provide quantitative assertions of linguistic findings, it should be pointed out that it is not always possible to perform statistics because of the type and/or the amount of data to be analysed in the case. Likelihood-ratios, for instance, are not suitable statistics when one does not have population data to process. It would be unscientific to perform likelihood-ratios if one knows that the necessary conditions to do so accurately do not meet and thereby, the results will be unreliable. For this reason, the probability scale-based approach seems to be more suitable than the likelihood-ratio-based approach in plagiarism detection.

Furthermore, the chapter attempted to demonstrate that text similarity analysis is a complex task that goes beyond identifying copied text into one work from another. Plagiarism requires a multi-layered approach, combining both quantitative and qualitative methods. Computer systems can automatically detect literal plagiarism (verbatim or slightly modified copied text) and measure how similar two texts are. However, computer systems leave the analysis of the data to the expert linguist. Through qualitative linguistic analysis and consultation of databases of natural language the expert linguist can assess the independent originality of the reference text and the questioned text.

The chapter has also addressed the significant development of research on computer-based methods for intelligent plagiarism detection since 2013. However, it should be noted that computer engineers mostly work with laboratory data. Thus, it is difficult to know the effectiveness of the latest advances in the field with live cases. Another important weakness is that the advances do not necessarily translate into the implementation of computer systems that can assist the expert linguist in detecting intelligent plagiarism. Furthermore, there seems to be a lack of transparency about the computer methods implemented in computer systems. If the expert linguist had access to such valuable information, she could make better decisions about which computer system is the best suited for each case. On the other hand, an added difficulty is that the vast majority of automated plagiarism detection systems in the market today are commercial because of the complexity and expenses involved in developing such systems. The essential idea that emerges from this discussion is that expert linguists need better tools for the trade of plagiarism detection that can ease validity measurements and smooth the admissibility of scientific linguistic evidence in the courts of justice.

We hope this chapter may provide theoretical and methodological guidance for scholars interested in language and the law in general and linguists who want to initiate a career providing professional service as consultants or experts in plagiarism detection.

Notes

1. European Parliament. (2018). *Copyright Law in the EU. Salient Features of Copyright Law across the EU Member States.* European Parliamentary Research Service. Study. Retrieved from https://www.europarl.europa.eu/RegData/etudes/STUD/2018/625126/EPRS_STU(2018)625126_EN.pdf.
2. Spanish law, a civil law jurisdiction, explicitly protects the authors' moral rights under art. 14. (Content and Characteristics of Moral Rights) of the *Intellectual Property Act 1/1996*: (1) The right to disclosure; (2) The right to determine how communication with the public should be effected; (3) The right to claim authorship; (4) The right to demand respect for the integrity of the work; (5) The right to modify the work with the permission of the copyright holder; (6) The right to withdraw the work due to changes in intellectual or moral convictions and (7) The right of access to the sole or rare copy of the work.
3. The other three enforceable limitations to the general public's freedom of speech are patents, trademarks—and service marks—and trade secrets.

4. Copyright limitations are transnational in scope for most countries due to international treaties such as the Berne Convention of 1886, the UNESCO Universal Copyright Convention of 1952, the World Trade Organisation's TRIPS Agreement of 1995 and the WIPO Copyright Treaty of 1996.
5. By way of example, the author has acted as an expert linguist in only four plagiarism cases over the last thirteen years, of which only two were court cases. In these two, the author acted as expert for the defendant. One case was relating to plagiarism between lawyers (Guillén-Nieto, 2020b), the other case concerned supposedly plagiarised electronic material into a teaching project.
6. Retrieved January, 3, 2021, from https://www.law.cornell.edu/wex/frye_standard.
7. Retrieved January, 3, 2021, from https://www.law.cornell.edu/wex/daubert_standard.
8. Retrieved from https://www.boe.es/buscar/doc.php?id=BOE-A-2000-323.
9. Retrieved from https://www.boe.es/buscar/act.php?id=BOE-A-1882-6036.
10. Kraus (2016) offers a comprehensive review of plagiarism detection systems and evaluation methods until 2012. Furthermore, Foltýnek et al. (2019) provide an exhaustive critical review evaluating the capabilities of computer-based academic plagiarism detection methods from 2013 to 2018. Over this period one can see major advances concerning the automated detection of obfuscated academic plagiarism forms.
11. PAN is a well-established platform for the comparative evaluation of authorship identification and plagiarism detection methods and systems. Retrieved from https://pan.webis.de/.
12. Retrieved from https://www.ithenticate.com/.
13. Retrieved from https://www.plagscan.com/es/?gclid=Cj0KCQiAx9mABhD0ARIsAEfpavR5s-cCrTnF608Lius5CnmZPtqJfK4JB0r5NZpKTjvN0OE9-mLhoBoaAoCKEALw_wcB.
14. Retrieved from https://www.turnitin.com/.
15. Retrieved from https://unicheck.com/es-es.
16. Retrieved from https://www.articlechecker.com/.
17. Retrieved from https://www.copyscape.com/.
18. Retrieved from https://antiplagiarist.softonic.com/.
19. Retrieved from https://www.duplichecker.com/.

20. Retrieved from https://www.plagium.com/.
21. Retrieved from https://plag.co/.
22. For confidential reasons, reference to the suspect translator is omitted.
23. Woolls (2012) explains that 'in order to avoid over-matching, function words, due to their high frequencies in a language, are collected together on what is termed a "stop-list" and discounted altogether for vocabulary comparison purposes' (p. 525).
24. CREA (3.2 June 2008) is a current Spanish database that contains 160,000,000 linguistic forms from written and oral texts produced in all Spanish speaking countries from 1975 until 2004. The written texts have been selected from books, journals and magazines.
25. CORDE is a database of diachronic Spanish. It contains 250 million linguistic forms from a wide range of genres from the Spanish language's origins until 1974.

References

Ainsworth, J., & Juola, P. (2019). Who wrote this? Modern forensic authorship analysis as a model for valid forensic science. *Washington University Law Review, 96*(5), 1161–1189.

Bakhtin, M. (1981). *The dialogic imagination: Four essays* (Ed. M. Holquist; Trans. C. Emerson, & M. Holquist). Austin: University of Texas Press.

Bazerman, C. (2004). Intertextuality: How texts rely on other texts. In C. Bazerman, & P. Prior (Eds.), *What writing does and how it does it* (pp. 309–339). Lawrence Erlbaum.

Butters, R. R. (2008). Trademarks and other proprietary terms. In J. Gibbons, & M. Teresa Turell (Eds.), *Dimensions of forensic linguistics* (pp. 231–247). John Benjamins Publishing Company.

Butters, R. R. (2012). Language and copyright. In P. M. Tiersma, & L. M. Solan (Eds.), *The Oxford handbook of language and law* (pp. 463–477). Oxford University Press.

Chaski, C. (2013). Best practices and admissibility of forensic author identification. *Journal of Law and Policy, 21*, 333–376. https://brooklynworks.brooklaw.edu/jlp/vol21/iss2/5

Chatterjee-Padmanabhen, M. (2014). Bakhtin's theory of heteroglossia/intertextuality in teaching academic writing in higher education. *Journal of Academic Language & Learning, 8*(3), A101–A112.

Copyright, Designs and Patents Act. 1988. https://www.legislation.gov.uk/ukpga/1988/48/contents

Coulthard, M., & Johnson, A. (Eds.). (2007). *An Introduction to forensic linguistics: Language in evidence*. Routledge.

Coulthard, M., Johnson, A., Kredens, K., & Woolls, D. (2010). Four forensic linguists' responses to suspected plagiarism. In M. Coulthard, & A. Johnson (Eds.), *An introduction to forensic linguistics: Language in evidence* (pp. 523–538). Routledge.

Daubert Standard. (1993). Retrieved on January 8, 2021, from https://www.law.cornell.edu/wex/daubert_standard

Daubert v Merrell Dow Pharmaceuticals. (1993). (US). https://caselaw.findlaw.com/us-supreme-court/509/579.html

De Luca, S., Navarro, F., & Cameriere, R. (2013). La prueba pericial y su valoración en el ámbito judicial español. *Revista electrónica de ciencia penal y criminología. Artículos RECPC, 15*(19), 1–14.

Eggington, W. G. (2008). Deception and fraud. In J. Gibbons & M. T. Turell (Eds.), *Dimensions of forensic linguistics* (pp. 249–264). John Benjamins Publishing Company.

Ehrhardt, S. (2018). Authorship attribution analysis. In J. Visconti (Ed.), *Handbook of communication in the legal sphere* (pp. 169–200). Boston.

European Parliament. (2018). *Copyright law in the EU. Salient features of copyright law across the EU member states*. European Parliamentary Research Service. Study. https://www.europarl.europa.eu/RegData/etudes/STUD/2018/625126/EPRS_STU(2018)625126_EN.pdf

Foltýnek, T., Meuschke, N., & Gipp, B. (2019). Academic plagiarism detection: A systematic literature review. *ACM Computing Surveys, 52*(6), 1–42. https://doi.org/10.1145/3345317

Franco-Salvador, M., Gupta, P., & Rosso, P. (2013). Cross-language plagiarism detection using a multilingual semantic network. In P. Serdyukov et al. (Eds.), *Advances in information retrieval. ECIR 2013. Lecture notes in computer science* (pp. 710–713). Springer. https://doi.org/10.1007/978-3-642-36973-5_66

Frye Standard. (1923). Retrieved on January 6, 2021, from https://www.law.cornell.edu/wex/frye_standard

Frye v United States. (1923). 293 F. 1013 (US). https://www.mass.gov/doc/frye-v-united-states-293-f-1013-dc-cir-1923/download

Gamini Fonseka, E. A. (2020). Sacrifice unacknowledged: A literary analysis of the nightingale and the rose by Oscar Wilde. *American Research Journal of*

English and Literature, 6(1), 1–8. https://doi.org/10.21694/2378-9026.20010

Gil, L., Soler, C., Stuart, K., & Candela, J. (2004). *TextWorks*. Departamento de Idiomas, Universidad Politécnica de Valencia.

Gipp, B. (2014). *Citation-based plagiarism detection*. In *Citation-based plagiarism detection* (pp. 57–88). Springer. https://doi.org/10.1007/978-3-658-06394-8_4

Green, S. P. (2002). Plagiarism, norms, and the limits of the theft law: Some observations on the use of criminal sanctions in enforcing intellectual property rights. *Hastings Law Journal, 54*(1), 167–242. https://papers.ssrn.com/sol3/papers.cfm?abstract_id=315562

Guillén-Nieto, V. (2011). The expert as witness in the CTM courts. *International Journal of Applied Linguistics (ITL), 162*, 63–83.

Guillén-Nieto, V. (2020a). Defamation as a language crime: A socio-pragmatic approach to defamation cases in the high courts of justice of Spain. *International Journal of Language & Law (JLL), 9*, 1–22.

Guillén-Nieto, V. (2020b). The relevance of context in plagiarism detection: The case of a professional legal genre. *Ibérica, 40*, 101–122.

Guillén-Nieto, V. (2021). 'What else can you do to pass…?' A pragmatics-based approach to quid-pro-quo sexual harassment. In J. Giltrow, F. Olsen, & D. Mancini (Eds.), *Legal meanings and language rights. International, social and philosophical perspectives* (pp. 31–55). de Gruyter Mouton. https://doi.org/10.1515/9783110720969

Hage, J., Rademaker, P., & van Vugt, N. (2010). A comparison of plagiarism detection tools. In *Technical report UU-CS-2010-2015* (pp. 1–26). Department of Information and Computing Sciences, Utrecht University. http://www.cs.uu.nl/research/techreps/repo/CS-2010/2010-015.pdf

Hussain, F., & Suryani, M. A. (2015). On retrieving intelligently plagiarized documents using semantic similarity. *Engineering Applications of Artificial Intelligence, 45*, 246–258. https://doi.org/10.1016/j.engappai.2015.07.011

Kraus, C. (2016). Plagiarism detection. State-of-the art systems (2016) and evaluation detection. Retrieved from arXiv:1603.03014v1 [cs.IR].

Kristeva, J. (1980). The bounded text. In L. Roudiez, T. Gora, & A. Jardine (Eds.), *Desire in language: A semiotic approach to literature and art* (pp. 36–63). Columbia University Press.

Love, H. (2002). *Attributing authorship. An introduction.* Cambridge University Press.

Lukashenko, R., Graudina, V., & Grundspenkis, J. (2007). Computer-based plagiarism detection methods and tools: An overview. *Proceedings of the 2007 International Conference on Computer Systems and Technologies, 18*, 1–6. https://dl.acm.org/doi/10.1145/1330598.1330642

Meuschke, N., Gipp, B., & Lipinsk, M. (2015). CITREC: An evaluation framework for citation-based similarity measures based on TREC genomics and PubMed Central. In *iConference 2015 Proceedings*. http://hdl.handle.net/2142/73680

Meuschke, N., Shubotz, M., Hamborg, F., Skopal, T., & Gipp, B. (2017). Analyzing mathematical content to detect academic plagiarism. *CIKM'17 Proceedings of the 2017 ACM on Conference on Information and Knowledge Management*, 2211–2214. https://doi.org/10.1145/3132847.3133144

Meyer zu Eissen, S., & Stein, B. (2006). Intrinsic plagiarism detection. *Lecture Notes in Computer Science, 3936*, 565–569. https://doi.org/10.1007/11735106_66

Mikolov, T., Chen, K., Corrado, G., & Dean, J. (2013). Efficient estimation of word representations in vector space. *Computation and Language*, 1–12. https://arxiv.org/abs/1301.3781

Nicklaus, M., & Stein, D. (2020). The role of linguistics in veracity evaluation. *International Journal of Language & Law (JLL), 9*, 23–47.

Osman, A. H., Salim, N., Binwahlan, M. S., Alteeb, R., & Abuobieda, A. (2012). An improved plagiarism detection scheme based on semantic role labelling. *Applied Soft Computing, 12*(5), 1493–1502. https://doi.org/10.1016/j.asoc.2011.12.021

Pennycook, A. (1994). The complex contexts of plagiarism: A reply to Deckert. *Journal of Second Language Writing, 3*, 277–284.

Pennycook, A. (1996). Borrowing others' words: Text, ownership, memory, and plagiarism. *TESOL Quarterly, 30*, 201–203.

Potthast, M., Stein, B., Barrón-Cedeño, A., & Rosso, P. (2010). An evaluation framework for plagiarism detection in COLING'10. *Proceedings of the 23rd International Conference on Computational Linguistics*, 997–1005. https://www.aclweb.org/anthology/C10-2115

Real Academia Española: Banco de datos (CORDE) [online]. (n.d.). *Corpus diacrónico del español*. Retrieved February 16, 2021, from http://www.rae.es

Real Academia Española: Banco de datos (CREA) [online]. (n.d.). *Corpus de referencia del español actual*. Retrieved February 16, 2021, from http://www.rae.es

Rieber, R. W., & Stewart, W. A. (Eds.). (1990). *The language scientist as expert in the legal setting. Annals of the New York academy of sciences, 606* (pp. 1–135). The New York Academy of Sciences.

Shuy, R. (2008). *Fighting over words: Language and civil law cases.* Oxford University Press.

Sousa-Silva, R. (2014). Detecting translingual plagiarism and the backlash against translation plagiarists. *Language and Law/Linguagem e Direito, 1*(1), 70–94.

Sousa-Silva, R. (2015). 'Reporter fired for plagiarism: A forensic linguistic analysis of news plagiarism'. In Simões, Barreiro, Santos, Sousa-Silva, & Tagnin (Eds.), Linguistica, informática e tradução: Mundos que se cruzam. *Oslo Studies in Language, 7*(1), 301–322.

Spanish Civil Procedure Act (LEC) 1/2000. (n.d.). BOE-A-2000-323. https://www.boe.es/buscar/doc.php?id=BOE-A-2000-323

Spanish Criminal Act (LECrim) 1882. (n.d.). BOE-A-1882-6036. https://www.boe.es/buscar/act.php?id=BOE-A-1882-6036

Spanish Criminal Code 2014. (n.d.). Clinter (Trans.). Ministry of Justice. Official State Gazette, *281.* https://www.legislationline.org/download/id/6443/file/Spain_CC_am2013_en.pdf

Spanish Intellectual Property Act 2012. (n.d.). Clinter (Trans.). Ministry of Justice. Official State Gazette, *97.* https://www.wipo.int/edocs/lexdocs/laws/en/es/es177en.pdf

Stamatatos, E. (2009). Intrinsic plagiarism detection. Using character *n*-gram profiles. In B. Stein, P. Rosso, E. Stamatatos, M. Koppel, & E. Agirre (Eds.), *Proceedings of the SEPLN'09 Workshop on Uncovering Plagiarism, Authorship and Social Software Misuse* (pp. 38–46). http://ceur-ws.org/Vol-502/pan09-proceedings.pdf

Stein, B., Lipka, N., & Prettenhofer, P. (2011). Intrinsic plagiarism analysis. *Language Resources and Evaluation, 45*(1), 63–82. https://doi.org/10.1007/s10579-010-9115-y

Turell, M. T. (2004). Textual kidnapping revisited: The case of plagiarism in literary translation. *International Journal of Speech, Language and the Law, 11*, 1–26.

Turell, M. T. (2008). Plagiarism. In J. Gibbons, & M. T. Turell (Eds.), *Dimensions of forensic linguistics* (pp. 265–299). John Benjamins Publishing Company.

Turney, P. D., & Pantel, P. (2010). From frequency to meaning: Vector space models of semantics. *Journal of Artificial Intelligence Research, 37*, 141–188. https://doi.org/10.1613/jair.2934

Turnitin. http://turnitin.com/
van Dam, M. (2013). A basic character n-gram approach to authorship verification. *Notebook for PAN* at CLEF 2013. http://ceur-ws.org/Vol-1179/CLEF2013wn-PAN-vanDam2013.pdf
van Dijk, T. A. (2015). Context. In K. Tracy, C. Ilie, & T. Sandel (Eds.), *The international encyclopedia of language and social interaction* (1st ed., pp. 1–11). John Wiley & Sons, Inc. https://doi.org/10.1002/9781118611463/wbielsi056
Willis, Sh. et al. (2015). *ENFSI Guideline for Evaluative Reporting in Forensic Science. Strengthening the Evaluation of Forensic Results across Europe (STEOFRAE).* https://enfsi.eu/wp-content/uploads/2016/09/m1_guideline.pdf
Woolls, D. (2002). *CopyCatch Gold v2*. CFL Software.
Woolls, D. (2010). Computational forensic linguistics. Searching for similarity in large specialised corpora. In M. Coulthard, & A. Johnson (Eds.), *The Routledge handbook of forensic linguistics* (pp. 576–590). Routledge.
Woolls, D. (2012). Detecting plagiarism. In P. M. Tiersma, & L. M. Solan (Eds.), *The Oxford handbook of language and law* (pp. 517–529). Oxford University Press.

Primary Sources

Baeza, R. (1980). *Oscar Wilde. El príncipe feliz y otros cuentos*. Bruguera.
Gómez de la Serna Puig, J. (1943). *Oscar Wilde. Obras completas*. Aguilar.
Montes, C. (1988). *Oscar Wilde. Cuentos completos*. Espasa Calpe.
Sarto, J. (2003). *El ruiseñor y la rosa*. Susaeta.
Wilde, O. (1888). *The happy prince and other tales*. Book from Project Gutenberg. [Online].

11

The Linguistic Analysis of Suicide Notes

Monika Zaśko-Zielińska

1 Introduction

In the realm of forensic linguistics, one of the aims of text analysis is to determine the authorship of a written text—author attribution—and to establish the authenticity of a text in case there is a suspicion of someone masking a murder by simulating the victim's suicide or involving third parties to induce suicide. In the case of suicide notes, it might be assumed that these two tasks overlap. To conclude that a suicide note is genuine it is necessary to examine whether there are any linguistic traces in the text that confirm that the author, while writing the text, experienced a suicidal situation and expressed his or her intentions described in the text. Therefore, a genuine suicide note is a text that was written or recorded through another medium by a person before committing suicide (Leenaars, 1988, p. 34). The suspect is also the same person who signed the text or is assumed to be the sender of the letter based on the indicated circumstances.

M. Zaśko-Zielińska (✉)
University of Wrocław, Wrocław, Poland
e-mail: monika.zasko-zielinska@uwr.edu.pl

V. Guillén-Nieto, D. Stein (eds.), *Language as Evidence*,
https://doi.org/10.1007/978-3-030-84330-4_11

The starting point of an analysis in forensic linguistics is a particular genre of text—in this case, a suicide note—and its linguistic features. The linguist's task while performing an expert analysis of the text is to establish 'what a given text says' and 'what it means' (Coulthard, 1988, p. 118; Coulthard et al., 2017). This task can be successfully undertaken only when the linguist examines a particular suicide note in a broader context of the genre that locates the text within social, psychological and cultural reality. The research, however, is always centred on the human being, whose universal biological properties imply that the investigations of suicide notes carried out in different parts of the world yield very similar findings (Chávez-Hernández et al., 2009, pp. 314–320; Girdhar et al., 2004, pp. 179–185).

This chapter overviews the current research on suicide notes, presents the available methodologies, and provides an analysis of genuine and contested suicide notes. The analysis is primarily based on the experience I gained while working on developing the Polish Corpus of Suicide Notes (PCSN) and the examination of the collected data. Through the research, I gathered linguistic determinants of text authenticity which can be used to investigate other suicide notes. The corpus consists of three parts: a subcorpus of 614 genuine suicide notes, 79 simulated suicide notes and 117 suicide notes forged during a linguistic experiment (Zaśko-Zielińska, 2013).

2 The State of the Art, Theories and Controversies in the Area

Previous research on suicide notes, in which corpus linguistics was applied, allows us to establish to what extent an utterance produced by a sender conforms to the typical properties of a suicide note as a genre. A text that strongly deviates from the rules of the genre may be considered forged, or it may result from special circumstances affecting the author at the time the text was written. Apart from the concept of genre, the idiolect—or individual variation within a language—is also relevant in the analysis of suicide notes and can be useful to identify the authorship of a questioned suicide note by comparing it with other known texts of the suspect.

2.1 The Suicide Note as a Genre

The suicide note is a genre that has been described in the framework of discursive suicidology as the culmination of a narrative related to suicide (Oravetz, 2004). It is preceded by various presuicidal verbal interactions, which include conversations with relatives, specialists (e.g. doctors, therapists and helpline employees), personal writings (e.g. letters, diaries, blogs and forum discussions), in which suicide ideations and declarations may appear with increasing frequency (Lester, 2004, 2014). A suicide note is written shortly before the act of suicide, and it is significantly different from other types of presuicidal narratives. The main feature that distinguishes a suicide note from other forms of expression in presuicidal discourse is the location of the text within the history of the individual's lifetime and the individual's assurance that s/he does not want to receive a response from the recipient, as it could affect the premeditated decision.

The section below presents the current state of research on the genre of a suicide note. It addresses the following issues: (1) the consistency and stability of the genre with respect to the discourse community (Swales, 1990, pp. 23–29), (2) the social context of a genuine suicide note and (3) the superstructure and microstructure of the genre (Van Dijk, 1995).

2.2 Suicide Notes—the Boundaries and the Stability of the Genre with Respect to the Discourse Community

It is very difficult to outline the boundaries of a suicide note clearly, as it may occur in different variants related to, for example, inter-genre variation, the valuation of suicide by the author and their genre competence. The text macrostructure may also be influenced by the implementation of other presuicidal genres, such as a personal diary, correspondence that mentions the topic of suicide, conversations with the family and helpline employees, and last will and testament. The earlier communicative activity on the part of a suicidal person may result in the inclusion of biographical fragments in the text, a request to read the letter or provide information about the death to the indicated persons by phone. The crossing of typical genre boundaries may also result from institutional, social and cultural contexts of suicide, which may affect the structure of a particular utterance. Furthermore, the scope of the implemented communication goals may be influenced by the author's individual prior linguistic experience and practice, leading to the inclusion of artistic elements, such as poems or songs, or samples of Internet communication. The stability and the schematic nature of genre structures depend on their availability in the genre reality. The types of texts that language users read frequently or the texts they are often exposed to during their regular life activities tend to have a more established template structure, as in the case in politeness formulas and official business texts. The same tendency can be observed in the case of genres that are studied at school. However, the suicide note is defined as an occluded genre (Swales, 1996). It functions outside the discourse community (Samraj & Gawron, 2015, p. 91), so it is not formed by genre users who jointly contribute to creating its rules that eventually become consolidated thanks to the presence and the activity of experts. Suicide notes usually represent a one-off communication (Abaalkhail, 2020, p. 8), and there are no publicly formulated rules for creating suicide notes.

Due to the reasons stated above, it is often assumed that suicide notes in general share very few macrostructural elements, although they seem to pursue a set of uniform communication goals. Moreover, despite the author's lack of genre competence, suicide notes written by different authors display certain affinities because of the authors' shared experiences and psychological, biological and social conditions. Therefore, one may observe similarities between suicide notes, regardless of the authors' linguistic and cultural differences. The knowledge of these common traits can be used to distinguish between the genuine and forged suicide notes (Shneidman & Farberow, 1957), as forged suicide notes are created outside the real experience of the suicidal process.

2.3 The Sender and the Recipient of a Suicide Note

A detailed description of the participants of the social context—that is the sender and the recipient—allows us to establish their social relationship (Bhatia, 1993, p. 64). Furthermore, a corpus-based analysis of the suicide note can help to identify its generic features.

The suicide note is a written genre that, on the one hand, implies the absence of a face-to-face contact between the sender and the recipient, and, on the other hand, includes the possibility of the sender taking into consideration the recipient's point of view in the text. Hyland (2005, pp. 175–182) describes two main methods of implementing an interaction between the sender and the recipient in written texts: stance and engagement. Stance is the sender's attitude revealed in the text through writer-oriented features, which can be expressed through hedges, for example epistemic expressions such as ['possible', 'perhaps']; modal verbs such as ['might']; boosters such as ['clearly', 'obviously'], attitude markers, that is verbs such as ['agree', 'prefer'] and sentence adverbs such as ['unfortunately']; and self-mentions, for instance ['me', 'mine']. Engagement, which is the sender's attitude towards the recipient, involves the application of reader-oriented features. They are used by the sender to adopt the recipient's point of view and to subsequently coax the recipient, often implicitly, into accepting the sender's point of view. Engagement is expressed by means of reader pronouns ['you', 'your'], directives (including imperatives and modal verbs such as ['must', 'should']), questions, appeals to shared knowledge and personal asides (metalinguistic comments addressed to the reader).

It is important to keep in mind the special communicative context of the interaction between the interlocutors in suicide notes. In general, written texts may be created as a result of an interruption in the personal contact between interlocutors due to, for example, physical distance and their inability to communicate via other devices, for instance by phone. Likewise, other types of written texts, such as academic textbooks, may be addressed to recipients that access them at different times and in different locations. These types of written texts involve a physical barrier, but there are no psychological barriers that may limit, for example, the possibility of a negotiation between the interlocutors. In the case of suicide notes, the reasons for the lack of actual contact between interlocutors are different. For the sender of a suicide note, the recipient's location is irrelevant. The choice of the written form of text only confirms the barriers in communication that have existed earlier, as is shown in the following extracts from the PCSN corpus: 'But you didn't think that I was telling the truth'; 'I didn't know how to talk to anyone about it...'; 'I didn't get a chance to have a conversation...'. Face-to-face contact is not possible either: although the sender wants to contact the recipient, s/he does not want the form of communication to be fully dialogical. Thus, the sender does not plan to take the recipient's opinion into consideration ('I did what I wanted') and does not expect an answer from the recipient, as the text will be read only after the author's death ('When you are reading this, I'll no longer be here'). The intended level of interaction allows for the following activities: the decision to convey the message to a particular person (though sometimes the mere act of conveying the message is deemed sufficient and the recipient may be a random person, unknown to the sender); the willingness to pass information about oneself to other people ('You are all probably asking yourselves why'); fulfilling the sender's own communication needs (e.g. through apologising, explaining or asking); giving advice and directions to others ('Don't cry for me...'). The recipients of the suicide note form a kind of auditorium. The interactivity in suicide notes is made explicit through the sender's direction of the text to a particular recipient and through the sender's performance of the statements by virtue of the recipient's participation in the communicative exchange. The exchange may involve, for example, giving explanations, apologising, taking the recipient's point of view into account in the statement. In the sender-recipient relation, the sender assumes a superior position. It is the sender who decides to initiate contact, blocks feedback, authorises himself or herself to provide the recipient with advice, instructions, guidance, and focuses on his or her own goals ('Maybe this writing will help me').

Suicide notes are unquestionably dominated by stance, as is evident in the ratio of self- mention to reader pronouns. The sender leaves no room for the recipient to negotiate the point of view, as the sender informs the recipient about the decision that has already been made and does not allow him or her to co-decide. Engagement can only focus on convincing the recipient or on giving them directives.

Although only a certain group of suicidal people leaves suicide notes (Callanan & Davis, 2009), it can be observed that the willingness to speak to other people is so strong that at the earlier stages of the presuicidal discourse, before the actual suicidal act, communication activity significantly increases, which is perceptible on social media such as Twitter (Lester, 2014, pp. 135–139).

The texts collected in the PCSN corpus reveal that while the sender of the suicide note is usually a single person (except for group suicides), the recipients of the text may be a group of people (Zaśko-Zielińska, 2013, pp. 145–149). The number of recipients may affect the number of suicide notes left by the sender (Shapero, 2011, pp. 83–89). The author can then direct a single text to a group of people or several texts to different recipients. The suicide notes included in the PCSN corpus display several properties related to the possible number of suicide notes and addressees, and the different ways in which the authors contacted the recipients. For example the sender of a suicide note may write a single suicide note to one recipient, a single suicide note addressing several people, or a suicide note requesting to provide information to other people: the number of these people may even exceed twenty. It may also be the case that the sender of a suicide note writes several separate suicide notes to different recipients, from two to fifteen. Hence, the sender and recipients of a genuine suicide note deviate from an ideal pattern. However, awareness of the communicative situation may provide a useful insight into the structure of a suicide note and the determinants of its microstructure. It may also improve the understanding of the material investigated, which may include several suicide notes, written by a single author and addressed to different readers.

2.4 The Communicative Situation—Genuine and Forged Suicide Notes

The main difference concerning the social context that occurs during the process of writing genuine and forged suicide notes is related to the number of participants involved in the communication. In a forged suicide note there are at least two participants on the sender's side: the forger and the sender, and the presence of the latter is overtly expressed in the text. In a genuine suicide note, there is only one sender unless the note has been written by a group of suicide participants. In the situation of a perfect forgery, the linguistic features of the forger (who acts as the putative sender) would not transpire. However, taking full control over text creation is a very demanding task for the author, especially when s/he does not have enough information about the idiolect of the person on whose behalf the text is written. Hiding the original authorship of a suicide note and attempting to assume the role of another person cause the forger to excessively concentrate on the author's identity in the text, which results in the decreased presence of the intended recipient in the text in comparison to genuine suicide notes, as the forger knows much less about the recipient than the authentic author. For example the PCSN corpus clearly shows that the occurrence ratio of second person pronouns is considerably higher in genuine suicide notes than in forged ones. Moreover, when creating a text, the sender, who is not a suicide person, does not possess an internal, personal perspective on suicide and may only relate to it through the knowledge and the point of view about suicide coming from the media, literature and films.

The author of a suicide note does not experience the receipt of his/her note; nonetheless, at the time of writing, s/he is addressing the message to the recipients and includes references to the intended audience in the message content. This is a very important feature that confirms the authenticity of a text. It relates not only to the way other people are addressed in the text but also to the way the author expresses his/her attitude towards them, by indicating distance or closeness, which often occurs beyond the author's awareness. For this reason, an important task in the analysis of suicide notes is to detect linguistic traces of the social context, which is different in genuine and forged suicide notes.

2.5 The Superstructure of Suicide Notes

The superstructure of suicide notes has been analysed within the genre theory of discourse moves developed by Swales (1990). Whereas a short suicide note may be written with a single intention, longer texts usually have multiple communicative purposes. Corpus analyses of suicide notes have demonstrated that not all rhetorical moves are present in suicide notes (Samraj & Gawron, 2015) and that some of them seem to appear more frequently than others. The most frequent obligatory moves are: (1)

addressing a recipient, that is, a direct statement to a specific recipient; (2) giving instructions to the recipients about what to do after the author's death, that is testamentary instruction; (3) justifying suicide, that is apology, expressing love or positive emotions on the part of the sender; (4) signing off, that is a formula that closes the text, which can be a farewell or a signature (Abaalkhail, 2020; Samraj & Gawron, 2015; Zaśko-Zielińska, 2013).

The linguistic concept of rhetorical moves and steps makes it possible to identify the communicative purposes that are inherent to one communication genre and to treat them in an overtextual way (Swales, 2004). Since moves and steps are rhetorical rather than grammatical tools, they can be often observed above the level of a sentence or a paragraph, and they can be implemented verbally and non-verbally (Schneider & Barron, 2014, p. 168). For this reason, the analysis of the rhetorical moves of suicide notes helps to abstract the repertoire of communication goals that occur, obligatorily or optionally, in suicide notes (Abaalkhail, 2020) and to detect their occurrence in particular statements. As some of the rhetorical moves observed in the suicide note have originated in other written genres, mainly in the genre of the private letter, it is worth drawing attention to the implementation of the text frame, which shows how a specific situation and the lack of discourse community affect the superstructure of the text and its incompleteness. Compared to private letters, suicide notes frequently have an incomplete frame, as the suicide note most often accompanies the suicide person's body, so the context identifies the sender's identity and thereby does not need to be explicitly mentioned. Alternatively, the suicide note is found at home, and it is known to whom it is addressed. The material collected in the PCSN corpus indicates that it is rare for an author to put the suicide note in an envelope—sometimes the function of the envelope is performed by the first page of the note—since suicide notes are not usually sent by post. Hence, instead of the address, the envelope may only contain information about the recipient and how to deliver the suicide note—for example 'to be hand-delivered'; 'please open at 10 pm'; 'open only after you have found me'. The most typical openings found in suicide notes are a salutation addressing the recipient (18%); a dateline (6%) or a heading—for example 'My Farewell' and 'Love' (4%). The closing of a suicide note typically includes the signature (43.9%), which may be illegible or simplified possibly due to lack of time or due to the obviousness of the sender; sometimes a final formula (17.9%); and very rarely a dateline (2.4%) (Zaśko-Zielińska, 2013, pp. 129–134).

2.6 The Microstructure of Suicide Notes

The analysis of the microstructure of a suicide note applies methods typical of forensic linguistics and it examines the text with respect to its morphological, syntactic, semantic and pragmatic properties. Specifically, the analysis focuses on the text properties that are important in determining authorship. These features include the quantitative style analysis, text layout, stylistic register of utterances, features of spoken and written language, the nature of lexicon and collocations, syntactic characteristics, punctuation, spelling correctness and morphology (McMenamin, 2002; Olsson, 2004).

All analyses of suicide notes, both quantitative and qualitative, are based on complete texts or separate paragraphs. The body of the suicide note may take the shape of a unitary text, but sometimes it may also have a fragmentary structure consisting of numerous paragraphs and notes, at times placed not only at the end of the text but also on the sides of the text or between the lines. As regards the graphic layer, the text may have a slightly unusual layout, which is adapted to the type of surface on which it was written, such as the margins of a doctor's prescription or an advertising leaflet. The chaotic structure of a suicide note may be caused by, among other possibilities, the author's mental state (stress, concentration difficulties), lack of time, lack of paper, the author's linguistic competence and his/her habits. The natural chaos that characterises the microstructure of a suicide note facilitates forgery, as it is relatively easy to add another paragraph to a suicide note when the preceding paragraphs differ from each other in size, line spacing or notation accuracy.

2.7 A New Approach to Idiolect—Idiolectal Style and Linguistic Identity

The idiolect, understood as an individual's unique and distinctive use of language in a given period of life, is an important feature to consider in the analysis of forensic texts. Such an analysis does not require an exhaustive description of an idiolect but rather an identification of certain linguistic features that can be considered typical of the author. These individualising features are meant to confirm or exclude the authorship of a suicide note when compared to the known texts of the sender, so the idiolect does not need to have the same detection power as the DNA or fingerprint (Coulthard, 2004; Olsson, 2004, pp. 31–32). Kredens (2002) argues that the factors that influence the form of an idiolect include biological features, such as age, sex and health condition; social features, such as family status, education, profession, personal interests, geographical origin and nationality; and interactive features, such as the social context, the subject matter of the text and the linguistic background of other interlocutors. In this way, Kredens highlights the influence of the sender's sociolinguistic history on the idiolect, the traces of which can be detected, for example, on the basis of the existing corpora or corpora created for the purpose of analysing a language used by a selected group (Kredens & Coulthard, 2012). This approach is indicative of a shift in the research on idiolect, which is now referred to by some scholars as idiolectal style (Turell & Gawalda, 2013, p. 498). This shift necessitates the use of corpus methods in the analyses of authorship attribution in forensic linguistics.

Johnston (2009) observes that an idiolect may also be influenced by the speaker's individual life experiences, affecting their values. The individual style can be observed on different levels of language use. Specifically, a written text may express the author's individual pronunciation features when, due to limited linguistic competence, the author uses a phonetic rather than the conventional notation in the text. However, idiolectal features are most clearly visible at the lexical level, although the usage frequency of some words, such as function words, is uniform across idiolects (Litvinova et al., 2018). Quite frequently, however, authorship can be determined not so much by the frequency of a feature but by a combination of various features present in the text, such as punctuation and syntax (Chaski, 2007).

The style markers used by a particular author may also include individual preferences concerning spelling, text layout, lexical, grammatical and syntactic structures, as well as discourse-related properties, such as the level of formality or informality of the written texts, which testify to the author's preferences and habits (Ainsworth & Juola, 2019, p. 1169). These properties are changeable, as they can be tailored by the author to specific interactions.

2.8 Stylistic and Idiolectal Features of Suicide Notes

The investigation of a genre from an idiolectal perspective must take into account its particular embedding in specific interactions, as these may determine particular variants of the genre implemented by the sender. A suicide note is a type of personal utterance where the author's idiolectal features are the easiest ones to observe due to the unofficial and frequently colloquial nature of the text. Therefore, a suicide note displays traces of the author's communication experiences, which Grant and MacLeod (2018, p. 87) refer to as 'an individual's sociolinguistic history'.

Suicide notes usually have a specific addressee, which allows tracking the sender's writing style in relation to a specific person who could be regarded as a representative of a selected communication group that is relevant for the sender's language contact. Suicide notes addressed to relatives, friends and acquaintances may contain, for example, affectionate names, kinship terms or names of places from the immediate surroundings that are appropriate for a given family, as well as dialectal or sociolectal expressions that the sender has been exposed to earlier in his/her life and uses them as part of everyday language contacts with selected people in informal situations. Due to the fact that these idiolectal features are characteristic of a particular author, they constitute a unique mosaic of linguistic properties. They make it difficult for a forger to imitate such a communicative complexity of the language style, further conditioned by the author's personal experiences. It is easier for a forger to create a text that is consistently based on a few select, conspicuous features. Thus, a comparison of genuine and forged suicide notes included in the PCSN corpus indicates that if a forger decides to incorporate dialectal features in a note, they dominate the entire text, whereas genuine suicide notes written by actual users of a dialect never exhibit the relevant dialectal features throughout the text in a uniform way.

A particular relation that exists between the sender and the recipient influences the actual stylistic choices made by the author of a suicide note. The sender may adjust the text and make it more alike to a spoken or written form, an unofficial or more formal writing style, which can be seen in the text frame, its syntax and vocabulary, as well as in handwriting accuracy. Furthermore, suicide notes are also more likely to exhibit individualised expressiveness than as-a-matter-of-fact tone; for example when they take the form of a report on the author's final stages of his/her life or contain a debt list. Deviations from the unofficial writing style include expressions typical of the sublime style related to the perception of the moment of death (as in the following examples from the PCSN corpus, 'I am leaving', 'I am falling asleep', 'I close my eyes', 'I am laying down my life'), the elements of the official style necessitated by the type of the recipient (such as the police, prosecutor's office or employer) or the inclusion of testamentary instructions in the text (Zaśko-Zielińska, 2013).

Individual authors may display different attitudes towards spelling, depending on the formality level of the contact and the use of prosodic or syntactic punctuation. This may be conditioned by their linguistic competence, but it may also be a result of the transition from one type of punctuation to another depending on the type of text (Kniffka, 2007, p. 182).

Given that suicide notes are conditioned by the situational context and that their style may be strongly influenced by social factors, the notes written by the same author addressed to different recipients may display different characteristics, which should be taken into consideration while performing an analysis.

3 Methodology

The corpus method is among the most important methods applied in the analysis of suicide notes. As Kredens and Coulthard (2012) argue, corpus analysis is crucial for determining the authorship of suicide notes. No suicide note can be correctly analysed without reference to a properly accommodated, single-genre corpus of suicide notes. These corpora are arranged according to a specific genre type, such as genuine, simulated, attempted, completed and fabricated letters (T. Litvinova et al., 2018; Marcińczuk et al., 2011; Pestian et al., 2012; Shapero, 2011; Shneidman & Farberow, 1957). Due to the corpus specialisation, it is also possible to compare different corpora, such as the corpus of genuine and simulated suicide notes (Jones & Bennell, 2007) as well as genuine and forged suicide notes (Zaśko-Zielińska, 2013). Even if such comparisons are not considered in a particular analysis, linguists always draw on their findings implicitly by referring to observations made in seminal studies, such as Shneidman and Farberow (1957).

Since suicide notes are relatively short (the suicide notes included in the PCSN corpus are from 1 to 890 tokens long, but the majority of them are 10–20 tokens long), which makes comparative analysis a necessity. The analysis of data samples requires a comparative examination of texts in terms of the genre or idiolectal features of their authors. Depending on availability, other texts written by the same author, such as private letters, email correspondence, as well as corpus sources, can be suitably used to determine the presence or absence of typical genre determinants in the analysed text and to identify the individual linguistic features of the author.

3.1 Corpus Data Transcription

Suicide notes included in a corpus must be transcribed regardless of how they were written. Handwritten suicide notes must be transcribed to enable their processing (Shapero, 2011, pp. 94–96). The transcription of handwritten suicide notes or suicide notes taken from electronic sources, such as text messages or email correspondence, is performed along with the annotation of text correctness and its adaptation for lemmatisation. During transcription, a linguist addresses problems caused by unreadable fragments and determines the degree of readability of other parts of the text. The PCSN corpus contains scanned versions of suicide notes, which are transcribed in a way that explicitly marks all the characteristic features of the author's writing style such as errors, highlights (underlining, bolding, capitalisation) and the layout, and it also includes revised versions of the suicide notes, which enables quick access to the content (Marcińczuk et al., 2011).

Text transcription is also of considerable importance in the analysis of a single document, as it allows an expert to explore the material in depth, which is not possible while reading isolated parts of the text.

3.2 Layers of Corpus Annotation

The type of data obtained from the corpus analysis depends on the annotation system used for the corpus creation. The annotation system applied in the PCSN corpus is based on the Text Encoding Initiative (TEI) system, designed for the transcription of handwritten texts. This system follows the basic rules of private letter transcription and has been used to prepare many corpora of private letters, such as DALF (*The Digital Archive of Letter in Flanders*) and *The Corpus of Ioannes Dantiscus' Texts & Correspondence*. In the PCSN corpus, the manually entered annotation covers several layers (Marcińczuk et al., 2011). At the level of text structure, the annotation involves marking the parts of letter structure (the opening, the body and the closing); the layout (the location of the header, the date and the signature); the physical division of the text into text blocks and lines, for example paragraphs, page and line breaking; text highlighting; non-verbal elements, such as ornaments and figures; the author's corrections; the editorial correction with several types of error marking, including spelling errors, errors concerning marking nasalisation; small and capital letters, joint and separate spelling, consonant voicing and devoicing, hypercorrection, errors related to marking palatalisation and a replacement of consonants or vowels. Other levels of annotation include the annotation of proper names, which facilitates text searching and anonymisation, as well as pragmatic annotation.

Due to the importance of explicit marking of positive and negative emotions in suicide notes, more recent corpora also contain emotional annotation (Ghosh et al., 2020; Pestian et al., 2012). With the advancement of the technical solutions offered by sentiment analysis and the emotive annotations in WordNets, there have been attempts to analyse suicide notes automatically. This analysis aims to distinguish genuine suicidal notes from forged ones and to recognise suicidal statements in Internet communication preventively.

3.3 Corpus Analyses

The analysis of extensive corpus material requires the application of quantitative methods. These methods allow obtaining information on the average numerical data for the collected material. The data include the average length of a suicide note measured in tokens, characters, the average sentence length, the average word length, Type Token Ratio and the parts of speech (POS) data: the number of nouns, verbs, adjectives, adverbs, pronouns and the syntactic and semantic relations that may occur between them.

The generated numerical data may provide general information about the corpus content, but it may also provide information adapted to the needs of an analysed text. For example it is possible to select authors of specific gender and age, the method of committing suicide and the length of the text. The calculations may apply to the entire text or to individual paragraphs whose authorship may be different.

In the context of the study of idiolectal features it is also important to use corpora that contain other types of texts than suicide notes, as they may show how similar or different the analysed text is with respect to typical stylistic implementations. For this purpose, national, Internet and specialised corpora can be used (Kredens & Coulthard, 2012).

3.4 Software in Corpus Analyses

The PCSN corpus was created as part of a Web-based system, Inforex, with the aim to establish qualitative corpora (Marcińczuk et al., 2011). The quantitative analyses were carried out using tools developed within the CLARIN project. To implement analyses of this type, researchers may also use tools such as Wordsmith Tools, LIWC (Linguistic Inquiry and Word Count—a tool for the analysis of 76 variables) (Pennebaker et al., 2001) or other authorship detection tools that have been tested in standard experiments (van Halteren, 2019). The increasing sophistication of IT tools may lead to automatic analyses of suicide notes (Piasecki et al., 2017).

3.5 Qualitative Methods in the Analysis of Suicide Notes

The quantitative methods are complemented by qualitative methods related to the pragmatic, stylistic and thematic analyses of the text. When an expert analysis is not concerned with a suicide note as a genre but with a specific text that needs to be examined, then the starting point for the analysis is the note, its content and form, which will indicate what features should be checked in regard to the quantitative data obtained from the corpus. It is also necessary to diagnose the communicative situation which affects the style of the text and its structure and establish the communicative goals. By combining the quantitative and qualitative methods, it is possible, for example, to determine which linguistic features of the analysed text may have the status of individual determinants of style that indicate an idiolect. As part of the qualitative approach, the content of suicide notes is also analysed. The quantitative data can also be used at this stage, but it is necessary to correlate various types of information; for example the choice of specific topics is conditioned by the purpose of the text and the author's relationship with the recipient. This is implemented through the selection of particular stylistic elements.

3.6 The Thematic Analysis of Suicide Notes

The macrostructure of a suicide note determines the communicative goals attained in the text and the implementation of the cognitive content of an utterance, such as the subject matter, the emotional marking of the text and the valuation of suicide. Following a psychological study carried out by ten suicidologists, Leenaars (1988) distinguishes several thematic repertoires of suicide notes. Sentences extracted from suicide notes were catalogued as representative of the theories analysed in Leenaars's (1988) study and then divided into eight groups: (1) Unbearable

Psychological Pain, (2) Cognitive Constriction, (3) Indirect Expressions, (4) Inability to Adjust, (5) Ego, (6) Interpersonal Relations, (7) Rejection—Aggression and (8) Identification—Egression (O'Connor et al., 1999). A linguistic analysis of the topics found in suicide notes makes it possible to attain the cognitive level of a text by examining rhetorical goals and frequency analysis of the thematic vocabulary. The analysis produces the ranking of topics typically addressed in suicide notes, divided into subject fields based on corpus data. The subject fields include Feelings (e.g. love, expressed by words such as 'love'); Life—its physical and social aspects (e.g. 'live', 'be born', 'die', 'school' and 'work'); Reasoning—memory and intellectual evaluation, motivation for actions (e.g. 'think', 'remember', 'please', 'unfair', 'plan'); Affective—intellectual and moral evaluation (e.g. 'good', 'bad', 'sad', 'pleasant', 'tragic'); Verbal behaviour (e.g. 'ask', 'say goodbye', 'forgive'); Characters (e.g. 'mother', 'child', 'family'); Time (e.g. 'already', 'now', 'yet', 'today'); Ownership (e.g. 'mine', 'have', 'give', 'property'). Knowing the themes of the suicide notes collected in the PCSN corpus makes it possible to evaluate the vocabulary included in a suicide note and compare the frequency of words used by the author to discuss individual topics. This comparison between the corpus data and the analysed text allows us to establish the occurrence of the most frequent words and to detect *hapax legomena* or words avoided by the author within the relevant fields.

3.7 Suicide as Taboo in Suicide Notes

Because a suicidal person may have a different perception of suicide than other people, it is worth paying attention to the tabooing of suicide in the analysis of suicide notes. The phenomenon of suicide is culturally conditioned and results from the author's personal life history. This history affects their system of values expressed in the suicide note, their awareness of the recipients' attitude towards suicide, and idiolectal features revealed in the suicide note (Johnston, 2009). One of the tasks in the analysis of suicide notes is to reveal the methods of euphemising suicide, which may be typical of a given language and culture, but it may also reflect the author's personal view of suicide (Zaśko-Zielińska, 2012).

4 Case Study

4.1 Genuine and Forged Suicide Notes in the PCSN Corpus

To determine the authenticity of suicide notes, investigators focus primarily on a comparison between genuine and simulated suicide notes. Furthermore, it is helpful to examine both content and structure variables (Jones & Bennell, 2007; Osgood & Walker, 1959). In forensic linguistics, studies may also involve comparisons of genuine and forged suicide notes; the latter are rare, but they are slightly different from the simulated notes.

The PCSN corpus includes a subcorpus of forged suicide notes. Since the purpose of the corpus collection was to prove authorship, the applied method of suicide note collection was different from the methods that are normally adopted during the collection of suicide notes for psychological purposes (Shneidman & Farberow, 1957). The authentic event during which a forged suicide note is written involves creating a suicide note by a different person than the suicide person. The suicide person is not the author of the suicide note because s/he was either murdered and his/her suicide was faked, or s/he was forced to commit suicide. To imitate an authentic context, the respondent does not write a suicide note on his/her behalf during the experiment, but instead on behalf of someone whose personal details have been added to a particular survey. To select the most representative information for the experiment, it was necessary to collect complete data about the people who committed suicide in Poland and left suicide notes in 1999–2008. The data became part of the corpus of genuine suicide notes. As an outcome of the analysis, several factors were selected (age, sex, marital status, education and the manner of committing suicide), which were then randomly grouped and assigned to individual fictitious persons on whose behalf the respondents wrote the suicide notes. Ultimately, a subcorpus of forged suicide notes with 117 texts was created. The corpus is systematically supplemented through the involvement of other research centres. Another 200 texts are currently being annotated.

4.2 The Genuine Suicide Note

The analysis of a genuine suicide note presented in this section was carried out on the basis of data obtained from the PCSN corpus. The examination included the following stages:

1) the layout features and graphic level;
2) the communicative situation;
3) the time and place orientation;
4) communication goals: moves and steps;
5) stylistic features of the text; and
6) the attitude to suicide as a taboo.

The length of the suicide note selected for the analysis represents the average note length within the suicide note subcorpus. The sender is an 18-year-old man who left behind 3 texts before his death: (1) a suicide note to everyone (58 words)[1], (2) a suicide note to his girlfriend (115 words) and (3) a poem (39 words).

Using the three texts left by one sender, it is possible to observe the way in which texts written in the same situation by the same sender and addressed to different people relate to one another. The analysis focuses on two suicide notes: the first text, the suicide note to everyone and the second text, the suicide note to the girlfriend. I do also refer to the third text, the poem, which indicates that suicidal situations may evoke the need for artistic expressions. Similar texts (songs and poems) have been created by well-known suicidal poets, such as Sylvia Plath, as well as ordinary language users.

4.2.1 Features of the Layout, Spelling and Punctuation Correctness

The suicide note to everyone shown in Fig. 11.1 and transcribed in Table 11.1, hereinafter indicated as (1), was written on a piece of paper. Its text forms a single, eight-line paragraph and two separate lines separated by two-line spacing. There is no topographically separate formula

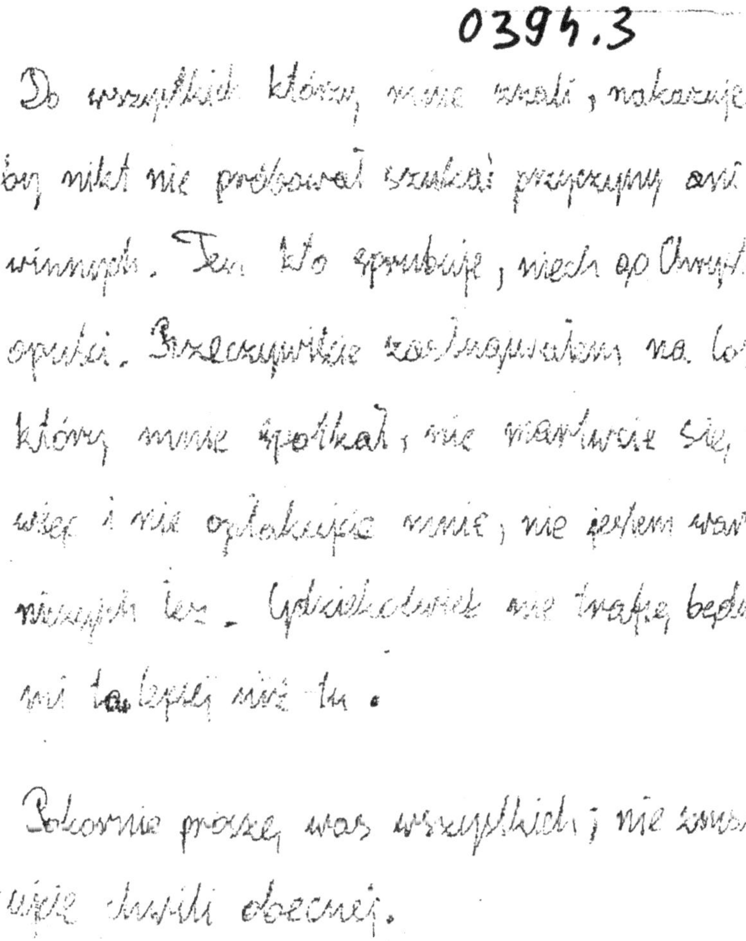

Fig. 11.1 Scan of the handwritten suicide note to everyone (source: PCSN repository)

specifying the addressee. The formula appears in the first line and its boundary is marked with a comma, but utterance continues within the same line.

The suicide note to the girlfriend shown in Fig. 11.2 and transcribed in Table 11.2, hereinafter indicated as (2), has the same layout: the

Table 11.1 Transcript and English translation of the handwritten suicide note to everyone in Fig. 11.1 (slashes indicate end of line in the Polish text)

Transcript of the suicide note to everyone	English translation of the suicide note to everyone
Do wszystkich którzy mnie znali, nakazuje/ by nikt nie próbował szukać przyczyny ani/ winnych. Ten kto sprubuje, niech go Chrystus/ opuści. Rzeczywiście zasługiwałem na los/ który mnie spotkał, nie martwcie się/ więc i nie opłakujcie mnie, nie jestem wart/ niczyich łez. Gdziekolwiek nie trafię będzie/ mi tam lepiej niż tu. Pokornie proszę Was wszystkich; nie zmarn/ -ujcie chwili obecnej.	To everyone who knew me, I order that no one try to find the cause or the guilty ones. Whoever tries, may Christ abandon them. Indeed, I deserved the fate that befell me, do not worry then and do not mourn me, I am not worth anyone's tears. Wherever I go, I'll be better off there than here. I humbly ask all of you; don't waste the present moment.[2]

addressee formula is also the part of the first line, and a subsequent part of the utterance is the part of the same verse. The whole text (2) also takes the form of a block paragraph, separated by line spacing from the farewell expression and the postscript.

There is no text highlighting in either of the suicide notes. The only highlighted element occurs in the poem shown in Fig. 11.3 and transcribed in Table 11.3, hereinafter indicated as (3), as the title was underlined. Each line starts with a capital letter, and the entire thirty-eight-word text is broken down into twelve lines. This property distinguishes the poem from the letters written in block paragraphs, though this type of writing is typical of poems as a genre.

4.2.2 Spelling Correctness

Some authors of suicide notes included in the PCSN corpus verbalise their awareness of the mistakes they have made in their texts and also report that they are not able to control them, as in the following fragment:

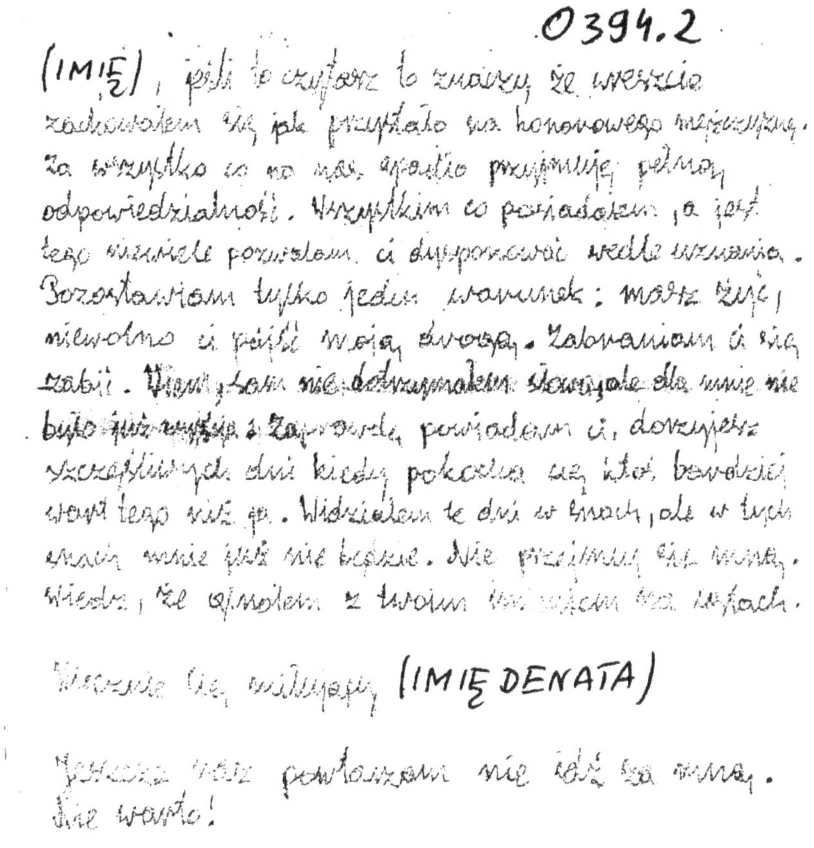
0394.2

(IMIĘ), jeśli to czytasz to znaczy, że wreszcie zachowałem się jak przystało na honorowego mężczyznę. Za wszystko co na nas spadło przyjmuję pełną odpowiedzialność. Wszystkim co posiadałem, a jest tego niewiele pozwalam ci dysponować wedle uznania. Pozostawiam tylko jeden warunek: masz żyć, niewolno ci pójść moją drogą. Zabraniam ci się zabić. Wiem, sam nie dotrzymałem słowa ale dla mnie nie było już wyjścia. Zapewne, powiadam ci, doczekasz szczęśliwych dni kiedy pokocha cię ktoś, kto będzie wart tego niż ja. Widziałem te dni w snach, ale w tych snach mnie już nie będzie. Nie przejmuj się mną. Wiedz, że odszedłem z twoim imieniem na ustach.

Kocham Cię, miłująca (IMIĘ DENATA)

Jeszcze raz powtarzam nie idź za mną. Nie warto!

Fig. 11.2 Scan of the handwritten suicide note to the girlfriend (source: PCSN repository)

> I apologise for the mistakes and the handwriting, but I cannot control myself when writing this suicide note. My hands are trembling with worry; sorry for the spelling and the bad handwriting, but I'm a bit nervous as I am writing this. It certainly looks a little messy because it is happening before the great tragedy.

Such statements indicate that errors in suicide notes are not always a sign of limited linguistic competence. We found several correctness errors in the analysed texts. There is one spelling mistake in the suicide note to

Table 11.2 Transcript and English translation of the handwritten suicide note to the girlfriend in Fig. 11.2 (slashes indicate end of the line in the Polish text)

Transcript of the suicide note to the girlfriend	English translation of the suicide note to the girlfriend
[The girl's name], jeśli to czytasz to znaczy że wreszcie/ zachowałem się jak przystało na honorowego mężczyznę./ Za wszystko co na nas spadło przyjmuję pełną/ odpowiedzialność. Wszystkim co posiadałem, a jest/ tego niewiele pozwalam ci dysponować wedle uznania./ Pozostawiam tylko jeden warunek: masz żyć,/ nie wolno ci pójść moja drogą. Zabraniam ci się/ zabić. Wiem, sam nie dotrzymałem słowa, ale dla mnie nie/ było już wyjścia. Zaprawdę powiadam ci, dorzyjesz/ szczęśliwych dni kiedy pokocha cię ktoś bardziej/ wart tego niż ja. Widziałem te dni w snach, ale w tych/ snach mnie już nie będzie. Nie przejmuj się mną./ Wiedz, że ginołem z twoim imieniem na ustach./ Wiecznie Cię miłujący [signature]/ Jeszcze raz powtarzam nie idź za mną./ Nie warto!	[The girl's name], if you are reading this, it means that I finally acted like an honourable man. I take full responsibility for everything that fell on us. Everything I have, and there is little of it, I let you administrate of it as you wish. I leave only one condition: you must live, you must not follow my path. I forbid you to kill yourself. I know, I didn't keep my word, but for me there was no way out. Truly I tell you, you will live to see the happy days when someone more worthy of you than me will love you. I've seen those days in my dreams, but I won't be in them anymore. Don't worry about me. Please know that I have died with your name on my lips. Loving you forever I urge you again, don't follow me. It's not worth it!

everyone (1): the Polish verb spelt as *sprubuję* instead of *spróbuję* ['to try'], which occurs in spite of the fact that the infinitival form of that verb occurs earlier, and it is then spelt correctly as *próbować* ['to try']. Moreover, one verb was spelt without the nasalisation marking (the letter 'e' in *nakazuje* ['I order'] should be spelt as 'ę'), which follows the common practice and the rules of contemporary Polish pronunciation. There is

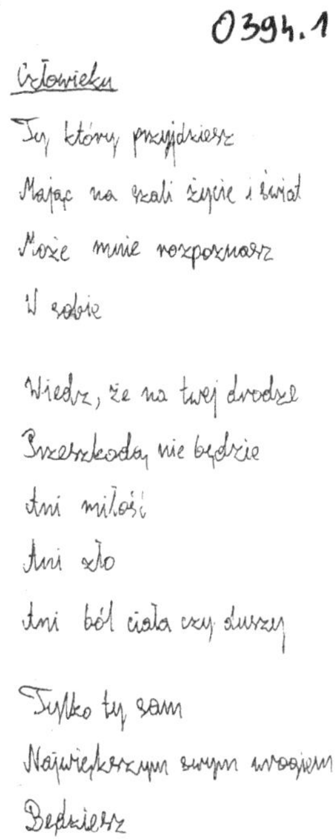

0394.1

Człowieku

Ty który przyjdziesz

Mając na szali życie i świat

Może mnie rozpoznasz

W sobie

Wiedz, że na twej drodze

Przeszkodą nie będzie

Ani miłość

Ani zło

Ani ból ciała czy duszy

Tylko ty sam

Największym swym wrogiem

Będziesz

Fig. 11.3 Scan of the handwritten poem (source: PCSN repository)

Table 11.3 Transcript and English translation of the handwritten poem in Fig. 11.3 (slashes indicate end of line in the Polish text)

Transcript of the poem	English translation of the poem
Człowieku/ Ty który przyjdziesz/ Mając na szali życie i świat/ Może mnie rozpoznasz/ W sobie/ Wiedz, że na twej drodze/ Przeszkodą nie będzie/ Ani miłość/ Ani zło/ Ani ból ciała czy duszy/ Tylko ty sam/ Największym swym wrogiem/ Będziesz/	Man You who will come With life and the world at stake Maybe you'll recognise me In yourself Know that in your way Love will not be the obstacle Nor evil Nor the pain of your body or soul Only you alone You will be Your own greatest enemy

also one case of hyperism: the incorrect spelling of *tam* ['there'] as *tą* ['this'], which contains the nasal vowel *ą* that must have been the result of auto-correction, as the letters have been bolded. The second person plural pronoun *wy* ['you'] is spelt with the initial letter in the lower case. This feature is somewhat unusual and disregards the Polish linguistic etiquette, according to which pronouns referring to specific recipients should be spelt with a capital letter. Interestingly, very similar types of errors are present in the suicide note to the sender's girlfriend (2). For example *dożyjesz* ['you will live'] is wrongly spelt as *dorzyjesz*. Furthermore, there are two spelling errors caused by actual pronunciation practice. Specifically, there is one spelling error related to nasalisation marking in the verb *ginąłem* ['I died'], which is spelt as *ginołem*. Another error concerns the negation marker *nie*, which is spelt as a single word together with the verb as *niewolno*, instead of the correct spelling *nie wolno* ['you are not allowed']. Finally, there is one error related to the wrong use of lower case with the personal pronouns referring to the reader: *ci* ['you'] $_{\text{DAT}}$; *twoim* ['your']$_{\text{GEN}}$. We find very similar types of errors in the suicide note addressed to the girlfriend (2).

4.2.3 Punctuation Correctness

The author used three types of punctuation marks in the suicide note to everyone (1): periods (which are used five times in the text to mark sentence boundaries), commas (four times) and a semicolon. The semicolon is a punctuation mark that is used least often by the Polish language users. It is most frequently found in the texts written by well-educated people who are either aware of the punctuation rules and apply them correctly or who are familiar with formal texts as their readers. In the case of this study, the latter motivation is more likely to hold, as the semicolon does appear, but it is used incorrectly. The commas used by the author in text (1) appear for prosodic reasons as the markers of pauses, rather than for syntactic reasons. If the commas had been used to mark the syntactic structure of the clause, they would have been used before the two instances of the relative pronoun *który* ['who'] and before the words *by* ['would'], *kto* ['who'] and *będzie* (the future auxiliary 'be'). In general, it can be concluded that both the spelling and punctuation in the suicide note to everyone (1) are correct, though inconsistent, which may be due to the writer's emotional state or his insufficient knowledge of the spelling and punctuation rules.

The ratio of the occurrences of punctuation marks in the suicide note to the girlfriend (2) is similar, with the comma and the period used most frequently, and the colon and the exclamation mark each used only once. In the suicide note to the girlfriend (2), as in the suicide note to everyone (1), the commas are used to mark pauses, as they do not consistently mark the syntactic structure of the clauses. There are no punctuation marks in the poem, as is common in the genre of poetry in general, therefore, their absence does not reflect on the author's punctuation competence.

4.2.4 The Communicative Situation

The author of the suicide note to everyone (1) reveals his presence in the text by using pronouns—three times the accusative form *mnie* ['me'] and once the dative form *mi* ['me'], and verbs in the first-person singular: *nakazuję* ['I order'], *zasługiwałem* ['I deserved'], *jestem* ['I am'], *trafię* ['I go'] and *proszę* ['I ask']; Polish is a null-subject language and thereby, the subject is not obligatory in the clause. The first-person pronoun *ja* ['I'] has a similarly high frequency (five instances) in the suicide note to the girlfriend (2). The high frequency of first-person pronouns is characteristic of suicidal notes in general, as their authors frequently focus on themselves. Namely, even though first-person pronouns are infrequent in the written texts included in the Polish National Corpus (NKJP), they are attested in as many as 64.88% of documents included in the PCSN corpus.[3] In both suicide notes (1, 2), the sender displays a negative vision of reality. The negative particle *nie* ['no'] is the second most frequent word occurring in the PCSN corpus. Negation is also a recurring category in the analysis of the suicide notes performed within LIWC. In the suicide note to everyone (1), the negative particle *nie* is found six times. Correspondingly, in the suicide note to the girlfriend (2), the negative particle *nie* ['no'] is used seven times.

The recipient of the analysed suicide note to everyone (1), on the other hand, is multi-personal and remains unspecified, as s/he is hidden behind the quantifier *wszyscy* [‘everyone’; ‘to everyone’; ‘I ask all of you’] and verbs marked for the second person plural: *nie martwcie się* [’do not worry’], *nie opłakujcie* [‘do not mourn’] and *nie zmarnujcie* [’do not waste’]. The poem’s (3) addressee is even more abstract, as the text begins with the addressing formula *Człowieku* [’Man’] in the vocative case. This addressing formula is also the title of the poem.

As in every suicide note, the sender assumes a superior attitude towards the recipient, as due to the suicide, the sender prevents any potential reaction to the utterance on the part of the recipient. Additionally, in the suicide note to everyone (1), the sender’s superiority is strengthened through the verb phrase *nakazuję* [‘I order’], which may be used by a person in a position of power or having the authority to influence someone’s decisions. Moreover, the verb *nakazuję* [‘to order’] is accompanied by prohibitions expressed through negated verbs: *nie martwcie się* [‘do not worry’], *nie opłakujcie* [‘do not mourn’] and *nie zmarnujcie* [‘do not waste’]. The sender’s superiority is also clearly rendered through the threat addressed to the reader who may fail to comply with his order: *Ten kto spróbuje, niech go Chrystus opuści* [‘Whoever tries, may Christ abandon them’].

The sender’s superiority above the recipient is not mitigated even by the request, ‘I humbly ask you’ in the last sentence. Rather, this sentence is meant to be understood as a stylisation through which the sender wants to convey a valuable truth to the recipient. The sender’s dominant position is also present in the note to the girlfriend (2), where it is expressed through the following phrases, *pozwalam Ci dysponować* [‘I let you administrate of it’], *zabraniam Ci się zabić* [‘I forbid you to kill yourself’] and *masz żyć* [‘you must live’], *nie wolno Ci pójść moją drogą* [‘you must not follow my path’]. The expression *Zaprawdę powiadam Ci* [‘Truly I tell you’] is also typical of this text; by appealing to the biblical style, the sender emphasises the large distance between the sender and the recipient as well as the sender’s superior position towards the speaker.

4.2.5 The Time and Place Orientation

The suicide note to everyone (1) displays a double perspective of time, which is a very typical property of genuine suicide notes: the perspective of time is different on the part of the recipient, who reads the suicide note after the sender's death: *do wszystkich którzy mnie znali* ['[t]o everyone who knew me']; *zasługiwałem na los* ['I deserved the fate'], and on the part of the sender, who is writing the suicide note: *nie jestem wart* ['I am not worth']; *gdziekolwiek nie trafię* ['wherever I go']. This situation is explicitly rendered through the adverbs *tutaj* ['here'] and *tam* ['there'], which refer to the time before and after the sender's death, rather than to a specific location. The only future reference that is made in the suicide note refers to the act of giving the recipients' instruction about what they are supposed not to do after the sender's death (*nie opłakujcie* ['do not mourn']; *nie martwcie się* ['do not worry']). However, this is the future time from the sender's perspective, and it is supposed to be the present time for the audience.

The suicide note to the girlfriend (2) contains analogous temporal inconsistencies. It begins with the sentence, *jeśli to czytasz to znaczy że wreszcie zachowałem się jak przystało na honorowego mężczyznę* ['If you are reading this, it means that I finally acted like an honorable man']. This sentence refers to the situation after the sender's death and corresponds to the expressions found in other suicide notes in the PCSN corpus, with statements of the type, *jeśli to czytasz, mnie już nie ma* ['if you are reading this, I'm no longer here'].

Because the suicide note to the girlfriend (2) does not contain any testamentary instructions concerning the body, particular objects or the people involved, there are no deictic references to space in the text.

4.2.6 Communication Goals: Rhetorical Moves and Steps

Both suicide notes (1 and 2) display five rhetorical moves of the same type. They constitute the implementation of the sender's goals. The difference between the two suicide notes concerns only some of the rhetorical steps. Below I present a list of rhetorical moves and steps attested in both suicide notes (1 and 2):

Move 1: Addressing the recipient: *Do wszystkich, którzy mnie znali* ['To everyone who knew me'] (1),[4] [the girlfriend's name] (2).

Move 2: Instructions for survivors. Step 1: Expressing directions: *Nakazuję, aby nikt nie szukał przyczyny ani winnych* (1), ['I order that no one try to find the cause or the guilty ones'], *Nie opłakujcie mnie* ['do not mourn me'] (1), *Nie martwcie się* ['do not worry'] (1), *Zabraniam Ci się zabić* ['I forbid you to kill yourself'] (2), *Pozostawiam tylko jeden warunek: Masz żyć, nie wolno ci iść moją drogą* ['I leave only one condition: you must live, you must not follow my path'] (2), *Nie przejmuj się mną* ['Don't worry about me'] (2). Step 2: Expressing wishes: *Pokornie proszę Was wszystkich; nie zmarnujcie chwili obecnej* ['I humbly ask all of you; don't waste the present moment'] (1), *Dożyjesz szczęśliwych dni kiedy pokocha Cię ktoś…* ['you will live to see the happy days when someone will love you…'] (2). Step 3: Testamentary instruction: *Wszystkim co posiadam, a jest tego niewiele pozwalam Ci dysponować wedle uznania* ['Everything I have, and there is little of it, I let you administrate of it as you wish'] (2). Step 4: Threat: (1): ['Whoever tries, may Christ abandon them'].

Move 3: Apologising. Step 1: Selfblaming: *Rzeczywiście zasługiwałem na los który mnie spotkał* ['Indeed, I deserved the fate that befell me'] (1). Step 2: Self-dispraise: *Nie jestem wart niczyich łez* ['I am not worth anyone's tears'] (1), *Ktoś bardziej wart tego niż ja* ['someone more worthy of you than me'] (2), *Nie warto* ['It's not worth it!'] (2). Step 3: Taking responsibility: *Za wszystko co na mnie spadło przyjmuję pełną odpowiedzialność* ['I take full responsibility for everything that fell on us'] (2), *Wiem, sam nie dotrzymałem słowa* ['I know, I didn't keep my word'] (2). Step 4: Justification: *Zachowałem się jak przystało na honorowego mężczyznę* ['I finally acted like an honorable man'] (2), *Ale, dla mnie nie było wyjścia* ['but for me there was no way out'] (2). Step 5: Describing one's state in death and afterwards: *Gdziekolwiek nie trafię, będzie mi tam lepiej niż tu* ['Wherever I go, I'll be better off there than here'] (1), *Wiedz, że ginąłem z Twoim imieniem na ustach* ['Please know that I have died with your name on my lips'] (2), *Widziałem te dni w snach, ale w tych snach mnie już nie będzie* ['I've seen those days in my dreams, but I won't in them any more'] (2).

Move 4: Farewell, expressing love: *Wiecznie cię miłujący* ['Loving you forever'].

Both suicide notes were written by the same author, but they were meant for different recipients. For this reason, they display somewhat different rhetorical steps. In the suicide note (1), there are no testamentary instructions, whereas the suicide note (2) contains the step 'expressing love'. Correspondingly, the threat *niech go Chrystus opuści* ['may Christ abandon them'] in suicide note (1) is intended to guarantee the fulfilment of the order not to focus on finding the causes or the culprits of the sender's death. These types of acts of threatening, cursing and frightening the reader are not frequent in the suicide notes included in PCSN corpus, but they do occur repeatedly. They complement the expression of negative feelings towards the recipient, as in the statements: ['may you be cursed forever'], ['I will keep visiting you after my death'], ['this sight will haunt you for the rest of your life'], ['I hope you will have me on your conscience'] and ['I wish you the worst'].

As far as the pragmatic content is concerned, both suicide notes implement rhetorical moves that have been distinguished for the genre of suicide notes based on the corpus analyses. In line with the theory of discursive moves and steps, the genre does not need to use the entire repertoire of pragmatic elements or an obligatory set of elements. In the analysed texts written by the same sender, we can observe a repetition of the applied rhetorical moves and a repeated occurrence of the same move, characteristic of genuine texts, which confirms the way suicide notes are written. They are unedited texts, written as statements that accompany the situation that has triggered their creation.

4.2.7 Text Stylistic Features

The analysed suicide notes are stylistically different from many other genuine suicide notes, but it is not an isolated example. The corpus contains a wide variety of texts. Apart from many colloquial texts that resemble spoken language, the PCSN also includes suicide notes that sound formal, resemble official documents or sound very solemn, typical of some artistic forms of expression. Some authors introduce elements of the official register into their texts, which may reflect the nature of the actual relation between the interlocutors or indicate that the sender wishes to increase the emotional distance from the recipient (e.g. ['I am referring to you as "madam" because you are not my wife anymore, and even when you were my wife, I never felt this way']). The formal style is also marked through the official forms of signatures, which may contain the first name and the surname; only the first name, the middle name or the surname; the surname preceding the first name, and kinship terms such as 'son', which are all included in private letters addressed to relatives. The fact that some authors adjust their signatures in each suicide note directed to a different recipient confirms that these are deliberate actions on the part of the sender.

On the other hand, the solemn style of texts may also be caused by the feeling of seriousness and the importance of the moment of dying, which affects the choice of artistic forms of expression (such as poems and songs), results in the introduction of fragments of prayers, religious references and vocabulary or expressions that are typical of literary or artistic texts (e.g. ['I give my life']; ['I close my eyes']). The suicide notes (1, 2) and the poem left by the eighteen-year-old author implement the latter style of communication.

For this reason, the style of the written texts predominates in all the suicide notes left by the sender, as evidenced by the sentence length (11.6 words per sentence (1); 9.58 (2)),[5] frequent subordinate clauses, formal vocabulary typical of literary works, such as *opłakiwać* ['to mourn'] (1), *nie jestem wart niczyich łez* ['I am not worth anybody's tears'] (2), and *gdziekolwiek nie trafię* ['no matter where I go'] (1). The religious style of the text is reflected in the particular communicative situation, in the direct references to Christ, but also in the post-nominal position of the adjectival modifier: (*chwila obecna* ['the present moment']) or in the final position of the future auxiliary: (*wrogiem będziesz* ['you will be an enemy']). The solemn style of the suicide note to everyone (1) also correlates with the usage of the hyperism represented by the incorrect spelling of *tam* as *tą* ['there'].

The orality of the text is manifested through its less extensive editing. Although the author modified the speech plan, he did not correct or adjust some parts of the text. Thus, a possible corrected version of the suicide note to everyone could be as follows: *Do wszystkich którzy mnie znali, nakazuję wam byście nie szukali przyczyny* ['To everyone who knew me, I order you not to try to find the cause']. Alternatively, the quantifier in composite form *do wszystkich* ['to everyone'] could be used in the dative form *wszystkim*. The actual text, however, begins with the quantifier ['everyone'], which functions both as a salutation and as a complement to the verb. Subsequently, the author applies ellipsis, which relates to the previous clause, *by nikt nie próbował szukać przyczyny ani winnych. Ten kto spróbuje to robić/szukać przyczyny, niech go Chrystus opuści* ['that no one try to find the cause or the guilty ones. Whoever tries to do that, may Christ forsake them']. Another strong marker of orality is the use of demonstrative pronouns and adverbs such as *tu* ['here'] and *tam* ['there'], whose reference would be ambiguous outside the context, as well as incomplete logical and syntactic orderings, such as the sequence of three incomplete clauses, which in a correctly written text would have been separated by periods, ['Indeed, I deserved the fate / that befell me, do not worry / then and do not mourn me, I am not worth / anyone's tears']. It seems that the observed incomplete syntactic ordering, characteristic of spoken language, has no justification in the actual communicative situation or in the subject of the text. Rather, it is the result of the author's temporary partial loss of control over the created text, which may have been caused by his emotional state or linguistic competence. The overlap of orality and literacy in a single text is a property of many genres, but its implementation may be characteristic of the author's idiolect, or it may be conditioned by the context in which the text is created. The stylistic inconsistency of suicide notes may correlate with spelling mistakes that in general occur there more often than in standard texts (Osgood & Walker, 1959; Shapero, 2011) and with reduced quality of handwriting.

The suicide note to the girlfriend (2) is written in a similar, solemn fashion. It includes formal words and expressions, such as *dysponować czymś* ['to administrate sth'], *miłujący* ['loving'], *pójść moją drogą* ['follow my path'], *ginąć z czyimś imieniem na ustach* ['die with someone's name on the lips'] and *być wartym czegoś* ['be worthy of something']. However, due to a more personal communicative situation, there are more colloquial and spoken language features. For example the sentences are slightly shorter (8.92 words per sentence) and a fragment of dialogue occurs that could be interpreted as a response to the girlfriend's reaction ['I know, I didn't keep my word']. There are four instances of demonstrative pronouns (in the fragments that correspond to the translations 'those days', 'these dreams', 'it is worth it' and 'there is little'), whose increased frequency is an indicator of spoken texts (Biber, 1988). The meta-textual commentary ['I urge you again'] seems characteristic of spoken language as well.

4.2.8 Suicide Is a Taboo

As many authors of suicide notes, the author of the suicide note to everyone (1) does not use the word ['suicide']. While referring to his situation, he remains silent about the suicide. He says ['that no one try to find the cause or the guilty ones'] but avoids expressing the required complements of the words ['cause'] and ['guilty']. These words could be complemented by the word 'suicide' or its euphemisms, such as 'death', 'step' or 'this'. A euphemistic reference to suicide occurs only once in the text, in the statement ['the fate that befell me'], though it is more likely to be the description of the process than of the death itself. In the suicide note to the girlfriend, the author uses the euphemistic expressions ['I finally acted like an honourable man'] and ['follow my path'], and he also uses the verb 'to kill', though, in the original Polish text, it appears in the negated form and about the addressee ['I forbid you to kill yourself']). However, when he talks about himself, he avoids the word 'suicide' again, as in ['I didn't keep my word'].

4.2.9 The Author's Idiolectal Features

To an outside reader, the analysed texts may seem unlikely to have been written by a young person. They are characterised by official style and contain elements that are typical of religious and artistic registers. This aspect is also confirmed by the transfer of the communicative situation from a concrete relation (between a man and a woman) in the suicide note to the girlfriend (2) to a more abstract level in the suicide note to everyone (1), which is confirmed by the addressing formula of the text ['To everyone who knew me'] and the underlined title of the poem ['Man'], with the noun in the vocative case. The author's ability to create a message in such a style confirms his linguistic competence; furthermore, it points to his reading experience, which may also be characteristic of a recipient of typical school readings.

If the sender were older, the religious dimension of the text would have most likely involved the inclusion of fragments of prayers into the suicide note, references to the category of sin in the apology, and requests concerning the religious dimension of the funeral. The knowledge of spelling and punctuation rules would have also correlated with the style and the content of the suicide note. Such a correlation is not observed in the analysed texts, despite the obvious signs of the author's knowledge of the language norms, which happens not to be complete. On the level of style, we observe incongruence in the juxtaposition of very formal rhetorical expressions and moves that dominate in the text with colloquial expressions and direct pragmatic instructions, such as a humble request and the threats in the suicide note to everyone (1), as well as the literary image of an honourable man, who, like a loving knight, dies with the girl's name on his lips, and at the same time expresses an order using a colloquial form of the imperative ['you must live'].

The analysis of the three texts written by the author shows that they display many common features, though they differ in the form and the addressees' choice. The solemn style of the poem is motivated by the genre and the content, but the suicide note to everyone (1) could have taken the form of an unofficial message directed to friends and family, while the suicide note to the girlfriend could have been even more direct than it is.

Both suicide notes are characterised by an almost identical set of moves and steps taken by the author, which are typical of the genre. The two texts are also very similar with respect to the communicative situation, style, language correctness and the tabooisation of suicide. The sentences are of similar length in both texts: 11.6 words in (1) and 9.58 words in

(2), and they contain a similar number of words: 5.94 in (1) and 4.97 in (2). All these properties confirm that the analysed texts were written by the same person and were created in an authentic situation.

4.3 A Contested Suicide Note—a Few Questions to the Reader

Below I include a contested suicide note that comes from a subcorpus of the PCSN. First, I present some information about the correctness of spelling and punctuation in the contested text. Then I ask several questions regarding the communicative situation, time orientation and the content of the suicide note, which will be helpful in assessing the authenticity of the text (Table 11.4).

4.3.1 Spelling Correctness and the Sender's Linguistic Competence

The spelling correctness of the suicide note provides information on the sender's linguistic competence or his/her perception of the linguistic competence represented by the textual subject, which s/he tries to reflect in the text during the process of forgery.

The following errors occurred in this suicide note:

1) a single use of the colloquial phrase *zrobić dziecko* ['to knock up a girl'];
2) two spelling errors—*życie* ['life'] spelt as *rzycie* and *ożenić się* ['to get married'] spelt as *orzenić się*—which affect high-frequency words that

Table 11.4 Transcript and English translation of the Polish suicide note

Original suicide note	English translation of the suicide note
Rzycie jest dla mnie bez sęsu. Brak pracy, orzeniłem	*Life has no meaning for me. No job, I got married*
się, bo zrobiłem dziecko. Kiedyś się upijałem, ale	*because I knocked up a girl. I used to tipple, but*
teraz to nie ma jusz sęsu. Nie widze miejsca dla siebie.	*now it doesn't make sense any more. I don't see any place for myself.*

belong to the basic vocabulary. These are so-called typical errors that appear in the texts written by school children or adults with significantly reduced linguistic competence;

3) an error that concerns the devoicing of the final consonant (*już* ['already'] spelt as *jusz*), which mirrors the pronunciation of the word, and the devoicing of the word-final consonant due to its assimilation with the initial voiceless consonant of the following word;
4) a hyperism *sens* ['sense'] spelt as *sęs* and repeated twice in the suicide note;
5) a mistake related to the marking nasalisation of the final vowel in the word *widzę* ['I see'], spelt as *widze*, which should rather be regarded as a graphic mistake made by the author, as this is a mistake that reflects a common way of pronouncing word-final nasal vowels by contemporary Polish speakers who, regardless of their education, often use such an erroneous notation, as has been independently confirmed by the data from the corpus of simulated suicide notes collected among university graduates (PCSN).

The actual differences in the spelling correctness between genuine and forged suicide notes concern not only the frequency of various types of errors, but mainly their co-occurrence. In genuine suicide notes, typical spelling errors are accompanied by the incorrect spelling of two words as a single word (as in *nie wiem* ['I don't know'] spelt as *niewiem*; correlation coefficient in PCSN—0.74), the incorrect notation of consonant palatalisation (in PCSN—0.63), errors in the spelling of *j* as *ji* (PCSN—0.62), inflectional errors (PCSN—0.61) and other spelling deviations. In the corpus of forged suicide notes, different types of errors usually occur in isolation, as they are not typically a result of the insufficient mastery of writing skills (apart from the errors in the notation of nasalisation), but instead were deliberately introduced into the texts. The same holds true for the analysed text, in which there is a rare correlation of spelling errors with hyperisms (PCSN—0.29) and an equally rare correlation of hyperisms with the final consonant devoicing in the spelling (PCSN—0.36).

An additional area that could be used as a test for the author's linguistic competence level is the application of punctuation rules. Despite introducing serious spelling errors into the text, the author adheres to the rules of syntactic punctuation: the commas appear before conjunctions (such as *bo* ['because'] and *ale* ['but']) and at the sentence boundaries; the only mistake concerns the usage of a comma instead of a period to separate the short utterance *Brak pracy* ['No job'] from the subsequent part of the text. There is no prosodic punctuation in the suicide note, which commonly appears in genuine suicide notes due to the influence of spoken language, and which is frequent among authors who have not fully mastered the written language rules and mark breaks in speech with punctuation marks. There are also no signs of emotional punctuation or inflectional errors. On the other hand, we observe preverbal and postverbal placement of the reflexive clitic *się* (as in *orzeniłem się* ['I got married'] and *kiedyś się upijałem* ['I used to tipple']), which may be an indication of advanced linguistic competence.

4.3.2 Communicative Situation

First, let us examine the communicative situation in the suicide note. Many genuine suicide notes in the PCSN corpus do not have an opening or a closing with a signature. Moreover, only 18.07% of genuine suicide notes contain an addressing formula, and only 5.24% contain a signature. The majority of the genuine notes feature a reference to the recipient located in the main body of the suicide note (59.93%).

Therefore, if we were to assess whether the text is genuine, we should examine the issues regarding the communicative situation in the text (see 4.3 herein for details). Moreover, we should also take the theoretical considerations into account (see 2.4: Communicative situation—genuine and forged suicide notes). Therefore, we should consider the following questions:

1) What information about the communicative situation can be found in the contested text?
2) Is it possible to obtain any information about the recipient of the text or about the interpersonal relations between the sender and the intended recipient from this suicide note?
3) Could the content of this suicide note be addressed to a loved one, for example a family member?

4.3.3 Time Orientation

Secondly, we should examine the relationship between the time orientation and the analysed text. Although suicide notes are frequently short, they often contain references to the sender's past, present and future. Sometimes, suicide notes take the time perspective of the recipient who reads the suicide note after the sender's death.

To properly analyse the time orientation in the contested suicide note (the text in 4.3), we should consider the questions below. The analysis should be conducted based on the theoretical considerations provided in 4.2.5:

1) Which statements from this suicide note refer to the past, to the present and to the future?
2) Imagine there is a timeline between the sender's past and the present time. In which position of the timeline the word *now* would be placed?
3) Does the sender of the text consider the prospect of the recipient reading the suicide note? Does s/he have any expectations of the recipient?

4.3.4 An Analysis of Rhetorical Moves

Thirdly, the rhetorical structure of the text also deserves attention. A suicide note does not need to include all the rhetorical moves determined for the genre, but it always includes at least one of the designated repertoire of moves and steps. Some of the rhetorical moves are considerably more frequent, including apologising, instructions for survivors and farewell.

Therefore, we should consider the following notions regarding the text's rhetorics regarding the contested text (from 4.3). To properly answer the questions below, the information from 4.2.6 will be of use.

1) What communicative goal did the sender want to achieve with his/her text?
2) What rhetorical moves can be observed in this suicide note?
3) Can the statements included in this suicide note be taken as an explanation of the cause of the suicide?

4.3.5 Content Analysis

Finally, we should examine the text's content. An analysis of the corpus of suicide notes made it possible to establish a ranking of the most common words attested in the suicide notes. These are words related to feelings, especially positive ones (to love, love, hope, happiness), personal belongings, first-person pronouns, verbal behaviour (to ask, to apologise), whereas there are few words that refer to cognitive processes (to think, to see).

To conclude this analysis, we should answer the questions regarding the style and the content of the contested text (from 4.3) based on the theoretical data from 3.6 and 4.2.7. The questions are:

1) Is the vocabulary in the analysed text concrete or abstract?
2) What is the emotional marking of the words in the text?
3) Is the analysed text characterised by the properties of formal language register (e.g. known from press) or rather informal (e.g. similar to the one from private correspondence)?

5 Conclusions

To satisfy scientific evidence requirements, the analysis of suicide notes must relate to the current state of research. Therefore, any person preparing an expert analysis needs to be active in forensic linguistics and follow its theoretical development to be able to apply the current methodologies.

As in all genres, the suicide note is immersed in the socio-cultural context, so any changes in the extra-linguistic reality may have an impact on the text form. It is crucial to have access to corpora which are regularly updated with new resources to grasp these changes. The most urgent need is to consider the influence of computer-mediated communication on the creation of suicide notes, which are written as parts of text messages or emails and transmitted through different types of communicators. By investigating the current writing practice, which involves an increased usage of electronic writing, one may observe new types of errors, which are different from those in handwriting. Moreover, the relatively infrequent use of handwriting by modern language users may result in a situation in which even adults may experience problems with handwriting a text, which in consequence may need substantial editing and correction. Thus, the additional corrections may prove not to result from the author's level of education or the emotional state but rather from the insufficient handwriting skills caused by the current prevalence of electronic writing.

Notes

1. All the calculations were made for the texts in the original Polish language version.
2. The texts are literal translations of the Polish texts.
3. Polish is a null-subject language, with rich subject agreement marking on the verb, so the subject pronoun is normally dropped in the clause.
4. Quotations marked with (1) were taken from the suicide note to everyone, whereas quotations marked with (2) were taken from the suicide note to the girlfriend.
5. All the calculations were made for the texts in the original Polish language version.

References

Abaalkhail, A. (2020). An investigation of suicide notes: An ESP genre analysis. *International Journal of Applied Linguistics and English Literature, 9*(3), 1–10. https://doi.org/10.7575/aiac.ijalel.v.9n.3p.1

Ainsworth, J. & Juola, P. (2019). Who wrote this? Modern forensic authorship analysis as a model for valid forensic science. *Washington University Law Review, 96*(5), 1159–1187. Retrieved from https://openscholarship.wustl.edu/law_lawreview/vol96/iss5/10

Bhatia, V. K. (1993). *Analysing genre: Language use in professional settings*. Longman.

Biber, D. (1988). *Variation across speech and writing*. Cambridge University Press.

Callanan, V. J., & Davis, M. S. (2009). A comparison of suicide note writers with suicide who did not leave notes. *Suicide and Life-Threatening Behavior, 39*(5), 558–568.

Chaski, C. (2007). Empirical evaluations of language-based author identification techniques. *Forensic Linguistics, 8*(1), 1–66. https://doi.org/10.1558/sll.2001.8.1.1

Chávez-Hernández, A. M., Leenaars, A., Chávez-de Sánchez, M. L., & Leenaars, L. (2009). Suicide notes from Mexico and the United States: A thematic analysis. *Salud pública de México, 51*(4), 314–320. https://doi.org/10.1590/s0036-36342009000400008

Coulthard, M. (1988). Making text speak: The work of forensic linguist. *Studia Anglica Posnaniensia, 33*, 117–130. Retrieved from http://ifa.amu.edu.pl/sap/Studia_Anglica_Posnaniensia_contents_33

Coulthard, M. (2004). Author identification, idiolect, and linguistic uniqueness. *Applied Linguistics, 25*(4), 431–447. https://doi.org/10.1093/applin/25.4.431

Coulthard, M., Johnson, A., & Wright, D. (2017). *An introduction to forensic linguistics: Language in evidence* (2nd ed.). Routledge.

Ghosh, S., Ekbal, A., & Bhattacharyya, P. (2020). CEASE, a corpus of emotion annotated suicide notes in English. In N. Calzolari, F. Béchet, P. Blache, K. Choukri, C. Cieri, T. Declerck, et al. (Eds.), *Proceedings of the 12th Conference on Language Resources and Evaluation (LREC 2020)* (pp. 1618–1626). The European Language Resources Association. Retrieved from http://www.lrec-conf.org/proceedings/lrec2020/LREC-2020.pdf

Girdhar, S., Leenaars, A., Dogra, T. D., Leenaars, L., & Kumar, G. (2004). Suicide notes in India: What do they tell us? *Archives of Suicide Research, 8*(2), 179–185. https://doi.org/10.1080/13811110490271362

Grant, T., & MacLeod, N. (2018). Resources and constraints in linguistic identity performance: A theory of authorship. *Language and Law/Linguagem e Direito, 5*(1), 80–96. Retrieved from http://ojs.letras.up.pt/index.php/LLLD/article/view/4548

Hyland, K. (2005). Stance and engagement: A model of interaction in academic discourse. *Discourse Studies, 7*, 173–192. Retrieved from https://journals.sagepub.com/doi/pdf/10.1177/1461445605050365

Jones, J. N., & Bennell, C. (2007). The development and validation of statistical prediction rules for discriminating between genuine and simulated suicide notes. *Archives of Suicide Research, 11*(2), 219–233. https://doi.org/10.1080/13811110701250176

Johnston, B. (2009). Stance, style, and linguistic individual. In A. Jaffe (Ed.), *Stance: Sociolinguistic perspectives* (pp. 29–52). Oxford University Press.

Kniffka, H. (2007). *Working in language and law: A German perspective.* New York: Palgrave Macmillan.

Kredens, K. (2002). Idiolect in forensic authorship attribution. In P. Stalmaszczyk (Ed.). *Folia Linguistica Anglica, 4*, 192–212.

Kredens, K., & Coulthard, M. (2012). Corpus linguistics in authorship identification. In P. Tiersma & L. M. Solan (Eds.), *The Oxford handbook of language and law* (pp. 504–516). Oxford University Press. https://doi.org/10.1093/oxfordhb/9780199572120.013.0037

Leenaars, A. (1988). *Suicide notes: Predictive clues and patterns.* Human Sciences Press.

Lester, D. (Ed.). (2004). *Katie's diary: Unlocking the mystery of a suicide.* Routledge Taylor & Francis Group.

Lester, D. (2014). *The "I" of the storm: Understanding the suicidal mind.* De Gruyter Open Ltd..

Litvinova, T., Litvinova, O., & Seredin, P. (2018). Assessing the level of stability of idiolectal features across modes, topics and time of text production. In S. Balandin, T. S. Cinotti, F. Viola, & T. Tyutina (Eds.), *Proceedings of the 23rd Conference of Open Innovations Association FRUCT* (pp. 223–230). FRUCT. https://doi.org/10.23919/FRUCT.2018.8588092

Marcińczuk, M., Zaśko-Zielińska, M., & Piasecki, M. (2011). Structure annotation in the Polish corpus of suicide notes. In I. Habernal & V. Matoušek (Eds.), *Text, speech and dialogue* (pp. 419–426). Springer. https://doi.org/10.1007/978-3-642-23538-2_53

McMenamin, G. R. (2002). *Forensic linguistics: Advances in forensic stylistics.* CRC Press.

O'Connor, R. C., Sheehy, N. P., & O'Connor, D. B. (1999). A thematic analysis of suicide notes. *Crisis: The Journal of Crisis Intervention and Suicide Prevention, 20*(3), 106–114. https://doi.org/10.1027/0227-5910.20.3.106

Olsson, J. (2004). *Forensic linguistics: An introduction to language, crime and the law.* Continuum.

Oravetz, R. (2004). Roots of discoursive suicidology. *Horizons of Psychology, 13*(1), 151–161.

Osgood, C. E., & Walker, E. G. (1959). Motivation and language behavior: A content analysis of suicide notes. *The Journal of Abnormal and Social Psychology, 59*(1), 58–67. https://doi.org/10.1037/h0047078

Pennebaker, J. W., Francis, M. E., & Booth, R. J. (2001). *Linguistic inquiry and word count: LIWC 2001*. Lawrence Erlbaum Associates.

Pestian, J. P., Matykiewicz, P., & Linn-Gust, M. (2012). What's in a note: Construction of a suicide note corpus. *Biomedical Informatics Insights, 5*, 1–6. https://doi.org/10.4137/BII.S10213

Piasecki, M., Młynarczyk, K., & Kocoń, J. (2017). Recognition of genuine Polish suicide notes. In R. Mitkov & G. Angelova (Eds.), *Proceedings of the International Conference Recent Advances in Natural Language Processing RANLP 2017* (pp. 583–591). Varna, Bulgaria: INCOMA Ltd. doi: 10.26615/978-954-452-049-6_076

Samraj, B., & Gawron, J. M. (2015). The suicide note as a genre: Implications for genre theory. *Journal of English for Academic Purposes, 19*, 88–101.

Schneider, K. P., & Barron, A. (Eds.). (2014). *Pragmatics of discourse*. Mouton de Gruyter.

Shapero, J. J. (2011). *The language of suicide notes* (Doctoral dissertation, University of Birmingham, United Kingdom). Retrieved from https://etheses.bham.ac.uk/id/eprint/1525/1/Shapero11PhD.pdf

Shneidman, E. S., & Farberow, N. L. (Eds.). (1957). *Clues to suicide*. McGraw-Hill.

Swales, J. M. (1990). *Genre analysis: English in academic and research settings*. Cambridge University Press.

Swales, J. M. (1996). Occluded genres in the academy: The case of the submission letter. In E. Ventola & A. Mauranen (Eds.), *Academic writing: Intercultural and textual issues* (pp. 45–58). John Benjamins Publishing.

Swales, J. M. (2004). *Research genres: Explorations and applications*. Cambridge University Press.

Turell, T. & Gawalda, N., (2013). Towards an index of idiolectal similitude (or distance) in forensic authorship analysis. *Journal of Law and Policy, 21*(2), 495–514. Retrieved from http://brooklynworks.brooklaw.edu/jlp/vol21/iss2/10

Van Dijk, T. (1995). On macrostructures, mental models and other inventions: A brief personal history of the Kintsch-Van Dijk theory. In C. Weaver, S. Mannes, & C. R. Fletcher (Eds.), *Discourse comprehension: Essays in honor of Walter Kintsch* (pp. 383–410). Erlbaum.

Van Halteren, H. (2019). Benchmarking author recognition systems for forensic application. *Linguistic Evidence in Security Law and Intelligence, 3*, Retrieved from http://www.lesli-journal.org/ojs/index.php/lesli/article/view/20/20

Zaśko-Zielińska, M. (2012). Tabu w listach pożegnalnych samobójców [Taboo in the suicide notes of suicidal persons]. In N. Długosz & Z. Dimoski (Eds.), *Tabu w oku szeroko otwartym [Taboo in the eye wide open]* (pp. 85–93). Wydawnictwo Rys.

Zaśko-Zielińska, M. (2013). *Listy pożegnalne: W poszukiwaniu lingwistycznych wyznaczników autentyczności tekstu [Suicide notes: On the search for linguistic indicators of text authenticity]*. Quaestio.

12

Fighting Cybercrime through Linguistic Analysis

Patrizia Anesa

1 Introduction

To fight cybercrime effectively, investigative procedures and legal policies need to keep pace with the challenges posed by crimes committed online at a global level. In particular, traditional justice paradigms continuously need to adapt to a fluid, dynamic and ever-changing phenomenon. This chapter discusses the main issues and difficulties that law enforcement agencies, forensic linguists and other stakeholders need to deal with in their daily activities to prevent, investigate and fight cybercrime. This work stems from the key consideration that it is timely and necessary to acknowledge novel theoretical and methodological frameworks for investigating cybercrime both from a legal and a linguistic perspective and to adopt an interdisciplinary, international approach to this field of inquiry, especially when linguistic data are involved. Only through this type of collaboration can researchers gain a finer understanding of the

P. Anesa (✉)
University of Bergamo, Bergamo, Italy
e-mail: patrizia.anesa@unibg.it

V. Guillén-Nieto, D. Stein (eds.), *Language as Evidence*,
https://doi.org/10.1007/978-3-030-84330-4_12

phenomenon and offer new insights that can contribute to an effective prosecution of the different forms of cybercrime and identification of its perpetrators.

This chapter starts with a discussion of cybercrime, concentrating on the main theories and controversies that arise in the attempt to provide definitions in this area. The introductory discussion is followed by a description of some of the key approaches adopted in the investigation of cybercrime discourse, focusing on the contributions made by forensic linguistics. Subsequently, an exemplary case of romance scams is analysed through the lexical features that characterise this type of discourse. More specifically, this chapter outlines an aetiology of romance scams and explains how scammers may acquire status and power in the eyes of victims through linguistic and discursive devices.

2 Cybercrime Discourse: State of the Art, Theories and Controversies

2.1 Definitional Issues

Cybercrimes include a vast range of phenomena such as, among other things, hacking, cyber grooming, romance scams, business frauds, trolling, online antisocial behaviour, online abuse, stalking, cyberbullying, Internet intellectual property crimes, hate speech and privacy violation. The area is so vast and differentiated that the analytical section of this chapter must inevitably limit itself to one specific type of crime, namely romance scams, with the awareness that its inclusion in a wider conceptualisation of cybercrime is essential.

In this respect, the very notion of cybercrime is subject to lively debate. Indeed, defining cybercrime from a holistic perspective is not easy, given its multifaceted and fluid nature (Donalds & Osei-Bryson, 2019), and definitions have often been fragmented, inconsistent and even contradictory. Yet, a clear positioning of cybercrime from a definitional perspective is key to a better understanding of the phenomenon, which is essential to developing appropriate responses to prevent and combat it (Barn & Barn, 2016).

Cybercrimes have been illustrated through several taxonomies. For example, Suleman (2016) describes a tripartite cybercrime framework which is, to a large extent, based on motivational factors and presents three main broad categories: socio-economic cybercrime, psychosocial cybercrime and geopolitical cybercrime. However, such a distinction is questionable, largely due to the extreme permeability of the boundaries between these groups, as these areas inevitably overlap when dealing with complex forms of cybercrimes. For instance, in this case, romance scams are listed under the socio-economic categorisation, but I contend that they additionally belong to the psychosocial one. The same issue emerges for crimes such as cyber prostitution or cyber blackmail. Although they are classified as socio-economic, they also have a strong psychosocial component. Thus, we may argue that, on the one hand, classification schemas are essential to offer a functional framework for grouping cybercrime but, on the other hand, such schemas need to be perpetually updated and must account for the inherent contextual and cultural intricacies that these malefactions entail.

Cybercrimes can be broadly classified into computer-assisted or computer-focused crimes (Furnell, 2002). Whereas in the former case the computer represents an enabler of the crime, in the latter it constitutes a contingent aspect of the crime. Computer-assisted crimes existed, for example, in the shape of fraud, money laundering and harassment, before the advent of the Internet and other new technologies. Instead, computer-focused crimes—where the computer itself becomes the target—have emerged as a result of the expansion of the Internet and the development of new technologies—for example hacking and viral attacks (cf. Bolton, 2014).

In a similar vein, Wall (2005) argues that the Internet has led to three distinct phenomena: (1) more opportunities for old crimes—for example fraud, money laundering, stalking and trading of pornographic materials; (2) new opportunities for old crimes—for example hacking, identity theft or advance-fee scams and (3) new opportunities for new crimes—for example, e-auction scams, spam, hate speech or intellectual property piracy. However, this distinction is also problematic. For instance, the proliferation of online hate speech, especially on social media, may be considered a new crime, enhanced by new technology, but related forms of this crime date back to the pre-Internet era. The same could be said about the phenomenon of scams (see Section 4).

2.2 Legal Framework

From a legal perspective, the EU's 2001 Convention on Cybercrime (ETS No. 185), also known as the Budapest Convention, was the first international treaty on Internet and computer crime. One of its main objectives, set out in the preamble, was to pursue a common criminal policy aimed at protecting society against cybercrime, particularly by adopting appropriate legislation and fostering cross-border co-operation. The Convention defines key terms such as *computer system*, *computer data*, *service provider* and *traffic data*,[1] but it does not define cybercrime as such. It does, nevertheless, list the following categories as forms of cybercrime: (1) offences against the confidentiality, integrity and availability of computer data and systems (Title 1); (2) computer-related offences (Title 2); (3) content-related offences (Title 3) and (4) offences related to the infringement of copyright and related rights (Title 4).

The European Commission, in its *Communication to the European Parliament, the Council and the Committee of the Regions—Towards a general policy on the fight against cybercrime*, dated 2007,[2] offered a similar categorisation by listing three key areas of cybercrime, which may be summarised as follows:

a) traditional forms of criminal activity, in which the Internet is used to commit crimes (e.g. fraud, phishing or as a consequence of identity theft);
b) the publication of illegal content (e.g. material inciting terrorism, xenophobia, homophobia or child abuse); and
c) crimes unique to electronic networks, which were unknown in the pre-Internet age, such as attacks on information systems.

These categories may also partly overlap, and a single crime may include a series of related criminal activities. For instance, a romance fraud may implicatively insinuate the publication (or threat of it) of confidential material online or lead to *sextortion*.

Given the dynamicity of the phenomenon, categorising cybercrime has to be intended as a fluid and constantly evolving process. Thus, its definition may benefit from transcending, to some extent, the debate on whether we should consider online crimes as either old crimes committed through new media or as new and unique crimes. Different types of illegal practices inevitably encompass a form of modernisation of old ones. However, the novel space where these crimes are committed, the different types of agents involved and the diversity of the victims differ from traditional criminal activities. Consequently, there is a need for new tools to investigate new crimes opportunely.

3 Investigating Cybercrime

3.1 Linguistic Perspectives

Cybercrimes, which have a disruptive impact on individuals, organisations, companies and governments, are deemed to remain endemic at a worldwide level, and the magnitude of the phenomenon is expected to grow even further (Blythe & Coventry, 2018). The fight against cybercrime cannot disregard an interdisciplinary approach that adopts multiple perspectives to explore a process with an ever-growing and ever-changing nature. In this regard, Linguistics can contribute to the investigation and the prevention of cybercrime in terms of theories and methods (Perkins, 2018). In this field, linguists can perform different roles. Firstly, the linguist can actively help to recognise cybercrime attempts; secondly, linguists can help to develop systems aimed at preventing cybercrime through the identification of the linguistic and discursive features of different forms of cybercrime; and thirdly, linguists can make an active contribution to the field of victimology, by helping those involved in the investigation of such crimes to implement improved communication strategies when interacting with the victims. This activity is essential to help the individuals become aware of the nature of the crime and encourage them to report it to the authorities. Therefore, linguists can support the investigative process and help with the prevention of re-victimisation, which is particularly common in criminal phenomena such as romance scams, as will be shown later in Section 4.

3.2 Forensic Linguistics

When dealing with cybercrime, forensic linguists require a multifaceted preparation encompassing various degrees of expertise in different areas. Three of these areas are: (1) knowledge of linguistics—that is phonetics and phonology, syntax, semantics, pragmatics, psycholinguistics, sociolinguistics and computational linguistics; (2) understanding aspects of computer science relevant to cybercrime analysis; and (3) some specific legal knowledge.

Forensic linguistics is constrained by several legal elements, such as the legal framework within which the analysis is to be conducted, ethical and deontological considerations, and the method employed needing to have a scientific basis for the forensic report to be admitted by the court of justice. In this respect, defining legal standards for the level of acceptability of forensic linguistics in a court of law is a complex matter, particularly when the issue goes beyond national boundaries. Given the international nature of cybercrime, defining the role of cyber-forensic linguists is challenging because of the specific constraints within which they have to work. Furthermore, the criteria adopted to define the level of expertise requested may vary. For instance, in the United States, the Daubert standard rule of evidence[3] specifies that expert witness testimony can only be accepted under given circumstances. Specifically, evidence can be admitted if the theory and method are reliable, validated and generally accepted by the scientific community and if the testimony is predicated on adequate scientific information. In particular, in the case of cybercrime, given its relative novelty and, above all, the rapid evolution that it undergoes, a constant redefinition of the validity of the methods involved in its investigation proves to be particularly significant.

Typically, forensic linguists play a significant role in different situations which may result in future prosecutions and their work often enhances the clarification of specific elements of criminal enquiries. The areas in which forensic linguists may be involved include voice identification, examination of police interrogations, transcript evaluation, linguo-cultural analysis and authorship attribution, among others (Danielewicz-Betz, 2012). Many traditional activities of forensic linguistics take place in cyberspace as well. For instance, forensic phonetics can be used in criminal investigations to analyse the voice on audio recordings that scammers may have sent to their victims. In this case, linguists may work on voice comparisons, disputes over the content of recordings, transcriptions of spoken language, authentications of recordings, among other possibilities.

In the case of scams, there is often a series of potential forensically pertinent text traces to be evaluated, including instant messages, text messages, emails, and audio and video recordings. In particular, in romance frauds, given that scammers often pretend to be native speakers of a certain language, geographical dialect/accent recognition also plays a crucial role, as do voice line-ups, to identify whether the same scammers have been involved in multiple crimes.

Furthermore, the forensic analysis of scams can also involve authorship attribution;[4] in this case, forensic linguists can be asked to identify the author of the questioned fraudulent texts. This type of forensic linguistic investigation can be combined with other data, such as identifying the IP address location from which the message is delivered so that the criminal organisation members can be located.

Various forms of communication, including email messages, text messages or instant messages,[5] may additionally be analysed for authorship attribution by observing indicators such as stylistic features. Indeed, stylistic variation is a key feature which can typify scam messages: it can be intratextual, when changes are detected within the same text, or intertextual, when variation occurs across different texts. From a practical perspective, a scammer typically presents himself or herself as the writer of all the texts of a given exchange, but author variation may emerge and may represent a potential indicator of the fraudulent attempt.

Statistical analysis can be conducted employing a specialised language database of a given genre to facilitate the analysis and contribute to the profiling process to offer information about demographic or social aspects (Danielewicz-Betz, 2012, p. 99). To proceed with the attribution, the linguist can analyse features such as, among other things, word and sentence length average, word frequency, type-token ratio, punctuation choices, lexical density, syntactic boundaries or word keyness (Danielewicz-Betz, 2012, pp. 98-99).

Generally, the linguist needs to process the text under investigation along with other texts to identify homogeneous attributes between the messages and contribute to the identification of templates utilised by the same criminal organisation. Some major issues have to be considered: firstly, the fact that consistent or inconsistent forms may be used at an intra-individual level; secondly, the scammer may fake a certain style, which may increase the likelihood of inconsistency and thirdly, scams are usually the result of collective work where multiple authors are involved in the creation of the message, thus complicating the analysis. Messages are often the replication or adaptation of standardised texts, an element that is concretely pertinent as the portion of reproduced texts can be identified automatically via detection software and indicate the lack of genuineness of a message.

4 Case Study: Romance Scams

4.1 Romance Scamming: A New Crime?

Romance frauds are not new, but their diffusion and impact have changed with the Internet revolution, contributing to determining a new, evolving paradigm for this type of crime. Hence, the investigation of these texts should abandon static perspectives (Herring et al., 2013) to account for their fluidity and flexibility, as has been done for other genres developed through computer-mediated communication (CMC).

Romance scams represent a deceitful scheme in which criminals typically contact their victims through dating or social networking sites, feigning romantic intentions. These frauds are based on digital deception because they are intended to create a false belief in a digital environment (Hancock, 2007; Hancock & Gonzales, 2013). Indeed, scammers use persuasive techniques to gain the victims' trust and affection and ultimately defraud them (Whitty & Buchanan, 2012). Untruthful emails and messages can be successful, despite their manifestly suspicious appearance, because of the criminals' ability to implement persuasion strategies and fulfil certain credibility requirements. In this respect, romance scammers have proved to be particularly skilful in employing psycholinguistic strategies to trigger emotional responses from their targets (Jones et al., 2015) and affect their cognitive behaviour (Modic & Lea, 2013).

Two main questions have often led the investigation of romance scams: Is it because of the immediacy of the Internet that impulsive forms of needing attention emerge? Or is it the dream of an emotional reward which fosters compliance with the scammers' requests? These questions focus exclusively on the victims' wants, as if a latent desire to be victimised was at the inception of the crime. Against this background, a common perception exists that these problems may only affect those who are more imprudent and irresponsible. Therefore, most people tend to believe that they are sufficiently sensitised towards online criminal behaviour and feel they would be immune to fraudulent attempts.

Whitty (2018) suggests that the risk of victimisation is higher among middle-aged females, especially when they display a predisposition for impulsivity, trustworthiness and a tendency to dependency. Other studies indicate that the inclination to have strong romantic beliefs and to idealise relations may also be an indicator of potential victimisation, but other psychological factors (such as a tendency to loneliness) do not seem to have a substantial effect (Buchanan & Whitty, 2014).

The notion of cyber victimisation is fraught with biases and preconceptions, which often lead to the acritical assumption that there exists a group of ideal targets, while other individuals are exempted from being defrauded (Lindgren, 2018). Contrary to common belief, research has demonstrated that victims of romance scams belong to different social classes and display heterogeneous cultural and educational backgrounds (Anesa, 2020).

4.2 Research Framework

This study adopts a multi-perspectival framework, coalescing Forensic Linguistics models with an approach which I would label as Applied Societal Discourse Analysis (ASDA). This approach is intended as an applied form of Discourse Analysis that addresses complex societal issues and whose purpose is to actively offer interpretive and strategic insights and practical recommendations which go beyond purely descriptive considerations. Thus, starting from acknowledging a given issue, ASDA aims to describe and explain romance scams, identify margins for manoeuvre and suggest potential solutions, employing both qualitative and quantitative approaches.

Due to the topic sensitivity, the difficulty in accessing data, and the ethical issues related to data collection and the analysis of such data, it is not always easy to conduct primary research on romance scamming. However, this linguistic study is based on a corpus of authentic online romance scams (ORSC) which was compiled for the purpose of this research project. It consists of a set of texts used by the international criminal organisation led by Olayinka Ilumsa Sunmola[6] as well as a set of instant messages and emails collected in Malaysia between 2016 and 2018.[7]

The investigation deals with selected linguistic techniques found in successful Internet romance frauds to identify persuasive appeals to entice the target to fall prey to the criminal. Specifically, the analysis focuses on the lexical items which characterise these cyber text types. The research questions addressed are: What are the typical words and expressions used by the scammer to create the profile of an attractive, credible and trustworthy online persona? What linguistic, discursive and rhetorical techniques are employed to trigger an emotional response—for example, love, affection, desire, interest, enthusiasm, fear, guilt or responsibility—that leads the victim to comply with the scammer's requests?

The language of romance scams can be investigated both qualitatively, by processing and coding the textual elements, or quantitatively, by observing features such as word frequency and keyness via corpus linguistics tools. The present study combines both methods. As the corpus is relatively small in size, it was possible first to conduct a qualitative analysis of selected codes—that is, words on specific semantic areas. The software used was *QDA Miner Lite* and two coders carried out the same procedure to evaluate the level of intercoder agreement, which reached 85%. In the case of discrepancy, a third coder was consulted. Subsequently, a quantitative analysis was conducted using *AntConc* (Anthony, 2019) to verify the findings of the qualitative investigation. In this case, particular attention was devoted to word frequency and keyness.

4.3 Analysis

Scammers use several strategies to coerce the victims into complying with their requests. Firstly, the anonymity provided by the Internet provides the criminal with a cyber-stature—that is, the possibility of creating an online persona. Consequently, the profile of the scammer is one of the aspects to be investigated. As the vast majority of the texts included in the corpus under scrutiny were produced by male scammers targeting female victims, this analysis focuses on male profiles and their self-descriptions.

In ORSC, the professions most frequently claimed relate to the military, engineering and business professions, in line with Suarez-Tangil et al.'s results (2019).[8] Furthermore, related research confirms that these professions are generally considered more desirable by selected targets and thereby, functional to the scamming process (Anesa, 2020; Whitty, 2013). It is important to note that the boundaries between the above-mentioned professional groups are not always clear-cut. For example, a scammer may claim to be both an engineer and the manager of a company. For this reason, it is difficult to offer a precise quantitative analysis. Therefore, the data are to be intended as merely indicative of the main professions mentioned in romance frauds. Besides, scammers often state that they work abroad—for example, on an oil platform or a military deployment, as illustrated in the excerpt below:

> I own my construction company. I deal basically with oil platforms, rig constructions, renovations, water bridges, interior decors, and some artworks.[9]

Table 12.1 Male profiles: claimed professions

Scam male profiles: freq. (based on Suarez-Tangil et al., 2019)	Real male profiles: freq. (based on Suarez-Tangil et al., 2019)	Scam male profiles: freq. (in ORSC)
Military 0.25	Other 0.15	Engineer 0.30
Engineer 0.25	Self 0.07	Military 0.20
Self 0.10	Engineer 0.07	Business 0.18
Business 0.06	Tech. 0.05	Building 0.16
Building 0.06	Student 0.05	Other 0.10
Other 0.04	Retired 0.05	Manager 0.08
Contract 0.04	Building 0.05	
Medical 0.03	Service 0.04	
Manager 0.02	Transport 0.04	
Sales 0.02	Manual 0.03	

Some of the main professions claimed in male profiles are listed in Table 12.1.

The analysis conducted by Suarez-Tangil et al. (2019) is based on the website datingnmore.com, which has an international platform of users. The ORSC, instead, draws on scams involving people located mainly in the US and Malaysia. The victim's geographical location may generate differences in data, in that, for example, the popularity of certain professions may vary across cultures. However, the distribution of the claimed professions displays a strong similarity between the two corpora. For instance, the military profession is frequent in scam profiles; indeed, it is functional to create a perfect character for the story that is narrated for fraudulent purposes (typically involving a man living abroad in very distant locations) and contributes to projecting a powerful and authoritative identity. Moreover, the scammer's claimed provenance is generally a well-known city in the west, such as New York or Paris. This aspect engenders a sense of familiarity in the victim and an interest in a location that is generally perceived to be beautiful, interesting or exciting.

Further demographic data emerging from the profiles or the scam messages are also revealing. As a case in point, the ethnicities declared by scammers differ from the statistics present in real profiles. Compared to the real male profiles, a higher proportion of scam male profiles claims to be *White*, while a significantly lower percentage is labelled as *Hispanic*.

Table 12.2 Male profiles: claimed ethnicity

Scam male profiles (%) (based on Suarez-Tangil et al., 2019)	Real male profiles (%) (based on Suarez-Tangil et al., 2019)	Scam male profiles (%) (in ORSC)
White 66%	White 44%	White 71%
Other 6%	Other 8%	Asian 11 %
Native American 11%	Native American 1%	Other 9%
Mixed 7%	Mixed 5%	Mixed 9%
Hispanic 2%	Hispanic 32%	
Black 6%	Black 6%	
Asian 2%	Asian 4%	

The claimed ethnicity may show some differences related to the victim's location, but the white[10] ethnicity is predominant, with most scammers declaring that they are either American or British (Table 12.2).

As far as marital status is concerned, scammers claim to be widowed in 28% of cases, while only 4% of real profiles belong to widowers. Furthermore, it is common for scammers to state that they have children. Therefore, the high frequency of words such as widower, boy, girl or child is one of the several lexical elements which can generate an alert. Indeed, these items are artfully used to build a narrative that can generate pity and empathy in the victim.

The scammers make other strategic lexical choices to align with the victims' desires, making it difficult for them to doubt the veracity of the message. For instance, criminals often employ religious words and expressions, aiming to create the identity of a moral, religious and ethically sound individual. When the victim's profile also shows a religious orientation, this approach is in line with perceived similarity. Consequently, these elements contribute to occluding the signs of a fraudulent attempt.

Another common feature is the presence of words that identify a particularly romantic, passionate, potential lover. This process includes different techniques:

1) citation of songs, poetry, quotes, all having a strong romantic vein;
2) paying compliments to the target—for example, *your beauty is divine*;
3) using affectionate expressions—for example, *I love you*; *you are my life*;
4) using forms of endearment—for example, *my angel*; *dear*; *honey*;

5) using commissive speech acts—for example, *I will always love you*; *I will love you till I die*;
6) using hyperbolic expressions—for example, *you saved my life*; *I cannot live without you*; *you are better than anyone on this planet*); and
7) figurative language, with the usage of several metaphors—for example, *you are a star*; *you my angel*; *my diamond*.

Once a relationship has been established, the scammers aim to create the identity of a lover who needs help. In this phase some of the following specific lexical elements are introduced:

1) words relating to worry and fears—for example, *Thank you for being the one who calms all my inner fears*. In this regard, it has been demonstrated that liars make use of emotional language more frequently than truth tellers and, in particular, online deception often includes negative affect words (cf. Hancock & Gonzales, 2013, p. 375);
2) begging and pleading language—for example, *My love, here I come on my knees, I will never ask you anything if I have other options. Though you come first, but I hate to take my woman through stress*;
3) introduction of third parties to corroborate the scammer's story—for example, *my lawyer*; *my colleague*; *my doctor*; *the bank manager*;
4) words and expression related to money delivery—for example, *bank transfer*; *money transfer*; *bank account*; and
5) words related to the secrecy of the process—for example, *It's a secret*; *nobody can know*; *only you know this*.

The examples depicted in Table 12.3 illustrate some of the main semantic fields to which strategic lexical items pertain.

Finally, victims often show a tendency to rely on a small number of simple, heuristic cues to assess the level of credibility. Lengthy self-descriptions (rather than their soundness and legitimacy) are automatically associated with high levels of credibility. Thus, the amount of information appears more significant than its reliability (Toma, 2017). Consequently, scammers introduce themselves through protracted descriptions, and the extent of a single email can be over 1000 words, even in the initial exchanges.

Table 12.3 Strategic semantic fields

Semantic field	Examples
Religion	*I have prayed last night and again this morning—I asked God and Archangel Michael to surround you—your work—your house and family with 65 million Angels to protect and guide you.*
Love	*I got your message and looked at your picture over and over again, you are a true diamond, you are priceless, a blessing and an angel.*
	I am sunk in love, crazy about you honey. I am at work but I can hardly leave the office cos I am waiting to hear from you every second of every minute of every hour. Please tell me, what have you done to me? (lol)... I love you soooooooooooooooooooooooooooooo oooo much .....
Money	*Since I got the money you sent, it has been much relief and great joy in the heart of every one.*
	I needed some of the cash for my flight and some other stuffs while the remaining should be put in an account I can access when I get to the States.
Secrecy	*Like I told you, honey, please keep my secret to you and you alone because I will never discuss my business with anyone except for love. This is how much I have given my life to you. I believe that husband and wife should not keep secret from each other if truly they are in love.*

5 Conclusions

Although it is not possible to span the wide canvas of cybercrime in just one chapter, this study has tried to draw attention to the need to refine the concept of cybercrime and highlight its multifaceted character. Furthermore, given the evolving nature of cybercrime in terms of shape, size and scope, it is apparent that any depiction of the phenomenon is inevitably a snapshot of what is happening *hic et nunc*. Thus, the malleability and the fluidity of cybercrime bring with them the need to constantly redefine the theorisation of this form of crime. In the specific case of online romance scams, the findings presented in this chapter are only a fragment of a complex reality. They must be considered as merely illustrating one of the several analytical approaches implemented to offer linguistic data that can contribute to the uncovering of processes by which frauds are constructed.

Romance scams represent a key instantiation of deception in CMC. Whereas the way deception emerges in cyber contexts has often been explored in laboratory settings, investigation in more naturalistic situations is relatively less spread (Hancock & Gonzales, 2013). Consequently, despite its limitations, this chapter has the merit of observing real examples of deceptive texts to define some of its key features.

In online romance scams, the perception of authenticity is determined by micro-level discursive strategies, especially in the use of lexical items and macro-structural aspects. Moreover, personalised recipient-focused cues appear to be more significantly used than in other types of scams, such as Nigerian letters (cf. Gill, 2013 on the unauthenticity of this form of business fraud).

The methodology used in this chapter may prove to be particularly appropriate for an early detection and prevention of romance scams. In this respect, the quantitative and qualitative lexical analysis of the corpus under study shows that specific words and expressions related to given semantic fields—for example, religion, love, money or secrecy—appear frequently in scams. However, in stark contrast with potential fraud indicators, victims, who display heterogeneous backgrounds, commit errors of judgement and comply with the requests they receive. Therefore, insightful reflections on the determinants that may stir such compliance are necessary. Furthermore, raising awareness about the strategies implemented in romance frauds can help to improve their early detection.

Research into cybercrime can also benefit from the implementation of other methodological approaches, including *in situ* observations, for instance, scambaiting (*online vigilantes*). In this case, the authenticity and validity of the data obtained are inevitably affected by the baiter's behaviour, but this approach can complement other investigation forms. Moreover, interviews with the victims[11] are currently being conducted within this project and will be used to gain new insights into the phenomenon and to acquire specific information from an emic perspective. This type of data can be crucial to confirm the hypothesis concerning the victims' errors of judgement that is formulated in the present study.

Notes

1. See Chapter 1, art. 1: 'For the purposes of this Convention: a) "computer system" means any device or a group of interconnected or related devices, one or more of which, pursuant to a program, performs automatic processing of data; b) "computer data" means any representation of facts, information or concepts in a form suitable for processing in a computer system, including a program suitable to cause a computer system to perform a function; c) "service provider" means: i) any public or private entity that provides to users of its service the ability to communicate by means of a computer system, and ii) any other entity that processes or stores computer data on behalf of such communication service or users of such service; d) "traffic data" means any computer data relating to a communication by means of a computer system, generated by a computer system that formed a part in the chain of communication, indicating the communication's origin, destination, route, time, date, size, duration, or type of underlying service'. Retrieved from: https://rm.coe.int/CoERMPublicCommonSearchServices/DisplayDCTMContent?documentId=0900001680081561. (Last access 30 March 2020).
2. See https://eur-lex.europa.eu/legal-content/EN/TXT/?uri=celex:52007DC0267. (Last access 30 March 2020).
3. US Supreme Court case, *Daubert v. Merrell Dow Pharmaceuticals, 509 US 579 (1993*).
4. Among the different approaches to authorship identification we can find two main models: generative (e.g. Bayesian) or discriminative (e.g. Support Vector Machine). Also, two main classes are identified: closed or open. In the closed class, the expert attributes the text to a single author drawn from a predefined group, while, in the open class, the possible author does not necessarily belong to a predefined set. On a final note, in the case of profiling, the expert identifies the author's general properties or characteristics—for example, socio-demographic features (Inches et al., 2013). For a general introduction to authorship identification practices, see Stamatatos (2009).
5. Instant messages tend to be very informal, short and unstructured. However, in scamming, the textual organisation may vary according to different variables, such as the replicability of the texts and the use of templates. In the case of conversational documents, the classical statisti-

cal models are unsuitable for authorship attribution, and ad hoc approaches need to be implemented to attain a high accuracy rate (Inches et al., 2013).

6. Olayinka Ilumsa Sunmola was the leader of a successful and far-reaching scamming organisation targeting female victims, especially in the US. The crimes were perpetrated between 2007 and 2014.
7. All texts were anonymised and potentially sensitive pieces of information were deleted.
8. The data obtained by Suarez-Tangil et al. (2019) are drawn from datingnmore.com and the related public scam list is available at scamdigger.com.
9. For the sake of authenticity, any errors or inaccuracies present in the original texts have been preserved in the excerpts quoted.
10. The term refers to the label adopted by the users themselves.
11. Qualitative research in this field is often based on a phenomenological approach. The project from which this study derives also includes interviews with the victims to offer an emic perspective on the phenomenon. Although these aspects are beyond the scope of this chapter, they are deemed essential to gain novel and authentic insights into the scamming process.

References

Anesa, P. (2020). Lovextortion: Persuasion strategies in romance cybercrime. *Discourse, Context & Media, 35*, 1–8.

Anthony, L. (2019). *AntConc*. Waseda University.

Barn, R., & Barn, B. (2016). An ontological representation of a taxonomy for cybercrime. *Research Papers, 45*. Retrieved from https://aisel.aisnet.org/ecis2016_rp/45.

Blythe, J. M., & Coventry, L. (2018). Costly but effective: Comparing the factors that influence employee anti-malware behaviours. *Computers in Human Behavior, 87*, 87–97.

Bolton, A. (2014). Virtual criminology. In J. M. Miller (Ed.), *The Encyclopedia of theoretical criminology* (pp. 924–927). Wiley Blackwell.

Buchanan, T., & Whitty, M. T. (2014). The online dating romance scam: causes and consequences of victimhood. *Psychology, Crime & Law, 20*, 261–283.

Danielewicz-Betz, A. (2012). The role of forensic linguistics in crime investigation. In A. Littlejohn, & S. R. Mehta (Eds.), *Language Studies: Stretching the Boundaries* (pp. 93–108). Cambridge Scholars Publishing.

Donalds, C., & Osei-Bryson, K. M. (2019). Toward a cybercrime classification ontology: A knowledge-based approach. *Computers in Human Behavior, 92*, 403–418.

Furnell, S. (2002). *Cybercrime: Vandalising the information society*. Addison Wesley.

Gill, M. (2013). Authentication and Nigerian letters. In S. Herring, D. Stein, & T. Virtanen (Eds.), *Pragmatics of computer-mediated communication* (pp. 411–436). De Gruyter.

Hancock, J. (2007). Digital deception: When, where and how people lie online. In K. McKenna, T. Postmes, U. Reips, & A. N. Joinson (Eds.), *Oxford handbook of internet psychology* (pp. 287–301). Oxford University Press.

Hancock, J., & Gonzales, A. (2013). Deception in computer-mediated communication. In S. Herring, D. Stein, & T. Virtanen (Eds.), *Pragmatics of computer-mediated communication* (pp. 363–383). De Gruyter.

Herring, S., Stein, D., & Virtanen, T. (2013). Introduction to the pragmatics of computer-mediated communication. In S. Herring, D. Stein, & T. Virtanen (Eds.), *Pragmatics of computer-mediated communication* (pp. 3–32). De Gruyter.

Inches, G., Harvey, M., & Crestani, F. (2013). Finding participants in a chat: authorship attribution for conversational documents. *International conference on social computing, Alexandria, VA, 2013*, 272–279. https://doi.org/10.1109/SocialCom.2013.45

Jones, H., Towse, J., & Race, N. (2015). Susceptibility to email fraud: A review of psychological perspectives, data-collection methods, and ethical considerations. *International Journal of Cyber Behavior: Psychology and Learning, 5*(3), 13–29.

Lindgren, S. (2018). A ghost in the machine: Tracing the role of 'the digital' in discursive processes of cybervictimization. *Discourse & Communication, 12*(5), 517–534.

Modic, D., & Lea, S. (2013). Scam compliance and the psychology of persuasion. *Social science research network*. doi: https://doi.org/10.2139/ssrn.2364464.

Perkins, R. C. (2018). The application of forensic linguistics in cybercrime investigations. *Policing: A Journal of Policy and Practice*. doi: https://doi.org/10.1093/police/pay097.

Stamatatos, E. (2009). A survey of modern authorship attribution methods. *Journal of the American Society for Information Science and Technology, 60*(3), 538–556.

Suarez-Tangil, G., Edwards, M., Peersman, C., Stringhini, G., Rashid, A., & Whitty, M. (2019). Automatically dismantling online fating Fraud. Retrieved from arXiv:1905.12593.

Suleman, I. (2016). Social and contextual taxonomy of cybercrime: Socio-economic theory of Nigerian cybercriminals. *International Journal of Law, Crime and Justice, 47*, 44–57.

Toma, C. L. (2017). Developing online deception literacy while looking for love. *Media, Culture & Society, 39*(3), 423–428.

Wall, D. S. (2005). The Internet as a conduit for criminal activity. In A. Pattavina (Ed.), *Information technology and the criminal justice system* (pp. 77–98). Sage Publications.

Whitty, M. T. (2013). The scammers' persuasive techniques model: Development of a stage model to explain the online dating romance scam. *British Journal of Criminology, 53*(4), 665–684.

Whitty, M. T. (2018). Do you love me? Psychological characteristics of romance scam victims. *Cyberpsychology, Behavior, and Social Networking, 21*(2), 105–109.

Whitty, M. T., & Buchanan, T. (2012). The online dating romance scam: A serious crime. *Cyberpsychology, Behavior, and Social Networking, 15*(3), 181–183.

13

Linguistic Approaches to the Analysis of Online Terrorist Threats

Julien Longhi

1 Introduction

According to Dean and Bell (2012, pp. 11–12), 'Web 2.0 social media technologies have allowed terrorism to become a massive "dot.com" presence on the internet'. The question of online terrorist threats is a topic of growing interest. While computer sciences have already invested a lot in this field, especially in terms of digital traces and the analysis of computer networks, linguistics has only recently taken an interest in this subject. Bérubé et al. (2020) confirm that forensic sciences have taken a growing interest in digital traces as the latter are 'invaluable sources of information, although using them effectively poses certain challenges' (p. 8).

J. Longhi (✉)
CY Cergy Paris Université, Paris, France

Institut Universitaire de France (IUF), Paris, France
e-mail: julien.longhi@cyu.fr

V. Guillén-Nieto, D. Stein (eds.), *Language as Evidence*,
https://doi.org/10.1007/978-3-030-84330-4_13

1.1 Internet, Technologies and Information

According to the report 'Investigations and intelligence-gathering' (2012), issued by the United Nations Office on Drugs and Crime (UNODC) in collaboration with the United Nations Counter-Terrorism Implementation Task Force:

> Technology is one of the strategic factors driving the increasing use of the Internet by terrorist organizations and their supporters for a wide range of purposes, including recruitment, financing, propaganda, training, incitement to commit acts of terrorism, and the gathering and dissemination of information for terrorist purposes. While the many benefits of the Internet are self-evident, it may also be used to facilitate communication within terrorist organizations and to transmit information on, as well as material support for, planned acts of terrorism, all of which require specific technical knowledge for the effective investigation of these offences. (p. 1)

Besides, in the fourth chapter of the above report, the authors admit that:

> Effective investigations relating to Internet activity rely on a combination of traditional investigative methods, knowledge of the tools available to conduct illicit activity via the Internet and the development of practices targeted to identify, apprehend and prosecute the perpetrators of such acts … [thus] different types of investigative techniques, both traditional and specifically relating to digital evidence, are employed in unison. (p. 53)

In this chapter we will work within the realm of *forensic computing* and thereby analyse complex data generated from the 'increased use of multimedia, combined with the rapid expansion of the Internet' (McKemmish, 1999, p. 5). Textual data—for example from social media, blogs and forums—require processing adapted to natural language. Indeed, if we consider the technological changes that have affected the way in which law enforcement agencies conduct their criminal investigations and gather intelligence (Bérubé et al., 2020, p. 8), natural language processing techniques can contribute to analysing online terrorist threats. Given their multifaceted nature, it is thus important for linguists to have a certain competence in computer science in order to be able to analyse these threats.

1.2 Language Processing

Chaski and Chemylinski (as summarised in Chaski, 2005) explain the usefulness of the 'method for decomposing the data into smaller chunks so that a larger set of variables can be used for the discriminant analysis' (Chaski, 2005, p. 11). They note that, on average, the method yields result accuracy above 95%. The work of Ainsworth and Juola (2018) allows us to take authorship attribution analysis further. They argue that 'language can be analysed by its objectively identifiable features' (p. 1173):

- forensic authorship analysis is objective, repeatable, and reproducible but needs to be based on empirical methods that clearly show how they work;
- applying the method of using big amounts of document sets in which the identity of the author is known, researchers can perform a number of calculations, measurements, and comparisons, which make it possible to compare texts in a corpus from different perspectives—that is word length, sentence length, term frequencies, grammatical categories, among others.

Let us consider, for instance, the concept of threats from a linguistic point of view. In a study by Ascone and Longhi (2017), 'starting from the rhetorical pattern characterising the jihadist propaganda, where threat represents only a facet of the jihadist discourse' (p. 96), we examined both the content and form of propositions conveying a threat. Ascone and Longhi's analysis yielded the following results that were subsequently confirmed by Ascone (2018):

- two magazines we looked at, *Dabiq and Dar-al-Islam*, presented different discourses and different types of threat but 'the Islamic State's propaganda aims at reinforcing the reader's adhesion to the jihadist

ideology, and at inviting him/her to act against its enemies in the name of the jihadist ideology' (p. 6);
- four kinds of threats were identified: direct threat against enemies, direct threat against Muslims, the description of threatening events and incitement to commit violent acts against the enemy.

The analysis of online threats requires both precise linguistic criteria and computer tools. For example the question of enunciation devices, the links between explicit and implicit aspects of discourse and sociolinguistic dimensions must be considered before conducting any data computer processing.

1.3 Looking for Clues

While linguistics alone cannot solve crimes, a better understanding of language data brings additional clues that can be useful for criminal investigations. Digital tools, as we will see in the case study, are useful in extracting clues from the linguistic traces that make up texts. According to Margot (2014), 'it is only based on the knowledge of the possible versions of the facts, or propositions, that the value as a clue or the quality of the information provided by the trace can be measured or assessed' (p. 79). This chapter tries to show the link between trace and clue and how textometric analysis works. A linguistic trace fits Margot's (2014) definition:

> A trace is only an object with no meaning of its own. Its link to a case, and to reasonable hypotheses explaining its presence, in a way gives it its fundamental *raison d'être*. It is the observed result that makes the reasoning possible, an inference about a past fact. Thus, a trace becomes a sign when it is used for investigative purposes, or a clue when it is involved in reconstruction or demonstration. (p. 86)

The term *sign* is particularly interesting because it is the founding term of linguistics, as used by Ferdinand de Saussure when he developed linguistics as a part of semiology. To link signs, clues and evidence, we can follow Ainsworth and Juola (2018) who explain that when we look for clues, 'linguistic analysts examine systematic language variation on many levels' (pp. 1168–1169). Language usage patterns can be called 'style markers', and analyses based on these markers become 'forensic stylistics'. Ainsworth and Juola (2018) distinguish different levels:

- Patterns of punctuation, spacing and spelling which can reflect an idiolect, regional dialects or slang;
- Grammatical choices;
- Narrative structures, levels of formality/informality, the use of irony, sarcasm, hyperbole, etc.

All these makers can be considered qualitatively and quantitatively, which works very well with the textometric method that will be presented and employed in the remainder of this article.

Therefore, these reflections on the links between traces, clues and evidence intersect with the debates and discussions that can take place in the fields of stylistics and stylometry. In his thesis, Wright (2014) investigates the advantages and disadvantages of the different approaches, highlighting three points: '(i) objectivity and reliability, (ii) theoretical and linguistic validity and explanation, and (iii) accessibility to lay judges and juries' (p. 19).

If qualitative stylistic approaches can be seen as too subjective, 'much of this criticism comes from the United States, where the admissibility of expert evidence is determined in relation to the standards of the Daubert Criteria' (Wright, 2014, p. 19). Thus, stylometric approaches are 'considered to be more objective, empirical, replicable, and ultimately more reliable than their stylistic counterparts', but they can hardly give information about theoretical aspects of linguistic variation.

2 Related Works

For Chen, Zhou, Reid and Larson (as cited in Dean & Bell, 2012, p. 15), terrorism informatics 'draws on a diversity of disciplines from Computer Science, Informatics, Statistics, Mathematics, Linguistics, Social Sciences, and Public Policy and their related sub-disciplines'. They point out that different approaches (e.g. data mining, data integration, language translation technologies, image and video processing) can be used in the prevention, detection and remediation of terrorism. Three problems can appear relating to digital aspects when applied to online terrorist threats: the amount of data, the specificities of computer processing and the way in which linguistic treatments of digital corpora can be computerised.

2.1 The Amount of Data

According to UNODC (2012, p. 60), 'there is a vast range of data and services available via the Internet which may be employed in an investigation to counter terrorist use of the Internet'. Whether as part of internal or external communication, terrorist organisations produce a large amount of textual data. Communications between members of the organisation, communication intended for potential recruits, propaganda messages or apologias for terrorism are all analysable data. However, the first difficulty concerns identifying relevant data among a myriad of messages. UNODC recommends 'a proactive approach to investigative strategies and supporting specialist tools, which capitalizes on evolving Internet resources, promotes the efficient identification of data and services likely to yield the maximum benefit to an investigation' (p. 60). Of all the existing resources, and because we are interested in analysing textual data, we will turn to natural language analysis methods and tools.

2.2 The Specificities of Computer Processing of Textual Data

To discuss this point in more detail we will start with the work of McKemmish (1999) who has set out the rules of forensic computing. The observance of these rules 'is fundamental to ensuring admissibility of any product in a court of law' (p. 3). For him, the rules of forensic computing are, in essence, the following:

- Rule 1: An original should be handled as little as possible
- During the examination of original data there should be minimum application of forensic computer processes. Since McKemmish (1999) considers this rule as the most important in forensic computing, it is important to note that the data processing that one will apply to textual corpora must be carried out with discernment and that the tool must be put at the service of the analyst.
- Rule 2: Every change should be examined
- Every change that occurs during a forensic examination needs to be documented in terms of its nature, extent, and reason for it. In the case of textual data analysis, this rule essentially concerns the corpus. Hence, by describing how the corpus is set up, its possible enrichment, and its relation to the problem raised, the analyst can take a measured look at the case study.
- Rule 3: Rules of evidence should be accomplished
- Rules of evidence should be complied with when applying or developing forensic tools and techniques. From my point of view, one of the fundamental precepts of forensic computing is the need to ensure that the application of tools and techniques does not lessen the final admissibility of the product. Consequently, the type of tools and techniques used, as well as the way in which they are applied, are essential elements in ensuring compliance with the relevant rules of evidence. We will go back to these elements later when we deal with the case study. Even if assisted by a reputable computer tool, the linguist must always contact investigators and, more generally, those who know the case to which the corpus relates. Linguistics thus interacts with other analysis components and can provide new information linked to specific skills.
- Rule 4: An expert should not exceed their knowledge
- A forensic computer expert should be aware of the scope and possible limitations of their experience. Furthermore, they must also keep in mind the degree of confidence of the methods and tools they employ in their analysis, and question the status of their results in terms of, among other things, what is certain proof or, on the contrary, only a possibility or a probability.

These four rules will be followed in our computer-based approach to the analysis of online terrorist threats.

2.3 How Far Can We Computerise the Processing of Complex Concepts?

While 'forensic science is constantly evolving and transforming in response to the numerous technological innovations in recent decades' (Bérubé et al., 2020, p. 1), in forensic linguistics determining authorship on the basis of habits of style questions the validity of stylometry. According to Totty et al. (1987), some difficulties appear with such methods and tools. First, in forensic applications, at times 'stylometry has been used to test the validity of claims by convicted persons that records of interviews, containing full or partial confessions, which formed part of the prosecution evidence at their trial, had been fabricated, in whole or in part' (p. 17). The utterances taken down by a police officer are typically the answers given by the suspect. Therefore, their validity as evidence is, in effect, based on statements made by police officers saying that the records are true and accurate accounts of what was said.

The second difficulty linked to corpus linguistics concerns the scope of corpora and admissibility criteria. For example, in politics the appearance of the political tweet as a genre of discourse (Longhi, 2013, 2018) has modified certain parameters for setting up political corpora. Nevertheless, if certain precautions are taken, digital textual data are an important source for the researcher, and also for the investigator. As a scientific discipline, stylometry must consider the variety of texts, and thus the variety of size, as a constraint. The work of Lam et al. (2021) opens up promising prospects in this respect.

The second difficulty relates to the authenticity of the corpora. The question of the author, and more broadly of the speaker or the enunciator, has long been dealt with by linguistics, and it seems that a good knowledge of the theories of enunciation would provide guarantees for the analysis conducted (Benveniste, 1966; Ducrot, 1981, among others). In the case study that will be described later, the analysis focuses on anonymous texts, which are a subject of interest to linguistics and stylometry in particular.

3 Description and Explanation of the Most Significant Methodologies

In this section I will present the type of mixed method used to explore corpora which combines qualitative with quantitative processing. This approach allows for a concrete analysis of corpora as presented at point 4, while bearing in mind the need for thoroughness and replicability.

3.1 A Methodological Mix: Combining Qualitative and Quantitative Approaches

As illustrated by a study I conducted together with Ascone (Ascone & Longhi, 2017, p. 87), an iterative approach to jihadist propaganda may consist of four stages:

1. Stage 1: A preliminary qualitative analysis of the jihadist ideology, the radicalisation process and the linguistic characteristics of hate speech has been essential to understanding the jihadist discourse and putting forward initial hypotheses. It is very important that the researcher knows the corpus, has read it, or at least browsed it if it is very voluminous, and knows the different criteria for structuring and setting up the corpus (extraction choices, variable selection). Using certain concepts or a qualitative analysis grid, the researcher or analyst can highlight a certain number of phenomena, make assumptions about the corpus, or extract a certain number of characteristics according to the knowledge acquired during the literature review.
2. Stage 2: A quantitative analysis whose goal is to verify the hypotheses' validity. The analysis can be performed with the help of software—for example using a pre-established lexicon to identify the discourse themes. This instrumentation is reasoned because it is based on specific observables and described in the literature. However, at the same

time, this approach allows unexpected results to emerge while objectifying analyses.

3. Stage 3: A deeper qualitative analysis of the themes. Textual statistics or data mining tools make it possible to return to the corpus. This criterion is fundamental for linguistic analysis. The results yielded by the tools are only a way of looking at textual data differently, by reorganising them or exploring them according to a certain hypothesis.
4. Stage 4: A final quantitative analysis to test the hypotheses and results yielded by the qualitative analysis. The last instrumentation can be useful to interact again with the corpus via a tool—Steps 3 and 4 can be performed repeatedly since the instrumentation should be seen as an aid to the researcher or analyst.

The above-mentioned methodology may seem tedious because it requires the mobilisation of human expertise and IT tools in several stages. However, it makes it possible to overcome the difficulties raised by Bérubé et al. (2020): 'The amount of data is often too large for a traditional qualitative analysis, computational methods of network and content analysis have been used, depending on the research objectives' (p. 2). Therefore, we were able to explain that the proposed methodological mix makes it possible to benefit from the advantages of qualitative and quantitative methods.

This progressive methodology makes it possible to work on both raw and processed corpora at different levels, according to needs and tools. From a methodological point of view, we highlighted the role of corpora, the importance of their structuring and the tools adapted to analyse them. We followed Ainsworth and Juola (2018) who explain how the community of forensic linguists can be structured:

> [T]he key to validating the science behind authorship attribution has been the development of accuracy benchmarks through the use of shared evaluation corpora on which practitioners can test their methodologies. These corpora consist of document sets with known 'ground truths' about their authorship. (p. 1176)

We thus found practices close to what could be done in textual data analysis or data science, with empirical comparisons of methods and results based on common corpora. This type of practice seems to have the virtue of improving the reliability and transparency of studies in this field. Likewise, we tried to draw inspiration from the work and discussions in the textometry community on the one hand, and deep learning on the other, in order to improve the replicability and thoroughness of analyses.

3.2 Ensuring Replicability

In the context of analysing corpora that include terrorist threats, it is crucial that the method used is replicable, the results are explicit and transparent and the conclusions can be clearly justified. This takes us to the concept of 'Forensic reproducibility' (Garfinkel et al., 2009, p. 3) in which two areas of interest stand out. First, reproducibility makes it possible 'for one researcher or research group to validate that they have mastered a technique and then to go off in a different direction'. This criterion therefore allows the community to discuss and compare results and make progress. Second, the criterion of validation, and more generally of consensus, also makes it possible to give a stronger social scope to academic disciplines, not least, in our case, corpus linguistics.

For the remainder of the article I will use the textometric approach which is the subject of regular work and discussions in the scientific community, including at the *International Conference on Statistical Analysis of Textual Data* or *Journées d'analyse des données textuelles* (JADT) which takes place in Europe every two years. Textometry offers an instrumented approach to corpus analysis, combining quantitative with qualitative analysis (Lebart & Salem, 1994). Functionally, textometry implements differential principles, using statistics and probabilities. The approach highlights similarities and differences observed in a corpus according to different criteria (words, grammar, n-gram, among others.). Textometry employs contextual and contrastive modelling, which makes it possible to perform objective 'measurements' on texts, but also to measure distances, proximities, similarities and differences between texts or parts of texts. Such a method makes it possible to ensure both the replicability of the results and their explanation (there is no 'black box' here).

4 Case Study

My own case study (Longhi, 2021) proposes a summary and an extension of this research with new analysis based on specific examples and the presentation of innovative methods (deep learning).

4.1 Characterising the Themes Running Through Criminal Acts and the Types of Threat

The French Gendarmerie provided material to help investigators with cases involving criminal acts that concerned especially terrorist groups with links to the far left. I collected 23 anonymous texts from various websites in which authors claimed responsibility for malicious acts. The analysis conducted aimed to help investigators by formulating hypotheses on the possible number of authors or the probability that, for example, texts x, y, z had one, two, or three authors. These characteristics should help investigators with other dimensions of forensic study.

The 23 texts contained 12,109 occurrences, 2534 forms with an average of 526 occurrences per text. This corpus size, although modest, was well suited to textometric methods. Such an approach could already be useful in proposing a thematic classification of articles. It could be represented using the descending hierarchical classification which resulted from the Alceste method and was provided by the Iramuteq software (Reinert, 1990)—see Fig. 13.1.

By means of the themes shown in Fig. 13.1 we were able to establish a link between terrorist threats and the subjects they applied to—for example energy sources, places related to animal husbandry, among others. Probst et al. (2018) explained that the communicative and semantic factors that determine the force of the motivating impact of a speech act of threat include: (1) the significance of punitive measures, (2) the

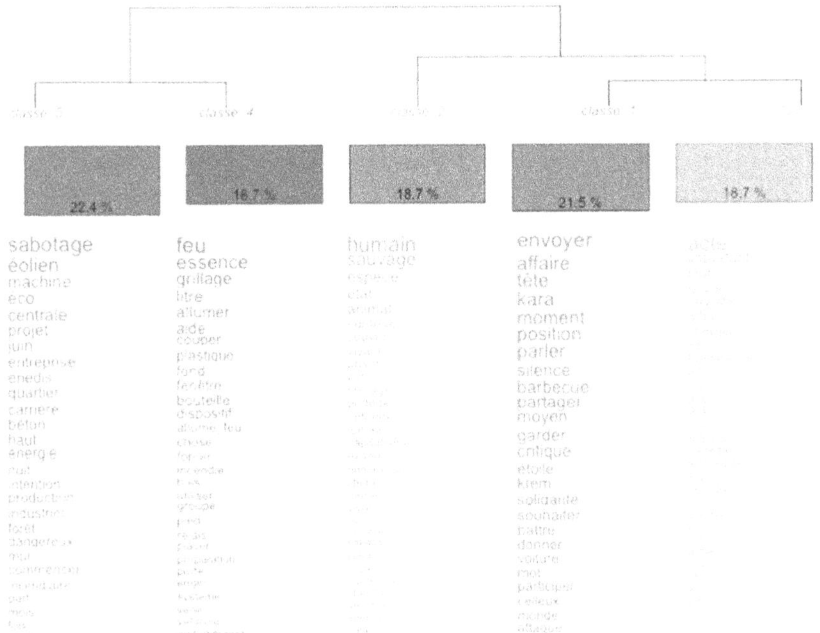

Fig. 13.1 Descending hierarchical classification (themes) of the corpus

possibility of punishment and (3) the high probability of negative actions stated or implied by the producer.

When looking for examples in the corpus which reflected these criteria, the following quotes stood out:

1. We don't live in the past, we don't expect anything from the future, our revolts have no future, so they can't be put off until tomorrow.
2. We are answering the call for a dangerous June because it expresses these nuances well.
3. On Thursday night we broke into the ENEDIS building in Crest, which supplies the energy that allows this shitty world to turn. We poured 10 litres of petrol inside and lit it with handheld flares (have a plan B in case the handheld flares fail). Ten litres of petrol give one hell of a blast. By the time we got back out, the building was in flames. We found out later it was destroyed to a large extent.

4. On the night of 25 to 26 October 2016 we set fire to the car of a chief of the Tuilières gendarmerie which was parked in the barracks compound. We committed this act of sabotage in solidarity with the migrants in the Calais Jungle.
5. An incendiary device was placed and lit under each of the three Enedis vans parked in the company car park. We were in a hurry to get to the karaoke night so we didn't have much time to watch them burn, but we do hope we started a nice bonfire. … They say June is going to be dangerous. Let's hope it's just the beginning.

Words such as 'revolts' that can't be 'put off' (1), 'a dangerous June' (2), 'lit it', 'flames' and 'destroyed' (3), 'set fire' and 'sabotage' (4), 'incendiary device', 'burn' and 'dangerous' (4) illustrate the way in which these acts echoed terrorist threats, reprisals and violent acts which, from the point of view of their perpetrators, were the consequence of actions contrary to what they stood for.

4.2 Textometric and Deep Learning Analysis[1]

However, to help investigators link authors of texts with perpetrators of malicious acts, we can resort to calculating specificities, making it possible to group texts according to their linguistic dimensions. The full analysis is developed in my study (Longhi, 2021). For example one can observe these distances between texts by focusing on grammatical variables as depicted in Fig. 13.2.

The analyst can thus formulate hypotheses on the proximities between texts, which they can compare with the survey data after returning to the corpus to examine these results in context. In order to increase the quantity of data to be analysed by relying on the most recent technologies, current projects focus on using deep neural networks. We will discuss this avenue in the next section.

Starting from the gendarmerie's initial data, I found some particularly interesting sites on which to test my approaches to linguistic analysis in security-related contexts (which were not necessarily akin to terrorism). The data retrieval work was carried out by Jeremy Demange, the engineer

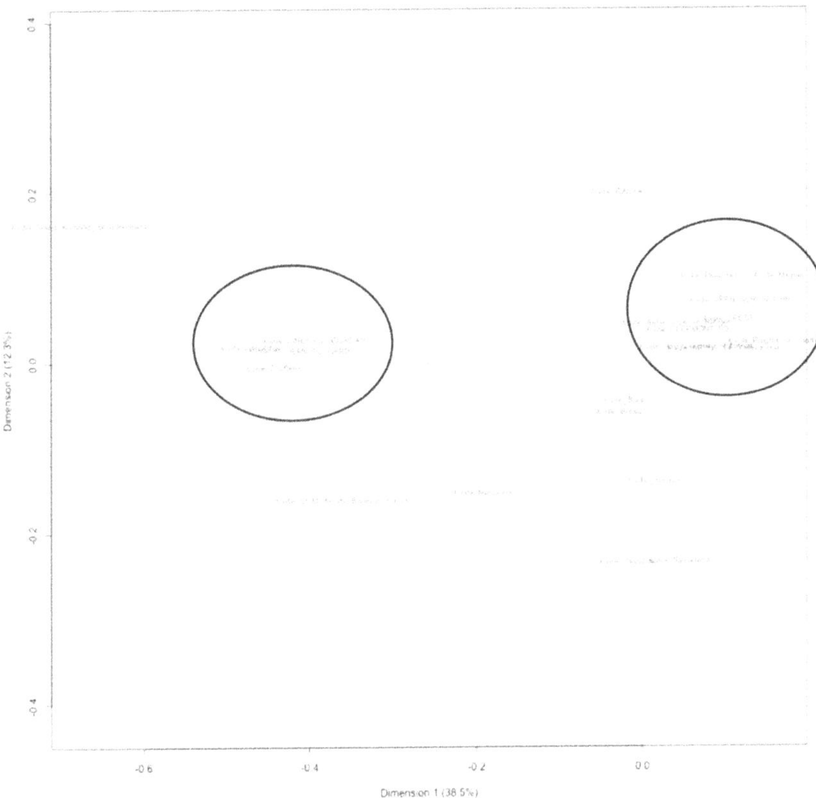

Fig. 13.2 Graphic grouping of texts based on their grammatical characteristics

from CY's (Cergy Paris Université) digital humanities institute. The data came from the site https://nantes.indymedia.org. We retrieved this site via a copy from the Common Crawl website (http://commoncrawl.org), which allowed us to avoid overloading the publisher site's server and also to obtain data quickly and easily. To retrieve the content, we used a suite of AWS tools such as Athena, which allowed us to retrieve all pages available on the site as of September-October 2020. This strategy allowed us to extract almost all of the articles published from 2003 (when https://nantes.indymedia.org was created) to September 2020. We were able to retrieve a total of 8126 unique articles from the site and detected a total of 4806 unique authors. The 'anonymous' author (without

Table 13.1 Names of authors listed in the articles

Author's name	Frequency
Anonyme	407
Zadist	232
nantesrévoltée	184
.	166
Anonymous	152
radiocayenne	82
unsympathisantducci	67
...	63
X	48
*	44

preprocessing) appears most often with a total of 287 frequencies. However, it should be noted that anyone can write any author's name on this site and be identified as *anonyme* ('anonymous'). Thus, I performed a preprocessing step to eliminate any results that appeared to me to be false—that is uppercase characters and spaces were removed. Table 13.1 depicts the top ten names of authors who wrote the most on the site (after preprocessing).

I trained a prototype Python model to test the author comparison on this corpus. I was able to achieve 93.48% accuracy (the model being improved). Figure 13.3 shows the details of the selected model.

For the analysis of similarities, an algorithm version was developed by Jérémy Demange in Python. The analysis focused on the first nine authors:

- author_anonyme
- author_zadist
- author_nantesrévoltée
- author_.
- author_anonymous
- author_radiocayenne
- author_unsympathisantducci
- author_...
- author_x

Figure 13.4 depicts the results of the analysis of the texts by the abovementioned authors.

```
Layer (type)                 Output Shape              Param #
==============================================================
input_1 (InputLayer)         [(None,)]                 0
--------------------------------------------------------------
expand_last_dim (ExpandLastD (None, 1)                 0
--------------------------------------------------------------
text_vectorization (TextVect (None, 512)               0
--------------------------------------------------------------
embedding (Embedding)        (None, 512, 64)           320064
--------------------------------------------------------------
dropout (Dropout)            (None, 512, 64)           0
--------------------------------------------------------------
conv1d (Conv1D)              (None, 508, 256)          82176
--------------------------------------------------------------
global_max_pooling1d (Global (None, 256)               0
--------------------------------------------------------------
dense (Dense)                (None, 256)               65792
--------------------------------------------------------------
re_lu (ReLU)                 (None, 256)               0
--------------------------------------------------------------
dropout_1 (Dropout)          (None, 256)               0
--------------------------------------------------------------
dense_1 (Dense)              (None, 671)               172447
--------------------------------------------------------------
classification_head_1 (Softm (None, 671)               0
==============================================================
Total params: 640,479
Trainable params: 640,479
Non-trainable params: 0
```

Fig. 13.3 Prototype of authorship attribution model

Therefore, we could observe the possible connection or distance between certain names of authors based on a larger body of text than at point 4.1. Of course, this work is in progress and needs further study, but there is promise in using this technology to help deal with online threats. Knowledge of the methods at 4.1 can help refine the results, for example, if we look at the themes of the texts or add information to the stylistic analysis of the authors, as shown in Fig. 13.5.

This analysis allows, for example, to distinguish specific subjects (political, economic) and help investigators concentrate on the classes that would perhaps be more relevant to them—for example class 5 which includes terms such as 'grenade', 'bullet' and 'injure', or class 2.

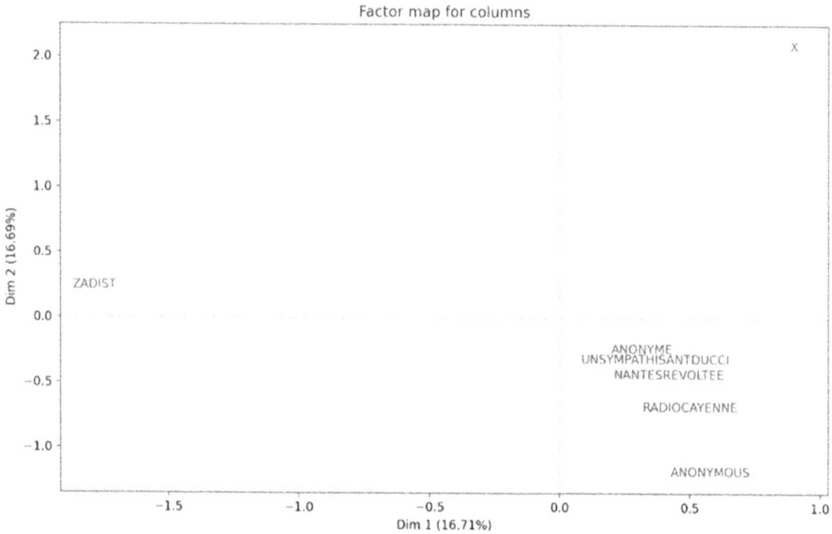

Fig. 13.4 Authors connected by the analysis model

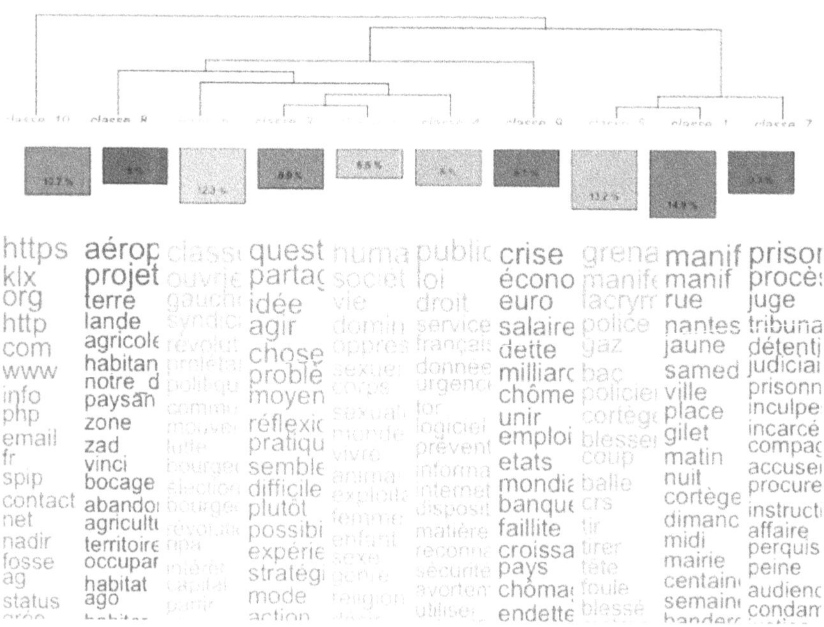

Fig. 13.5 Descending hierarchical classification (themes) of the second corpus

What I wish to highlight at the end of the analysis of this example is the possible complementarity between deep learning and textometry for the purposes of corpus analysis: while textometry allows for an efficient instrumentation of the analysis and the exploration of texts, it may present some limitations in producing clear results on certain issues (text authorship, content similarity, among others). Thus, textometry can be used to make connections, filter certain parts of the corpus and orientate the analysis. Deep learning can provide analysis procedures that are more efficient but also more explicit and easier to understand (the 'black box' aspect of some algorithms). Textometry can be used at the end of the study to interpret and verify the obtained results.

5 Conclusions

This chapter has highlighted several dimensions of online threat analysis, particularly in the context of terrorism. The evolution of technologies and their efficient use for criminal purposes makes it necessary to consider the linguistic aspects of these threats in a thorough and systematic way. In this chapter, I have presented the challenges of a method that combines qualitative and quantitative approaches and seeks to emphasise the replicability and thoroughness of such analyses. This serves a dual purpose: to ensure the quality of analyses, but also to provide institutions, professionals and society at large with the assurance that these analyses are reliable and can be verified and redone.

To this end, I have presented a model that combines textometry with deep learning: while textometry provides the means to measure, compare and explore corpora, deep learning can then efficiently produce results on certain research questions that can initially be addressed from a statistical point of view. Textometry can also help to better understand the results provided by artificial intelligence algorithms, contextualising and exemplifying the results. I have thus highlighted examples of online threats involving violence, malicious acts or reprisals. Authorship identification in such threats is a major goal, particularly when it comes to dealing with terrorist acts and their tragic consequences.

Note

1. The paragraph on deep learning was written in collaboration with Jeremy Demange, engineer at CY IDHN.

References

Ainsworth, J., & Juola, P. (2018). Who wrote this: Modern forensic authorship analysis as a model for valid forensic science. *Washington University Law Review, 96*, 1161–1189.

Ascone, L. (2018). Textual analysis of extremist propaganda and counter-narrative: A quanti-quali investigation. *JADT*, June 2018, Rome, Italy. https://hal.archives-ouvertes.fr/hal-02317752

Ascone, L., & Longhi, J. (2017). The expression of threat in jihadist propaganda. *Fragmentum, 50*, 85–98.

Benveniste, E. (1966). *Problèmes de linguistique générale*. Gallimard.

Bérubé, M., Tang, T. U., Fortin, F., Ozalp, S., Williams, M. L., & Burnap, P. (2020). Social media forensics applied to assessment of post-critical incident social reaction: The case of the 2017 Manchester Arena terrorist attack. *Forensic Science International, 313*, 110364. https://doi.org/10.1016/j.forsciint.2020.110364

Chaski, C. E. (2005). Who's at the keyboard? Authorship attribution in digital evidence investigations. *International Journal of Digital Evidence, 4*(1), 1–13.

Chen, H., Zhou, Y., Reid, E. F., & Larson, C. A. (2011). Introduction to special issue on terrorism informatics. *Information Systems Frontiers, 13*(1), 1–3.

Coulthard, M., & Johnson, A. (2007). *An introduction to forensic linguistics: Language in evidence*. Routledge.

Dean, G., & Bell, P. (2012). The dark side of social media: Review of online terrorism. *Pakistan Journal of Criminology, 3*(4), 191–210.

Ducrot, O. (1981). Langage, métalangage, et performatifs. *Cahiers de linguistique, 3*, 5–34.

Garfinkel, S., Farrell, P., Roussev, V., & Dinolt, G. (2009). Bringing science to digital forensics with standardized forensic corpora. *Digital Investigation, 6*, S2–S11.

Lam, T., Demange J., & Longhi, J. (2021). Attribution d'auteur par utilisation des méthodes d'apprentissage profond. *Proceedings of the Deep Learning for NLP workshop*, EGC 2021.

Lebart, L., & Salem, A. (1994). *Statistique textuelle*. Dunod.

Longhi, J. (2013). Essai de caractérisation du tweet politique. *L'Information Grammaticale, 136*, 25–32.

Longhi, J. (2018). *Du discours comme champ au corpus comme terrain. Contribution méthodologique à l'analyse sémantique du discours*. L'Harmattan.

Longhi, J. (2021). Using digital humanities and linguistics to help with terrorism investigations. *Forensic Science International, 318*, 110564.

Margot, P. (2014). Traçologie: La trace, vecteur fondamental de la police scientifique. *Revue Internationale de Criminologie et de Police Technique et Scientifique, 67*(1), 72–97.

McKemmish, R. (1999). *What is forensic computing?* Australian Institute of Criminology. https://www.aic.gov.au/sites/default/files/2020-05/tandi118.pdf

Probst, N., Shkapenko, T., Tkachenko, A., & Chernyakov, A. (2018). Speech act of threat in everyday conflict discourse: Production and perception. *Lege Artis, 3*(2), 204–250. https://doi.org/10.2478/lart-2018-0019

Reinert, M. (1990). Alceste une méthodologie d'analyse des données textuelles et une application: Aurelia de Gerard de Nerval. *Bulletin of Sociological Methodology/Bulletin de méthodologie sociologique, 26*(1), 24–54. https://doi.org/10.1177/075910639002600103

Totty, R. N., Hardcastle, R. A., & Pearson, J. (1987). Forensic linguistics: The determination of authorship from habits of style. *Journal of the Forensic Science Society, 27*(1), 13–28.

United Nations Office on Drugs and Crime (UNODC). (2012). *The use of the Internet for terrorist purposes*. https://www.unodc.org/documents/terrorism/Publications/Use_of_Internet_for_Terrorist_Purposes/ebook_use_of_the_internet_for_terrorist_purposes.pdf

Wright, D. (2014). *Stylistics versus statistics: A corpus linguistic approach to combining techniques in forensic authorship analysis using Enron emails*. Unpublished doctoral thesis, University of Leeds, England.

Index[1]

[1] Note: Page numbers followed by 'n' refer to notes.

V. Guillén-Nieto, D. Stein (eds.), *Language as Evidence*,
https://doi.org/10.1007/978-3-030-84330-4

GPSR Compliance
The European Union's (EU) General Product Safety Regulation (GPSR) is a set of rules that requires consumer products to be safe and our obligations to ensure this.

If you have any concerns about our products, you can contact us on

ProductSafety@springernature.com

In case Publisher is established outside the EU, the EU authorized representative is:

Springer Nature Customer Service Center GmbH
Europaplatz 3
69115 Heidelberg, Germany

www.ingramcontent.com/pod-product-compliance
Lightning Source LLC
Chambersburg PA
CBHW071639030826
49219CB00005B/270
* 9 7 8 3 0 3 0 8 4 3 2 9 8 *